Eurabia
The Euro-Arab Axis

By the Same Author

Les Juifs en Egypte. Geneva: Editions de l'Avenir, 1971. Revised and enlarged Hebrew edition: *Yehudai Mizrayim.* Foreword by Hayyim Ze'ev Hirschberg. Translated from the French by Aharon Amir. Tel Aviv: Maariv, 1974.

Le Dhimmi: Profil de l'opprimé en Orient et en Afrique du Nord depuis la conquête arabe. Paris: Editions Anthropos, 1980.

The Dhimmi: Jews and Christians under Islam. Preface by Jacques Ellul. Revised and considerably enlarged English edition. Translated from the French by David Maisel, Paul Fenton, and David Littman. Rutherford, NJ: Fairleigh Dickinson University Press, 1985. (Sixth printing, 2003.)

Ha-Dimmim: B'nai Hasoot. Enlarged Hebrew edition. Translated by Aharon Amir Preface by Jacques Ellul. Introduction by Moshe Sharon. Jerusalem: Cana, 1986.

The Dhimmi: Jews and Christians under Islam. Russian edition. In 2 vols. Jerusalem: Society for Research on Jewish Communities / "Aliyah" Library, 1991.

Les Chrétientés d'Orient entre Jihâd et Dhimmitude, VIIe-XXe siècle. Preface by Jacques Ellul. Paris: Les Editions du Cerf, 1991.

The Decline of Eastern Christianity under Islam. From Jihad to Dhimmitude. Seventh-Twentieth Century. With a Foreword by Jacques Ellul. Translated from the French by Miriam Kochan and David Littman. Madison, NJ: Fairleigh Dickinson University Press, 1996 (Fourth printing, 2002.)

Juifs et Chrétiens sous l'Islam: Les dhimmis face au défi intégriste. Paris: Berg International, 1994.

Der Niedergang des orientalischen Christentums unter dem Islam. German edition. With a preface by Heribert Busse. Translated from the French and English by Kurt Maier. Munich: Resch Verlag, 2002.

Islam and Dhimmitude: Where Civilizations Collide. Translated from the French by Miriam Kochan and David Littman. Madison, NJ/Fairleigh Dickinson University Press, 2002. (Second printing, 2003.)

Eurabia

The Euro-Arab Axis

Bat Ye'or

Madison • Teaneck
Fairleigh Dickinson University Press

Associated University Presses
2010 Eastpark Boulevard
Cranbury, NJ 08512

The paper used in this publication meets the requirements of the American National Standard for Permanence of Paper for Printed Library Materials Z39.48-1984.

Library of Congress Cataloging-in-Publication Data

Bat Ye'or.
   Eurabia : the Euro-Arab axis / Bat Ye'or.
      p.   cm.
   Includes bibliographical references and index.
   ISBN 0-8386-4076-1 (alk. paper)—ISBN 0-8386-4077-X (pbk. : alk. paper)
   1. Europe—Politics and government—20th century.   2. Europe—Politics and government—21st century.   3. Islam—Influence.   4. Islam and state—Europe. 5. Jihad.   I. Title.
D1053.B38   2005
303.48′240174927—dc22   2004025171

FOURTH PRINTING 2005

PRINTED IN THE UNITED STATES OF AMERICA

Contents

Part III: The Functioning of Eurabia

Part IV: The Making of Eurabia

Part V: Dialogue on Trial

Preface

Broad historical movements that profoundly transform human societies are difficult to discern in the short term. They extend over decades, often centuries, and affect the social fabric in multiple ways that are scarcely noticed by contemporary commentators but become perceptible in times of accelerated social change. This pattern of historical development applies to the dynamic of Islamic *jihad*. For over a millennium, *jihad* has been a potent political force that has subjugated and in some cases extinguished once powerful centers of Judeo-Christian, Hindu, Buddhist and other civilizations in Asia, Africa, and Europe. This historical process can be observed today on all three of these continents. In the 1970s, *jihad* reappeared as a powerful factor in European affairs but, for nearly three decades, the revival of *jihad* passed with little comment in both popular and academic journals. European statesmen remained silent. The murderous September 11, 2001 jihadist attacks in America broke the silence. President Bush's war on terrorism forced Europeans to take sides, while investigations revealed the presence of extensive and well-established networks of *jihad* terrorists throughout Europe. The Madrid bombing of March 11, 2004 heightened awareness of this grim reality. However, constructive public debate has been hampered by profound ignorance of the *jihad* dynamic and by the tendency of Europe's political elite to continue to appease jihadist driving forces.

This book describes Europe's evolution from a Judeo-Christian civilization, with important post-Enlightenment secular elements, into a post–Judeo-Christian civilization that is subservient to the ideology of *jihad* and the Islamic powers that propagate it. The new European civilization in the making can be called a "civilization of dhimmitude." The term dhimmitude comes from the Arabic word "*dhimmi.*" It refers to subjugated, non-Muslim individuals or people that accept the restrictive and humiliating subordination to an ascendant Islamic power to avoid enslavement or death.[1] The entire Muslim world as we know it today is a product of this 1,300 year-old *jihad* dynamic, whereby once thriving non-Muslim majority civilizations have been reduced to a state of dysfunctional dhimmitude. Many have been completely Islamized and have disappeared. Others remain as fossilized relics of the past, unable to evolve.

9

For over a millennium, following the seventh-century Muslim military offensives against Byzantium, European powers instinctively resisted *jihad*—militarily when necessary—to protect their independence. The response of post–Judeo-Christian Europe of the late twentieth century has been radically different. Europe, as reflected by the institutions of the EU, has abandoned resistance for dhimmitude, and independence for integration with the Islamic world of North Africa and the Middle East. The three most apparent symptoms of this fundamental change in European policy are officially sponsored anti-Americanism, antisemitism/anti-Zionism and "Palestinianism." These increasingly visible aspects of European policy are merely components of an overall vision for the transformation of Europe into a new geopolitical entity—Eurabia.[2]

The decisive shift in European policy came as a result of the oil crisis of 1973 when the European Economic Community (EEC), at the initiative of France and the Arab League, established the Euro-Arab Dialogue (EAD). Since then, the EAD has been in the vanguard of engineering a convergence between Europe and the Islamic states of North Africa and the Middle East. The EAD promotes a specific conception of international politics that determines Europe's relations with the Arab/Muslim world, and with America and Israel. It has also formulated a vision of European history, religion and culture, both past and future. Under the rubric of "dialogue," the EEC and its Arab League partner created a formidable political and legal superstructure that encompasses the entire Euro-Arab relationship and fostered increased joint Euro-Arab diplomatic initiatives.

The following chapters describe the origin and development of the little-known EAD. EEC and subsequently EU documents reveal the development of a new ideology that is producing demographic and cultural change for the purpose of creating conditions for the fulfillment of the Eurabian vision. Eurabia's cultural preconceptions include the "new Judeophobia," as well as resurgent anti-Americanism. The intensity of Judeophobia and anti-Americanism reflects increasing Islamic penetration of Europe and its growing influence on European policy. Judeophobia has been a characteristic of European and Islamic societies since medieval times. The Islamic elements of the modern European Judeophobia, together with its related anti-Americanism, have been incorporated into policies emerging from the EAD. They are as much anti-Christian and anti-Western as they are anti-Jewish. I do not believe that Judeophobia and anti-Zionism are common among the majority of Europeans. These attitudes, instead, are imposed *nolens volens* on an often reluctant public by political, media, and religious elites through methods that I will elucidate.

It is now obvious that Islam in Europe has not followed a process of Westernization; instead, the West becomes increasingly compliant to accommodate the religious and political norms of Muslim immigrants out of a fear of social unrest and terrorism. Policies aimed at the integration of Muslim immigrants and their offspring have generally failed. Many Europeans have perceived this profound civilizational shift. A significant minority of Europeans have responded by voting for rightist or even extreme right-wing political parties. Despite popular protests, European immigration policies were not substantially altered until 2003.

Observing this disturbing phenomenon, one gets the impression of a sinking continent, a colossal Titanic wreck, where the passengers run from one desperate situation to another. Indeed the situation does seem hopelessly compromised, as the European political authorities responsible for a state of affairs that they have knowingly created refuse obstinately to confront it. Instead, they tend to escape into a virtual world of rhetoric that replaces reality.

Over the past three decades, the EEC and the EU's political and cultural organizations have invented a fantasy Islamic civilization and history. The voluminous historical record of violations of basic human rights for all non-Muslims and women under the *shari'a* (Islamic Law)—throughout the past, and in contemporary Muslim societies—is ignored, or dismissed. Immunized from criticism by this fabricated historical construct, Europeans could engage in mutually fruitful business transactions and diplomatic ventures—particularly at the United Nations and other world bodies—with dictatorial regimes. It is in this context of international relations—pompously called "international legality"—that "old Europe" driven by France, the main architect of this policy, opposed America and supported Palestinian terrorist organizations.

In this book, Euro-Arab Judeophobia will be examined only as an indicator of the common Euro-Arab culture that is permeating, even overwhelming, all levels of West European society. It is no easy task to avoid an analysis of the current European Judeophobic trend. Under the euphemism of "peace process," the EU has made Israel the cornerstone of its relations with the Arab states, with the USA, and of its own security—as a quid pro quo against Islamist terror. Hence, from whatever angle we observe these three positions, we find that Israel is at the core of Europe's strategies. In fact, as it will become clearer in the following pages, under Arab pressure, the EU has willingly made Israel hostage to its own Arab policy and its security.

Fostering and promoting such hate through policies, speeches, and the media impact both the elite responsible for its expression, and the larger society.[3] For Jew-hatred, as abetted by EU policy decisions, does not concern only the Jews, but also non-Jewish Europeans—either as active or passive supporters of this dynamic, or in opposition to it.

Judeophobia does affect the way Europeans—whether Christian, "post-Christian," or atheist—understand their past and conceive their future.

This understanding of history, and conception of the future, is also influenced by European anti-Americanism. The nexus between European Jew-hatred and anti-Americanism becomes apparent when Americans resist Islamization and perceive their identity and culture as an emanation of biblical history and values—a heritage scorned by contemporary Eurabia.

The recurrence of antisemitism across Western Europe is mentioned here as a reliable indicator of more fundamental changes that impact, ultimately, all of Western civilization. It relates to a profound structural transformation of the western part of the European continent that affects its demography, culture, and religious orientation. These tectonic shifts have deep sociopolitical divisions, which came to the fore during the acrimonious public debates and demonstrations that surrounded the American-led Coalition War against Iraq in Spring 2003.

European anti-Americanism is not a new phenomenon. During the Cold War, it was perceived as an almost exclusively, albeit widespread, Soviet-inspired phenomenon. However, a contemptuous anti-Americanism among some Europeans—particularly certain French and Germans trends—reflected a sense of cultural superiority and compensated for the Nazi, Fascist, and Communist defeats. The collapse of the Communist system exposed other currents of anti-American hatred, manifested by Third-Worldists, neo-Communists, and Islamists reoriented into a powerful jihad-ist coalition against Western democracies and their values. This recast ideological war is deeply rooted in a Euro-Arab political alliance and growing cultural symbiosis, which propagates—and expresses, often unabashedly—virulent antisemitism and anti-Zionism.[4]

The Euro-Arab Dialogue implemented in the 1970s a new sociopolitical and cultural conception, which has now affected profound changes within Western Europe. In the following pages, I use the terms "Europeans" and "Eurabians." Eurabia designates a new entity—with political, economic, religious, cultural, and media components—superimposed on Europe by powerful governmental lobbies. While Europeans live within Eurabia's constraints, few are really conscious of them on a daily basis, beyond a somewhat confused awareness. Eurabians are the agents and enforcers of this all-encompassing new Eurabian policy and culture. The tension between Europeans and Eurabians arises from fundamental and uncompromising differences over political, societal, and cultural values, as well as core religious identities. This tension is also apparent in disputes regarding the strength and durability of the European-American transatlantic alliance and the cohesion of what we still call Western civilization. The divisive European-Eurabian arguments over the war in Iraq, or the larger global war on *jihad* terrorism, reflect a deeper religious and cultural confrontation between Western and Arab/Islamic civilizations where, consciously or not, Eurabians have become the agents of Islamic political ambitions in Europe.

This book will elucidate the origins of contemporary European dhimmitude and examine its propagation. Similar developments, at a much more inchoate stage, have been discerned in America, through examination of school textbooks and university curricula.[5]

Switzerland, October 2004

Acknowledgments

This book was written directly in English, a daring enterprise for a French writer. I am most grateful to all those friends who carefully read through the manuscript and gave useful grammatical, editorial, and other advice.

Without the constant support and encouragement of Dr. Andrew Bostom this study would never have been written. He also provided me with some additional research material and documentation. I am deeply indebted to him for his trust and precious help till the end.

Lastly, I wish to thank my husband, who undertook the difficult task of reading and correcting the early and final manuscript several times, offering his experienced suggestions which allowed me to improve the final version.

It is my earnest hope that this venture into an unexplored domain will serve as an introduction for more comprehensive research projects on the long-term political, cultural and ideological geopolicy of dhimmitude that led Europe toward Eurabia.

Author's Note

Quotations from the Qur'an are taken from Richard Bell's authoritative translation of *The Qur'an, with a critical re-arrangement of the Surahs* (1937), and occasionally from *The Koran Interpreted* (1964), by Arthur John Arberry.

The word "antisemitism" is spelled throughout following the preferred usage initiated by Dr. James Parkes in his pioneer work, *The Conflict of the Church and the Synagogue. A Study in the Origins of Antisemitism* (London, 1934). An alternative word, "Judeophobia," is sometimes used with the same significance.

Appendix 1 and 5 contain extracts published in *Euro-Arab Dialogue. The relations between the two cultures* (1983). These, and other passages quoted in the main text are reproduced with the kind permission of the editor, Derek Hopwood and Taylor & Francis Books Ltd. London.

Abbreviations

AIPU	Arab Inter-Parliamentarian Union
CFSP	Common Foreign and Security Policy
CIE	Council on Islamic Education
CMIP	Center for Monitoring the Impact of Peace
DAI	Documents d'Actualités Internationale
EAD	Euro-Arab Dialogue
EC	European Community
ECF	European Cultural Foundation
ECSC	European Coal and Steel Community
EEC	European Economic Community
EIB	European Investment Bank
EPC	European Political Cooperation
EU	European Union
EURATOM	European Atomic Energy Community
EuroMeSCo	Euro-Mediterranean Study Commission
FEMIP	Facility for Euro-Mediterranean Investment & Partnership
GATT	General Agreement on Tariffs and Trade
IEA	International Energy Agency
ICRC	International Committee of the Red Cross
IFRI	Institut Français des Relations Internationales
IIIT	International Institute of Islamic Thought
IPU	Inter-Parliamentary Union
JHA	Cooperation in the Fields of Justice and Home Affairs
MEDA	Euro-Mediterranean Partnership Program
MEDEA	European Institute for Research on Mediterranean and Euro-Arab Co-operation
MEP	Member of the European Parliament
NGO	Nongovernmental Organization
OCDE	Organization for Economic Cooperation and Development
OIC	Organization of Islamic Conference
OLAF	European Union Fraud Office
OPEC	Organization of the Petroleum Exporting Countries
PA	Palestinian Authority
PAEAC	Parliamentary Association for Euro-Arab Cooperation
PLO	Palestine Liberation Organization

SEA   Single European Act
TEU   Maastricht Treaty on European Union
UAR   United Arab Republic of Egypt and Syria
UDHR   Universal Declaration of Human Rights
UNCHR   United Nation Commission on Human Rights
UNESCO   United Nations Educational, Scientific and Cultural
               Organization
UNRWA   United Nations Relief and Works Agency for Palestine
               Refugees in the Near East
WCCP   World Conference of Christians for Palestine
WHO   World Health Organization

Journals, Press, and Others

ADL   *Anti-Defamation League* (New York)
AI   *Antisemitism International* (Jerusalem)
AFP   *Agence France Presse* (Paris)
AP   *Associated Press* (New York)
CMIP   *Center for Monitoring the Impact of Peace* (Jerusalem)
FPM   *FrontPageMagazine* (New York)
IHT   *International Herald Tribune* (Paris)
JCPA   *Jerusalem Center for Public Affairs* (Jerusalem)
JC   *Jewish Chronicle* (London)
JP   *Jerusalem Post* (Jerusalem)
Le Temps   *Le Temps* (Geneva)
MEMRI   *Middle East Media Research Institute* (Washington, DC)
MEQ   *Middle East Quarterly* (Philadelphia)
NRO   *NationalReviewOnline* (New York)
NYT   *New York Times* (New York)
OMJ   *Observatoire du Monde Juif* (Paris)
Reuters   *Reuters* (London)
REP   *Revue des Etudes Palestiniennes* (Paris)

Eurabia
The Euro-Arab Axis

Part I
Eurabia: The Project

1

Eurabia Revealed

In her forceful book, *La Forza della Ragione*, Oriana Fallaci ponders the steady Islamization of Europe, noting, "it was all there for years and we didn't see it."[1] This "all there" relates to burning questions. Why have generations of Europeans been taught in universities to despise America and harbor an implacable hatred for Israel? Why has the European Union (EU) proposed a Constitution that willingly renounces and even denies its Judeo-Christian roots? Has the 1930s–World War II alliance of Arab jihadists with European Nazis and fascist trends been resurrected today? Is the European Union's covert war against Israel, through its Palestinian Arab allies, the secret *schadenfreude*[2] fulfillment of an interrupted Holocaust?

Is the issue of the "Palestinian refugees" Eurabia's duplicitous mechanism to destroy Israel by a "return invasion"? Has Europe helped to fund, coddle, and sacralize them for this reason? And why does Europe call "inviolable international boundaries" the 1949 armistice lines between Jordan and Israel, which were never recognized then as international boundaries by the Arab/Muslim world, nor by other states? Has Europe chosen this position in order to delegitimize Israel by calling its citizens "colonizing settlers on Arab Muslim lands"? This implies that Europe now adopts knowingly the *jihad* conception of "Judea" and "Samaria" as permanent territories in the *Dar al-Islam* (the land of Islam), where an apartheid theocratic system, i.e., the *shari'a*, discriminated against and persecuted the indigenous non-Muslim population from the seventh century until the British Mandate period.

Has the European Union, through the Euro-Arab Dialogue superstructure, become the instrument for the neutralization of America? What would a Euro-Arab dominion represent for America and the freedom of the world? Does an Arab-Palestinian *jihad* against Israel aim at the elimination of the Jewish state only? Or is this *jihad* focused deceptively on Israel to conceal its true global ambitions and designs? How are such policies conceived and implemented, and what might be their consequences, for Europe and America? As Fallaci has surmised, these overall policies were not created in a clandestine fashion. They were developed, as I will demonstrate, during what became routine meetings and forums between the European Economic Community (EEC), later the European Union (EU), and the Arab League states.

Eurabia emerged at the outset of the third millennium as Judeophobia, later accompanied by massive anti-American demonstrations, swept across Western Europe. These overt manifestations of Europe's creeping transformation into Eurabia began during the interval following September 30, 2000—the date Arafat's *al-Aqsa* war intensified. It was no mere coincidence: European governments, some of the Churches and much of the media had supported anti-Americanism and the PLO for decades. That support was just the most visible manifestation of EU policy toward Americans, Israelis and Arabs, and heralded a larger societal and cultural transformation of Europe itself.

The political convergence that took place from 2000 to 2003 between the Arab League, the European Union, and the Palestinian Authority, its funded agent in the Middle East, was the result of a long-term process. Consequently, European politicians often asserted that America's "unilateralism" and Israel's "injustice" were the root causes of Islamist and Palestinian terrorism against America or Israel.[3] Terms such as "misery," "humiliation," and "injustice" often serve as code words for the alleged "domineering arrogance" of America, or the "oppression" caused by Israel's very existence. The problem is said to be not so much Islamist ideology but misguided American policies that have created Arab despair and poverty. The terror strategy devised by the Palestinian leadership for use against Israelis was given the whitewash of a moral justification: Israel's self-defense policy, analysts claimed, merely increased Palestinian terrorism.

In 2003, the EU, which for years had cultivated excellent relations with Syria and its surrogates in Lebanon, refused to place Hezbollah on its list of terrorist organizations. When, in America's war against terrorism, President Bush urged Europe in June 2003 to block Hamas funds, France adamantly refused. Because the EU has generally dismissed the danger of Arab/Islamic terrorism, European leaders—especially French politicians—cultivated friendly relations with states and organizations sponsoring terror, including Iran, Iraq, Syria, Libya, and the Palestinian Authority. France's stand at the UN Security Council just before the Iraqi war earned President Chirac the gratitude of the Arab and Muslim world. His state visit in April 2003 to Algeria was a triumph—during which he made no mention of that country's pitiful human rights record or its internecine war that has claimed over 150,000 lives in a decade.

In 1988–89, Saddam Hussein ordered the gassing of 5,000 and the massacre of more than 100,000 Kurds. In 1991 after the First Gulf War, he was responsible for the killing of a similar number of Shiites. On June 4, 1994, Saddam's regime issued Decree 59, which prescribed—in accordance with traditional *shari'a* rulings—amputation of the right hand for a theft of less than ten dollars, amputation of the left foot for a second theft, and death for a third.[4] Decree 109, issued on August 18, 1994, prescribed tattooing or branding with an "X" between the eyebrows all persons who had undergone legally sanctioned amputations. Decree 115, which was issued on August 25, 1994, ordered the "cutting off of the auricle of one ear of each person evading military service" or deserting, as well as of those who sheltered such offenders. Any journalist, politician, businessman, or diplomat could have noticed the mutilated Iraqis punished by Saddam's judiciary. Yet, those crimes remained little known to the Western public until quite recently. In reliable polls, millions of Europeans backed Saddam Hussein against America in 2003 and even hoped for his success on the battlefield.

Until early 2004, European governments did not officially recognize the reality of Islamic terrorism as such. Instead, they blamed terrorism upon Israel's "occupation and injustice" toward the Palestinians, which allegedly provoked terror as an understandable reaction. Likewise, they refused to acknowledge the extent of antisemitism in Europe, and tended not only to vindicate anti-Israeli terrorism but also to justify or ignore the anti-Jewish aggression in Europe, in effect providing impunity for the attackers. Arab Judeophobic outbursts on European soil were blamed on Ariel Sharon's policies; thus, even though such acts often bordered on terrorism, they have generally gone unpunished.[5] Israel's "evil policies" somehow mitigated the crimes committed by immigrants of Arab-Muslim origin against European Jews and their community property, especially in France and Belgium.

The EU could not denounce its closest allies in the Middle East, the Palestinians; to do so would offend them and the Arab/Islamic countries. Attacks against European Jews were routinely ignored or denied in order to protect European political and economic interests in the Muslim world. Despite overwhelming factual evidence—the torching of schools and synagogues in France, the slaying and mutilation of a Jewish victim (which took place in Paris on November 19, 2003), and hostage taking—the European Union's ambassador in Israel declared that, while he could not say whether there was an increase in European antisemitism, there had definitely been an increase in anti-Muslim and anti-Arab feeling worldwide.[6] For such a high-ranking official to skirt around Judeophobia by changing the subject is in itself an antisemitic act. European leaders' efforts to represent antisemitism as criticism of Israeli policy cannot explain why the religious, civil, and human rights of European Jews in EU countries are not protected by their own governments. Furthermore, by maintaining that Israel's policies are largely responsible for antisemitic violence in Europe, the EU manipulates its terrorized European Jewish communities, as part of an overall anti-Israeli and pro-Arab strategy.

With slight nuances, the anti-American and anti-Israel discourse that was heard through 2003 into early 2004 on both shores of the Mediterranean is identical. It unfurled across Europe's national boundaries and spread within the context of the Euro-Arab informal diplomacy and alliances of the last thirty years. This process led to Europe's subservience to Arab/Muslim jihadist goals, cloaked in Western moral rhetoric as the pursuit of "justice and peace."[7] But official Muslim texts reveal a coalescence of European anti-Americanism, antisemitism, and jihadist tactics threatening Israel's right to exist and attempting to subvert America to Euro-Arab political dominance. Because *jihad* targets mainly Christianity worldwide, Europe's deliberate support of a jihadist demonization of America and Israel has become self-destructive.

The Arab-Israeli conflict, deliberately blown out of all proportion by the Euro-Arab associative diplomacy, is just one arena of an incessant global *jihad* that targets the entire West. PLO practices of airplane piracy since 1968, random killings, hostage takings, and Islamikaze bombings have been adopted worldwide as effective jihadist tactics against Western and other civilians, including Muslims.

The most notorious example of this *jihad*, the 9/11 attacks, was condemned by the European Union. However, some European leaders attributed *jihad* terrorism to American "arrogance." This apologetic rationale was already part of the European discourse. In 1999, former French Foreign Minister Hubert Vedrine defined the United States as a "primary international problem tending to inadmissible hegemony and unilateralism." Analyzing the French position soon after the Coalition's military victory over Saddam's regime in April 2003, *New York Times* correspondent John Vinocur stated, "If anything, for the French, this description has since been amplified through the war in Iraq."[8]

For decades, anti-Americanism has been festering among Washington's European allies, despite claims that Bush's current antiterror policies have actually created this phenomenon. The 9/11 atrocities inflamed Islamist fervor and provoked an explosion of euphoria, not only in many Muslim countries but also in certain segments of the European population. The casual European political pattern of blaming the victims of Islamic terror rather than its perpetrators was repeated, more as a knee-jerk reaction in this case than as a considered decision to outrage the memory of the American and other victims. Yet "Old Europe," accustomed as it was to ignoring Arab terrorism against its own European citizens and Israelis for political and commercial gain, now brought its anti-Americanism out into the open—with far more weighty consequences for itself than the abhorrence and disdain it routinely cast on Israeli victims.

The sudden awareness in certain Western countries, especially the United States, of the global extent of Islamic terrorism—as well as the worldwide media coverage it received and Washington's post-9/11 anti-terrorism measures—all offended Arab/Muslim sensibilities. In response, accusations that Jews, Israelis, and even the American government actually perpetrated the Islamist attacks on New York and Washington were circulated fast in both Muslim countries and Europe.[9] This thesis was published by a French author, Thierry Meyssan, in his book translated into English, *The Appalling Fraud.* Distributed in twenty-nine countries, the book benefited from powerful international support by European media, political, and literary figures. On April 13, 2004, the European television channel Arte showed a two-hour documentary program on the neo-Nazi and Arab networks involved in this book's success. The panel, composed of French and German intellectuals, discussed the cooperation and complicity of the national media in France and Germany, including publishers and academics, and all agreed that antisemitism was feeding such rumors.[10] Simultaneously, numerous Internet sites contended that Muslims were being calumniated and Islam's prestige and honor tarnished by the reactions to 9/11 and by the new antiterrorist security regulations, while lamenting that sympathy for Israel and Americans was increasing.[11]

Muslim "humiliation," in turn, caused European Jews to suffer more violent attacks and further defamation by the mass media. This violence and incitement evoked a number of carefully calibrated, "neutral" government declarations consistent with the long-standing policy of not distinguishing between the perpetrators and supporters of such acts, and their victims. Panicked by the fear of renewed terror on its own soil, the EU increased its financial and moral support for the Palestinians while blaming "American unilateralism" for endangering the peace of the planet. Israel's retaliation against terrorist bases in the Palestinian controlled areas, following a wave of jihadist bombings targeting Israeli civilians, brought crowds of European pacifists into Bethlehem, Ramallah, and Gaza to act as "human shields" for the Palestinians. Some Muslim immigrants in Europe expressed their rage by attacking individual Jews or damaging schools, shops, synagogues, and cemeteries.

The campaign of hate against Israel increased in 2002, as America successfully uncovered the Arab/Islamist terror network in Afghanistan and elsewhere—further humiliating the Arab/Muslim world. European opinion focused on the disadvantages suffered by Muslims from antiterror operations, while anti-Americanism reached new heights. As incredible as it may seem, well-established European newspapers often affirmed that Israel should not benefit from the wave of sympathy shared by other victims of *jihad* terror.[12] The year 2001 saw a sixfold increase in acts of violence in Europe against Jewish people and property. More than 70 percent of the violent racist acts reported to police, as well as other racist deeds such as threats, insults, and graffiti, were against Jews.[13] The Jewish community of

France was the target of over thirteen hundred hate crimes and incidents between September 2002 and March 2003. America's wars against Islamist terrorism had provoked Euro-Arab retaliation against Jews.[14] Roman Catholic Cardinal Roberto Tucci declared on Radio Vatican, "Antisemitism that is rife in the Islamic world today is comparable to the antisemitism of the Nazi era."[15] Jews were not the only victims. As the Asian subcontinent conflicts flared up, Hindus and Sikhs in England, mainly in Bradford, were targeted by Muslim violence. Antiwhite prejudices incensed riots in Oldham in 2001.

Meanwhile, America's decision to destroy Saddam Hussein's terror regime raised European anti-Jewish demonstrations to a fever pitch not seen since World War II. Gigantic rallies took place in most European cities; many participants cursed America, Bush, Israel, and the Jews; demonstrators burned flags; handwringing prelates and clerics who had never denounced attacks on Jews in Europe and Israel, or the persecution of Christians in the Palestinian territories and throughout the Islamic world, made appeals for peace and fraternity. Millions protested against America, Britain, and Israel, thereby proclaiming their sympathy for two of the world's worst tyrants: Saddam Hussein and Yasser Arafat. Enormous demonstrations against the war, which in fact were in solidarity with the dictatorial regimes of Saddam's Iraq and Arafat's Palestinian Authority, were staged across Europe and the Muslim world. Those in Europe often outdid those in the Middle East. The frequent accusations by French officials and media figures that Israelis and Jewish hawks had hijacked the American government aroused Arab and European violence against Jews. Americans and Britons were harassed too. In France, they were advised to take extra precautions—even to the extent of avoiding speaking English in sensitive places. At its core, this anti-American and anti-Jewish vitriol expressed not only a deep-seated antisemitism but also the European politicians' tremendous fear of Islamist terrorism.

Rancorous anti-American slurs were reiterated by the European media, and overwrought anti-American demonstrators filled Europe's streets: had the Mediterranean Sea suddenly evaporated, making Europe an extension of the Arab/Muslim world? Jihadist gangs were now trying to dictate European policies and elections, as in Spain after the Madrid bombings of March 11, 2004, which killed nearly two hundred. The Iraqi kidnappers of four Italian hostages demanded that the Italian government, specifically Prime Minister Silvio Berlusconi, issue an apology for Italy's insult to Islam and Muslims.[16] After killing one of them, they ordered the Italians to demonstrate in the streets to save the life of the remaining three. Thousands obeyed out of solidarity with the hostages, but they were not liberated then, only later. Another Italian hostage was decapitated soon after.

In her latest book, *Oriana Fallaci intervista Oriana Fallaci*, the Italian writer, in her courageous style, strongly denounces European antisemitism and, in a wider perspective, the betrayal of Europe.[17]

How did Europe arrive at such a crossroads? Was Europe the target of a war of political and cultural subversion, undertaken by its own politicians, media, and intellectuals? What is the current meaning of Europe? Is there still a Europe at all, or are we witnessing its mutation into a conglomerate Euro-Arab continent?

This brief study will endeavor to trace the main steps of a transformation that has already begun in Europe, the birth of a new *dhimmi* civilization: Eurabia.

2

Historical Background

Although extensive Islamic territories lie close to some Western countries and millions of Muslim immigrants have settled in European cities, a number of Western politicians prefer not to recognize that this phenomenon might be problematic. However, it is ultimately against their best interests to pretend to be blind and deaf to the hostility that emanates from these nearby, overcrowded Islamic lands and now reverberates in Western European towns and neighborhoods. Neither American policy nor Israel's perversity have bred this hostility; it is nourished by a culture of aversion toward, and hatred of, infidels. Clearly, a large percentage of Muslims do not share this Islamist view; many have totally rejected these traditional interpretations, and many also ignore them. Nonetheless, it would be criminal and suicidal for those whom such hatred targets to deny its existence as a major trend among the illiterate Muslim population, and their religious leaders, in the fifty-six states and the Palestinian Authority that constitute the Organization of the Islamic Conference (OIC).

European obsequiousness, or its policy of weakening Israel while defaming America and whitewashing Christian sufferings in Muslim countries, will not help to alleviate this hatred, entrenched as it is in religion, history, and tradition. Westerners should have the moral courage to acknowledge its reality instead of hiding behind an appeasement policy that targets scapegoats.

Jihad is central to Islamic history and civilization. It has not been fundamentally questioned or changed since the founders of Islamic jurisprudence propounded it in the eighth and ninth centuries—although some modern Muslim scholars, living mainly in the West, have initiated some new critical interpretations. The Syrian-born scholar Bassam Tibi, currently Director and Professor of International Relations at the University of Göttingen in Germany, has written an incisive critique of *jihad*. Soheib Bensheikh, the mufti of Marseilles, France, has advocated a desacralization of the *shari'a* but has balanced his progressive views with anti-Zionism. Sheikh Abdul Hadi Palazzi, an active pro-Israeli imam in Milan, Italy, strongly critical of Arafat and the Hamas leadership, is, nonetheless, a staunch supporter of the idea that *jihad* is only a moral struggle.

Ibn Warraq, a former Muslim, is one of the few intellectuals from the Islamic world who has had the courage to criticize Islam in a systematic way—scrutinizing every tenet; examining the language, content, and origin of the Qur'an; and critically evaluating the historical sources of our knowledge on the rise and spread of Islam in several books he edited, of increasing scholarly depth, after his initial work, *Why I Am Not a Muslim* (1995).[1]

Nevertheless, reforming trends in Islam remain marginal, while *jihad*'s traditional legal regulations are reiterated today by luminaries like Sheikh Yusef al-Qaradhawi, the spiritual leader of the Muslim Brotherhood and head of the European Council for Fatwa and Research, and Sheikh Mohammad Sayyid Al-Tantawi, the Grand Imam of the prestigious Al-Azhar University in Cairo. Such jurists, for example, interpreted the 2003 Coalition war against Saddam Hussein as an attack by infidels against the whole Muslim *umma*, mandating the participation of all Muslims, in conformity with *jihad*'s rules. In Egypt, the Islamic Center for Research at Al-Azhar issued a communiqué, approved by Tantawi, emphasizing that *jihad* becomes an individual obligation for every Muslim when enemies raid an Islamic land, "because [otherwise] our Muslim nation will be subject to a new Crusader invasion targeting the land, honor, belief, and homeland."[2]

The call for *jihad* came also from the grand mufti of Syria, Ahmed Kuftaro: "I call on Muslims everywhere to use all means possible to thwart the aggression, including martyr operations against the belligerent American, British and Zionist invaders."[3] In *Onward Muslim Soldiers*, Robert Spencer has documented many of the calls by Muslims for a general *jihad*, issued in the Arab countries, Europe, the Philippines, Indonesia and Malaysia, before the operations in Iraq.[4] More recently, Patrick Sookhdeo, in his *Understanding Islamic Terrorism*, provides a concise and clear picture of the traditional and modern foundations of *jihad* and its application and interpretations today in the Muslim world and in Europe. He examines the modern Muslim critical trend and its opponents and recalls that even Sheikh Tantawi of al-Azhar University "teaches that it is permissible for Muslims to fight non-Muslims in other countries for no greater injury than that the non-Muslims are 'actively condemning or belittling' Muslims or the religion of Islam."[5]

Thus, wherever the ideology of *jihad* and its precepts have not been rejected, Muslims relate to non-Muslims within its conceptual framework. Although the call to *jihad* is often pronounced in European, as well as in Muslim capitals, few Westerners have understood what it really means. Analysts deliberately mislead the public by using the Crusades in order to create a sense of moral equivalency between Christianity and Islam and to calm European concerns about *jihad*.

They ignore, of course, that *jihad*, as an ideology and a praxis, was unremittingly active in Asia, Africa, and Europe four centuries before the Crusades. Beginning early in the eighth century, a formal set of rules to govern relationships between Muslims and non-Muslims was elaborated, based upon Islamic conquests, practices, theology, and jurisprudence. This theological-juridical conception is called *jihad*. In the early centuries of Islam, Muslim theologians and jurists endeavored to give a religious and legal structure to *jihad*. Living during and after the great wave of Arab-Muslim expansion over the mainly Christian lands they had conquered, they built their theory of *jihad* on their interpretations of the Qur'an and the *hadith* (the words and acts attributed to the prophet Muhammad). Their elaboration of the concept and doctrine of *jihad* established the relationship between Muslims and non-Muslims in terms of belligerency, temporary armistices, and submission. These scholars defined the aims, tactics, and strategies of *jihad*, as well as specific rules concerning troops, compulsory conditions for treaties, the treatment of prisoners, and the division of booty.

The ideology, strategy, and tactics of *jihad* have constituted throughout history a fundamental part of Islamic jurisprudence and literature, since it is through *jihad* that the Islamic community developed and expanded. Muslim theologians explained that *jihad* is a collective religious duty (*fard al-kifaya*) binding the entire Muslim community and each individual (*fard al-ayn*) in certain situations and circumstances. The collective effort can be pursued by military means or peaceful methods—propaganda, speech, or subversive activities—within a non-Muslim nation. The "enemies" are those who oppose the establishment of Islamic law or its spread, mission, or sovereignty over their lands. The world of infidels is considered as one entity, called *dar al-harb*, the region of war—until, through *jihad*, it comes under Islamic rule. The hostilities between the region of Islam (*dar al-Islam*) and the region of war (*dar al-harb*) must continue as long as unbelief exists.

The universality of *jihad* was proclaimed from the beginnings of Islam. *Jihad* has been ordered not only against specific groups or for specific times, but, like Muhammad's mission (Qur'an 34:28), it is a universal injunction that will endure until the only religion remaining is that of Allah (Qur'an 2:189). This ongoing striving "in the path of Allah" triggers the process that Huntington has called "Islam's bloody borders";[6] that is, Islam's continuous expansion through attacks on its neighbors, in accord with the Qur'an's command to "fight the unbelievers who gird you about" (9:124).

There are countless treatises on *jihad* written today by Muslim jurists and theologians. They reaffirm this standardized interpretation and conceptualization of international relations. Thus, Ismail Raji al-Faruqi (d. 1986), who taught in the Universities of Chicago and Syracuse, and was a professor in the Department of Religion at Temple University, wrote that all Muslims hope that the Islamic state will some day include the whole world. He affirmed: "The doctrine of Jihad or Holy War is valid in Islam."[7]

The *jihad* conception classifies infidels under three categories: 1) those who oppose the Islamic call with arms; 2) those who belong to the countries of truce; 3) those who have surrendered to Islamic domination, exchanging their land for peace; they become "*dhimmis*," "protected" from the ongoing *jihad* war against non-Muslims by a treaty of subjection and protection (*dhimma*).

The infidels of the first category are called *harbis;* they belong to the *dar al-harb*, the region where warfare is mandatory as long as they refuse to recognize Islam's supremacy.

The infidels of the second category are in a situation of respite between two wars since, in principle, the truce with infidels cannot exceed ten years, after which *jihad* must resume. They live under the regime of *dar al-sulh,* the land of temporary truce. There are two possible motivations for Islamic authorities to conclude a truce with infidels: 1) Muslims are too weak to win the war; 2) the infidel leaders agree to pay a tribute to the Muslim ruler to obtain the cessation of hostilities, those latter including rampages, abductions, enslavement, and killings.[8] The countries of *dar al-sulh* must also abstain from hindering the development of Islam in their lands. In the event of war, they should provide military contingents to the Islamic armies.[9] Moreover, only the treaties that conform to the stipulations of Islamic jurisprudence are valid, and they must be renewed every ten years. If those conditions are not fulfilled the treaties are invalidated. The refusal to allow the propagation of Islam in the lands of truce is tantamount to a casus belli, and *jihad* can resume.

Forty years ago, French scholar Charles-Emmanuel Dufourcq noted as a basic point, the difficulties in the elaboration and maintenance of treaties between Christian and Muslim countries. He explained that according to the juridical concept of *jihad*, war was the normal state of relations between Muslims and Christians. All trade and other treaties between them were called "truce treaties," or, in effect, declarations of peace, rather than of war: "It was not war that was proclaimed but peace." The duration of each treaty was specified.[10] Every Muslim ruler, including the Ottoman sultans, through the nineteenth century, enforced such "peace proclamation" treaties in their relationships with non-Muslim societies and governments.

The infidels of the third category are those who have surrendered without fighting to the Muslim ruler. Their lands are integrated into the *dar al-Islam*, the territory of Islam, and their non-Muslim vanquished inhabitants are protected from the *jihad* onslaught by a treaty, the *dhimma*, which establishes their rights and duties. They become *dhimmis*, whose *dhimma* protection pact safeguards them as infidels against the rules of *jihad* targeting non-Muslims. The peace of *jihad* is founded on the principle "peace and security in exchange for land": peace and security are conceded by the *jihad* armies if the infidels cede their territory and submit to the rules of dhimmitude.

I have called "dhimmitude" this condition of "subjection with protection" of non-Muslims in their own countries, obtained by the cession of their land to the Muslim ruler. Subjection, because the infidels submit to the Islamic law which expropriates them, and protection because this same law protects them from *jihad* and guarantees limited rights under a system of discriminations that they must accept, or face forced conversion, slavery or death. Dhimmitude is the direct outcome of *jihad*.

Jihad thus represents a unique ideology of continuous and universal religious war. People unfamiliar with its history might believe that it remained an abstraction. Quite the contrary: in the course of one century, beginning in 641 after *jihad* armies had already conquered Arabia and advanced into the surrounding areas, Islamic conquests expanded over Christian lands from Armenia to Portugal. By the second decade of the eighth century, Muhammad bin Qasim's *jihad* campaigns had extended the Muslim empire to Sind, on the Indian subcontinent. Other conquests in Byzantine and European lands followed in the next centuries. The newly conquered countries around the Mediterranean had been populated by Christians, with large Jewish minorities. Waves of colonists from Arabia followed the Muslim armies of occupation.[11] These settlers gradually became majorities through the occupants' policy of colonization, land dispossession, fiscal oppression and, at times, slavery and deportation.[12]

Yet Muslims do not view their *jihad* campaigns in this context, despite extensive historical documentation by both Muslim and non-Muslim chroniclers. Because mandatory *jihad* and dhimmitude rules are justified by Islam's sacred texts, criticism is prohibited. The oppression and persecution of the infidels, including Jews and Christians, are the rightful punishment deserved by the *kuffar* (infidels) for refusing Islam's truth. Any derogatory comments of Islamic rule enshrined in the *shari'a*, the religious Islamic law, is tantamount to blasphemy. For Muslims, the Qur'an is the verbatim uncreated word of Allah. Those who create obstacles for the propagation of Islam and refuse to submit to conversion or Islamic world governance are responsible for the wars that follow. Infidels are to blame because they oppose the will of Allah. In his critical examination of *jihad* theory, Bassam Tibi—a scholar and a moderate Muslim—observes that, according to Islamic doctrine, "Any war against unbelievers, whatever its immediate grounds, is morally justified."[13]

The Muslim conquerors could not have maintained their hold over the overwhelmingly Christian populations of the lands conquered by *jihad* had it not been for the support and collaboration of Christian princes, patriarchs, and army commanders.[14] This collusion derived from a context of inter-Christian dynastic and religious rivalries or personal ambitions. Coming from the highest levels of power and authority in administrative, eccle- *arians* siastical, and military bodies, these betrayals triggered the Islamization of millions of Christians. Whereas in a Christian realm the Church would be subject to a Christian king who would interfere in theological definitions, control the patriarch's treasury and curtail his power, under the Islamic caliphate the patriarch was given exclusive responsibility for his Christian flock. But this prerogative was conceded on his total compliance with the caliph's service and orders. The patriarch thus became the instrument of the caliph's anti-Christian policy and oppression, guaranteeing the steady trend toward Islamization.

A historical overview of the complex and numerous intricacies that led to the Islamization of powerful Christian civilizations spread over the Middle East, North Africa, the Iberian Peninsula, Anatolia, and Southeastern Europe reveals several unchanging key elements. Permanent factors of Islamization constitute fixed components of the *jihad* policy toward Christendom. Within this context, with its alternate periods of wars, conquest, temporary peace treaties, terrorlike practices and alliances, three important factors emerged throughout the period of Islamization:

1) The gradual erosion of resistance within the societies targeted but not yet conquered by *jihad*, concurring with their growing economic weakness due to the tribute required for the Muslim overlords' renewal of the truce. During and after their subjugation, their demographic decline followed as a result of warfare, massacres, slavery, abduction of women and children, and deportation, until the situation stabilized;[15]

2) The insecurity caused by the constant mass immigration of foreign populations and the subsequent process of alteration and substitution of one civilization by another, hostile to the indigenous inhabitants;

3) The emergence of powerful collaborationist parties economically and politically linked with Muslim rulers.

Hence it was within the religious, political, intellectual, and economic domains of the Christian world that the system of dhimmitude developed and grew. The culture of dhimmitude was characterized by surrender and passive submission, imposed by leaders who had been won over to the service of Islam by ambition and financial interest.

Now in the twenty-first century, we again live in a context of *jihad*, and the Islamists have made it clear that they still subscribe to the traditional classification of the infidels into these three categories. *Jihad* is being waged today on all continents through terrorist activities, abductions for ransom, the indiscriminate killing of civilians and, in Sudan, ongoing slavery. While some countries—America, India, Israel, Russia, the Philippines, Sudan, Kenya, Nigeria and now Spain—are directly targeted by jihadist forces, others are considered to be *dar al-sulh*, countries of temporary treaties. In the Islamic view of international relations, the European Union can today be placed in the category of "lands of temporary truce," as Osama bin Laden implied in his summer 2004 message.

Benefiting from the Dialogue policy, millions of Muslims have immigrated into Europe, where they have built hundreds of mosques and powerful Islamic centers. In these mosques and cultural centers, they influence strongly both religious and political developments, without hindrance. Arab and Muslim newspapers, propaganda books, and leaflets are widely distributed in every European capital—including *The Protocols of the Elders of Zion* in Arabic—as well as in the many cities and universities where Euro-Arab dialogues and encounters are frequent events. Islam and Islamic issues have become paramount everywhere, imposing a preemptive control on minds and thought, and fusing religion, propaganda, and politics. What is emerging is a new Eurabian culture with its own dogma, preachers, axioms, and rules.[16]

The traditional Islamic international politic was confirmed at the Lahore second Islamic Conference in 1974 by the secretary-general of the conference, Mohammed al-Tohami, when he called for the building of a broad base of faithful men capable of leading the Islamic state in all fields to outstrip non-Muslim countries. "Such leadership would set an example for those who wish to stem the tide of aberration and perdition and to protect the sons of our contemporary generation against the blind and meaningless limitations of the ways, customs and concepts of non-Muslims."

A contemporary Iranian shi'ite scholar in Islamic jurisprudence, Abbasali Amid Zanjani, recently devoted a book to the examination in modern terms of the Islamic principles of jurisprudence, according to what he calls "the Law of the Tribute Agreement"—which is, in fact, the *jizya*, resulting from the *dhimma* pact of protection given to Jews and Christians subjected by a successful *jihad*.[17] Zanjani expresses the standard Islamic position when he states that Islamic law forbids cultural dependence and any cultural accord that subordinates Muslim culture to that of foreigners (non-Muslims). As he put it, "Islam strongly rejects such a friendship and forbids the Muslims from engaging in such a treason."[18] He quotes numerous Qur'anic verses prohibiting friendship with non-Muslims in order to preserve Muslim's prestige and leadership.[19] Adopting ideas and following ways of non-Muslims "would involve the loss of independence and leadership in favor of others, transformation of the Islamic morals and ways, and inclination towards those of the non-Muslims, and ultimate perversion."[20]

Zanjani justifies the struggle against these polluted ideas, foreign to the *shari'a*, by quoting the Qur'anic verse 4:140: "And Allah will never give the disbelievers a way against the believers," and the hadith, "Islam surmounts, not surmounted."[21]

On 20 December 1999, the *Shari'a* Court of the United Kingdom issued a *fatwa* prohibiting any Muslim from participating in Christmas or Christian New Year celebrations taking place in the Millennium Dome.[22] Sheikh Omar Bakri Muhammad, the Principal Judge of the Court and leader of the al-Muhajirun movement, gave several reasons for this. For example, it is forbidden for Muslims

> to imitate the non-Muslims (i.e. Kuffar) in their religious or ritual celebrations such as celebrating Christmas or the Christian calendar. There are many sayings of the Messenger Muhammad (saw) forbidding the Muslims to copy the Mushrikeen (polytheists) and Jews and Christians. There are also narrations ordering Muslims to be different from the Mushrikeen, the Jews and Christians, in relation to following anything which is part of their religion. (Parentheses explanations in the original)[23]

At the beginning of the nineteenth century, when the modernization of the Ottoman Empire was in progress, the same problem relating to the adoption of Western laws provoked strong opposition to the reforming policy of the sultan.[24] Only through direct rule and colonization could Western concepts be propagated among resentful Muslim populations in Asia and Africa. Today, at the dawn of the twenty-first century, a conflict of civilizations is reemerging on European soil in the context of Islamic immigration. Western politicians choose to circumvent, rather than confront it. Many even claim that secularism is a Qur'anic not an original Western conception, in the hope of facilitating the integration of Muslim immigrants into their modern secular societies. Numerous Muslims have successfully adapted to Western democracy, but they are still the exceptions. Despite the EU's conciliatory policy, preachers in mosques continue to call Christians and Jews "infidels," descendants of "apes and pigs," "enemies of Allah belonging to the camp of Kufr (unbelief)" and to request Muslims to educate their children in the spirit of *jihad*.[25]

For al-Faruqi *jihad* can be waged for two reasons: defense and, as he wrote,

> the undoing of injustice wherever it takes place. Like the Muslim individual within *Dar al-Islam*, the Islamic state regards itself, and does so rightly, as viceregent of God in space and time, a vocation which lays a great responsibility upon the Islamic state . . . to redress injustice wherever men have caused it—even if that has been [on] the other side of the moon.[26]

The word "injustice" conforms here to the *shari'a* legal definition of justice.

Iranian ayatollah Morteza Mutahhari explains the legitimacy of *jihad* against non-Muslims—albeit with different arguments. Religion—that is *tawhid*—pertains to the universal rights of humanity, and as it is legitimate to defend the rights of humanity, so it is legitimate to defend *tawhid* against others. He argues that as polytheism is evil, it is allowed to Muslims to fight in order to suppress this evil. Moreover, if *tawhid* pertains to the rights of humanity and represent a condition for its welfare and prosperity, it is permissible to start a war against the *mushrikin* (polytheists), in order to uphold religion (Islam) and uproot corruption. He makes a distinction between freedom of thought and freedom of belief to affirm that war is allowed to free humanity from the bondage and internal chain of wrong beliefs.[27]

America's current policy of withstanding jihadism uncompromisingly acknowledges its imminent danger to Western civilization. In contrast, denying this peril, European countries have engaged consistently in policies of appeasement and are often opposed to confronting the jihadist threat—including threats against modernist European Muslims living in their midst. During the millennium of encounters between Islam and non-Muslims, this latter type of behavior, motivated by fear and greed, has a name: dhimmitude.

3

Knitting the Threads Together

After World War II, Charles de Gaulle began the reconstruction of France. He retained many of the officials of the Vichy collaborationist government, including even those who could have been condemned as war criminals for their participation in the deportation of Jews to the death camps.[1] During the war, the Pétain government established on French territory twenty-eight main detention camps where Jews were confined by the French police. From there they were deported to Nazi death camps in Eastern Europe.

De Gaulle had been humiliated by France's exclusion from the 1945 Yalta negotiations between the U.S., Britain, and Soviet Russia about Europe's future. Furthermore, during the next fifteen years France's loss of its colonial empire significantly reduced Paris's prestige as a great power. Gaullist practitioners of realpolitik had formulated a strategy to restore France's influence. This entailed two convergent policies, which they hoped to implement both in Europe and in the Arab-Muslim world: the unification of Europe as an international counterweight to America and an alliance with the Arab and African Muslim world, which they considered an economic and geopolitical element of France's postcolonial sphere of influence.

The latter position was strongly advocated in 1945 by Haj Amin al-Hussaini, the former mufti of Jerusalem and a notorious Nazi ally who was Hitler's guest in Berlin from 1941. After the German defeat he was declared a war criminal and was actively hunted by the British for having fomented a coup d'état in Iraq in 1941 to establish a pro-Nazi government. This led to hundreds of Jews being killed and wounded in a three-day pogrom (May 31–June 2, 1941). Haj Amin also recruited an SS division with Arab and Bosnian Muslims in the Balkans, and collaborated with the Nazis in the genocide of European Jewry. The mufti claimed that he was handed over to the Red Cross to escape from American arrest.[2] He failed to obtain refuge in Switzerland in 1945, and after surrendering to the French forces in Germany, he was brought to France on May 19, 1945, with Marshall Pétain,[3] and then transferred on de Gaulle's orders to a Paris suburban residence under French protection.

39

De Gaulle refused to let him be judged as a war criminal by the Nuremberg tribunal. A preeminent leader among the Muslim masses, and especially the Muslim Brotherhood, the mufti became an agent of French influence in the Arab countries. He pleaded for a Franco-Arab alliance against the British and the Zionists, stressing French and Arab common interests. Through his powerful Arab networks, he proposed a French policy of solidarity with the Arab world. Meanwhile, public knowledge of his close collaboration with the Nazis and his war crimes, led the French to facilitate his escape on May 29, 1946, from the Paris villa to which he had been moved. He then returned to Egypt, maintaining his contact with the French embassy in Cairo and with French diplomats, calling for a Muslim-Catholic alliance against the Protestants and the Jews.[4] He finally settled in Lebanon in 1962.

On his return to power in 1958, de Gaulle maintained the pro-Israel socialist government policy from the mid-1950s. In 1961, he received Israel's Prime Minister David Ben Gurion at the Elysée calling Israel "notre ami et notre allié" (our friend and our ally). After Algeria gained its independence in 1962, de Gaulle set out to reorient France's policy toward the Arab/Islamic world. He pursued economic and strategic long-range planning designed to unite the European and Arab countries of the Mediterranean into a single, interdependent economic bloc that would oppose America. Since the mid-nineteenth century, France had adopted an Islamophile orientation determined by its ever-growing Arab-Muslim empire in Africa and the Middle East. Its conquest of Algeria (1830), Guinea, Gabon (1843–44), Mauritania, Senegal (1854–65), Tunisia (1882), French Equatorial Africa (1910) (today Chad, Gabon, Congo, and Central African Republic), Madagascar (1895–96), the Comoros, Morocco (1912) and the Mandates over Syria and Lebanon after World War I, made France an "Islamic Empire." From the 1880s, Paris has been one of the most antisemitic cities in Europe, competing with Vienna, a tendency that led the Vichy government to collaborate fully with Nazi and Arab anti-Jewish racism. Because of its components and the history of both parties, France's Arab policy included a strong underlying antisemitism.

Haj Amin's calls for an active Franco-Arab alliance were abetted by influential French politicians and intellectuals who urged the government to adopt a coherent policy toward the Muslim world. They cherished France's ambition since the days of Bonaparte and Napoleon III: a grand Arab Empire stretching from Algiers to Syria, under French control, with Eastern Christians as the agents of Paris. They believed that France's association with a Muslim federation extending over North Africa and the Middle East would bring it an ascendancy that would impress the Soviet Union and rival the United States. Pierre Lyautey—nephew of Marshall Lyautey, the first French governor of Morocco—championed a Franco-Muslim association in several studies on Euro-Arab relations. In May 1962 he stated, "A French Islamic policy carried out together with the new Algeria, Morocco and Tunisia, perhaps linked tomorrow with a North African federation, and with the states of the Middle East, would bring us a prestige which would impress the United States and the USSR."[5] De Gaulle shared with his collaborators his wish to build a community with all the Mediterranean countries, different from the American model.[6] At the prestigious Collège de France in Paris, the influential scholar of Islam, Louis Massignon (1883–1962) delivered his lectures on Islamic subjects with a pro-Islamic fervor, contrasting with a violent Judeophobia and anti-capitalism.[7]

French Arab policy coalesced with de Gaulle's greatest ambition: the creation of a unified Europe whose centerpiece was an unprecedented rapprochement between two traditional enemies, France and what was then West Germany. In 1951, these two countries, along with Belgium, Italy, Luxembourg, and the Netherlands, signed the Treaty of Paris. This Treaty formed the initial basis for an economic European community: the European Coal and Steel Community (ECSC). In 1957, these same countries signed the treaties of Rome, founding the European Economic Community (EEC) and the European Atomic Energy Community (EURATOM), which aimed at economic integration. De Gaulle, displeased with London's close links with America, rejected Britain's application to join the European Community in 1961 and again in 1967.

As strange as this may have seemed in the years immediately following America's rescue of France from Nazi tyranny, French hostility toward America ran high. It was fed on the left by the communists and their sympathizers and on the right by pro-Nazi collaborators from the Vichy regime. They remained influential and continued to serve even at the uppermost levels of the postwar French government. Anti-American animus in French government circles was so intense that the eminent French philosopher Raymond Aron noted in 1968 that France "was supporting wittingly and deliberately all those in the Third World who professed the most hostile feelings to Americans and Westerners." He wondered: "Is every friend of the United States an enemy of France?" Aron commented, "in fact everything transpires as if General de Gaulle's supreme objective was to oppose everywhere and always the United States. . . . Does not the current anti-American obsession resemble the anti-British obsession of Vichy in 1940?"[8]

In 1948, the nascent State of Israel defeated five invading Arab armies. Israel had a minuscule territory devoid of any natural resources and its population included the remnants of the Jews who had lived in their ancestral homeland since biblical times, together with three contingents of Jewish refugees. One comprised the Jews expelled during the 1948 war from the British mandate areas of Palestine (Gaza, Judea, Samaria, and the Old City of Jerusalem) by the armies of Egypt, Syria, Transjordan, and Iraq, helped

by their Arab Palestinian allies. Along with these Palestinian Jewish refugees who had lost their land, homes, and synagogues, came two larger contingents of Jewish refugees who were equally dispossessed. One was
returning from the ashes of Europe, leaving behind the death camps of
Europe's recent history; the other was fleeing the Arab countries of the
Middle East and North Africa, where they had long suffered discrimination, expropriations and confiscations, imprisonment, massacres, and ex-
pulsions.

While Israel was establishing itself, the network that had united European Nazis and fascists with Arabs before World War II was reemerging. In
the early 1950s, many Nazi criminals and collaborators had found asylum
in the Arab world, mainly in Egypt and Syria. There they lived under false
names and worked in anti-Zionist propaganda centers, such as the Institute
for the Study of Zionism, which was founded in Cairo in 1955. Its director,
Alfred Zingler (alias Mahmoud Saleh), worked together with Dr. Johannes
von Leers (d. 1965, alias Omar Amin), who had been a specialist on the
"Jewish question" in Josef Goebbels's propaganda department. Zingler's
main assistants were Dr. Werner Witschale and Hans Appler (Saleh Sha-
far), who had also served on the staff of Goebbels's ministry, as well as
Louis Heiden. Heiden was the editor of one of the many Arabic versions of
The Protocols of the Elders of Zion and of a translation of Hitler's *Mein Kampf*
into Arabic. In 1955, the Cairo Egyptian special services for anti-Jewish and
anti-Zionist propaganda hired Appler.

Other Nazis settled in Egypt as well. Most of them worked with the Egyptian government as advisers on anti-Zionist propaganda or assisted with the
organization of police forces or as military trainers in Palestinian terrorist
camps. In 1957, according to the *Frankfurter Illustrierte*, the number of Nazis
in Egypt was over two thousand.[9] Erich Altern (Ali Bella), the chief of the
Jewish section of the Gestapo in occupied Galicia during the war, escaped
to Egypt in the early 1950s, where he served as a military instructor in the
Palestinian camps. Baumann (Ali Ben Khader), who had collaborated in
the extermination of Jews in the Warsaw ghetto and went into hiding, became a military specialist in Egypt for the army of the Palestine Liberation
Organization (PLO).

By the 1960s, Arab activities in Europe had greatly increased. Arab diplomats, Arab League offices, and thousands of Arab students in European
universities all contributed to a much stronger Arab presence. Networks
were established between Arabs and neo-Nazi and fascist movements eager
to build close links with the Arab world. They planned to issue propaganda
leaflets, pamphlets, and books on the "Jewish Question," as well as distribute Arab League literature dealing with the Middle East. They circulated
the *Protocols of the Elders of Zion* and anti-Zionist propaganda.

A European Nazi-Arab network emerged to exchange information on world affairs and facts concerning Jewish activities in all countries. It also fostered suitable liaisons with Arab representatives. Many of these Nazi and fascist groups aimed at building a European Middle East policy. In Germany, the head of the Arab office in Bonn, Hassan Awat Fakoussa, an attaché at the Egyptian Embassy, published a weekly information bulletin that contained much material from the neo-Nazi press (*Deutsche National-Zeitung, Deutsche Wochen-Zeitung*). One of the leading figures in the German neo-Nazi movement, a former SS officer named Karl Ernst Priester, was a founding member of the European Social Movement. After his death, a police investigation revealed that he was one of the chief European agents for the Arab League.[10]

In Austria, the right-wing organs were *Reichsruf* and *Nation Europa*, a monthly for intellectuals. In Belgium, Paul E. Laurent, a former Belgian SS sympathizer, headed the Centre de Documentation pour la Collaboration avec les Peuples Arabes and kept links with the fascist movements *Jeune Europe*, *EuropaFront*, and *Europe Réelle*. In the United Kingdom, the British leader of the Nazi National Socialist Movement, Colin Jordan, maintained Arab-Nazi cooperation. In Sweden, the C. E. Carlberg Foundation in Stockholm supported this collaboration and close contacts with Arabs, particularly with what was then the United Arab Republic of Egypt and Syria (UAR). Such links developed also with Italian fascist movements.

Thus, postwar fascist and neo-Nazi groups endeavored to establish a widespread network throughout Europe. Many were funded by the Arab League. Despite their racist ideology, some sought the Arab alliance because they shared the same hatred of Israel. They opened offices in various key cities—Strasbourg, Vienna, Lausanne, and Malmö, an important conference center in Sweden, and elsewhere. James Parkes, historian and Anglican clergyman, has listed some of these organizations in his 1963 book, *Antisemitism*.[11]

Although numerous, these organizations failed to gain large numbers of members and were forced to operate in a semiclandestine fashion. They all rejected parliamentary democracy and shared a profound hatred of the Jews, Israel, and America—the power that had destroyed the Nazi-fascist dream of world hegemony.

In May 1967, the expulsion of the UN Peace Corps from Sinai by the Egyptian leader Gamel Abdel Nasser, along with the closure of the Straits of Tiran at the Gulf of Akaba to Israeli shipping, provided a casus belli. Israel tried diplomacy for three weeks without success. On June 2, de Gaulle announced an embargo on all military equipment to the Middle East—in fact only Israel was affected. When Jordan joined Egypt and Syria for a three-pronged attack, Israel launched a preemptive strike on June 5. De Gaulle immediately declared Israel the aggressor. Raymond Aron recorded that an Israeli politician who was known to be a reliable source had

told him that if Nasser had not had implicit French support, he would
never have decreed the blockade of the Gulf of Akaba.[12] Quite unexpectedly, Israel won the war rapidly and decisively on all fronts in six days.

French officials did not congratulate Israel for its lightning victory over
Egypt, Syria, Jordan, and the Palestinian Arabs—who were all supported by
the rest of the Arab and Muslim world. Five days after the UN Resolution
242—rejected by the Arab countries—de Gaulle, in a press conference on
November 27, 1967, condemned Israel's foreign policy. He presented
France's cooperation with the Arab world as "the fundamental basis of our
foreign policy."[13] The Association of Franco-Arab solidarity was created at
that time, with the blessing and participation of distinguished Gaullist diplomats, ministers, and intellectuals. The Catholic Church was also wholeheartedly behind the Arab cause, despite the fact that Arab Christians
tended to promote a modern version of the replacement theology that had
been rejected as un-Christian by the Second Vatican Council (1962–65).
The Church's support for the Arab cause was praised at the Lahore Islamic
summit in 1974, although the pro-Palestinian militancy of many Churches
had drawn strong criticism from individual clergymen. At international forums, France voted consistently in favor of Arab League anti-Israeli resolutions. In December 1968, Arab terrorists destroyed an El Al plane in
Athens; Israel answered by destroying planes at Beirut airport. In retaliation, France backed a unilateral boycott of arms sales to the Jewish state
(1969). After the 1967 Six–Day War, France also began to agitate for a European anti-Israel stand; French diplomats set out to steer the EEC policy
in a pro-Arab, anti-Israel direction.

Two elements thus cemented the Franco-Arab alliance in the 1960s:
French anti-Americanism fed by frustrated power ambitions, and a conver-
gence of French Vichy antisemitism with the Arab desire to destroy Israel.
From then on, America and Israel were inextricably linked in this policy.

In January 1969, the Second International Conference in Support of the
Arab Peoples was held in Cairo.[14] Scores of delegates attended from
seventy-four countries and fifteen international organizations. They represented a wide spectrum of politicians, opinion makers, and intellectuals,
including the British historian Arnold Toynbee and the French Arabist Jacques Berque. The chief object of the conference was to demonstrate hostility to Zionism and solidarity with the Arab population of Palestine. In its
appeal, the conference stressed

> that all information media should be mobilized to enlighten world public
> opinion, kept in ignorance and confusion by deceitful propaganda on the
> part of Israel and its supporters. It is an incumbent moral and political duty
> of all participants to this conference to reveal the truth and spread it
> through the press, the radio, television, demonstrations, visits of delegations,

and the organization of seminars and conferences in the West and through all continents.

The conference issued twenty-three resolutions on pro-Arab world mobilization, including six practical measures. It called for special committees to be established in each country and the coordination of their activities in the most suitable conditions. The seventh resolution demands that all international and national organizations and committees organize public demonstrations, exhibitions, publications, and films "dealing with the background, causes, current events, Israeli atrocities, refugees, Palestinian resistance, etc., according to the possibilities in each country." Countries with pro-Israeli governments needed special emphasis for the mobilization of public opinion (resolution 9).

Resolution 15 is most important as it originated the Euro-Arab policy and its overall development for thirty years in European domestic and foreign policy. It stated that "The conference decided to form special parliamentary groups, where they did not exist, and to use the parliamentary platform for promoting support of the Arab people and the Palestinian resistance."

Resolution 22 declares that representatives would organize, on return from the conference, special meetings and publications, and utilize the press, radio, and television media to popularize the conference's decisions in the most appropriate way for each individual country.[15]

These ideas were widely disseminated, as this conference brought together delegates from all over the world. Among the fifty-four members of the conference's Sponsoring Committee, forty-three were from Europe, including thirty-two from Western Europe (France, Italy, England, Belgium, and Cyprus). Eleven were from Communist countries (Yugoslavia, Poland, East Germany, and Hungary); two were from Chile and one from the United States.

In concert with the wishes of the Cairo Conference, in the 1970s national groups proclaiming "Solidarity with the Palestinian Resistance and the Arab peoples" appeared throughout Europe—as well as at the United Nations, particularly in pursuance of General Assembly resolution 32/40 B of December 2, 1977, when the Committee on the Exercise of the Inalienable Rights of the Palestinian People was set up. Members of these European groups joined a left-wing Catholic group called Témoignage Chrétien (Christian Witness) in several anti-Israel demonstrations. Georges Montaron, its director, had played a vital role in the Cairo Conference's French delegation. Afterward, he organized what became known as the first World Conference of Christians for Palestine (WCCP).

The WCCP opened in Beirut on May 7, 1970, inaugurated by the Christian president of Lebanon, Charles Helou.[16] Two thousand people from thirty-seven countries assembled. The organizers of the conference rejoiced at the ecumenical nature of the meeting with the participation of more than three hundred Christians—Catholics, Greek Orthodox, Anglicans, and other Protestants—coming from some thirty countries and with many "prestigious and influential" personalities.

According to the Geneva bulletin of the League of Arab States, the WCCP had a considerable impact on the Christian populations of the West. One of the WCCP's aims was to inform Christians around the world about the plight of the Palestinians. The Arab League's Bulletin stated that Middle Eastern Christians were "anxious to bring to their brothers in the West and in Eastern Europe, a testimony not only of their solidarity, but also of their identity with the Arab peoples of the region where they form an integral part."[17] For the League, it was also a major victory for unity between Muslim and Christian Arabs, and for Arab solidarity in general.

Despite all this talk of unity, cracks were already appearing in the fraternal edifice. Many Eastern Christians opposed antisemitism and anti-Zionism on principle, and thus never accepted the basic premises of the WCCP. Moreover, clashes occurred as early as April 1969 between the Lebanese army and the PLO in southern Lebanon and in the Bekaa Valley. Within a few years, the PLO would become instrumental in the destruction of Lebanon. After the PLO had contributed to Lebanon's devastation in the mid-1970s, Bashir Gemayel—Lebanon's president-elect when he was assassinated in 1982—denounced the tragic fraud imposed upon his country in the name of Arab solidarity. Amid the blood and ruin, he appealed for help to European politicians and the Western Churches. But his appeal was in vain: many were backing Lebanon's enemies in their common war against Israel.

Thus, the politico-religious axis of Euro-Arab Judeophobia that had re-emerged after World War II now drew Middle Eastern Christianity into its web. This was the beginning of the great pro-Arab, pro-Islamist offensive in the West. *Dhimmi* Churches and Arab-Christian intellectuals became enthusiastic soldiers and propagandists for Islamic causes.

On November 22, 1970, Témoignage Chrétien's director Georges Montaron gave a lecture at Cairo's Dar Es-Salam Center entitled "The Arab World and Western Opinion." He cited three fundamental reasons for European ignorance of the Arab world: lack of information, the great humility and lack of assertiveness of Christian Arabs, and Zionist propaganda. Referring to the successes of European Jews, Montaron told his Arab audience: "If you succeeded in making from authentic Oriental Arabs, authentic Frenchmen or Englishmen—what an influence you would wield [in Europe]!"[18]

European pro-Palestinian lobbies labored to create a Euro-Arab population that would fight in Europe for Arab causes against Zionism and

"American imperialism." This goal also motivated the Third World solidarity movement, which arose in the 1970s among clergymen, intellectuals, and politicians in favor of massive Muslim immigration to European countries. Pro-Arab lobbies attributed to Zionist propaganda the natural sympathy that the majority of Europeans felt in those years for Israel—that is, to what they regarded as false and misleading information that a Palestine solidarity movement had set out to "unmask." In his speech, Montaron called for an Arab information network all over Europe that would serve as an effective anti-Zionist tool. Arab Christians, meanwhile, would play the role of ambassadors on behalf of Islamic causes to their fellow Christians in Europe.

In December 1969, France sold 110 Mirage jets to Libya's new dictator, Muammer al-Qaddafi. Beginning in the early 1970s, it became a major supplier of arms to many Arab states, while maintaining the strict boycott of Israel imposed soon after the Six-Day War. Against this backdrop, France—having developed a network of friendly relations throughout the Arab world—began to explore with Libya the concept of a Euro-Arab Dialogue (EAD).[19] Paris became the advocate of the Arab cause in the European Economic Community (EEC) and set out to build a unified European position against Israel. On an official visit to Lebanon in July 1971, Jean de Lipkowski, the French secretary of state for foreign affairs, told a press conference that there was no way that the Israeli policy of a separate, partial settlement could be negotiated in the Middle East, hence endorsing the Arab position. He pointed out that the six EEC countries had unified their views regarding the Middle East conflict, while, in the previous year, France had been isolated at the EEC in its anti-Israel stance. Previously, European Community critics accused the French of bias toward the Arab world, he commented, but that had now changed, and there was a real possibility of a common European policy on this highly important matter.[20]

The Oil Embargo: The Trigger

The Egyptian-Syrian war against Israel of October 1973 and the Arab oil embargo, used as a weapon to manipulate international policy, favored these French schemes. Mortified by the Arab defeat in a war that had begun well for them, the Arab oil-producing countries met in Kuwait on October 16–17. There they decided unilaterally to quadruple the price of oil and to reduce their production of crude oil by 5 percent each month, until Israel withdrew from the territories that Egypt, Syria, and Jordan had lost in the 1967 Six-Day War and had failed to recover in 1973. Moreover, they imposed an embargo on oil deliveries to the countries that they considered friendly to Israel: the United States, Denmark, and the Netherlands. Oil-consuming countries were classified as friendly, neutral, or enemy.

Bellicose threats aggravated these measures: "We will do like Samson, we will destroy the temple with all its occupants, including ourselves," said Qaddafi. Saudi Arabia's King Faisal declared, "There will not be any softening or compromise except if our demands are met without conditions . . . in no circumstances would we abandon Arab Jerusalem." Sheik Ahmed Zaki Yamani, the Saudi oil minister, threatened that the oil-producing countries could "reduce production by 80%. How could you survive with that?"[21]

Thus, unable to annihilate Israel militarily, the Arabs used the oil threat as a weapon to coerce the West to support their war, despite the fact that they were totally dependent on the West for their industrial development, foodstuffs, and any modernization that was taking place in their countries. Western nations responded to this threat from a united Arab front in divergent ways. America, on the one hand, stood firm and disregarded the Arab threats. But France and Germany panicked. Throughout the oil crisis, France was careful to maintain good relations with Arab leaders, even the most radical—such as the Saudi, Algerian, Syrian, and Iraqi leaders. The French even established semiofficial relations with the PLO at this time and renewed a unilateral embargo on arms sales to Israel.

Ignoring Washington's objections, the EEC insisted on making an approach to the oil-producing countries. The nine countries of the EEC met in Brussels on November 6, 1973, and issued a joint Resolution based on their dependence on Arab oil. This Resolution was totally in line with Franco-Arab policy toward Israel.[22]

The Snare

At Brussels, the EEC added three new points to its Israel policy. Its Resolution declared:

1. the inadmissibility of acquiring territory by force, which had already been stated by the UN Security Council's Resolution 242;
2. that Israel must withdraw to the armistice lines of 1949;
3. that "the legitimate rights of the Palestinians" must be included in any definition of peace for the Middle East.

The first proposal seemed admirable, but was in fact absurd: throughout history, territories have always been acquired by force. What constitutes the international legitimacy of states? Ottoman Palestine was conquered by force by the British in 1917. In the 1948 war against Israel, Egypt took Gaza by force. Abdullah's Arab Legion—under the British General Glubb Pasha—occupied Judea and Samaria by force, as well as the Old City of Jerusalem. All the Palestinian Jewish inhabitants of these areas were expelled. *1917* Moreover, except for Arabia itself, all the countries that today are called "Arab" had been conquered by Arab *jihad* armies. What criteria should determine the irreversibility of a conquest and an injustice: the occupation of a land, or its liberation? Did non-Muslim populations "occupy" their own countries: Spain, Portugal, Sicily, Greece, Bulgaria, Yugoslavia, Romania, and Armenia? Was it not rather the indigenous populations of these countries who freed themselves from Muslim occupation? Is the State of Israel the legitimate expression of a free people, whose land had been Arabized and Islamized by one of the cruelest forms of persecution against its indigenous Jewish and Christian population, or an unjust usurpation of a land conquered by *jihad* and ruled by the dehumanizing laws of dhimmitude?

The second point of the Brussels Resolution was significant in showing that the European Community had adopted the Arabs' denial of their 1967 defeat. In this way, the EEC put its seal of approval on the Franco-Arab-Islamic interpretation of the UN Resolution 242. The Resolution's original and authoritative English version refers only to "withdrawal *from territories*"—very carefully chosen words hotly debated before its adoption. But after Brussels, no parcel of Judea and Samaria was considered as administered territories open to negotiation in a final peace treaty, all was declared "occupied Arab territories"—that Israel had to evacuate immediately.

The third point of the Resolution introduced an innovation into the Middle East conflict that would prove dramatic for Europe in the future. Until the late sixties, the expression "Palestinian people" had not been used in this context. Arabs who had settled in the Byzantine Holy Land after the early Arab conquest had never manifested any political or cultural autonomy that differentiated them from other Muslim Arab conquerors in the surrounding regions. The idea of an Arab Palestinian people distinct from the larger Arab–Islamic nation was not only utterly new, but contrary to two fundamental historic concepts: that of the *umma* (the worldwide Islamic community), and of the Arab Nation—the ideology, dating from the 1890s, that promoted a pan-Arab totalitarian nationalism proclaiming the Arabs a superior people and combined with pan-Islamism.[23]

Under the Arab rule, Muslim clerics had seen themselves as the guardians of the Islamized Holy Land; there they oppressed and reviled Jews and Christians even more so than in other provinces of the Arab Empire. Although anarchy and abuses diminished under the Ottomans, the conditions of the indigenous Jews and Christians living under the *shari'a*'s rules did not improve for centuries.

Among numerous testimonies, we can quote Canon Antoine Morison, from Bar-le-Duc in France. During his travels in the Levant in 1698, he noted that the ancient Land of the Bible could not be conceived from the actual desolated state of "Judea in particular, or Palestine in general." He commented that the Jews in Jerusalem are "there in misery and under the most cruel and shameful slavery," and although a large community, they lived under regular extortion. He observed that descendants of Moors who had been expelled from Spain were numerous in the Holy Land.[24]

With the emergence of Zionism, Muslim clerics in Palestine began to emphasize their role as a spearhead of the Arab–Islamic *jihad*. Before 1967, an autonomous "Palestinian people" had never claimed independence or sovereignty over the Old City of Jerusalem—or even over the territories conquered in the 1948–49 war by the Jordano-Palestinian armies backed by Egyptian, Syrian, and Iraqi contingents. Even at the beginning of the 1970s, the political concept of a "Palestinian people," as distinct from the larger Arab nation, was still relatively inchoate. Article 1 of the revised Palestinian National Covenant of 1968 states: "Palestine is the home of the Arab Palestinian people; it is an indivisible part of the Arab homeland and the Palestinian people are an integral part of the Arab nation." Likewise, the Declaration of the Algiers Conference in 1973 and subsequent declarations spoke of the *Arab Nation* determined to recover *its* territories. Israeli land was considered as belonging not to a distinct Palestinian nationality but to a global Arab nation, whose members supported their brethren in Palestine.[25]

It was therefore normal practice then to refer not to the "Palestinian people," as did the Brussels Resolution, but only to "Arabs"—people who were no different from the Arabs in the other countries of the Arab League, to say nothing of the Arabs in Transjordan (the Palestinian area that became the Hashemite Kingdom of Jordan in 1949). Jordan today covers 78 percent of the area designated by the League of Nations in 1922 as Palestine. Great Britain drew the borders of this vast Palestinian region in 1922, transforming it into an exclusively Arab country named the Emirate of Transjordan, where Jews could not settle nor own land. Even the 1967 UN Resolution 242 recommended a global solution to the refugee problem—Arabs and Jewish. Ten years later President Jimmy Carter confirmed that a solution to the refugee problem also concerned the Jewish refugees who had fled from Arab countries, leaving all their possessions behind.

The creation of a "Palestinian people" ex nihilo after the Arab oil embargo in 1973 was accompanied by a European policy that buttressed the legitimacy of this new Palestinian people with rights that were not only equivalent to, but even superior to those enjoyed by Israelis. To do so, European policy went hand in hand with the ancient and condemned Christian theology of "replacement." Constantly nourished with propaganda demonizing Israel, this theology justified the demise of the Jewish state. It confirmed the EEC on its path of active collusion since 1974 with the Arab scheme to eliminate Israel "by stages"—a goal based in the Arab world on Islamic Judeophobia and the PLO's *jihad*, reformulated in the PLO Phased Political program by the Palestine National Council, at its 12th session held in Cairo, June 9, 1974.[26] The Euro-Arab alliance encouraged and legitimized Palestinian Arab terrorism against Israel, thereby facilitating the introduction of widespread international air piracy, hostage taking, and the indiscriminate killing of civilians in a worldwide *jihad* strategy. In the name of Palestinian rights, new horrors would soon be unleashed upon Israel and the world.

4

The Emergence of a Euro-Arab
Political and Economic Bloc

The EEC's Resolution of November 6, 1973, met the conditions that Arab
League states had set for opening a dialogue after their defeat in the October 1973 war against Israel. They rewarded the EEC with an immediate increase in oil supplies. Both sides viewed the Euro-Arab Dialogue (EAD),
born of the oil embargo, as a trade-off. The EEC countries adopted a pro-
Arab policy toward Israel in return for the benefits of economic agreements with Arab League countries.[1] The Arab side was less concerned with
the economic aspect of the Dialogue than with securing a European political commitment against Israel, and promoting Western European independence from Washington's Middle East policy and as a world power opposed
and rival to the U.S.A. The economic dimension thus became an integral
aspect of a Euro-Arab political solidarity pact that was hostile to both Israel
and America.

In his book on the EAD, Saleh A. al-Mani recalled that the idea for the
Dialogue began to take shape in discussions between France and Libya in
1973:

> The Euro-Arab Dialogue (EAD) was conceived initially by the French and
> the idea was explored in contact with Libya prior to the outbreak of the 1973
> war. The French leadership, in an attempt to enhance France's prestige and
> establish a new network of relations between the North and South, showed
> great faith in the effectiveness of personal contacts, which are well served by
> diplomatic interactions and dialogue.
>
> At a meeting on 26–27 November 1973 between French President
> Georges Pompidou and West German Chancellor Willy Brandt, the two lead-
> ers reaffirmed European intentions to engage in a dialogue with the Arabs.
> In Cairo, Abdul-Salam Jalloud, the Libyan premier actively enlisted support
> for a dialogue with the Europeans.[2]

The Pompidou-Brandt November 1973 meeting coincided with the Sixth
Summit of the Arab Conference held in Algiers on the following day, November 28. There Arab heads of state addressed a Declaration to the EEC

countries, stating that they had noted with interest "the first manifestations of a better understanding of the Arab cause by the states of Western Europe." They specified that their conditions for cooperating with the EEC were that Europe would defend Arab claims to Jerusalem and the "occupied territories" and that European states would recognize an autonomous Palestinian people. This enabled the Arab states to keep the Palestinian refugee problem alive as a weapon against Israel; under the older designation "Arabs"—used in UN Resolution 242—the Arabs of Palestine might easily have been settled in the neighboring Arab states, and especially in Jordan—formerly part of Palestine.

The Arab Declaration of Algiers prompted President Pompidou to call for an EEC summit to meet in Copenhagen on December 15, 1973. European heads of state and government examined the Middle East crisis and the planning for cooperation between Arab League and EEC countries. Four Arab foreign ministers delegated by the Arab Algiers summit and invited to monitor the project suggested various strategies and presented the conditions that the Arab states placed on any accord with the EEC.

The Political Component: The Arab Conditions

Two months later, on February 24, 1974, the Second Islamic Conference, which had been organized by the recently created Organization of the Islamic Conference (OIC), opened in Lahore. Three points of its Declaration set out clearly the policy of Muslim countries toward Israel:

2. Full and effective support should be given to the Arab countries to recover, by all means available, all their occupied lands; . . .
4. The restitution of the full national rights of the Palestinian peoples [*sic*] in their homeland is the essential and fundamental condition for a solution to the Middle East problem and the establishment of lasting peace on the basis of justice; . . .
7. The constructive efforts undertaken by the Christian Churches, all over the world and in the Arab countries, notably in Lebanon, Egypt, Jordan and Syria to explain the Palestinian question to the international public opinion and to the world religious conferences and to solicit their support for Arab sovereignty over Jerusalem and other holy places in Palestine should be appreciated.[3]

It is interesting to note that article 4 mentions the restitution of the national rights of the Palestinian people(s), for, as we saw in chapter 2, since the Islamic conquest in the seventh century there had never been "national rights" in that region. The Holy Land was divided into administrative provinces in the successive Muslim empires. This had been the policy in the Roman and Byzantine empires as well. In the territories conquered by Islam, the population was composed of Muslim settlers and indigenous *dhimmis*. The rights of both groups were determined by religion, not by territorial sovereignty: Islamic law, *shari'a*, recognizes only religious rights, not national rights. Palestine as a distinct entity was created after World War I by the League of Nations. Its population was made up of Muslims, Christians, and Jews. The former claimed to belong to the Arab nation whether they lived in the reduced Palestine of 1923 or in the Palestinian Emirate of Transjordan where, by British law, Jews were not allowed to settle. Thus, this notion of the "restitution of national rights" is clearly a European construct.

Article 7 stresses the worldwide engagement of the Churches against Jewish sovereignty in Jerusalem and over Christian holy places. This policy was a modernization of the Roman Emperor Hadrian's prohibition in 135 C.E. against the resettlement of Jews in Jerusalem, to which the Church gave a theological justification two centuries later. The OIC was attempting to stimulate Christian anti-Zionism by capitalizing upon the notion, still held by some Christians, that the Jewish deicide people had been condemned to wander in exile.

Britain, which had joined the EEC in 1973, vetoed the Euro-Arab Dialogue in protest that Holland was under an Arab embargo for being pro-Israeli.[4] After the Arabs ended their oil embargo against Holland, the European states began to discuss the "Dialogue" at a June 10, 1974, meeting in Bonn of the foreign ministers of the nine EEC countries. The foreign ministers adopted a text that specified areas in which they hoped to improve relations with Arab countries, as well as strategies for doing so. The main areas included agriculture, industry, sciences, culture, education, technology, financial cooperation, and civil infrastructure.

On July 31, 1974, in Paris, the first official meeting at the ministerial level took place between Europeans and Arabs to discuss the organization of the Dialogue. Attending were the Kuwaiti foreign minister, the secretary-general of the Arab League, the president of the European Communities Commission and the current president of the European Community (EC). In the course of meetings that followed, the European foreign ministers of the Nine laid the foundations for their cooperation with the Arab countries, through an institutionalized structure linked to the highest authorities in each EC country.[5] This formula made it possible to harmonize and unify the EC policy of trade and cooperation with Arab League countries.

A European Parliamentary Association for Euro-Arab Cooperation was founded by the nine countries of the European Community in order to improve political, cultural, and economic cooperation between Europe and the Arab world. Its executive committee subsequently met regularly every six months. Its membership spanned the spectrum of European political groups. This association's role was to keep European parliamentarians informed of developments involving the Arab world; to coordinate actions to improve relations between Europe and the Middle East; to organize regular meetings with the Interparliamentary Arab Union; and to visit Arab countries and receive delegations from them. The association was in regular contact with European governments, the Presidency of the European Council of Ministers, and the EC Commission.

The formation of the Association for Euro-Arab Cooperation was a direct fulfillment of the decision recorded, as already mentioned, in Resolution 15 of the International Conference in Support of the Arab Peoples, which met in Cairo on January 25–26, 1969, and which stated: "The conference decided to form special parliamentary groups, where they did not exist, and to use the parliamentary platform for promoting support of the Arab people and the Palestinian resistance" (see above p. 45).

Biannual Euro-Arab Parliamentary meetings were held alternately in European and Arab countries. About one hundred Arab and European members of parliament attended the meetings, together with observers from the Commission of the European Union, the Arab League and other international organizations.[6]

The Damascus Conference of September 14–17, 1974, which was organized by the interparliamentary Association for Euro-Arab Cooperation, brought together representatives of all the parliamentary parties of the EEC except Denmark. Here the Arabs set out their political preconditions for economic agreements with Western European countries. Specifically, the Arab delegates demanded:

1. The unconditional withdrawal of Israel to the 1949 armistice lines;
2. Arab sovereignty over the Old City of Jerusalem;
3. The participation of the PLO and its leader, Yasser Arafat, in any negotiations;[7]
4. Pressure by the EEC on the United States, to detach it from Israel and bring its policies closer to those of the Arab states.

These indispensable political preconditions of the Euro-Arab Dialogue were confirmed at the Seventh Summit of the Arab Conference a month later. At this summit, held in Rabat in October 1974, Arab heads of state emphasized that the Euro-Arab Dialogue must develop within the context of the Declaration of the Sixth Summit of the Arab Conference in Algiers, which had been transmitted to the EEC on November 28, 1973, establishing Arab political requirements concerning Israel. No time limit was placed on the Dialogue: it would continue until its objectives were achieved. For the Arab side, the interdependence of the political and economic aspects of Euro-Arab cooperation was not negotiable.

At this point, a permanent EAD secretariat of 350 members devoted to Euro-Arab cooperation was created, with its seat in Paris. The Euro-Arab Dialogue was organized into various committees charged with planning joint industrial, commercial, political, scientific, technical, cultural, and social projects.

The Economic Component: The EEC's Conditions

During the 1970s, the composition and the organization of the EEC were transformed. In January 1973 the UK, Denmark, and Ireland became members. The rise of international terrorism in the following years contributed to the EEC's integration policy and later the European Union, adding the instruments of a Common Foreign and Security Policy (CFSP) to its initial economic focus. After 1970, the European Political Cooperation (EPC) that dealt with foreign policy cooperation was increasingly used for matters outside the explicit boundaries of various treaty frameworks. This set a pattern for the conduct of the Euro-Arab Dialogue. The EEC had been conceived of as an economic institution, dealing with markets, finance, and trade. But Arab pressure for a unified European policy in relation to America and Israel required a modification of EC institutions, furthering the development of a unified foreign policy among the member states. Indeed, from its beginning, European heads of state regarded the Euro-Arab Dialogue as a tool for constructing a common, unified European foreign policy. Therefore, collective hostility to Israel became a linchpin of European unity.

Euro-Arab Dialogue representatives and experts gathered for their first meeting in Cairo on June 10, 1975. A delegation from the EEC met a delegation from twenty Arab countries and the PLO. More than thirty countries were represented by a general committee at the ambassadorial level, as well as by numerous experts. The European Community and the Secretariat of the Arab League were represented at the political level. The Jordanian spokesperson of the Arab delegation, Nijmeddin Dajani, stressed the political aspects and implications of the Euro-Arab Dialogue. The agreement between the two parties was emphasized: economic deals with Europe in exchange for European alignment with Arab policy on Israel. A Joint Memorandum of the Mixed Committee of Experts gave a preliminary formulation of the general principles and aims of the Euro-Arab Dialogue (see chapter 5).

Euro-Arab cooperation deepened in the years that followed, strengthened by various activities on an international scale and frequent EAD meetings: in Rome (July 24, 1975); Abu Dhabi (November 27, 1975); Luxembourg (May 18–20, 1976); Brussels (several meetings in 1976); and

Tunis (February 10–12, 1977). During the 1976 Luxembourg meeting, the organization and procedures of the Euro-Arab Dialogue were defined; they were published as appendix 4 of the final Communiqué. The Dialogue was composed of three organs: a General Committee; the Working Committees; and the Coordinating Committee. These committees involved officials of the highest rank of both sides.

The General Committee was made up of delegates of ministerial and ambassadorial rank from both sides: members of the League of Arab States and of the European Communities, of the General Secretariat of the Arab League, and of the European Commission, as well as the copresidents and rapporteurs of the Working Committees. The heads of the Arab and European delegations hold the presidency of the General Committee jointly. The General Committee represents the central body of the Dialogue, in charge of the general conduct of the Dialogue. It monitors its developments in different areas and is responsible for keeping it on track toward its political, cultural, social, technological, and economic goals, as well as for approving the Dialogue's overall program and tasks.

General Committee meetings take place behind closed doors and without recorded minutes. At the end of each meeting, the General Committee can, if it so wishes, publish a summary of the decisions it has made and issue a joint press release.[8]

The composition of the Working Committees follows the same principle: each group is made up of experts—business, economists and oil specialists—from both sides, as well as representatives of the General Secretariat of the League of Arab States and of the Commission of the European Communities. The Arab and European groups each appoint their respective president, who presided jointly over each working meeting, as directed by the General Committee. Each Working Committee can create specialized subgroups, whose experts are chosen in consultation with the General Secretariat of the League of Arab States and with the EC Commission.

The Coordinating Committee is composed of representatives of the General Committee, the General Secretariat of the League of Arab States, and the European presidency. The two sides presided jointly each meeting. The Committee is responsible for coordinating the work of the various working parties under the direction of the General Committee. The General Secretariat of the League of Arab States and the Commission of European Communities transmit all information and documentation.

The Euro-Arab Dialogue established the conditions for a genuine Euro-Arab symbiosis. There followed an intertwining of Arab and European policies, involving the European states at the highest level, as well as the presidency of the EC with the Arab League representatives. The Arab states had other demands besides their insistence that Europe champion a Palestinian state with Yasser Arafat as its leader and spearhead a campaign to bring

worldwide political and economic pressure upon Israel in order to force it
to withdraw to the 1949 armistice border. They also called for the implementation of an international boycott of Israel and opposed any separate
peace treaties.

To fulfill these demands, the Working Committees studied suitable
methods to condition European and world public opinion to support the
PLO—although its revised 1968 Charter stipulated the elimination of the
State of Israel. European members of the permanent secretariat of the Parliamentary Association for Euro-Arab Cooperation (PAEAC) traveled frequently to the United States where they tried to influence American policy
in favor of the PLO and against Israel. From then on, the organization of
the international anti-Israeli media propaganda formulated at the January
1969 Cairo Conference in Resolution 15, proceeded within the EAD framework, under the tutelage of the EEC heads of state.

Euro-Arab cooperation was not free of difficulties. In his study of the
Euro-Arab Dialogue, Saleh al-Mani notes that the Arab states in the 1970s
were irritated at Europe's failure to gain general recognition for the PLO.
Nonetheless, the Arabs saw the overall value of continuing the Dialogue:

> Despite the failure of the EAD to result in recognition of the PLO, the latter
> was, nevertheless, one of the most active supporters of the EAD. The PLO
> may have wanted to use the EAD as a channel for airing its demands, and in
> this regard it may have been successful.
>
> Although failing [sic] short of achieving formal recognition for the PLO,
> the EAD did, however, succeed in persuading the Europeans of the need to
> establish a "homeland for the Palestinians" and in "associating" the PLO
> with future negotiations on the Middle East. Thus the EAD has served cer-
> tain limited Arab objectives.[9]

Al-Mani's disappointment indicates that in the 1970s the European public and the majority of politicians were still reluctant to side unequivocally—at least officially—with the Arabs against Israel. By linking the EAD
with the recognition of the PLO, al-Mani provides further confirmation
that such recognition was an essential condition for the EEC to be granted
huge markets in the Arab world. EAD meetings customarily concluded with
declarations by the European delegation that echoed the Arab line. In the
late seventies, at EC meetings in London (June 29, 1977) and Brussels (October 26–28, 1978), the Europeans called for virtually everything the Arabs
wanted: Israel's withdrawal to its 1949 borders; Israel's obligation to recognize the national rights of the Palestinians; and the invalidation of all measures and decisions taken by Israel in the administered territories outside
the 1949 borders, including Jerusalem. Judea and Samaria (the "West
Bank") and Gaza were described as "occupied Arab territories."

In a speech on August 26, 1980, Lebanon's future President-elect Bashir

Gemayel described the PLO's terrorist war in Lebanon and then denounced the influence this organization had in Europe: "This is a recapitu-
lation of the doings of those [Palestinian] people on whose behalf the
chancelleries of the civilized world are striving throughout the year, and
for whose favors the old nations of Europe are competing."[10]

Those favors could be lucrative indeed. Al-Mani writes of the benefits
enjoyed by European countries that were involved in EAD: "A case in point
is Belgium, which seems to have been able to secure major constructions
[sic] contracts in Saudi Arabia and other Gulf states, due in large part to its
hosting of several EAD meetings in 1976."[11]

The euphoria was lessened somewhat by the 1977–78 Israeli-Egyptian
peace negotiations that were held at Camp David under the auspices of
American President Jimmy Carter. These put a damper on the EAD. The
Arab League totally rejected the Camp David negotiations, and even expelled Egypt from its ranks. France initially sided with the Arab League and
abstained from recognizing the Camp David peace agreements. The other
EEC countries, however, accepted them—though (under French pressure)
with reservations. Arab leaders were furious over the success of American
influence in the region, which undermined the European diplomacy that
they had so assiduously cultivated.

Nevertheless, the EAD lived on. The fourth meeting of the General Committee, held in Damascus on December 9–11, 1978, approved the creation
of a Euro-Arab technology-transfer center in Kuwait.

Al-Mani sums up the spirit of the EAD:

> A disinterested observer would conclude that the EAD has reflected Euro-
> pean concern over energy supplies and Arab concern over Western Euro-
> pean recognition of the PLO. These two imperatives explain the reactivation
> of the EAD in the autumn of 1980, after a cessation of nearly two years. The
> Europeans were worried about declining oil production in Iran, and the
> Arabs were concerned by the separate peace treaty signed between Egypt
> and Israel.[12]

Henceforth, Europe would consider the question of Israel's right to exist
only in connection with the European oil supply. In the decade to come,
economic realities and *jihad* terrorist threats would tip the scales in Europe
markedly against Israel. But in the heady first years of the EAD in the 1970s
and the euphoria of billions of petrodollars, the European participants in
the Dialogue could not forsee that one day Europe's hidden war against
Israel would threaten the security—and, indeed, even the survival—of Europe itself.

Part II
The Birth of Eurabia

5

A New Political and Cultural Entity

Eurabia was the title of a journal initiated in the mid-1970s by the European Committee for Coordination of Friendship Associations with the Arab World.[1] It was edited by Lucien Bitterlin, president of the Association of Franco-Arab Solidarity, and published jointly by Middle East International (London), France-Pays Arabes (Paris) and the Groupe d'Etudes sur le Moyen-Orient (Geneva). These associations initiated a virulent anti-Israel-campaign. Other publications by *Eurabia* included, in November 1978, a study on the *Three Myths of the Old Testament* by Georges Vaucher, their Swiss representative in Geneva, and secretary general.[2]

In its second issue, which appeared in July 1975, *Eurabia* published resolutions that had been passed unanimously by the general assembly of the Parliamentary Association for Euro-Arab Cooperation (PAEAC), at its Strasbourg meeting on June 7–8, 1975. The PAEAC comprised two hundred West European parliamentarians then representing the major trends of the political spectrum.[3] Thus, the program of a Euro-Arab entente was approved by a broad consensus, covering the entire European political scene.

The European Communities (EC) and their parliaments coordinated and integrated the EAD plan. This two-pronged approach helped promote what was, from the European perspective, a fundamental goal of the Dialogue: continent-wide foreign policy unity, so as to become a global alternative to American power. As was indicated in chapter 4, the foreign ministers of the nine EC countries had agreed on June 10, 1974 on the need to adopt a common foreign policy, bringing member states' positions closer in order to place Euro-Arab cooperation within a secure political framework. This common foreign policy enhanced European integration. It is one of history's ironies—as well as a revealing fact—that Europe's unification and integrative process was anchored in an anti-Israeli policy and an alliance with Israel's most rabid enemies.

This unifying policy was underlined by a *Eurabia* editorial which stressed "the necessity for a **political** entente between Europe and the Arab world as a basis for economic agreements," and the obligation for Europeans to "understand the **political** as well as the economic interests of the Arab world." The Euro-Arab Dialogue had to express "a joint **political** will" (emphasis added). To fulfill its part of the bargain, European authorities had to create "a climate of opinion" favorable to the Arabs.[4] The editorial continued:

> If they really want to cooperate with the Arab world, the European governments and political leaders have an obligation to protest against the denigration of Arabs in their media. They must reaffirm their confidence in the Euro-Arab friendship and their respect for the millennial contribution of the Arabs to world civilization.

The Arab world's conditions for the Dialogue were not limited to requiring European statements and actions against Israel; they also concerned Europe itself. Tilj Declerq, a Belgian member of the PAEAC submitted a study on the conditions for this cooperation to the economic commission of the association. It was later summarized in the July 1975 issue of *Eurabia* as "A European point of view."

Declerq declared that "the political interests of this cooperation must . . . be recognized." He emphasized that economic exchanges between Europe and the Arab world were subordinate to the EEC's support of the Arabs League's campaign against Israel. Declerq advocated increased economic ties that would benefit both sides: the Arab world could contribute manpower and raw material; the Europeans, technology. "A medium and long term policy must henceforth be formulated in order to bring about economic cooperation through a combination of Arab manpower reserves and raw materials, and European technology and 'management.'"

Declerq was thus an early advocate of a permanent Arab-Muslim immigrant population in Europe. This policy was already being stimulated by the EEC's economic agreements with the Arab world and through family reunification, from 1975 onwards, of a previously transient migrant population. According to Declerq, this sharing of technology on one side and manpower on the other would bring about the interdependence of Western Europe and the Arab countries, in order "gradually to reach as complete as possible an economic integration."

However, Declerq insisted that this integration would remain unrealizable so long as the fundamental political condition of support for the Arab campaign against Israel was not met. Therefore, "[a] genuine political will must be at the base of concrete plans for cooperation and must be demonstrated at three levels: the national level; the level of the continent; and at world level." In order to accomplish this, "Euro-Arab cooperation and solidarity has to be brought about through international organizations and international conferences." Joint Euro-Arab preparatory meetings and symposiums had "to be multiplied at every level—economic, monetary, commercial, etc.—in order to reach common positions."

Declerq's proposals were not simply the musings of an isolated theorist. At its Strasbourg meeting, a month before their publication in *Eurabia*, the Parliamentary Association for Euro-Arab Cooperation had unanimously approved them and integrated them into the resolutions. The political section of the Strasbourg resolutions targeted three areas: European policy on Israel, the creation of a European climate of opinion favorable to the Arabs, and Muslim immigrants in Europe.

Concerning Israel, the association predictably went along with Arab demands for Israel's total withdrawal to the 1949 armistice lines, thereby misinterpreting Resolution 242, which had called only for peace negotiations and withdrawal "from territories" (not "from all the territories"). In addition, the association called on European governments to recognize the PLO as the sole representative of the Palestinian Arabs. This was a fundamental point of joint Euro-Arab policy, which the association asked European governments to stress in all their initiatives. The association requested each EEC country to force Israel to accept the rights of a Palestinian nation represented by the PLO and its leader, Yasser Arafat. The EEC was expected to oblige Israel to accept a Palestinian state in Gaza lost by Egypt in 1967, and on the entire "West Bank"—occupied by Jordan in 1948–49 and lost with East Jerusalem during the 1967 war when King Hussein joined Egypt and Syria and shelled West Jerusalem.

Regarding Europe, the association called for news coverage more favorable to Arab causes, as well as special conditions for Arab immigrants:

> The Association requires European governments to arrange legal provisions concerning the free movement . . . and respect for the fundamental rights of immigrant workers in Europe: these rights must be equivalent to those of national citizens.
>
> The Association considers the political settlement of the Arab-Israeli conflict an absolute necessity for the establishment of a real Euro-Arab cooperation.

In the same vein, the association expressed the hope that "the harmonious development of cooperation between Western Europe and the Arab nation" would benefit from the free circulation of ideas and citizens. The economic resolution expressed concern about past political choices that

> had been prejudicial to Euro-Arab cooperation, such as the creation of the International Energy Agency and the signing of an agreement between the EEC and Israel, before the negotiations between the EEC and the Arab countries had been completed. On this subject, it made a formal request that economic cooperation between the EEC and Israel should not apply to the occupied territories.

Eurabia: A New Cultural Entity

The Strasbourg PAEAC meeting reaffirmed the resolutions that had been adopted by the preparatory Conference of the Parliamentary Euro-Arab Cooperation held in Damascus on September 14–17, 1974 (see chapter four, p. 55). It also issued several statements about the necessity of recognizing "the historical contribution of Arab culture to European development" and of the importance to stress "the contribution that the European countries can still expect from Arab culture, notably in the area of human values."

In line with these goals, the association asked European governments to create a more hospitable environment for Arab immigrants by expanding the presence of Arab culture and religion (Islam) in Europe. It demanded that European governments "make it possible for the Arab countries to create generous means to enable immigrant workers and their families to participate in Arab cultural and religious life."

The association requested "the governments of the Nine to approach the cultural sector of the Euro-Arab Dialogue in a constructive spirit and to accord the greatest priority to spreading Arab culture in Europe." This demand was followed by another appeal directed toward the Arab governments asking them "to recognize the political consequences of active cooperation with Europe in the cultural domain."

The association urged the press and friendship groups to work to improve public opinion regarding the Arab world. Finally, the Strasbourg Resolution concluded with condemnations of Israel, particularly the "Zionist wish to substitute Jewish culture for Arab culture on Palestinian territory, in order to deprive the Palestinian people of its national identity." It considered "that by carrying out excavations in the holy places of Islam (the Temple Mount)—the occupied part of Jerusalem—Israel has committed a violation of international law, despite the warning of UNESCO." Consequently, the association "Regrets that UNESCO's decision not to admit Israel into its European regional grouping should have been exploited, sometimes with a great lack of objectivity."[5] The people or organizations alluded to were not identified.

In their article on the Dialogue in the same issue of *Eurabia*, Bichara and Naïm Khader, two Palestinian economists, stressed that the success of Euro-Arab cooperation—which involved twenty-nine countries—required an identical vision in all domains. The authors deplored that the countries of the EEC had adopted differing policies in relation to the Middle East. They argued that Europe's interests in the Arab world were actually opposed to those of the United States and insisted that the Euro-Arab Dialogue could only succeed if Europe were entirely independent from America. Thus, the people involved in strengthening Euro-Arab relations within the various bodies of the EAD could not be pro-American or pro-Israeli.[6]

To illustrate their point, the authors questioned whether the pro-Israeli Henri Simonet, who later became a Belgian member of the European Commission, and Etienne Davignon, a backer of the Atlantic Alliance, should participate at all in the EAD. They were displeased with the fact that Davignon was the director of the Political Committee of the EEC, and thus was in charge of articulating the European position on the Middle East conflict, in addition to being president of the International Energy Agency (IEA). In September 1977, Simonet, then Belgian foreign minister and president of the Council of the EEC, endorsed the Euro-Arab policy in a speech he delivered at the UN General Assembly in New York, which illustrated the shift in official positions (see chapter 7).

Two days after the Strasbourg meeting, European and Arab representatives and experts met in Cairo (June 10–14, 1975) in order to prepare a preliminary formulation of EAD general principles and objectives.[7] The introduction to this meeting's joint Memorandum specifies that

> The Euro-Arab Dialogue is the fruit of a common political desire which emerged at the highest level and which aims to establish special relationships between the two groups.
>
> The two parties are mindful that the Dialogue had originated in their exchanges at the end of 1973, and, particularly, the declaration made by the nine States members of the European Community, 6 November 1973, concerning the situation on the Middle East as well as the declaration addressed to the Western European countries by the 6th Summit conference of Arab countries in Algiers on 28 November 1973.[8]

It is clear, therefore, that the basis for the Dialogue was the endorsement by the EEC of Arab policy concerning Israel, in accordance with the Algiers declaration. The next paragraph of the joint Memorandum states that the "political dimensions of the dialogue proceeded essentially from the attempt to rediscover, to renew and to reinforce the ties which are of interest to the neighboring regions." They stem "from the desire to remove the misunderstandings that had provoked difficulties in the past; and from the intentions to build the foundations of a future cooperation encompassing a vast area of activities, which would be for the benefits of the two parties." The development and growth of the Euro-Arab economic cooperation based on this entente would contribute to encourage stability, security, and equitable peace in the Arab region and to advance the cause of peace and the security in the world.

The joint Memorandum emphasizes that

> The establishment of a cooperation of the two groups is inspired by neighboring ties and a common cultural heritage, as well as by their complementary and convergent interests.

This cooperation should contribute to reinforce the relations that already exist and to develop the friendship between the states and the people concerned. It should improve their comprehension and their mutual trust and open new horizons in the political, economical, social, and cultural domains.

The EAD from its inception thus emphasized that the many aspects of the Euro-Arab entente depended entirely on the EEC's adherence to Arab anti-Israeli policy: the Arabs would dictate the criteria for peace, stability, security and justice. Meanwhile, in the economic sphere the dialogue aimed at "establishing the fundamental conditions for the development of the Arab world as a whole and at narrowing the technological gap, which separates Arab countries from the European countries."

The areas of cooperation listed by the Cairo meeting included cooperation in nuclear technology, finance, business, scientific research, technological development, technical and professional training, the utilization of nuclear power, the planning and building of cities, infrastructures, industrialization, transportation, urbanization, health, education, telecommunication, tourism, and more. The training of specialized personnel for the numerous projects envisioned would take place "either by sending teams of European experts with a view to training the Arab workforce, or by training this workforce in established centers in the EEC countries." The intention was to set up "effective [cooperation] and exchange of information between Arab and European universities" in research procedures, programs, and projects.

The section on "Cooperation in the fields of culture and civilization" stressed that the principal objective of the Euro-Arab Dialogue was to bring closer two civilizations that had considerably enriched the patrimony of humanity. Their cooperation in the area of culture and civilization should embrace education, the arts, science, and information. Hence, the Joint Memorandum affirmed that the principal objective of such cooperation was the consolidation and deepening of cultural understanding, along with an intellectual rapprochement between the two regions. To achieve this aim, the two parties would encourage discussions by scholars from existing institutions and the creation of a joint Euro-Arab cultural institution. The two parties would "strive to encourage and deepen the study of the European and Arab languages and cultures."

The Memorandum mentioned various measures, such as exchanges of experts and the development of contacts in education and tourism. The problems of the Arab workforce in Europe were to be settled by equality of treatment between citizens and immigrants in three areas: employment; working and living conditions; and social security benefits.

Thus, during the following decades, three theoretically independent sectors—economic and commercial exchange, Arab immigration, European politics and culture—were woven together by policies tying Europe to the Arab world in a web of anti-Israeli/antisemitic hostility and anti-Americanism. The expansion of terror as these policies were being formulated, as well as police complacency toward Arab terrorists, clearly indicate that a large motive for EAD supporters was a pervasive fear of Arab hostility. This was associated with a no less pervasive ambition for full Euro-Arab economic and political interdependency, exclusive of American interference.

Three decades later, one might ask: have these policies really benefited Europe?

6

The Spiral: The European Community as an Instrument of Arab Policy

By 1973, the member states of the European Communities had increased from six to nine. As mentioned previously, the Common Market was built on a policy aimed at general economic integration and monetary stability.[1] The EAD developed a community of interests between Arabs and Europeans. The European Political Cooperation (EPC), the body responsible for coordinating the foreign policy of the EC member states, supported the EC Commission and the European Council of Ministers in the meetings and activities of the Euro-Arab Dialogue. The interconnected engagements with the Arab world that came about through these three top bodies, which directed the policies and economy of the EC, helped establish a strong solidarity between Europe and the Arab world.

Al-Mani notes that in the 1970s the Euro-Arab community of interests thrived

> especially between high-ranking bureaucrats in the League of Arab States and the EC. The EAD has been a major interest of Chadli Kalibi [Klibi], secretary-general of the League of Arab States. He organized a special unit for the EAD that is attached directly to his office, and members of that unit engage in a certain amount of lobbying within the League. Similarly in Europe, members of the Commission's Developpement [*sic*] Directorate are responsible for the EAD work on its behalf.[2]

However, the development of the EAD almost immediately demonstrated the differing perspectives of the European and Arab states—particularly in regard to the correlations between the economic and the political networks imposed by the Dialogue. The EEC sought economic benefits through expanded oil, commercial, and industrial markets. Its actions were characterized by the businesslike pragmatism of management technocrats who formulated aid and regional development programs. It also facilitated massive sales of arms, as well as of industrial and nuclear equipment (e.g., the French Osirak nuclear reactor in Iraq, destroyed by Israel in 1981).

Arab Anti-Israeli and Anti-American Policy: The Oil Weapon

The Arab approach was different. It exploited the economy as a political instrument: a radical means of manipulating the European Council of Ministers in the service of its long-term political strategy for Europe, Israel, and America. The Arab political grip on the EC's economy rapidly imposed upon the Council Arab political directives vis-à-vis Israel. One of the Arab delegates to the EAD, Dr. Ibrahim A. Obaid, Saudi Arabia's director-general of the Ministry of Petroleum and Mineral Resources, aptly expressed the spirit of the Dialogue at a 1975 meeting of Euro-Arab Cooperation experts in Amsterdam: "Together and as equals, the Europeans and the Arabs can through a 'strategy of inter-dependence' forge ahead to remove the thorn from their sides—the Israeli problem—and attend to the Herculean task ahead of them."[3]

In his statement, "Political Preconditions for Cooperation with Western Europe," Obaid stressed that for the sake of peace, the European Community should stop all military and economic assistance to Israel and work toward "an Israeli withdrawal from occupied Arab territories foremost of which is Jerusalem." He affirmed that it was in the interest of Western Europe to attempt to assume a more active role in the Middle East and this would be facilitated, if the PLO were recognized by the European Community as the official representative of the Palestinians. "The Arab-Israeli conflict and the oil problem are not only related but inseparable. Had it not been for the said conflict the oil weapon would not have been unleashed," he declared. Then he explained that during the 1973 war against Israel "we had to act in order to defend our [Arab] rights and regain our occupied [Arab] territories, but at the same time we endeavored not to disrupt the economies of the free world."[4]

It is interesting to note here that Israeli territory—in accordance with the ideology of *jihad*—is regarded as belonging to a united and undifferentiated Arab-Islamic nation. Obaid and the other Arab delegates always referred to "Israel's aggression" while complaining of wars, refugees, and loss of territories. However, it was the Arabs that initiated the 1947–48, 1967, and 1973 wars to annihilate Israel. The Arab/Muslim meaning of "Israel's aggression" is just an expression of their conviction that Israel's very existence is an aggression against the twenty-two countries of the Arab League.

All the Arab EAD delegates consistently stressed the political aspects of the Dialogue. Nijmeddin Dajani, the Jordanian minister of industry and commerce, expressed it clearly, referring to several of the pivotal meetings and conferences when the Arab side had always maintained and emphasized that the Dialogue has been conceived and nourished within a political framework and that its momentum and success required the maintenance of an appropriate political climate. He recalled that the political aspect of the Dialogue was emphasized by the Seventh Arab Summit Conference held in Rabat in October 1974, at which time it was decided amongst other things that: 1) the Euro-Arab dialogue should proceed within the framework of the principles contained in the Declaration of the Sixth Arab Summit Conference in Algiers and addressed to Western Europe on November 28, 1973; and 2) that steps should be taken to proceed with the Dialogue so as to achieve tangible cooperation in the political, economic and cultural area for the mutual benefit of both sides.

He underlined the central issue as follows: as much as the Arab side attaches utmost importance to the economic development of their countries and the improvement in the standard of living of the Arab peoples, the Arabs were not ready to let the Dialogue proceed at the expense of the national interests, foremost of which was the Palestine problem. He continued,

> In other words, the Arabs insist on maintaining a certain balance between the economic needs and the other interest particularly the political and national aspiration of the Arab people. The growth and flourishing of Arab-European economic cooperation should proceed hand in hand with political relations between the two groups based upon mutual interests and a proper understanding of the basic interests of the Arab region.[5]

Thus, the economic agreements between the EEC and the Arab world were far more significant than most treaties regarding trade: they led directly to Europe's progressive subjection to Arab political objectives. Nor was there reluctance on the European side. The EAD—and France in particular—required an associative Euro-Arab diplomacy in international forums. There, the EC quickly fell into line with the Arab League's anti-Zionist positions.

The Dialogue, therefore, also became a primary vehicle for the legitimization of the PLO quest for international and diplomatic recognition. For the first time the PLO began to enjoy respectability and international standing, thereby counteracting its well-deserved reputation as a terrorist group.

The PLO for which the EAD labored so assiduously was a primary initiator of international terrorism, including the hijacking (1968) and blowing up of civilian airliners (1970). Beginning in 1965, the PLO had planned and executed virtually continuous sabotage, terrorist operations, and the capture of civilian hostages. It even carried out assassinations of Arab dissidents in Israel and abroad. In 1968, it became an umbrella organization for various terrorist groups led by Arafat's own movement, al-Fatah. In February 1969, Arafat became chairman of its Executive Committee as well as the PLO's leader and commander in chief.

The EAD's efforts to legitimize the PLO produced immediate results. In an immense propaganda victory, Arafat began to be treated as a statesman. The Arab Summit in Rabat in 1974, which recognized the PLO as sole legitimate representative of the Palestinians, helped pave the way for success: in November 1974, Arafat addressed the UN General Assembly in New York. Less well-publicized but even more beneficial was the help the PLO received from Europe's dark side: European fascists, French Vichy collaborators and old Nazis established links with Arafat's group, providing it with military training and teaching it the most effective propaganda techniques.[6]

By legitimizing the PLO, Europe was giving tacit approval to the 1964 PLO Charter that called for the destruction of Israel. The PLO's grievance against Israel was based on Islamic *jihad* ideology and Judeophobia, not on land claims. The revised Charter of 1968, which contained the same points, was never revoked according to its article 33—although the article calling for the destruction of Israel was ostentatiously dropped at a public session in Gaza in December 1998 to convince American President Bill Clinton. This decision was never ratified.

An entire war policy for the delegitimization of Israel was constructed by the EAD and propagated at the national and international levels within the European Community, in trade unions, the media, and the universities. From its beginning, the EAD served as a mouthpiece to popularize throughout Europe the demonization and defamation of Israel. This constituted an essential aspect of the EAD, necessary in order to create "the maintenance of an appropriate political climate" required for its success, as explained above by Dajani.

France, Belgium, and Luxembourg became the EAD's most active agents. The French government was the first to lend its support to Arab demands that PLO representatives participate in any negotiations regarding Israel. The French also began pressing for international recognition of a Palestinian state. Palestinians were prominent among the Arab delegates to the Euro-Arab Dialogue: during the 1970s and 1980s, Ahmed Sedki al-Dajani, a PLO representative, chaired the Arab side. The first General Committee meeting in Luxembourg, held from May 18 to 20, 1976, was chaired on the European side by Ambassador Jean Wagner of Luxembourg representing the presidency of the European Political Cooperation (EPC) and the EC Council of Ministers, and by Dr. Klaus Meyer, deputy secretary-general and representative of the EC Commission. The Arab delegation was chaired by Ambassador Abd el-Aziz al-Shamlan of Bahrain, representing the Presidency of the Political Council of the League of Arab States, and by Ahmad Sedki al-Dajani, representing the PLO—which was a full member of the League of Arab States.

According to al-Mani, the "Luxembourg meeting was important since it elevated the level of representation and brought the political aspects of the EAD to the fore." He stressed that "the Arabs succeeded in extending the scope of the EAD to state level in addition to regional organization level." He recalled that by this time,

> the EAD encompassed most of the European and Arab states in addition of the original initiators, the EC and the League of Arab States. Inclusion of the PLO, and European acceptance of this inclusion, indicated to the Arab side an indirect recognition of the PLO by the Europeans. The elevation of the EAD to the political level meant that the EAD not only represented the two respective regional organizations, but also the individual member states as well.[7]

At this meeting, Ambassador Wagner declared, "the Nine believe that the right of the Palestinian people to the expression of its national identity must be recognized." Speaking on behalf of the EC Commission, Klaus Meyer called for common action between Europe and the Arabs "increasing solidarity in all matters of mutual interest for our common economic future."[8] It is clear that the Arab war against Israel rekindled much enthusiasm in certain European leaders. The opening of PLO information offices in some European capitals satisfied the Arabs and encouraged them to demand a European arms embargo against Israel. France had already declared one in 1967. According to al-Mani:

> the PLO's representative, al-Dajani, was pleased by the EAD consensus on several grounds, but he criticized the Europeans for their adoption of '**a certain style of expression which tends to do its utmost to obscure a clear, undeniable fact**', and for their 'hesitancy in dealing with the case of the Palestinian people and calling things by their proper names.' [Emphasis added][9]

These comments imply that European anti-Israeli policy was couched in cautious terms that irritated their PLO and Arab allies who requested a more public support, as will be seen in the next chapter.

The PLO did not give up terrorism in line with its new respectability. On the contrary, its terrorist activities flourished on an international scale during the 1970s and 1980s with the 1972 massacres of the Israeli athletes at the Munich Olympic Games, the blowing-up of airplanes, the attacks and murder of civilians by the Black September group, and the bloody war against the Christians in Lebanon. Nonetheless, with France's support, the PLO was admitted to various UN bodies. Leading French statesmen enhanced Arafat's burgeoning legitimacy by meeting with him in 1975. France was also among the first European countries to open a PLO office in Paris.

For the Arab League countries, the EAD's importance lay in its ability to impose: (a) diplomatic recognition of the PLO with its leader Arafat as the sole representative of the Palestinians; (b) the request by France, alongside Arab countries, that any peace agreement be comprehensive, and secure a Palestinian state with Arafat as its leader—despite his terrorist activities. Hence, as al-Mani wrote,

> For the PLO, the EAD has been a successful exercise in symbolic politics. Through the EAD, the PLO has succeeded in specifically addressing the Europeans, and engaged in a successful effort to secure international diplomatic recognition of Palestinian representation. Through the dialogue, the PLO has transformed itself from an Arab regional factor to an international force that must be addressed in any differentiation of Middle Eastern political calculuses [sic].[10]

The EAD also served the Arab League as an instrument for applying pressure on America. Mindful of their new obligations to the Arab states, European diplomats labored to persuade the U.S. to align itself with Arab policy on Israel. However, hostility to America was deeply ingrained in European communists, Left-wingers, Third-Worldists and neo-Nazis. As we have seen, the Euro-Arab cooperation and alliance was from its inception also directed against America. For the Arabs, Euro-Arab cooperation became a political instrument to exacerbate anti-Americanism in Europe, to divide Europe from America—thus weakening both—and to encourage mutual hostility.

Arab Policy in Europe

For the Arabs, the EAD aimed at three more goals that are important:

1) attaining economic and industrial parity with the West by the transfer to Arab countries of modern technology, particularly military and nuclear technology;
2) implanting in Europe a large Muslim population, which would enjoy all the political, cultural, social, and religious rights of the host country;
3) imposing the political, cultural, and religious influences of Arab Islamism on European countries, through an immigrant population that remained politically and culturally attached to its countries of origin.[11]

The Arab countries also worked to implement the decisions made at the 1974 Islamic Conference of Lahore. As we saw in chapter three, Muslim kings, princes, and presidents had assembled there from all over the world

to decide the political future of Islam on a global scale. The general secretary of the Islamic Conference, Mohammed Hasan Mohammed al-Tohami,
spoke of an Islamic State that would work to propagate Islam in non-Muslim countries. He called on Muslim experts to coordinate their efforts to
bring about an intellectual upsurge that would realize the Islamic "nation's
hopes in building a broad solid base for this generation and coming ones."
That base should be built by the "faithful and thoughtful men capable of
leading the Islamic state in the various fields outstepping non-Muslim
countries and saving future generations. Such leadership would set an example for those who wish to stem the tide of aberration and perdition and
to protect the sons of our contemporary generation against the blind and
meaningless limitation of the ways, customs and concepts of non-Muslims."[12]

He proposed worldwide intellectual activities for Muslim youth, aiming
at enhancing their thinking "through debates, meetings, lectures, publications, and scientific, objective and meaningful comparisons." It would revive Islamic thought "and develop the lofty Islamic school of thought at
the international level." In this connection, he put forward two basic projects for the assembly's approval and support. The first envisaged setting up
a Council for scholars of the Islamic states at the international level. This
projected council would offer expert opinion to the Islamic nation and
"prepare the integral constitution of the Islamic nation in the various
sphere of life. Its profound studies and legislation would be put at the disposal of member countries that may wish to apply this evolutionary Islamic
programme in order to bring about the advent of the Islamic State with all
her spiritual, moral and practical values."

Al-Tohami's second proposal concerned the establishment throughout
the world of Islamic universities. These would base their curricula on Islam
and serve as centers to propagate the faith. Two universities had already
been planned in Central and West Africa, explicitly in order to help Muslims resist "alien thought and foreign ideology." Tohami reminded the
delegates that at the Conference of Islamic Cultural Centers (held in London in May 1973) Islamic leaders had agreed to support and fund such
centers not just in Africa but also in Europe, as "a great need was felt for
propagating the tenets of Islam and helping Muslim communities in Europe to play this role effectively and fruitfully." He referred to the 1973
London Conference that had

> decided to establish the Islamic Council of Europe to serve as an organ of
> co-ordination among all Islamic institutions and centres. Besides, it will help
> propagate the true teachings of Islam throughout Europe. Undoubtedly, the
> convening of such conferences would result in stepping up the activities of
> the Islamic Da'awa [proselytism] and propping [up] the Islamic Cultural
> Centre.

Al-Tohami then invited the assembly to send delegates to a meeting the following month:

> We hope that Ministers concerned with the Islamic call [the call for non-Muslims to convert to Islam] would take part in this Conference and to bring with them [*sic*] their programmes and plans in all fields—cultural, scientific and material so that Allah may guide us to achieve this objective and to undertake our duty in a well-studied and concerted manner on a universal level, in order to implemented the Benghazi Resolution [Benghazi Conference, March 1973] regarding the establishment of the Jehad [Jihad] Fund.

After examining Islamic thought, culture, economy, finance, investment, cultural centers and universities worldwide, as well as the international Islamic news agency and Da'awa, al-Tohami summed up his report, which contained the following points, summarized here:

1. Establishing an International Islamic News Agency and putting its programme into effects. . . .
5. Urgent convention of a meeting of specialists in the propagation of Islam on a world level and the establishment of Jehad Fund as a preliminary step for the definition of the tasks of that fund in accordance with the previous resolutions and putting them into effect wherever possible. Subscription to this fund is open with no restrictions in accordance with the progress of the plan of action in all fields of Jehad as mentioned earlier in this connection. . . .
7. Caring for the affairs of cultural centres and organizations in Europe, and the establishment of two cultural centres in the continent. . . . Besides, the existing centres should be cared of [for] and the cultural activities should be resumed in America and Africa.

As we shall see in the coming chapters, the EAD became the primary instrument for attaining these goals in the following decades. The educational and cultural programs of the European Islamic Centers, which were introduced by the EAD into European schools, seem to reflect the concept of the Jihad [Holy War] Fund that al-Tohami mentioned. These programs were wholeheartedly embraced, applied and monitored by European leaders, intellectuals, and activists.

On the international level, the associative policy of the Euro-Arab Dialogue has led the EU to defend Muslim causes, and particularly the Palestinians at every opportunity. The huge sums that the EU pays to Arab Mediterranean countries and the Palestinians amount to another tribute exacted for its security within the *dar al-sulh*. Europe thereby put off the threat of a *jihad* aimed at the *dar al-harb* by opting for appeasement and collusion with international terrorism—while blaming the increased world tensions on Israel and America so as to preserve its *dar al-sulh* position of subordinate collaboration, if not surrender, to the Islamists.

7

The Political Alignment of
the European Community

In 1969, various international organizations began a series of maneuvers that tended to isolate Israel, bringing it condemnation and ostracism from the international community. The Arab League—with the backing of the Soviet bloc, Third World countries and the European Community, the latter on France's initiative—stepped up its defamation campaign against the Jewish state. These attacks increased in 1974–75, soon after Arafat addressed the UN General Assembly. The Euro-Arab political collaboration was set on the June 10, 1974 meeting, followed by Euro-Arab contacts in Paris at the ministerial level three weeks later. The Nine established the structure of the European cooperation at the first interparliamentary conference for Euro-Arab cooperation in Damascus on September 14–17, 1974, two months before Arafat's appearance at the UN. From that time on, the PLO was granted observer status in UN bodies including the General Agreement on Tariffs and Trade (GATT), the World Health Organization (WHO), the United Nations Educational, Scientific and Cultural Organization (UNESCO), and the UN Commission on Human Rights. On November 10, 1975, the UN General Assembly adopted Resolution 3379, labeling Zionism a form of racism. It was a year after Arafat's speech, and the thirty-seventh anniversary of the 1938 Nazi *Kristallnacht*.

By 1977 the EC had fully aligned itself with the directives concerning Israel that had been formulated by the Arab League and the Algiers Arab Conference in November 1973. The Declaration of the Nine on the Middle East, issued in London on June 29, 1977, changed the wording of the original UN Resolution 242, which had been refused by the Arab countries.[1] Some passages of this Declaration repeat word for word the formulations of the Second Islamic Conference of Lahore (1974). Thus, article 2 of the Declaration of the Nine specifies "the necessity for Israel to end the territorial occupation it has maintained since the 1967 conflict," while UN S.C. Resolution 242 only mentions withdrawal "*from* territories" (French: *de* territoires, improperly translated as *des* territoires) linked to peace negotiations. The London Declaration also includes the statement that Israel must, in the interests of establishing a just and lasting peace, take account of the "legitimate rights" of the Palestinians—a condition also not to be found in the original English version of Resolution 242.

Article 3 of the London Declaration contains further reflections of the Arab position:

> The Nine are convinced that a solution of the Middle East conflict will only be possible if the legitimate right of the Palestinian people to give effective expression to its national identity is translated into a reality which will take account of the need of a homeland for the Palestinian people. They consider that the representatives of the parties to the conflict, including the Palestinian people, must participate in the negotiations in an appropriate manner, to be defined in consultation among all the interested parties. In the framework of an overall settlement, Israel must be prepared to recognize the legitimate rights of the Palestinian people. Likewise, the Arab party must be prepared to recognize Israel's right to live in peace within secure and recognized frontiers.

This declaration had actually been prepared by the General Commission of the EAD when it met in Tunis on February 10, 1977.[2] At this meeting the Arab delegates proposed to the Europeans the establishment of a joint political consultation committee within the EAD—a proposal that the Europeans promised to study. Concerning Jerusalem, the Tunis communiqué stated, "the European side . . . has also marked its opposition to any initiative tending to alter the status of Jerusalem unilaterally. The Arab side said how much it appreciated this attitude."

On September 26, 1977, M. Henri Simonet, the Belgian foreign minister and president of the Council of the EEC, declared at the UN General Assembly in New York that the Middle East conflict could only be resolved by implementation of Security Council Resolutions 242 (1967) and 338 (1973). He meant the Franco-Arab interpretation of these Resolutions. The language of the French version of Resolution 242 modifies the original English; the EEC adopted this nonbinding interpretation of Resolution 242 after the Arab oil embargo in 1973.[3] In his statement, Simonet affirmed in paragraph 50 that the EC backed Israel's withdrawal to the 1949 armistice lines, the territorial integrity of each state, and the establishment of peace by the recognition "of the legitimate rights of the Palestinians." Article 51 stressed the position of the nine countries of the EC: there will be no solution to the conflict "unless the legitimate right of the Palestinian people to give effective expression to its national identity becomes a reality. This would take into account, of course, the need for a homeland for the Palestinian people." In paragraph 52, another Arab principle was adopted by the EC spokesman: "It remains the firm view of the nine countries that

all of these elements constitute an indivisible whole." This meant: no separate peace between Israel and its neighbors—a position rejected by Israel
and America and supported by the Arabs and Europe. Like its Arab associ-
ates, the EC voiced its concern "over the illegal measures taken recently by
the Government of Israel in the occupied territories."[4]

The third session of the EAD General Commission took place at Brussels
on October 28, 1977. The king and queen of Belgium received the two
delegations at the Palais d'Egmont to emphasize the importance of this
Euro-Arab meeting. At this meeting, the Arab side expressed its satisfaction
with the June 1977 London declaration. The Brussels Commission's Communiqué confirmed the EC's alignment with the Arab position and recalls
the Arabs' repeated demand concerning the PLO.[5] The delegates stressed
that the time had come for the Nine to assert that the legitimate representative of the Palestinian people was the Palestine Liberation Organization
(PLO), which had already been recognized as such by all the Arab states
and a majority of other countries, as well as by the United Nations. At the
Brussels meeting, the Arabs offered $15 million to finance EAD projects,
and the Europeans' $3.5 million for the feasibility studies. Both parties con-
tributed $250,000 for a symposium on relations between the two civiliza-
tions. At the Tunis meeting, the Arab League budgeted $350,000 for EAD
activities.

The EAD General Commission met again in Damascus on December 9,
1978 in an atmosphere overshadowed by the Camp David peace negotiations between Egypt and Israel under the American aegis. Here again it
reaffirmed the Arab position concerning the territories and the peace conditions concerning Israel and the Palestinians.[6] It is ironic that this talk of
peace conditions went on at a time when the destruction of Lebanese
Christian political power by the PLO (supported by its Muslim and European allies) had already been going on for three years.

Pio Manzù Research Centre Symposium, Rimini, 1979

The Iranian Khomeini revolution in 1979 revitalized the Euro-Arab Dialogue, which—as described in chapter 4—had been frozen by the Israel-
Egyptian peace process of 1977–79. Although opposed to a separate peace,
the Europeans were divided. Germany and England were inclined to support the American Middle East initiative, while the others were afraid of
the Palestinian reaction. These internal divisions and the adamant Arab
opposition to peace contributed to a gloomy atmosphere at the EAD meetings, despite the EC's strong reservations about the peace process. Al-Mani
records that German Foreign Minister Hans-Dietrich Genscher, speaking
at the UN on behalf of the EC in September 1978, went out of his way to

reassure the Arab world of the Community's resolve for a comprehensive settlement based on recognition of Palestinian rights. The Arabs had totally rejected the Camp David agreement at the Fez Islamic Conference of 1980 (see appendix 2, article 12).[7]

The Pio Manzù Research Centre, an international research center on geopolitical and environmental issues that enjoys consultative status at the United Nations, organized a symposium that opened in Rimini, Italy on September 30, 1979. In planning this symposium, the Centre worked in cooperation with the United Nations, the European Communities, the League of Arab States, OPEC, and numerous ministries of foreign affairs, trade and industry. The symposium's title makes its intentions clear: *Europe Arab World. From clashing on petroleum to cooperating for a new economic order. Development-Interdependence-Cooperation, 5th International Study Days.*

During the discussions, the Arab delegates recalled that the dialogue had begun in 1973. Mana Ben Saeed Al-Otaiba, the chairman of OPEC and minister of petroleum and mineral resources of the United Arab Emirates, declared that the current reopening of the Euro-Arab Dialogue would facilitate "a much wider scope, including the Arab States, or rather the whole Arab World, and the whole of Europe." The importance of oil for the development of the Arab world as well as for Europe, he emphasized, formed the basis of this alliance. Commerce, economy, oil, the transfer of technology, industry, culture, and information constituted the foundation of the Dialogue. But he also wished the revival of the cultural relationship of former times. He then underlined the linkage between oil supplies and the EC's policy toward Israel:

> Maybe another aspect should be included in this dialogue—**most probably, our European friends, will not want to mention it** [emphasis added]—that is the political side of things. If there is no political harmony between us, how can we talk about commercial and economical harmony? Economy and politics are two sides of the same question.

He emphasized that the political problems were closely tied to economic and oil questions, and explicitly declared,

> All we ask is that Europe and the industrialized countries recognize Palestine as a nation and the Palestine Liberation Organization (PLO) as its sole representative. All dealings and discussions should be held with our brothers the Palestinian Arabs who can defend their cause better than anyone else.
>
> Europe and the other oil consuming countries want us to guarantee them oil and petroleum products. You all know that this is a highly volatile and inflammable product and that it is located in an area dominated by military and political disturbances.
>
> We must all work together to calm this situation—**this smouldering in the oil fields must be damped down otherwise it will burst into flames and then**

there would be no more oil to supply the industrialized countries with [emphasis added]. We must all face this reality if we want to find a peaceful solution to the Palestinian problem and to the problem of the Middle East.

Thank you for your patience in listening to me so far and for having considered many questions together, some of which are rather delicate ones for some of you. Between friends, one must be sincere and this sincerity is a proof of a firm desire to open up a dialogue with you.[8]

During the symposium Mohammed Jabir Hassan, the undersecretary for planning at the Iraqi Oil Ministry, recalled the importance of Palestine for the stability of Euro-Arab relations. The link between oil and the PLO was clearly expressed in the following threat:

Our cooperation should therefore be based on moral educational principles so that Europe should play its part in putting an end to injustice and restoring the people of Palestine to their rights. **Unless these aims are adhered to, it will be difficult for Europe to have her petroleum supplies guaranteed. With the help of collaboration on these matters, we shall be able to place the question of petroleum supplies on a different level without considering our reserves as a means of defending our rights and our homeland.** A true cooperation between ourselves and the European nations must begin from an analysis of the Middle Eastern question and the finding of a way to stop injustice and restore the people of Palestine to their legitimate rights. These questions are very important for us, although they may not be of very great interest to European public opinion, **and we think it should be a matter of international concern** that matters be righted [emphasis added].[9]

Jabir Hassan assured the Europeans that their energy problems deeply concerned the Arabs who felt it their duty to help and to do their best to ease international difficulties. But in the same way, therefore—he continued—the European nations should demonstrate "a similar duty in helping the Arab peoples to resolve their difficulties and ensure the people of Palestine their legitimate rights."

The Pio Manzù summit was followed by intense Arab diplomatic pressure on the European media. This coincided with an increased anti-Israeli campaign in Europe and the Arab world—a reaction to the direct peace negotiations between Egypt and Israel. In a lecture to the diplomatic press association in Paris on December 6, 1979, Arab League secretary-general Chedli Klibi, announced the opening of an Arab information campaign in the widest sense. He reminded his audience that the Tunis summit had made very precise recommendations for a concerted campaign to be initiated, aimed at all friendly countries, and particularly Europe. In effect, at its session in Tunis (February 10–12, 1977), the General Commission of the Euro-Arab Dialogue had decided to established a program for intensifying Euro-Arab cooperation in the media and information domain. The

Arabs—Klibi affirmed—attribute a particular importance to Western Europe, "because we believe that Europe can and must play a key role, first for itself, and to influence international, and especially American, opinion. Thus, we think that the campaign that will be directed toward Western Europe will be crucial."[10]

Klibi recalled that the UN General Assembly resolution 3236—which had been adopted by the Soviet–Third World "automatic majority" on November 22, 1974, after Arafat's UN address—had for the first time referred to the "Palestinian people", rather than to "refugees." Asked by a journalist how the UN Security Council's Resolution 242, which only referred to "refugees," could be modified, Klibi replied,

> That is where your role as Europeans can be effective. To start with, the concept of "refugees" should be replaced by that of "Palestinian people." And the consequences of this theoretical modification should also be realized so that this people would be placed in a position to have their state. That is where Europe can play a specific role, a dynamic role, a driving role. . . . I would like France to play a role in this direction and to be, within the European Community, a sort of driving force—that France should take the role as leader, and that the whole European Community would play a role in this direction.

Klibi explained that the Arab League rejected the Israel-Egyptian peace treaty that had been signed in March 1979, and that it would fight against Israel in every possible way—particularly through political means. He declared that such an information campaign was going to assume a special, primary role in this strategy and would be directed toward all the international communities, especially Europe and America.

To a journalist who expressed approval of the Egypt-Israel peace treaty, Klibi replied, "If you think that the principal belligerents are Egypt and Israel, you are mistaken. The principal belligerents are the Arabs on one hand, and Israel on the other."

Thus, the Arab League's propaganda campaign was directed toward the West with the full collaboration of the EAD organization, involving the approval of the EC countries leaders and the European Council. Six months later, in June 1980—and two months before the Fez Islamic Conference—the European Community issued the Declaration of Venice. The Declarations of Venice and Fez carry many similar points in relation to Israel and Jerusalem and apparently European EAD delegates were involved in both. This united European and Islamic outburst against Israel stemmed from Israeli Prime Minister Menahem Begin's firm declaration that Jerusalem was "the eternal capital of Israel."

The 1980 Declaration of Venice and the Fez Islamic Conference

The 1979 Iranian Revolution created a second oil crisis for the world's economies, especially those of Western Europe. The Islamic Republic and the OPEC countries together reduced their oil production, thus provoking a world recession and 11.5 percent inflation for the countries of the OCDE (Organization for Economic Cooperation and Development). Between 1973 and 1980, crude oil prices had increased tenfold.

By then, the EC had confirmed the demands of the Arab League concerning Israel. After the two-year interruption of the Dialogue following the Israeli-Egyptian peace treaty of 1979, the EC endorsed, in its Venice Declaration of June 1980, all the Arab political requests.[11] It confirmed the national rights of the Palestinians, "which is not simply one of refugees."[12] The European Community also required the participation of the PLO in all negotiations,[13] despite the fact that its 1968 Charter still called for the total destruction of Israel. The Nine member states stressed that they would not accept "any unilateral initiative designed to change the status of Jerusalem."[14] They condemned, as usual, Israel's "territorial occupation which it has maintained since the conflict of 1967" and affirmed, "the Israeli settlements constitute a serious obstacle to the peace process in the Middle East. The Nine consider that these settlements, as well as modifications in population and property in the occupied Arab territories, are illegal under international law."[15] The term "Arab territories" endorsed Arab terminology, and as for the international rules alluded to, they only apply to territories delimited by the borders of another nation-state. This was not the case in the 1967 war but should have been applied previously to those same territories when they were occupied by Egypt and Jordan after the 1948 war, with the expulsion of all Palestinian Jews and the confiscation or destruction of their synagogue and properties.

The UN Security Resolution 242 formulation of withdrawal "from territories"—not *Arab* territories—in exchange for peace was, thereby, discarded even though it had been sponsored by Britain and America. The EC had now officially adopted the Arab world's most radical positions. Barely two months later, from September 18 to 20, 1980, the Islamic Conference of Foreign Ministers on the Question of Jerusalem held a special session in Fez, Morocco (see appendix 2). All the speakers proclaimed their solidarity with the PLO *jihad* against Israel. Al-Hajj Ahmed Sekou Toure, president of the Revolutionary People's Republic of Guinea, declared that the Israeli decision to annex Jerusalem posed a challenge to humanity as a whole. President Leopold Senghor of Senegal—very close to France and a Christian—recalled that his country, a former French colony, had been the first to recognize the PLO as the sole representative of the Palestinians. He emphasized that two billion Muslims and Christians were protesting Israel's claim on Jerusalem.

According to the minutes of the Fez Conference, Agha Shahi, minister for foreign affairs of the Islamic Republic of Pakistan, recalled that "the Al Quds [Jerusalem] Committee, in its last meeting in Casablanca, had approved a comprehensive plan to be implemented by the Islamic states on both the national and international levels, and in the United Nations, to prevent Israel from using force and oppression to complete the annexation of Al Quds, and continue obliterating its Muslim and Christian features." Then he pointed to a new, encouraging development, "a change in favor of the Palestine issue: **the abstention by the European countries from voting at the Special General Assembly Session on the resolution on Palestine; the resolution on Al Quds submitted by the European countries to the Security Council; the condemnation of Israel's policy [by] prominent religious bodies, such as the World Church Council**" (emphasis added, see appendix 2). This, he said, indicated an increasing recognition of the Islamic position on the Palestinian issue.

After having called for a declaration of *jihad*, the Fez Islamic Conference issued a list of Resolutions. One set forth a plan of international dimensions to deny Israel's right to Jerusalem, thereby joining the European position stated in the Venice Declaration that had preceded it. In its Resolution 2, it declared its intentions to reaffirm the commitment of Islamic countries to mobilize all their political, financial, petroleum, and military potentials to counter the Israeli decision of annexing Al Quds (Jerusalem). They threatened with political and economic boycott any country that would recognize Israel's decision, contribute to its enforcement, or establish an embassy in Al Quds Al Sharif (Jerusalem).

Resolution 3 reiterated the same threat, requesting all the countries of the world to refrain from dealing with Israeli authorities in any way that could be exploited by these authorities as an acceptance of the fait accompli in Jerusalem and in all other occupied Palestinian and Arab territories; otherwise they would be liable to boycott measures. Those threats still today determine the policy of the world's nations toward Israel. The fact that the EC issued its Venice Declaration two months before the Fez Conference provided a fictitious impression of European political independence from the Arab World. For, as Hans-Dietrich Genscher, the minister of foreign affairs of the German Federal Republic, declared at the EAD Hamburg Symposium in 1983, the Venice Declaration aimed at soothing Arab anger and renewing the Dialogue.

The fourth Resolution calls on the Security Council to adopt military and economic sanctions against Israel. In the following one, the Conference expressed its full satisfaction at the response of the countries that had transferred their embassies from Jerusalem, at the appeal of the Islamic states.

It underlined the unanimous opposition of the international community to the Israeli measure of annexing Jerusalem, and declaring it the capital of Israel. Resolution 11 criticizes the American policy and threatens that any support extended to Israel "to sustain its illegitimate occupation and desecration of holy places, be it direct or indirect, overt or covert, constitutes a challenge to the Islamic world."

The EAD apparatus provided European assistance for this campaign, downplaying Palestinian international terrorism and hostage taking in Lebanon. Euro-Arab militancy began to show its influence not only in state policy and in widespread anti-Israel media coverage, but in the close association and collaboration at the highest level between European and Arab politicians, intellectuals, journalists, and even clergy, as a result of the EAD Tunis summit and the Fez Resolution that had appealed to these groups. They had been requested "to initiate political action at the UN with the Big Powers, notably the European Community, with a view to enlisting further support to the Palestine Question and to tightening Israel's isolation" (Resolution 13). Resolutions 18 and 19 recommended the intensification of contacts with the Holy See and Christian circles to request their support on behalf of the Palestinian people, their recognition of the PLO, and to initiate a wide-scale, anti-Israeli information campaign.

The statements and publications of the time show that the PLO's ideology, strategy, propaganda, and phraseology were conceived, formulated, and imposed on a reluctant European public opinion by a strong Arab and Western political and ideological alliance, including Third Worldists, Leftists, Communists and the extreme Right. These Arab positions were confirmed at the Eleventh Arab Summit Conference, held in Amman, Jordan, from November 25 to 27, 1980. The conference stressed the need to strengthen the role of the Latin American States and to exploit the EAD to further the Arab policy (see appendix 3).

> The Conference affirmed the determination of the Arab States to pursue the Euro-Arab dialogue with a view to the promotion of joint interests and the achievement of greater understanding of the justice of Arab demands, particularly with regard to the question of Palestine.
>
> The Conference stressed the need for endeavours to ensure the continued support and backing of the group of socialist States for Arab rights and to strengthen co-operation with that group with a view to the promotion of joint interests and the furtherance and development of the support of those States for Arab rights in such a way as to increase Arab steadfastness capabilities. . . .
>
> The Conference stressed the need for the continuation of contacts with the Vatican and with other Christian religious organizations and institutions in order to ensure their support for the recovery of full Arab sovereignty over Jerusalem.

Strong ties were forged between the OIC, the Arab and European states, as well as between various factions of the Left, the Vatican, and the World Council of Churches. They led, under Arab threats, to Israel's demonization at all levels of European society as well as in international bodies. In fact, this Euro-Arab collusion appears mainly in Arab texts; in European sources, it is carefully disguised as a humanitarian concern for "the suffering Palestinians abandoned by the world." Anglican Canon Kenneth Cragg described this identification with the Palestinians as "to be on behalf of the people in the voicing of despair, so that evil is not silenced, dismissed, disregarded—which is the way of untruth—but held, pilloried, taken for the evil it is."[16] Israel's metaphysical identification with evil had to be constantly exposed by shedding light on the sufferings of those who worked for its destruction.

The creation and dissemination of the image of the victimized and abandoned Palestinian was therefore of pivotal importance. The coalition of churches and mosques, of European and Islamic states, was cemented in a joint attack against four million Jews living on less than half of their historical land—survivors of the tyranny of both.

This militancy led to the establishment of Euro-Arab networks in the West that took place within the context of an international toleration of terror, in which several governments connived. It was in this way that the first seeds of dhimmitude were implanted in Europe,[17] as will be described later. It also accelerated the disintegration of the *dhimmi* Eastern Christian communities of the Middle East, a development that went largely unnoticed due to the European compliance with the Arab/Islamic propaganda war against Israel. Many distinguished non-Jewish and Jewish authors and intellectuals subsequently denounced the violent upsurge of Judeophobia and pro-Palestinianism that spread hatred over the world. However, they were too weak to prevail against the perversion of truth fabricated by governmental bodies at the highest levels.[18]

Beginning in 1974, radio, television, the press and UN educational publications (including those of UNESCO) spread anti-Zionist dogma worldwide. They particularly stressed the equation of Zionism with racism, based on the 1975 UN General Assembly Resolution 3379. Along the lines of Chedli Klibi's program detailed above and the Islamic and Arab Summits, France became the engine of Arab League strategy. Historian Robert Wistrich describes the next development:

Above all, the French televisual media created a climate of disinformation and unprecedented hostility towards Israel with its ceaseless use of emotionally charged Holocaustal [*sic*] terminology, which undoubtedly intensified latent antisemitic sentiment that had never altogether disappeared in France. The French Communist Party, through its manifold channels of influence, added its own Soviet-inspired legends of fascism and Zionism as inseparable "Siamese twins"; to this motley chorus one would have to add the left-wing Catholics of *Témoignage Chrétien,* a section of the French Socialist Party, the various Franco-Arab and Franco-Palestinian associations and the myriad promoters of anti-American Third World ideologies in France.[19]

The delegitimization of Israel was gradually integrated into Europe's strategic and economic interests. It became a central element of the policy of the French socialist-communist coalition governments actively involved in creating a Euro-Arab bloc hostile to the United States and Israel. This fundamental reason explains European opposition, particularly in France, to the Gulf war of 1990–91.[20] The eminent Arabist and French scholar Jacques Berque—the ideologue of Palestinian terrorism and of Israel's destruction—was an ardent admirer of the Arab world and of Saddam Hussein. He called him the "secularist" tyrant and recommended his regime that has become "a redoubtable potential adversary for Israel."[21]

A strange imbalance arose between the permanent pro-Palestinian militancy sustained by the states, the political parties, and the media, and the process, still ongoing, of rapprochement with Judaism. European officials cautiously restricted the latter, which was already limited solely to the religious level, to modest publications so as not to irritate the many Muslim states of the powerful Organization of the Islamic Conference (OIC), which today numbers fifty-six member states and the Palestinian Authority. Intellectuals, writers, and clergymen who dared to defend Israel were silenced and dismissed from their posts. Their manuscripts and articles were refused by editors and publishers, frightened by the OIC's threats and Palestinian terrorism. In private conversations and correspondence with the author in the 1980s, the eminent French sociologist and Protestant theologian Jacques Ellul complained that his articles were refused by many newspapers and even Protestant publications because of his pro-Israeli position. William Nicholls, Professor Emeritus of Religious Studies, University of British Columbia, Vancouver, suffered a boycott for the same reason. Such cases were not exceptional, as demonstrated by the present author's private exchanges with numerous authors and clergymen. They illustrated the strenuous resistance against intellectual totalitarianism by an intelligentsia that soon added to this campaign the defense of Christian victims in Islamic lands.

On June 9, 1982, following the start of Israel's war in Lebanon, the Council of Ministers of the European Community decided to defer signing the new EEC-Israel financial protocol in order to put pressure on Israel. However, no pressure was applied upon Syria and the PLO over their terrorist war in Lebanon. This kind of inequity, tacitly endorsing Arab impunity, became commonplace.[22]

The Hamburg Symposium, 1983

The Hamburg Symposium of the Euro-Arab Dialogue was inaugurated with great pomp on April 11, 1983. In his opening address, German Foreign Minister Hans-Dietrich Genscher, the minister of foreign affairs of the German Federal Republic, spoke strongly of Europe's debt to Islamic civilization and emphasized the importance of the Dialogue in cementing Euro-Arab solidarity. He referred to the beginning of the Dialogue in 1973, and underlined that its political aspects must not be ignored—in other words, he framed the EC's anti-Israel policy in the Middle East as the foundation of the entire economic edifice of Euro-Arab cooperation. He then declared:

> The Euro-Arab Dialogue would indeed remain incomplete if the political side were to be ignored or not taken seriously.
> Both parties to the Dialogue, both partners, should always remind themselves of the joint Memorandum issued in Cairo in 1975, the Charter of the Dialogue. The Memorandum contains the following quote: "The Euro-Arab Dialogue is the outcome of the common political will which strives for the creation of a special relationship between the two groups." We Europeans spoke out in a clear and convinced manner for a revival of the Euro-Arab Dialogue in the Venice Declaration of June 13, 1980. Since then, the various working groups within the Dialogue have become more active and the prospects for the future are now promising.[23]

In clear words, "the common political will" represents the common Euro-Arab anti-Israeli policy as proven by Genscher's reference to the Venice Declaration, one of the harshest against Israel. Five years later, in 1988, the European Parliament again put pressure on Israel. It refused to approve three new protocols until Israel allowed direct Palestinian exports to Europe. Israel had signed a commercial agreement with the EEC on May 11, 1975, under which its goods had enjoyed preferential treatment. The Arab Ambassadors in Brussels had immediately and jointly protested this agreement as contrary to the spirit of the Dialogue. A year later Morocco, Algeria, Tunisia, Egypt, Syria, Jordan, and Lebanon in their turn signed preferential cooperation agreements and benefited also from financial aid. The 1988 decision represented another concession to the Arab war against Israel.

In January 1990, the Commission of the European Communities applied a partial freeze on scientific cooperation with Israel until Arab schools in the administered territories were reopened. Israel had closed them following a terrorist upsurge. Again, no such pressures were ever exerted on Syria when it occupied Lebanon and settled hundred of thousands of Syrians there.[24] Nor did Europe raise its voice against Arafat when Palestinian schools were used to promote terrorist activities and anti-Jewish hate.

This pattern has continued in Europe. As, for example, in December 2003, when Ehud Olmert, Israel's industry, trade and labor minister, agreed to an EU request to label goods made in Israel with their city of manufacture. Clearly, this was another step in the tightening of EU economic sanctions against Israel and compliance to Arab requests, as it made it more difficult for Israeli exporters to market their products in Europe.[25]

Since the 1980s, the EC/EU has engaged in a policy of political discrimination against Israel, a corollary of the rising Islamist terrorist threat and its anti-Western fever. This tacit and silent collusion with the Islamic/Arab resolutions of 1980 aims at control of the direction of world politics, including America's course of action. The EC chose to protect its economic interests and oil supply by repeatedly indicting Israel and America rather than confront the looming global *jihad*. This strategy was accompanied and strengthened by a parallel cultural development, which will be examined in the next chapter.

8

The Cultural Alignment:
Euro-Arab Seminars

University of Venice, 1977

Arab cultural inroads into Europe were intimately bound up with the immigration of millions of Muslims from Africa, the Middle East, and Asia, who were encouraged to bring with them their mores and culture.[1] This cultural Arabization and Islamization was actually planned at a Euro-Arab Seminar that was held at the University of Venice from March 28 to 30, 1977. The topic was "Means and Forms of Cooperation for the Diffusion in Europe of the Knowledge of Arabic Language and Literary Civilization."

The seminar was organized by the Instituto per l'Oriente in Rome in conjunction with the Arabic literature section of the foreign languages faculty of the University of Venice. Arab participants came from fourteen universities in Arab countries. They represented Algeria, Tunisia, Egypt, Jordan, Iraq, Saudi Arabia, Qatar, and Sudan.[2] Nineteen Arabists from European universities participated, as well as numerous other personalities connected with the Muslim world, including a representative of the Pontifical Institute of Arab Studies in Rome (Pontificio Instituto di Studi Arabi e d'Islamitica/PISAI). The seminar was integrated into the framework of the Euro-Arab Dialogue and thus conducted under the auspices of the European Community and the Arab League.[3]

During this seminar, which consisted of four sessions under joint European and Arab chairmanship, the European participants presented reports on the diffusion and knowledge of Arabic and of Arab civilization in their respective countries. The Arab delegates, for their part, described the simplified methods they practiced for teaching Arabic to non-Arabs and recommended them for Europe. The seminar ended with the adoption of a number of recommendations. Their general tenor advocated the establishment in European capitals of centers for the diffusion of the Arab language and culture throughout Europe, in coordination with Arab countries. This project envisaged appointing to European institutes and universities Arab professors specialized in teaching Europeans—a rather sibylline formula. The recommendations in relation to this project are summarized below, but the full text of the recommendations is in appendix 1. The participants in the seminar unanimously proposed them for consideration by the governments of the member states of the European Community and the League of Arab States. They included "Coordination of the efforts made by the Arab countries to spread the Arabic language and culture in Europe and to find the appropriate form of cooperation among the Arab institutions that operate in this field."

The participants called for the creation of joint Euro-Arab Cultural Centers in European capitals for the diffusion of the Arabic language and culture, and support for "European institutions either at University level or other levels that are concerned with the teaching of the Arabic language and the diffusion of Arabic and Islamic culture." They demanded state involvement in joint cultural projects for cooperation between European and Arab institutions in "the field of linguistic research and the teaching of the Arabic language to Europeans." However, this teaching should not be left to Europeans. The demand to supply European institutions and universities with Arab teachers to teach Europeans is reiterated several times in the same document, and in nearly all of them over the years. In fact, it is no more than a cover for *da'wa,* which set the pro-Islamic and pro-Palestinian orientation of European universities. It is strange that European professors whose profession is precisely teaching Arabic and Islamic culture should themselves accept their incompetence in their own field and demand to be replaced by Arab teachers. They even added that the teaching of Arabic should be linked to Arab-Islamic culture and contemporary Arab issues. In other words, distinguished European scholars were ceding their place to foreign Arab colleagues to teach their disciplines in European institutions and universities and to spread their propaganda. In very cautious terms, recommendation 11 called on the governments of the EC to recognize the "necessity of cooperation between European and Arab specialists in order to present an objective picture of Arab-Islamic civilization and contemporary Arab issues to students and to the educated public in Europe which could attract Europeans to Arabic studies." This would end, in effect, critical thought in European public discourse about Islam and the Islamic world, as European governments and universities adopted the Arab perspective on virtually all relevant issues. In order to create a perfect Euro-Arab harmony between Arab and European universities the participants emphasized the need to train European teachers of Arabic in Arab universities and institutions.

Other resolutions delineated forms of cooperation that the seminar participants wished to see between Arab and European universities and their respective specialists. The seminar also discussed how to obtain and distribute the funds necessary for this Arabization project within the EC. Finally, the seminar recommended the establishment of "a permanent committee of Arab and European experts to follow up on the recommendations for disseminating Arabic and Arab culture in Europe; this to be within the framework of the Euro-Arab Dialogue."[4]

This EAD framework implies the approval of the foreign ministers of the EC countries and of the EC presidency, and their collaboration with the secretary of the Arab League and other Arab state ministers and diplomats on the EAD General Commission. Since the EAD General Commission's meetings were closed and the proceedings not published, the adoption of these proposals by the EAD can only be deduced from the fact of their subsequent implementation. Commentators on the Dialogue's organization have praised its practical and flexible framework, saying that the General Commission's secrecy frees it from treaties and legalism: European and Arab heads of state could work together unimpeded.[5] However, this structure also shielded from scrutiny and democratic control the proceedings conducted by national governments.[6]

The Venice seminar thus not only paved the way for the large-scale Arab and Muslim migration into Europe; it also envisioned the creation of a common culture encompassing the north and south shores of the Mediterranean. In his revealing book, Alexandre Del Valle describes the various sources that fed the growing current of Islamophilia among the European intelligentsia. The new Islamic vogue drew from the ranks of the respectable and from the disreputable, including clerics, communists, converts to Islam, and Nazi sympathizers.[7]

The philosophy of René Guénon in particular exercised a pervasive influence. Guénon was a French Nazi who had converted to Islam and lived in Cairo. He preached hatred of Western civilization and modern Western secularism, and maintained that Europe could be redeemed only through Islam. He was not alone in thinking that Islam would be the redeemer of the decadent West, as the tenacious Judeophobic current in the Church saw the Islamic destruction of Israel as a Christian victory.[8] This atmosphere encouraged the flow of immigrants from Muslim countries and the further development of EAD policies along these lines.

Beginning with the first meeting in Cairo on June 14, 1975 (see chapter 4), every EAD meeting passed resolutions in support of Arab immigration, labor, and employment in Europe. This policy, which developed jointly with the confirmation of the common Euro-Arab position regarding Israel and the PLO, was stated at the first session of the General Committee in Luxembourg (May 18–20, 1976) and reaffirmed in Tunis (February 1977), Brussels (October 1977), Damascus (December 1978), and at all subsequent meetings. The expansion of European markets in Arab countries was synchronized with the arrival in the EC of several million Muslim immigrants, whose religious, cultural, and social requirements the European host countries had committed themselves to satisfy. In France, Prime Minister Jacques Chirac—in President Valéry Giscard d'Estaing's government— issued a decree of April 23, 1976, allowing the reunion of immigrant families; temporary Arab immigration thereby became permanent.

The 1975 Cairo meeting that formulated the general principles and objectives of the Euro-Arab Dialogue stated that this cooperation would open new horizons in every domain: political, economic, social, and cultural. It specified that the principal objective of cooperation in the cultural field would be to consolidate and deepen the basis for cultural comprehension and intellectual rapprochement between the two regions. Thus the spread of Arab-Muslim language and culture, particularly in the universities, followed general EAD policy. The speed and scale of this operation were unique in history. Even the emigration of Europeans to their Arab colonies during the colonial period took place at a far slower pace. The number of European colonizers and their descendants in Arab countries, even after a century or more, were a fraction of the present-day Muslim immigrants in Europe after just three decades. This speedy transfer could not have happened were it not for the Euro-Arab Dialogue—in other words, without the explicit approval of all the governments and heads of state of the member states of the European Community.

Having encouraged this rapid Muslim immigration, European governments then had to consider the living and working conditions of the migrants. Al-Mani explained:

> As a reflection of the concern of the Maghreb countries over the living and working conditions of their citizens working in Europe, on 11 December 1978, at Damascus, the EAD adopted a joint declaration on the principles concerning the living and working conditions of migrant labour in the two regions. The fourteen-point declaration stressed the economic equality of migrant workers with the citizens of the host countries, legal representation of the workers, and vocational education for the workers and their children.[9]

The EAD texts mentioned reciprocity. However, this was entirely theoretical for no Arab country was likely to grant economic equality and legal representation to hundreds, let alone millions, of European migrants having—over the centuries— consistently denied that same equality of rights to their non-Muslim indigenous minorities.

The 1978 Damascus meeting of the General Commission involved the nine EC states at the ambassadorial level. The Declaration issued at this meeting began with a political statement expressing the joint Euro-Arab position concerning Israel's obligations. It also reaffirmed the importance of scientific and technological cooperation. Concerning cultural cooperation, it requested that a significant demonstration of the close relations between the two civilizations be made at the Hamburg symposium, which was scheduled for September 17–21, 1979. The participants planned a vast program of cultural events to publicize this initiative. They listed other proposals on cultural cooperation, including the publication of the conclusions of the 1977 Euro-Arab seminar of Venice, which according to those assembled in Damascus was "organized in order to promote the diffusion in Europe of the knowledge of the Arab language and civilization." The General Commission made several decisions at Damascus, among which was the creation of a special group of experts to examine the history books of the two regions. Other recommendations again touched on economic and industrial projects, and the protection and well-being of Arab migrants in Europe.

The political laxity of the European governments was worsened by the permission they granted to Arab countries to export their culture and their customs together with their population, as formulated by the Damascus EAD Declaration. Thus from the 1970s on, these immigration policies, correlated with the economic and political goals of the EAD that had been dictated by the Arab states and their European lobbies, did not envisage scattered immigration by individuals who wanted to integrate into the host country. Nor were they framed for genuine seekers of political asylum, as was the case for those who fled Eastern Europe before 1989. Rather, it planned throughout the European Communities an implantation of homogeneous ethnic communities, which in two decades would number millions.

The EAD conceptions facilitated the creation of fundamentalist trends among people who came with no intention of integrating into European society and culture. Instead, they arrived with the desire and the legal right, granted by the EC itself, to impose their own culture upon the host country. These immigrants rejected Europe's secular institutions as inferior to those of the *shari'a*, which they believe have been revealed by Allah through the Qur'an to the *umma*, the universal Muslim community. Whereas the EAD claimed for Arab immigrants the rights conferred by European legal secular institutions, many of the immigrants despised these institutions and preferred their own. Thus, from the start of this mass immigration, integration was compromised if not rendered impossible. The European host countries seemed to have heeded, implicitly, the call of the 1974 Islamic conference in Lahore to protect Muslims from "the ways, customs and concepts of non-Muslims."

There were also other sources of immigration. Since the 1950s, European economic development—as in the U.S.—has been linked to the availability of cheap and unskilled labor. Within Europe, this generally stimulated migration from poorer to richer regions: notably the successive waves of emigrants from Italy, Spain, and Portugal. However, none of these migration flows developed within a framework comparable to the EAD. In the 1980s, opposition to mass immigration became the banner of xenophobic extreme-right parties; thus, any critical discussion immediately provoked accusations of racism, Arabophobia, or Islamophobia. A sober, comprehensive, and regular assessment of the impact of Muslim/Arab immigration into Europe was impossible: it was shrouded with a taboo or identified with Nazi antisemitism. Since all main European parties were associated with the Parliamentary Association of Euro-Arab Cooperation, the future of Europe would develop according to the plans of the EAD's architects.

The Hamburg Symposium, 1983

At the Hamburg Symposium in 1983, both European and Arab speakers presented reports about the integration of the two civilizations. Participants were divided into three workshops. The first, "Prospects for Cultural Exchange," examined the potential for future cultural exchanges in all areas. The discussion covered "exchange agreements between universities, exchanges between students and teachers and others, in the field of creative arts, of audio-visual materials, co-operation in translation, in transmitting Arabic publications to Europe, exhibitions and publications." The areas of this cultural cooperation were to be defined "by a general cultural agreement between the Arab League and the European Community. This agreement would provide a framework for more specialized agreements to operate." A small joint committee within the framework of the Euro-Arab Dialogue would be "set up to monitor the working of the agreement, to examine and accept proposals for future projects and to ensure their execution."

The workshop suggested various schemes, such as the publication twice yearly of a Euro-Arab journal of Arab and European contributors on specific subjects, and a newsletter that would inform on cultural developments in the Arab world, emphasizing intellectual debates, important publications, and theatrical performances. Arab professional Unions and their members would be invited to conduct further cultural cooperation and exchange with their European counterparts. The Arab side was specially interested in an agreement with the Unions of Arab Writers and of Publishers. Periodical meetings were to be encouraged between European and Arab Unions of Radio and Television and between Associations of Film Producers and Actors to promote joint productions. The participants recommended the organization of small specialized or professional seminars on selected themes: "religious dialogue, Arab historiography, book publishing and librarianship, investigation of the content of text books at all levels in the history of the two regions."[10]

The second workshop focused on the "Social and Cultural Consequences of the Migration of Workers and Intellectuals." The participants noted that, since Arab immigration was becoming permanent, the December 1978 Damascus Declaration was inadequate to deal with the situation of 1983. It was considered particularly necessary to supplement the article stipulating the rights of Arab migrants and the members of their families to "enjoy equality of treatment as to living and working conditions, wages and economic rights, rights of association and the exercise of basic public freedoms"—the more so as participants felt that not enough was being done to implement these tenets.[11] The participants recommended the creation of a permanent institution to improve knowledge on the migrants and to formulate policies and programs "with the purpose of ensuring the highest level of welfare for the migrants themselves and maximum benefit for both countries of origin and employment with a spirit of genuine cooperation among the countries involved in the Dialogue" (article 4).

This workshop made several other proposals for the assimilation of migrant workers—none of which, however, involved the latter adapting to the customs of the host countries. It recommended that the social integration of migrant workers and their families in the host countries should be facilitated by providing equal rights in lodging, work opportunities, schooling, and vocational and professional training. It was recommended to make the general public more aware of the cultural background of migrants, by promoting cultural activities of the immigrant communities or "supplying adequate information on the culture of the migrant communities in the school curricula." Special training and educational course were required for civil servants, medical staff, members of the police force, teachers, social workers, and others who had functional relations with the immigrants. Access to the mass media had to be facilitated to the migrants in order to ensure "regular information in their own language about their own culture as well as about the conditions of life in the host country." Another proposal called for broadening cooperation between immigrant groups and the indigenous population. The participation of immigrant groups in trade union activities and their participation in political life were to be encouraged by special measures. Point 6 stated, "It is recommended that the Arab countries of origin strengthen their cultural support to Arab migrants in Europe."[12]

The third workshop examined cooperation in the field of Arabic and European language teaching. This group stressed that this question was of the greatest importance; indeed, it formed a basic principle of the Euro-Arab Dialogue. Again, the decisions of the Venice Seminar (1977) were supplemented. The workshop reiterated the necessity for teaching and dis-

seminating the Arab language and culture in Europe under the auspices
of Arab countries and institutions, as well as through the Euro-Arab cultural centers that were to be created in European capitals. It emphasized
the importance of teaching Arabic to the immigrants' children; of ensuring
the publication and distribution of Arabic newspapers and books aimed at
an educated, cultured European public; and of giving an "objective" and
attractive picture of Islamic civilization. A five-year schedule was planned
for implementing this program.

Reading the proceedings of the numerous EAD symposia, one is struck
by the difference in the discourse of the two parties. The Europeans are
cautious and emphasize their respectful admiration for Islam. They pay excessive tribute to the great Islamic civilization from which the civilization of
Europe has allegedly drawn inspiration (cf. the speech of German Foreign
Minister Hans-Dietrich Genscher, at the Hamburg Symposium). They formulate platitudinous, humble excuses for colonization and Europe's anti-
Arab prejudices. The Arab side's representatives, on the other hand, adopt
the tone of a schoolteacher wielding the stick. Convinced of the tolerance,
humanism, and greatness of Islamic civilization, they emphasize its position
as the spiritual and scientific fountainhead of Europe.

Reproaches are not absent, particularly for the inadequacy of European
measures against Israel, which of course is a central and essential point of
the whole Dialogue. The Arab speeches reiterate Europe's obligation to
deal severely with Israel, using the customary venomous language: "Zionist
usurpation," the "hand of Zionism seeking to kill the Arabs in every country," a "policy of institutionalized racism" (the UN Resolution 3379 equating Zionism with racism had been hammered through the UN General
Assembly in November 1975). The Arab delegates remind their European
colleagues of the duty to recognize and teach at university level the greatness and superiority of Islamic civilization and of the Islamic religion. Religious scholars affirm the Islamic origin of Judaism, Christianity and all
mankind—initially born as Muslim, in its original purity.

Such vain discourse was listened to with respectful silence by the representatives of the world's most powerful and educated nations. At this time,
no one foresaw the impact that these policies would have upon Europe in
the course of one generation.

Part III
The Functioning of Eurabia

9

Foreign Policy

The economic foundations upon which Eurabia grew cannot be examined adequately in a brief study: the topic deserves volumes for itself. There is ample documentation in the records of EU exchanges with the Arab/Muslim world of the astronomical sums involved in the commercial, industrial, construction, and arms markets, as well as in the oil and energy industry. It is enough to say that during those thirty years Western ingenuity and know-how raised luxurious new cities out of the Arabian sands, as European industry and modernization transformed the Middle East and North Africa. Against this big business backdrop, European governments, although continuing to preach the universality of human rights, increasingly lent tacit approval to Palestinian and Lebanese-based international terrorism, while turning a blind eye to the discrimination that weighed upon Eastern Christian populations in the Middle East and beyond.

However, the Arab states would have been powerless without Western technology, and were dependant on the West for their very subsistence. This alone—stressed by the United States during the oil crisis of 1973—should have rendered Arab threats during that crisis, and thereafter, empty. Analyzing the oil crisis in her book *Energy and Europe* (1975), Mary Mauksch emphasized that "most of the OPEC countries are dependent entities. They have been able to assert themselves because of disunity among and the unwillingness of importing countries to take any firm position vis-à-vis this confrontation."[1] They relied totally on the West for "technical and industrial know-how and capacity; and indirectly through its investment opportunities."[2]

Thus, when it was confronted by Arab League threats, Europe had the means to keep its dignity and independence, yet failed to use them. Mauksch commented that although the EEC declaration of November 6, 1973 on the Middle East "was a political necessity given Europe's dependence on Arab oil," it was also a consequence of Europe's traditional ties with the Arab countries, "including the most radical Arab elements." She stated,

France in particular had these special links and it was France which refused to participate in the consumer's cooperation group dominated by the

United Sates. France thus maintained its good relations with the Arab countries and underlined this by sending its Foreign Minister to hold talks with the leader of the Palestinian Liberation movement.[3]

For France had not only sent its foreign minister to engage in dialogue with the not-yet-legitimized Arafat, it also initiated the Euro-Arab dialogue in order to counterbalance the new cooperation on energy between Europe (without France) and America. "It was France, too, that took two initiatives which were particularly welcomed by the Arab world—the opening of a Euro-Arab dialogue aimed at initiating economic and technical cooperation in non-oil sectors, and the convening of a preliminary conference between the rich consumer countries, the developing countries and the oil producers (to lead eventually to a permanent energy dialogue between the three factions)."[4]

Was the anti-Israeli policy that was so central to the Dialogue, therefore, a course positively chosen by the French and Germans, rather than a mere adjunct of the opening of Arab markets? After all, the oil crisis brought about immediate Franco-German compliance with the Arab countries' anti-Israeli scheme—an agenda ultimately embraced by the whole EEC— although there was no political or economic necessity for them to yield so quickly. Even before the oil crisis, when it looked as if Israel might lose the 1973 war, Europe—with the exception of Spain, which was not yet a member of the EC—closed its airspace to American planes transporting munitions and spare parts to an Israel beleaguered by the armies of Syria and Egypt.

The anti-Israel policy also gave a new boost to France's old imperial dream. Whether the Euro-Arab convergence against Israel, based on an oil embargo, was originally conceived in Paris or in Riyadh, will intrigue historians for years to come. However, its growth by the early-twenty-first century into a system that is venomously anti-American as well as anti-Israeli, with a relentless Judeophobic passion, indicates that it is firmly entrenched in France and Europe. In just thirty years (1973–2003), the Euro-Arab Dialogue has successfully brought about the mutation of European civilization, giving birth to a hybrid culture: Eurabia—as foreseen in 1969 in Cairo by the European Committee for Coordination of Friendship Associations with the Arab World.

Over the years, new state members and new treaties modified the composition and legal framework of the European Community. The 1992 Maastricht Treaty on European Union (TEU) established three pillars upholding the European Union: the European Communities; a Common Foreign and Security Policy (CFSP); and Cooperation in the Fields of Justice and Home Affairs (JHA).[5] Treaties aiming at fuller integration of the member states have unified EU policy on economic and trade relations with non-EU states.

Similarly, the CFSP imposes a common foreign policy on all EU countries, covering highly sensitive international issues. In 1986, the EC countries signed the Single European Act (SEA). Among its requirements was that member states "shall endeavor jointly to formulate and implement a European foreign policy."[6] The Maastricht Treaty specified that the EU and its member states should collectively define and apply a common policy covering all areas of foreign relations and security. The Council of the EU would define a common position; member states would then issue guidelines to ensure the conformity of their national policies. The third pillar (JHA) established common rulings pertaining to asylum and immigration policies.

Over the years, the legal instruments created by the many treaties binding the EC/EU member states established a juridical and political institutional structure that weighed heavily on Europeans. "Eurocrat" decisions micromanaged the economies and markets of EU states. The EU nations' media and educational systems have been indoctrinating and conditioning Europeans to accept the new sociopolitical directives. The Euro-Arab Dialogue and its Arab lobby, the Parliamentary Association for Euro-Arab Cooperation (PAEAC), were already interwoven within the European parliaments. They were also represented in the European Parliament and in the EC structures pre-dating the European Union. The combination of a powerful Eurabian lobby with compliant European political, media, and educational systems produced throughout the EU that uniform political thinking known as "political correctness," so implacably opposed to any divergent opinion. Dissenters were harshly censured in universities, books and the media.

The Creation of a Virtual Arab/Muslim World

During the last three decades, the EC, and then the European Union which replaced it, has strengthened immensely Europe's economic and political ties with Arab/Muslim countries. Before 1989 the PAEAC had increased its membership to around six hundred, from the eighteen national parliaments of the member states of the Council of Europe, as well as from the European Parliament. Several institutional bodies have been created within the framework of the Dialogue. In 1995, the European Institute for Research on Mediterranean and Euro-Arab Co-operation (MEDEA) was established at Brussels to contribute to cooperation, stability, and development in the Mediterranean basin, as well as to improving Euro-Arab relations.[7] It aimed mainly to promote: 1) the exchange of information and ideas among politicians, academics, journalists, and concerned nongovernmental organizations (NGOs) from both sides; and 2) the communication of research findings to opinion and political decision makers, particularly members of European parliaments.[8] This focus on European rather than the Arab politicians proceeds from the difference between democracies and dictatorships; in the latter, policies are decided by the ruler, and parliaments are toothless if they exist at all. However, this imbalance also reveals a willingness among European parliamentarians to act as agents of Arab propaganda. In fact, MEDEA is another form of Arab lobby.

The MEDEA Institute has engaged in many information-oriented activities, such as the production of a weekly review of the Arab press and a monthly selection of the Turkish press (both in French), as well as a weekly news page in Arabic on European and Euro-Mediterranean developments. It organizes monthly conferences and smaller informal meetings that bring together diplomats, members of parliament, European officials, experts, and journalists for discussions on Euro-Mediterranean and Euro-Arab cooperation.

All these activities have led to the concept of a comprehensive Euro-Mediterranean Partnership, based on three pillars: Political and Security Partnership; Economical and Financial Partnership; and Social, Cultural and Human Partnership. Those objectives were defined at the first Euro-Mediterranean Conference, held in Barcelona on November 27–28, 1995.[9] This conference assembled the foreign affairs ministers of the fifteen member states of the European Union, along with those of Algeria, Cyprus, Egypt, Israel, Jordan, Lebanon, Malta, Morocco, Syria, Tunisia, Turkey, and the Palestinian Authority—two years after the Oslo Accords of 1993.

The delegates stressed their "will to give their future relations a new dimension, based on comprehensive cooperation and solidarity, in keeping with the privileged nature of the links forged by neighborhood and history." Israel was granted the privilege of participating in this august assembly. Yet, in spite of the numerous other sources of conflict in the Mediterranean—including Syria's colonization of Lebanon, the division of Cyprus, the Spain-Morocco dispute, the ongoing massacres of civilians in Algeria, the oppression of the Kurds in both Turkey and Iraq, the discrimination against non-Muslims and women enforced by *shari'a* rules in Arab countries, as well as anti-Israel and anti-Western Arab racism, and the funding of terror—the delegates singled out only one country for censure, Israel:

> The participants support the realization of a just, comprehensive and lasting peace settlement in the Middle East based on the relevant United Nations Security Council resolutions and principles mentioned in the letter of invitation to the [1991] Madrid Middle East Peace Conference, including the principle land for peace, **with all that this implies** [emphasis added].

The principle of land for peace and security is the foundation of the Islamic *jihad*-dhimmitude system. It figures in the Hamas charter as a basic regulator of Muslim relations with Jews and Christians. The Islamic empire was able to expand into Christian lands through *jihad* and the treaties of Islamic protection (*dhimma*) granted to the subdued non-Muslim populations. The subjugated people bought peace by surrendering their land to Islamic sovereignty and political control. But in today's international relations, which assume general recognition of basic, non-negotiable human rights, peace, and security for nations are not transactional rights that can be weighed according to a *jihadist* ideology of surrender by the infidels. Moreover, the formula "with all that this implies" is left purposefully unclear. In fact, it implies the "ghettoization" of Israel and its disintegration—according to the erroneous Franco-Arab interpretation of UN Security Council Resolution 242, which excludes territorial negotiations but imposes Israeli concessions.

The Barcelona delegates also expressed their convictions on important civilizational values: peace, human rights and democracy, the independence of the judiciary from politics, freedom of speech and religion, and equality in gender and human rights. They affirmed their intention to turn the Mediterranean basin into an area of dialogue, exchange, and cooperation that would guarantee peace, stability, and prosperity. Such goals required the "strengthening of democracy and respect for human rights, sustainable and balanced economic and social development, measures to combat poverty and promotion of greater understanding between cultures which are all essential aspects of partnership." In this view, the participants agreed to establish a comprehensive Euro-Mediterranean partnership based on three main pillars: a political dialogue strengthened on a regular basis; economic and financial cooperation; and a greater emphasis on the social, cultural, and human dimension.

The Barcelona Declaration overflows with good intentions. It projects an image of people sitting in a cozy salon, discussing abstract and fashionable ideas: the rule of law; democracy; an area of peace; stability, justice, and good faith between nations; dialogue of civilizations; democratic principles; gender equality; freedom of speech and religion. Yet none of these ideals is high on the list of Europe's Arab state partners, who are for the most part corrupt and ruthless dictators who suppress any opposition and allow cruel persecution of their own minorities. Some sponsor terrorism, either actively or by justifying it in calling their own terrorists mere "freedom fighters."

In no Arab country today is there effective democracy or the universal recognition of fundamental human rights. Nor is there gender equality, the equality of non-Muslims with Muslims, or full religious freedom. European statesmen, of course, know this perfectly well. However, the Barcelona Declaration gives the impression that the EU, with all this high-minded language, prefers to deal with an imaginary Arab world, invented to make possible this type of dialogue, rather than to face intractable Arab/Muslim realities.

Thus, the Declaration's statement that the participants agree to conduct a political dialogue based on observance of essential principles of international law, and undertake "to act in accordance with the United Nations Charter and the Universal Declaration of Human Rights (UDHR) as well as other obligations under international law" seems to emanate from a dream world. Although Muslim states have subscribed to the UDHR—with the notable exception of Saudi Arabia, one of the fifty-three member states of the UN Commission on Human Rights—they generally do not fully recognize its primacy. For them, the UDHR was effectively replaced by the 1990 Cairo Declaration of Human Rights in Islam, which was approved by the Nineteenth Islamic Conference of Foreign Ministers. Muslim states abide by the Cairo Declaration because it specifically conforms to the *shari'a*, and is considered "as a general guidance for member states in the field of human rights."[10]

For the same reason, international law made by humans (as opposed to the *shari'a*, which Muslims revere as the law of Allah) and based on secularism is only considered binding as long as it does not contradict the divine *shari'a* principles. In Europe, where Muslims are still a minority, they call for partial incorporation of *shari'a* into European civil law in matters concerning marriage, family, and education. In 1982, at Birmingham, England, the "Islamic Shari'a Council of the UK and Ireland" was created to apply Islamic law and issue *fatwas* and verdicts. Many other Shari'a Courts have since developed, creating a parallel unofficial Islamic legal system. The main area of legal and societal conflict concerns polygamy—practiced in some Muslim circles in Europe—forced marriage of girls, repudiation, female genital mutilation, guardianship of children in case of mixed marriages, and honor killings. If the EU cannot obtain from new Muslim immigrants the respect of its own laws, how will it bring Arab Muslim States to comply with two contradictory set of principles and rules? Yet at Barcelona, the participants agreed to

> respect human rights and fundamental freedoms and guarantee the effective legitimate exercise of such rights and freedoms, including freedom of expression, freedom of association for peaceful purposes and freedom of thought, conscience and religion, both individually and together with other members of the same group, without any discrimination on grounds of race, nationality, language, religion or sex.

But in Egypt, Christians are discriminated against on religious grounds and often even killed. Christian women are frequently abducted. Even though Egypt does not fully implement the *shari'a*, Egyptian Christians still suffer from the culture and the legacy of the *shari'a* rules of dhimmitude that were fully enforced in Egypt for more than a millennium.[11] In all Arab countries, women and non-Muslims suffer discrimination under laws taken directly from or derived from *shari'a* law. In Algeria, a party to the Barcelona Declaration, a barbaric internal terrorist war killed well over 150,000 people in the past decade since 1992.

The Declaration calls on participants for dialogue and exchanges of information on matters of human rights, fundamental freedoms, racism, and xenophobia. They are to ensure respect for diversity and pluralism in their societies, to promote tolerance and combat manifestations of intolerance, racism, and xenophobia. Although this last phrase is repeated several times one may wonder what effect these worthy intentions had on any of the dictatorial Arab regimes represented in Barcelona, or with the Palestinian Authority—where a culture of hate, xenophobia, and racism flourishes against Jews, Christians, and the West.

The participants agreed to strengthen their cooperation in preventing and combating terrorism in particular, by ratifying and applying the international instruments they have signed, and by taking any other appropriate measure. But as for terrorism, large numbers of Arabs consider that jihadist bombers and terrorists are martyrs (*shahid*) and "freedom fighters". In his well-documented book on modern *jihad*, Robert Spencer has amply provided the religious sources and motivations of jihadist terror.[12]

The psychology and religious fervor of "Islamikaze" jihadists have been studied with an innovative insight by Raphael Israeli as "manifestations of Islamic martyrology." He points out that both characterizations of *shahid* and *fida'i* for killers of infidels are Islamic religious notions.[13] The Islamikazes, writes Israeli, "fulfil a societal-family ideal, by preparing the grounds in Paradise for their entire family to follow."[14] They become mediators also on behalf of others (*shafa'a*), being invested by the *umma* with a holiness linked to the demonization and killing of the infidel. As long as the West covers up the *jihad* culture, the intrinsic dehumanization of the non-Muslim will confer upon the terrorist the aura of a *shahid*, whatever services are paid by European *dhimmis*. The need to confront *jihad* ideology is well discussed by Sookhdeo.[15] Challenged with such a fundamental and religiously inspired hatred, which Europe has persistently denied, the political correctness of the Barcelona Declaration on the campaign against "racism, xenophobia and intolerance" is a manifestation of a profound delusion, especially since the EU itself is motivating a racist campaign against Israel in Europe, coordinated with the Arab one.

The Barcelona Declaration also contains a section entitled "Partnership in Social, Cultural and Human Affairs: Developing Human Resources, Promoting Understanding between Cultures and Exchanges between Civil Societies." The subsection *Dialogue between cultures and civilizations* states:

- Given the importance of improving mutual understanding by promoting cultural exchanges and knowledge of languages, officials and experts will meet in order to make concrete proposals for action, inter alia, in the following fields: cultural and creative heritage, cultural and artistic events, co-productions (theatre and cinema), translations and other means of cultural dissemination, training.

- Greater understanding among the major religions present in the Euro-Mediterranean region will facilitate greater mutual tolerance and cooperation. Support will be given to periodic meetings of representatives of religions and religious institutions as well as theologians, academics and others concerned, with the aim of breaking down prejudice, ignorance and fanaticism and fostering cooperation at grass-roots level.

- Close interaction between the media will work in favour of better cultural understanding. The European Union will actively promote such interaction, in particular through the ongoing MED-Media programme. An annual meeting of representatives of the media will be organised in this context.

What did this elegant prose actually produce? A crescendo of Arab anti-Zionism and anti-American violence climaxed at the Durban Conference Against Racism—particularly at the prior NGO Conference.[16] The Conference ended two days before the *jihad* attack of September 11, 2001 when nearly three thousand American and foreign civilians going peacefully to work in New York were brutally exterminated. This was an act that filled many millions of Muslims throughout the world with pride and joy. Islamic terrorism had extended its secret cells in the West, the Palestinian war of terror waged against Israel increased, and thousands of civilian victims were killed by jihadists protected in Syria, Iraq, and Iran. Islamist preachers in the Arab countries that were party to the Barcelona Declaration encouraged, morally or actively, the *jihad* against the West.

In view of such harsh realities, the entire Euro-Arab Dialogue seems to be nothing more than an exercise in cynicism. It could even be said that the blindness to the facts manifested in such abundance amounts to a whitewash that encouraged criminality.

The MEDA program is an outcome of the Barcelona Declaration. It is the principal financial instrument of the European Union for the implementation of the Euro-Mediterranean Partnership. It accounted for €4.685 billion allocated for financial cooperation between the EU and its Mediterranean partners from 1995 to 1999. This sum, from European taxpayers, was increased for the period 2000–2006 to 5.35 billion euros (which currently amounts to about $6.5 billion). The European Union added to this an almost equivalent sum, lent by the European Investment Bank. Some

90 percent of MEDA resources are channeled to Algeria, Egypt, Jordan, Lebanon, Morocco, Syria, Tunisia, Turkey, and the Palestinian Authority. Israel is left out. The remaining 10 percent goes to regional activities.

The Euro-Mediterranean Parliamentary Forum is another of these numerous and costly organizations for dialogue or, more accurately, for Arab lobbying. It was set up in Brussels on October 27–28, 1998, and assembles the parliamentarians of the countries associated in the Barcelona process, the national parliaments of the member states of the European Union and the European Parliament.

The Gulf War of 1991 fired anti-Western hostility in the Arab countries. Thus, from the European standpoint a new initiative was needed to regain Arab hearts. The EU had to win back its lost prestige. This called for money and more pressure on Israel, especially since America was supervising the Oslo peace process. Hence, in the aftermath of the Gulf War the Europeans delivered an abundance of vehement anti-Israeli and pro-Palestinian declarations. The EU has become the largest donor of financial and technical assistance to the Palestinian Authority, providing over 50 percent of the international aid to the Palestinians. From 1994 to 1998, total EU aid to the PA amounted to 2 billion euros in grants and loans.

The EU was the largest single donor to the United Nations Relief and Works Agency for Palestine Refugees in the Near East (UNRWA), supporting 38 percent of its budget. Thus, Europe indirectly shares responsibility for the Palestinian culture of hatred and terrorism against the Israelis, which has grown correspondingly since 2000. Arafat broke off from the Oslo peace process in October 2000 with his *al-Aqsa* war. The EU's funding of the PA implied an indirect collusion with Palestinian terror against Israelis, which, beginning in October 2000, coincided with an extremely violent and coordinated anti-Israeli press campaign in the European Union, as well as criminal attacks against Jews, synagogues, their schools and centers. This was intended to intimidate the European Jewish communities, forcing them to side with the Palestinians and support the European policy of Israeli demonization. The persecutions, defamation, and racism against Jews and Israel replicate in the EU the discriminatory treatment in Arab countries of indigenous Christian minorities that are perceived, because of their religious affiliation, as close to the West. European governments— particularly the French—and the press turned a blind eye to this Euro-Arab Judeophobia until a vigorous denunciation from U.S. President George W. Bush and the American press in 2002 forced them to react. Suddenly the press incitement diminished noticeably and conferences on antisemitism were held in Vienna (June 2003), Brussels (February 2004), Berlin (April 2004) and at the UN in New York on 21 June 2004.

In its European Council Conclusions of March 20–21, 2003, the EU de-

clared that it would continue to make use of the "considerable opportunities offered by the Barcelona Declaration." This somewhat cryptic
statement became clearer during the following months, with the coordination on both Arab and EU sides of a scarcely veiled media campaign against
America—particularly the Bush Administration—and Israel.

10
An Anti-Zionist, Antisemitic Policy

The European Union's policy toward Israel consists of four major elements. The first two constitute the very foundation and structure of the Dialogue. One is Europe's need of the Arab bloc in order to establish itself as a strategic rival to America; the second is the Arab stranglehold on Europe created by oil and the economic ties of the EU with the Arab world. Already in 1983, Al-Mani perceptively noted that each crisis of oil supplies, such as in 1974 or during the Iranian crisis of 1979–80, immediately gave a new urgency to the EAD—accompanied by a hardening of European anti-Israeli policy. The same thing happened during the Gulf War of 1990–91 when France and the Vatican—as a service to the Arabs—insisted on establishing a linkage between Iraq's invasion of Kuwait and the Israel-Arab issue. The delusive Oslo agreement followed.

In 2003, during the American-British coalition-led war against Saddam Hussein, the EU intended to force Israel to submit to the decisions of the Arab League and the OIC. EU strategists criticized Israel's reaction to Arafat's terror war, alleging that such resistance fed terrorism; the words "occupation" and "apartheid" were continually repeated by the EU propaganda networks to mitigate Palestinian killings of Israeli civilians. Each crisis between the West and the Arab world triggers an anti-Israeli step from Europe, to placate the Arab party.

The third major element of EU policy toward Israel adds a moral imperative: it portrays this unbreakable bond between politics, oil, and economics as a just cause. As we saw in chapter 7, Mana Ben Saeed al-Otaiba, the minister of petroleum and mineral resources of the United Arab Emirates, asked Europe in 1979 to endorse the Palestinian cause from moral rather than economic motives. The Arab side has often demanded that Europe widen its relationship from the economic-political plane to the moral. Thus, already in the 1975 Euro-Arab meeting in Amsterdam, the Saudi minister of petroleum, al-Obaid, stated,[1]

> I am of the opinion that the morality of the Arab relationship needs to be faced up to by the Europeans as surely as the historical awakening and the

111

new power realities. There has been too much discussion of Europeans adapting to the Arab world just because of oil and surplus capital. Although those are unquestionably relevant, we expect your interests on firm and moral grounds as well, because a European-Arab relationship based only on the cynicism of power and materialism would not survive the real test of time. A precondition for a genuine and lasting relationship must be based on what is in our hearts and conscience.[2]

This request for a Euro-Arab moral symbiosis ends with the statement quoted in chapter 6: "Together and as equals, the Europeans and the Arabs can through a 'strategy of inter-dependence' forge ahead to remove the thorn from their sides—the Israeli problem—and attend to the Herculean task ahead of them."[3]

Mohammed Jabir Hassan, the Iraqi undersecretary of the oil ministry, also stressed the need to place the Palestinian war on a moral level.[4] The EU adopted this moral gloss expressed in the usual formulas—"the just Palestinian cause," "the legitimate rights of the Palestinians"—that ultimately imply the "injustice" of Israel's very existence.

This talk of morality also manifested a desire to place Israel and the Arabs of Palestine in a false ethical symmetry in relation to Europe. The *shoah* perpetrated by Europeans on Jewish victims became the equivalent of the *nakba* inflicted by Israelis on Arabs. Obviously, Jewish martyrdom in its own land under the dhimmitude system does not enter into this neat picture of moral equivalence. Nor did the numerous Arab attempts to destroy the State of Israel beginning in 1947, which provoked the wars leading to Jewish and Arab refugee exchanges. As we have seen, only the Arab refugees in those exchanges received care and assistance from the international community; there was no concern for the more numerous Jewish refugees who—though far from the war zone—were obliged to flee Arab countries from 1948 to 1974, either from persecution or insecurity.

It is important to examine the foundations of this Arab notion of morality as it concerns Israel, since European governments have now embraced it. At the 1974 Lahore conference, the secretary-general of the Islamic Conference, Mohammed Hasan Mohammed al-Tohami, describes the *jihad* conquest of Jerusalem in the seventh century in these terms: "[Jerusalem] was liberated by the Muslim armies and purged from the remnants of Romans [the Byzantines] and Zionists [*sic*]."[5]

He refers to the Christian and Jewish indigenous populations that were killed, enslaved, deported, or became *dhimmis* during the Arab invasion of Palestine. Al-Tohami also reaffirms the classical interpretation of *jihad* as a war to liberate a land from the oppression of governance by non-Muslims. He then mentions, in accordance with Islamic doctrine, various biblical figures as being Muslim prophets. This reflects the Islamic belief that Judaism and Christianity are later false emanations from the original Islamic faith, which preceded the other two monotheistic religions:

> Jerusalem has been Islamic since the Father of all Prophets, Ibrahim Al Khalil the friend [Abraham], has known Islam and pronounced it: as he said: "I am the first of all Muslims." He had called us Muslims, and he had inhabited Jerusalem after his journey through the land of Iraq and Syria.
>
> On this earth, there are no Muslims except the Islamic nation. God the Almighty does bequeath the land to whomsoever He wishes; and only those chosen by God shall inherit the earth; and God the Almighty has chosen that the Muslim nation should shoulder this trust. And God the Almighty does not alter the conditions of any people, unless they themselves change. May God protect us from deviation [from Islam], and from oblivion of this trust in the midst of current world events.[6]

In adopting Arab policies, the EU has lent its tacit endorsement to statements that would confer rightful world governance on Islam and challenge Israel's legitimacy in its own biblical homeland, which is considered by Muslims as rightfully theirs—a part of the *dar al-Islam*. This doctrine provides the ethical basis to the Arab-Palestinian war against Israel. The EU's moral commitment to the Palestinian *jihad* has thus compromised the very foundations of freedom and Western culture—for the forces of *jihad* also target Europeans as infidels and obstacles to the propagation of the faith of Allah in European lands, and beyond.

The fourth element of EU policy toward Israel is another Arab demand to which the EU has submitted: the internationalization of what was essentially a regional conflict. The Israeli/Palestinian dispute could have been settled decades ago by an adjustment of frontiers and the integration of Arab and Jewish refugees by each side in an exchange of populations—in the same way that many other conflicts were resolved throughout the twentieth century. But the Arab-Israeli conflict has been kept alive by the imposition of unacceptable conditions on Israel and European support for the most radical Arab leaders. The conflict is used as a tool against America to strengthen EU influence and interests in the Islamic world, while working for the disintegration of Israel. In all its declarations, the EU has boasted that it seeks peace, but its conditions to attain that "peace" involve only capitulation or endless strife, as dictated by the harsh "justice" of Islamic *jihad*, which applies to Europe too.

European politicians did not fall into line instantaneously. In his book on the EAD, Al-Mani frequently alludes to political reservations to the Arab agenda expressed within the EC, and in particular to the repugnance that some states felt in submitting to Arab demands concerning Israel. Certain governments—such as France and Belgium—willingly adopted an anti-Israeli policy for commercial and other reasons. Traditional antisemitism was repackaged as a universal moral duty to defend the Palestinian cause. However, other governments were constrained by specific Arab threats and pressures on their economy.

Nevertheless, those hesitations generally vanished as the EU solidified its unified foreign policy and deepened its symbiosis with the Arab–Muslim world through Muslim immigration and population growth in Europe, as well as through cultural synergy and institutional networks. Saleh A. al-Mani noted in 1983, "In examining the structure and processes of European associative diplomacy, we have found that the least publicized activities of this form of diplomacy have been the most successful."[7]

Whereas the EU offered and continues to offer Israel nothing but vague assurances of a "just and lasting peace" and "secure and recognized frontiers"—promises that can only be meaningless when viewed within the context of a *jihad* ideology—it demands concrete actions from Israel: (1) cession of territories; (2) redivision of Jerusalem; (3) the creation of a second Muslim state within the former mandated Palestine; (4) negotiations with Arafat,[8] regardless of the fact that he had been recognized internationally as a terrorist leader up to the time of the Oslo accords (1993), and reverted to terrorism in October 2000; (5) peace conditional upon a global settlement with the Palestinians and the neighboring Arab states, including Syria; (6) Israel's admission of its alleged responsibility for the problem of the Arab refugees by acknowledgment of a "right of return"—whereas their flight was provoked by the Palestinian leadership's military alliance with the invading armies of five Arab states, and their defeats.

The Declaration issued by the Eleventh Arab Summit Conference, held at Amman, Jordan from November 25 to 27, 1980 (see appendix 3), underscores the similarity of the EU and Arab positions.

> The Conference reasserted the right of the Palestinian Arab people, as represented by the Palestine Liberation Organization, its sole legitimate representative, to return to its land, to determine its own destiny and to establish an independent Palestinian State on the soil of its homeland, while pointing out that it was the Palestine Liberation Organization which alone has the right to take upon itself the responsibility for the future of the Palestinian people.

The EC repeated Arab rhetoric concerning the creation of a second Palestinian state, ignoring the fact that Jordan was created in 1922 by Britain from the Palestinian Mandated area with an Arab population.[9] The Europeans complied with the Arab League demand to recognize Arafat as the sole representative of the Palestinians, thus, as has been shown, conferring respectability and legitimacy on this sponsor of international terrorism, the unrelenting enemy of the State of Israel and of Lebanese Christians, and the symbol of the Arab *jihad* against the infidels.

Pretending that the 1949 armistice lines guarantee "security," the EC/ EU required that Israel withdraw to those lines, called "international boundaries" although never recognized as such.[10] Its refusal to acknowledge Israel's right to any part of its ancient capital, Jerusalem, implied a delegitimization and denial of the history of the Jewish people—a history to which Europe, by virtue of its Christian origins, is still a witness par excellence. Two sources motivated Europe's denial of Israeli sovereignty over the Old City of Jerusalem: theological Judeophobia and subservience to Islamic threats—as stated in the Resolution of the Special Session of the Islamic Conference of Foreign Ministers on the Question of Jerusalem (Fez, Morocco, September 18–20, 1980, see appendix 2). In article 2, the Muslim states affirm their commitment to apply a political and economic boycott to any state that recognizes Jerusalem as Israel's capital and establish its embassy there. A threat still valid today.

The EU has adopted the Arab perspective that locates all evil in Israel, eclipsing all other conflicts and tragedies of the world. Euro-Arab international policy thus explains, justifies, and morally legitimizes an Arab strategy that seeks the destruction of Israel as an absolute and universal priority. By implicitly enlisting in the Arab-Islamic *jihad* against Israel—under labels such as "peace and justice for the Palestinians"—Europe has effectively jettisoned its values and undermined the roots of its own civilization. It even struck a blow against worldwide Christianity, abandoning the Christians in Lebanon to massacres by Palestinians (1975–83), those of Sudan to *jihad* and slavery, and the Christians of the Islamic world to the persecutions mandated by the *dhimma* system.

On April 15, 2004, President Bush endorsed Israel's plan for unilateral withdrawal from Gaza and parts of the West Bank, in exchange for U.S. concessions regarding Israeli settlements on other land there claimed by the Palestinians. Bush also embraced Israel's rejection of any "right of return," other than those within the boundaries of a newly defined Palestinian state. Europe indignantly rejected Bush's position because it would exclude a massive Palestinian migration to Israel. Its declaration had the merit, at least, of clarifying Europe's definition of "peace" for Israel. These positions reemphasized the growing chasm between America and the EU, the latter being the mouthpiece of the PLO, as well as the Palestinian Authority. British Prime Minister Tony Blair, who endorsed Bush's position, received a letter signed by fifty-two British former ambassadors, high commissioners, and governors asking him to pressure Washington to align itself with Arab policy—in subservient EAD style. The signatories called the pressure on Bush "a matter of the highest urgency."[11] These diplomats pretended that the Israeli-Arab conflict "more than any other, has for decades poisoned relations between the West and the Islamic and Arab worlds."[12]

Plainly put, the West is expected to deliver Israel to the Arabs, and any European resistance, however weak it may be, enrages the Arab sympathizers.

According to Lord Robin Renwick, former British ambassador in Washington, "many of the signatories were former Arabists in the Foreign Office, affectionately known as the Camel Corps. Some members of the Corps have shown a tendency over the years to develop a quite passionate attachment to the Arab world that, unfortunately, has not always been reciprocated by the Arabs. They have tended to concentrate on the crimes of the Israelis, rather than those of the Palestinians. Most of us would prefer to be more even-handed."[13] *The Telegraph* (London) soon after uncovered evidence that several key signatories of the letter to Prime Minister Tony Blair are paid by pro-Arab organizations—including Oliver Miles, the former British ambassador to Libya, who instigated and drafted the letter. Some hold positions in companies seeking lucrative Middle East contracts, while others have unpaid positions with pro-Arab groups. This discovery prompted allegations that these former diplomats were promoting the interests of their clients.

This letter was followed by a similar protest sent on May 4, 2004 by a group of sixty former American ambassadors and diplomats condemning U.S. policy in the Middle East. Like the British diplomats, the former U.S. foreign service officers were "deeply concerned" by Bush's opposition to a Palestinian "return" to Israel. They accused him to "have placed U.S. diplomats, civilians and military doing their jobs overseas in an untenable and even dangerous position."[14] This sentence says a lot about the security of Western diplomats if they fail to abide by Islamic rules, and explains the West's total lack of awareness of the jihadist war that targets its whole population. European and American Middle East policy was based on the biased reports and analysis of those diplomats, fearful of their own security. One of the signatories was James Akin, former U.S. ambassador to Saudi Arabia, the greatest purveyor of international terrorism and of anti-American hatred, a situation that was carefully hidden before 9/11.

1998: European Actions Against Israel

On April 28, 1998, in London, a delegation of the Parliamentary Association for Euro-Arab Cooperation (PAEAC) met the representative of the British presidency of the EU, Derek Fatchett, minister of state for commonwealth and foreign affairs. In its internet files, PAEAC stated that it was customary for a delegation to contact each new European presidency in order to present Arab demands to them. This delegation consisted of the two co-chairmen of the Association, Henning Gjellerod, a Danish MP, and Editha Limbach, a German MP. Also attending were the MPs Roselyne Bachelot of France and John Austin of the United Kingdom, along with Jean-Michel Dumont, the secretary-general. The delegation's members had succeeded in blocking the ratification of a Euro-Israel accord, the EU-Israel Mediterranean Association Agreement—in the French and Belgian parliaments. Now they sought its suspension by the EU.[15] The Parliamentary Association demanded that the Council of Europe and the Commission apply pressure on Israel. It wrote a letter to the fifteen Offices for Foreign Affairs of the member states of the EU, pointing out that Israel did not respect the principles of the Barcelona Declaration.[16]

The annual Conference of the Euro-Arab Parliamentary Dialogue convened in Damascus on July 11, 1998, under the auspices of Hafiz al-Asad, then president of Syria.[17] It was organized jointly by the Arab Inter-Parliamentary Union and the PAEAC. Parliamentarians from sixteen Arab parliaments and fourteen European national parliaments, as well as the European Parliament, participated in the deliberations. Representatives from the League of Arab States and the European Commission, as well as observers from the Senate of Canada and the International Committee of the Red Cross (ICRC) also attended. The conference's Final Communiqué expressed the participants' deep thanks to the Syrian president, the Parliament, the Syrian people for their efforts which contributed to the success of their Dialogue, and to the European Commission for its financial contribution. This amazing statement is addressed to a terrorist dictatorship that was occupying another country. It gives the measure of the high moral standard the EU and the European Commission pretend to represent.

On the Middle East Process, "the participants in the Conference stressed the close connection between the achievement of peace in the Middle East and security and stability in Europe." In fact, the official Reports of the Dialogue constantly reiterated this point. However, this link would only be relevant if Arab terrorists threatened to retaliate against European interests, or in Europe itself, should European officials ignore the Arab requests concerning Israel that are transmitted through the PAEAC. This significant sentence revealed that Europe might have felt constrained to consider Israel, like America, as a threat to Europe because, if they resisted the *jihad* strategy, it would trigger Islamist retaliation against Europe.

The participants of the Damascus Conference reaffirmed their previous resolutions on Israel's return to the vulnerable 1949 armistice lines, including a total withdrawal from East Jerusalem, which was intended as the future capital of the new Palestinian state. They praised the European Commission's economic pressures on Israel, as well as the European policy that has consistently supported upgrading the Palestinian status at the UN. A few statements are worth quoting more fully:

> The participants also welcomed the stand taken by the Foreign Affairs Committees in the Belgian Parliament and the French National Assembly not to

ratify the Euro-Israeli Partnership Agreement whilst Israel continues to block
the peace process.

The participants considered that saving the peace process is a common
international responsibility which requires the collective action of all those
interested in establishing peace and stability in the Middle East. In the light
of the current conditions, the revitalization of the peace process requires a
firm international stand that compels Israel to abide by the [1991] Madrid
terms of reference which include the principle of land for peace and the
implementation of UN Security Council Resolutions 242, 338 and 425, and
to resume the negotiations on the Syrian track from the point they reached
with the previous Israeli government. . . .

The participants called upon Arab and European governments concerned
to suspend Israel's participation in the Euro-Mediterranean partnership
until the Israeli government fulfills its commitments within the framework
of the Barcelona Declaration of November 1995. . . .

They deeply regretted the lack of consistency of the United States as sponsor of the peace process in its dealing with the Israeli government. . . .

They also welcomed the important role played by the EU Special Envoy,
Ambassador Moratinos, and his proposals for the EU to assume an enhanced
role and responsibility in overcoming the current deadlock in the peace
process.

Over one third of the Declaration is devoted to the "Middle East Peace
Process." Most of this is directed systematically against Israel, the only non-
participant from the region. Other themes received only a summary treatment. The participants expressed their "deep concern" over the suffering
of the Libyan people because of the UN Security Council sanctions imposed on Libya as a consequence of its involvement in the 1988 explosion
of Pan Am flight 103 that killed 270 people over Lockerbie, Scotland, and
the French UTA flight 772 over Niger, Africa, in 1989. They stressed the
need for a dialogue with the Libyan government. They also demanded the
removal of the embargo on Iraq, as soon as its government finalized implementation of UN Security Resolutions. They requested European assistance
to Iraq, the renewal of cultural ties (which France had already initiated),
and a European diplomatic presence. They also made recommendations
for EU cooperation with both Sudan and Algeria. The participants called
for a Euro-Arab development partnership and the improvement of Euro-
Arab financing mechanisms.[18]

In another theme under the subtitle "On terrorism," the participants
reiterated their condemnation of all kinds of terrorism and of all countries
"which give sanctuary to terrorists and finance them." A cynical comment
made in Syria, haven for terrorists. They also called for the convening "of
an international conference for the definition of terrorism," a statement
that elucidates the condemnation. Muslim leaders, in general, do not recognize jihadists and suicide-bombers as terrorists, but only as "freedom

fighters." On October 6, 2001, Sheikh Wajdi Hamzeh al-Ghazawi, speaking in one of the main mosques of Mecca, gave the Islamic definition of terror:

> The [kind of] terror [in Arabic, "striking of fear"] that is permissible according to Islamic law is terrifying the cowards, the hypocrites, the secularists, and the rebels, by imposing punishments [according to the religious] law of Allah. . . . The meaning of the term "terror" that is used by the media . . . is the jihad for the sake of Allah. Jihad is the peak of Islam. Moreover, there are religious scholars who view it as the sixth pillar of Islam. . . . Jihad— whether speaking about the defensive jihad for Muslim lands and Islam like in Chechnya, the Philippines, and Afghanistan, or whether speaking about jihad whose purpose is the spread of religion—is the pinnacle of terror as far as the enemies of Allah are concerned.[19]

Syrian Foreign Minister Farouk al-Sharaa met the Conference delegation and expressed the Syrian foreign ministry's interest in the Euro-Arab parliamentary deliberations. He spoke of Syria's continuous support for a European role in the peace process and the deeply rooted Arab-European Dialogue relationship. He referred to "the moral values the Arabs have in dealing with others in accordance to justice and tolerance, on the ground of which the 'sublime message of Islam has been transferred to the whole world.' "[20]

As had become usual at these conferences, the beginning of the Euro-Arab Dialogue was recalled. Al-Sharaa emphasized that it took official shape after the war of Syria and Egypt against Israel in October 1973 and the sharp increase in oil prices. "The Dialogue would not have been launched unless certain European countries adopted objective stances. France was in the foremost [among] the countries that denounced Israel's aggression of 1967 and suspended all military aid to it."[21]

This friendly gathering of Europe's political and moral leaders in Syria, including the ICRC, lent an air of respectability to a country whose army had occupied, terrorized, and colonized Lebanon for over twenty years. Moreover, the Syrian regime was known to harbor and protect terrorist organizations like Hezbollah, Islamic Jihad, and other PLO terror groups, which for years have planned their attacks against Israel and which raises funds and recruits terrorists from Syria. Those facts were clearly restated by American Secretary of State Colin Powell on May 3, 2003, when he denounced Syria as a state sponsoring terrorism. Conversely, the EU— especially France—has continued to downplay Arab-Islamic terror, not only that of Arafat against Israel but also in refusing to consider Hamas as a terrorist movement in spite of its Charter's statements declaring its dedication to the destruction of Israel and to terrorist acts. Only in September 2003, at an EU meeting, were those facts reluctantly acknowledged. Yet France still maintained an ambiguous position.

After the Damascus conference, PAEAC met the Austrian EU presidency on October 1, 1998, as well as the Belgian presidency and all the following EU presidencies, in order to remind them of "the current freezing of the ratification of the EU-Israel cooperation agreement." The PAEAC insisted on the need for a "carrot and stick approach."

At the 100th Inter-Parliamentary Union (IPU) Conference, which was held in Moscow in September 1998, the PAEAC co-chairman, Henning Gjellerod, raised a number of issues concerning the peace process in the Middle East; Palestinian membership in the IPU; terrorism; the embargoes imposed on various Arab countries; the civil war in Sudan; and the need for Europe to distance itself from America. The Middle East conflict provoked the customary accusations against Israel:

> Concerning the Middle East conflict, a conflict rooted in the control of water [sic], we all witness that the current Israeli government practises ethnic cleansing in East-Jerusalem, is limiting the role of the Palestinian Authority to the management of bantoustans and multiplies provocations with the obvious aim of blaming the Palestinian Authority for breaking up the peace process. We think that the international community should do more than merely issuing declarations condemning these policies.

The speaker proposed the recognition of a Palestinian state, stressing the Arab position endorsed by the EU, that peace must "be global or not at all." On the Sudan, where a *jihad* war had taken over two million lives since 1983, he strongly warned that European countries should totally distance themselves from an American policy in Sudan that "widens the enlarging rift between the Muslim world and the West." A staunch advocate of the Arabs, he attributed the cause of terrorism to Israel. The Jewish state, he charged, was the real source of the deep frustration of the Arab and Muslim populations, who were complaining of "double standards" that allegedly favor Israel.[22]

A month later, the Euro-Mediterranean Parliamentary Forum held its first meeting in Brussels.[23] Its noteworthy Final Declaration stated that it was dedicated to implementing the Barcelona Declaration, and that the participants were committed to ever-closer partnership between the European Union and the Arab Mediterranean partner countries "based on the principles of solidarity, respect for national sovereignty, justice, dialogue, a global approach, shared prosperity and good faith." The participants declared their awareness "that positive progress in the Middle East peace process is of vital importance to the durability and consolidation of the Euro-Mediterranean partnership process." The actual meaning of this sentence, which is constantly reiterated, stresses the organic link between the Euro-Mediterranean Partnership and European pressure on Israel. This pressure aimed at satisfying the Arabs, with whom the EU is ever more closely associated through the preservation and consolidation of the Partnership. The coded language of Eurabian technocrats avoids the terms "Arab" and "Muslim" in the formulas "Euro-Mediterranean Partnership," and "Mediterranean partner countries," there they are usually replaced by the "South" or the "Neighbourhood." The Final Declaration expressed the participants' conviction:

- that parliaments are the genuine expression of democracy and of the will of the peoples they represent, and that their cooperation is essential for the consolidation of the democratic principles enshrined in the Barcelona Declaration,

- determined to lay the lasting foundations of a Euro-Mediterranean parliamentary dialogue which will contribute to consolidating, developing and preserving the Euro-Mediterranean Partnership, and to enhancing awareness of its importance in the societies of the European Union and the Mediterranean partner countries.

Article 7, the longest section of this Declaration, dealt with the 1993 Oslo Declaration and the Israeli-Palestinian peace negotiations. The Forum supported the agreements signed between Israel and the PLO, in accordance with the Oslo Declaration of Principles, and called upon the parties to resume negotiations on the Lebanon-Israeli and Syrian-Israeli tracks, in order to achieve a comprehensive peace in the region. It stated that the "problems and injustices now impeding the Middle East peace process represent a hindrance to the Barcelona process" and that the partner states, especially those of the EU, must make every possible effort to achieve a settlement on the basis of the "land for peace" jihadist principle, the Oslo Agreements and UN Security Council Resolutions 242, 338, and 425.

Again, the Declaration centered on Israel alone. It had nothing to say about the occupation of Kurdistan by Turkey, Syria, and Iraq, or these states' current repression of the Kurds. It was likewise silent about the Turkish occupation of Cyprus, the Syrian colonization of Lebanon, and the severe discrimination against Christians in Egypt. Instead, it recommended the participation of Libya in all aspects of the Barcelona process. It even called for the full membership of Mauritania, where slavery remains prevalent. The linkage between Israeli-Arab peace and Israel membership in the Euro-Mediterranean Partnership was a reminder of Europe's EAD obligation to impose upon Israel the Arab conditions for their alliance. No other conflict is considered a hindrance to peace. Only the Israeli-Arab conflict is regularly highlighted in the Dialogue's documents and texts. In fact, the Forum more or less repeated the preceding Communiqué given in Syria three months earlier.

As a result, Israel was accused of violating the Barcelona Declaration. It was to be punished and pressured by an international campaign of vilification, while the French and Belgian parliaments suspended the ratification of the Agreement with Israel. The Barcelona Declaration did not exclusively focus on the Oslo process, which Arafat was to break two years later by resorting to terrorism. Most of its tenets promoted democracy, the rule of law, respect between religions, freedom of conscience and expression, human rights, and the eradication of discrimination based on race, nationality, language, religion, or gender. It also contended with intolerance and xenophobia.

Which Muslim/Arab countries, signatories of the Declaration (and the same applies to the UN's International Covenants), were themselves meeting these obligations? Even the EU, that great moral preacher, was failing to meet them, since—by the very nature of the pressure it put upon Israel, and only on Israel—it was violating the articles of the Declaration that call upon states

> to refrain, in accordance with the rules of international law, from any direct or indirect intervention in the internal affairs of another partner; respect the territorial integrity and unity of each partner; settle their disputes by peaceful means, call upon all participants to renounce recourse to the threat or use of force against the territorial integrity of another participant.

EU hostility to Israel was coupled with an upsurge of violence directed at Jews within the EU itself. Jewish communities were forced to take exceptional security measures in response. Xenophobia against Israel and criminal aggression against Jews made a mockery of those very freedoms of which the EU boasted.

At the 101st Inter-Parliamentary Union (IPU) Conference, which was held in Brussels in April 1999, Henning Gjellerod, still the co-chairman of PAEAC, was happy to inform the delegates that their colleagues in France and Belgium "have maintained their refusal to even consider the ratification of the new Association Agreement between the European Union and Israel signed in November 1995." The strong condemnation of Israel's policy at the previous month's summit in Berlin of the European Council of Ministers reportedly made the delegates rejoice.[24]

The proceedings of the numerous Euro-Arab meetings, which involved the highest levels of leadership, would convince most informed observers that the EU and Arab League policies in relation to Israel are now—and have been for some time—one and the same. They employ the same logic and reasoning and are essentially interchangeable. The EU, which likes to think of itself as an honest broker in the peace process, has become—in this respect, at least—an appendix to the Arab/Muslim world in such matters. The Euro-Arab duo has chosen to play cat and mouse with Israel, while heaping on it denigration and vilification. Although the EU solemnly affirms Israel's "right to live in security," it would deny Israel that very right to self-defense that differentiates freedom from dhimmitude. Through the "Dialogue," Arab League politicians and economists have gained a firm ascendancy over Europe's policy and economy. There is no similar example of a foreign lobby infiltrating the parliamentary system of other countries as has the PAEAC, the Parliamentary Association for Euro-Arab Cooperation, which has managed to impose Arab League policy toward Israel and America upon Europe, with European leaders' full approval. This overwhelming Arab ascendancy, unparalleled anywhere in the world, is nevertheless brushed aside by Arab leaders—who never cease complaining about alleged EU sympathies for Israel.

Nowhere is Euro-Arab foreign policy fusion more seamless than in the EU's total acceptance of "Palestine." To this cause, the EU devotes all the passionate fervor of a senile lover who sacrifices to his lust the ultimate shadow of an illusory dignity. The PLO/PA is totally dependant on EU money, which it has received in enough abundance to facilitate its status as a powerful global organization of murder, crime, and hatred directed against Israel and Jews.

In November 2000, Members of the European Parliament (MEP), including François Zimeray (France) and Olivier Dupuis (Belgium), vigorously protested EU funding of Palestinian hate literature against Israel. EU Commissioner Chris Patten (UK) rejected the MEPs' request to open an inquiry into this matter. Instead, the European Commission decided to allocate 8 million to the PA, in addition to the monthly 10 million it was already giving. Finally, on February 2, 2003, 170 MEPs demanding accountability signed a petition to open a parliamentary investigation regarding the hundreds of millions of euros provided to the Palestinian Authority. Substantiated allegations were made that EU funds had been used by Arafat to finance Palestinian terrorist activities. Yet on February 14, 2003, the European Parliament rejected this petition, which Patten had strongly opposed.

In December 2003, German Green activist Ilka Schröder declared in a New York lecture: "It is an open secret within the European Parliament and the European Commission that EU aid to the Palestinian Authority has not been spent correctly."[25] She accused the European Parliament of having no intention "to verify whether European taxpayers' money could have been used to finance anti-Semitic murderous attacks. Unfortunately, this fits well with European policy in this area." According to Schröder, "The primary goal of the EU is the internationalization of the conflict in order to underline the need for its own mediating role." On this, Arab and European policies converge. Schröder acknowledged that Germany was no friend to Israel, but "of course, France and Belgium are much worse when it comes to Israel."

In one short sentence, she condensed the essence of the current European political culture: "The terror against Israel must also be seen in the context that Europeans don't want to see the Jews and Israelis as victims." The EC and then the EU's occult alliance with Israel's enemies, along with the weight of the past, explains this attitude.

EU diplomats, particularly from France, blocked American and Israeli efforts to leave Arafat out of peace negotiations because of his proven involvement in terrorism. There were nonetheless exceptions. Silvio Berlusconi, the Italian prime minister, provoked other European leaders' rage by meeting with Israeli Prime Minister Ariel Sharon and not with Arafat during his July 2003 trip to the Middle East. But France, Britain, and other EU member states refused to limit their contacts with Arafat. Since the 1973 EU declaration at Copenhagen, Arafat has been the arm of EU policy against Israel, and its surest means of rapprochement with the Arab/Muslim world. This is the same kind of thinking that considers Israeli and American self-defense and antiterrorist measures as the sources of terrorism, deflecting attention and responsibility away from the Palestinian Arab *jihad* war.

According to a poll conducted in 2003 for the European Commission in the fifteen EU countries, Europeans consider Israel the greatest threat to world peace—greater than Islamic terrorism or North Korea.[26] Such is the result of thirty years of vilifying Israel. This is not far from Hitler's reiterated claim that the Jews were responsible for World War II while he himself fomented it. European antisemitic abuse is a calculated response to America's war against Islamic terrorism, a spiteful attack on Israel, and a groveling service to the Muslim states, which are only too ready to resuscitate the myth of "The Jewish Peril" and the *Protocols of the Elders of Zion* that led to the *shoah*. Israeli Diaspora Affairs Minister Nathan Sharansky declared that the survey was proof that antisemitism lay behind political criticism of Israel. "The European Union, which shows sensitivity on human rights issues, would do well to stop the rampant brainwashing against and demonizing of Israel before Europe deteriorates once again to dark sections of its past," he told the *Yediot Aharonot* newspaper.[27]

Rabbi Marvin Hier, founder and dean of The Simon Wiesenthal Center, voiced his outrage directly to European Commission President Romano Prodi: "This poll is an indication that Europeans have bought into the vilification and demonization campaign directed against the State of Israel and her supporters by European leaders and media. . . . [I]t defies logic and is a racist flight of fancy that only shows that antisemitism is deeply embedded within European society, more now than in any other period since the end of World War II."

Margaret Brearley, advisor to the archbishop of Canterbury on the Holo-caust, declared in her address on the demonization of Israel in the British press: "Ample evidence exists that anti-Zionism in the British media—as in intellectual life generally—has intensified in the past two years."[28]

Like anti-Americanism, the anti-Israeli/antisemitic culture that has spread throughout Europe is integrated into the Euro-Arab partnership network and the ongoing workings of the EAD. The EEC's anti-Israeli directives, as well as its biased French interpretation of the 1967 UN Security Resolution 242, was a by-product of Arab demands. The EEC constructed its whole Arab policy in tandem with the Arab demonization and delegitimization of Israel, precisely because the Arab League had demanded an anti-Israeli policy and the promotion of the PLO as a condition for Euro-Arab eco-nomic exchanges and oil supply. The obsessive Arab desire for Israel's destruction earned the Jewish state an excessive importance on the world stage despite its tiny size—less than a fifth of the original Mandate's Palestine.

Islamic Judeophobia became an instrument of world geopolitics, like France's anti-Americanism. Israeli resistance to this exterminatory drive was defined as a "world threat to peace." The rage Israel provoked led to the rancorous scrutiny and denunciation of virtually every security measure by teams of observers, sent by the EU to protect Arafat and other Palestin-ian terrorists. Billions of euros were paid without any form of accountability to his central organization of terror, the PA, "to make the Palestinian terri-tories a better, safer neighbor for Israel," as Christopher Patten ex-plained.[29]

The sharp upturn in Judeophobia since 2000 resulted from the develop-ment of the Euro-Arab Partnership in social, cultural, and human affairs. This policy led to cooperation in political, cultural, and audio-visual pro-grams between the EU and its Arab and PA partners, as well as with NGOs as announced by Patten at the European Parliament on January 31, 2001, after Arafat's rejection of the Oslo agreements. Patten stressed that Eu-rope's "Southern flank"—in clear terms: the Arab world—"should enjoy a special place in our external relations." He underlined that the consider-able significance of the Middle East Peace Process for EU policy in the Mediterranean called for Europe to play a more active role in the Middle East—in other words to increase EU support for the PA. Patten concluded:

I am glad to note the agreement all round on the need to raise the visibility of the partnership. I warmly welcome the Parliament's activities in this re-spect through international contacts at all levels. And we shall be supple-menting our existing activities through the introduction of <u>dedicated programmes</u> using all the modern techniques at our disposal to ensure that the value of what we are doing is appreciated as widely as possible, both in the EU and among the Mediterranean partners. (Bold and underline in the original)[30]

This raised visibility of the Euro-Arab partnership "through international contacts at all levels," seems to indicate that the strategic center of antisemitism and anti-Israel propaganda is the European Union body itself. This can also be said about international anti-Americanism. The Partnership has supported and morally sustained Palestinian terror against Israel. It has done so in tandem with a European anti-American and anti-Zionist campaign intended to justify this terror and to intimidate, terrorize and silence the Jewish diaspora (see chapter 11). On the church level, Michael Sabbah, the Palestinian Latin Patriarch of Jerusalem, was elected president of the transnational and powerful Pax Christi International in 2000—just before Arafat, his mentor, triggered a war against Israel. Because of the strong networks binding the EU with Arab universities and with the publishing, film, news media, social, economic, and particularly the political spheres, the new European Judeophobia was the product of a compact yet comprehensive system permeating all social and political strata.

The MEDEA Institute—the European Institute for Research on Mediterranean and Euro-Arab Cooperation, which enjoys the support of the European Commission—allowed for strong links and concerted actions between Europeans and Arabs among politicians, academics, opinion makers, and NGOs. Its publications are designed to influence European parliamentarians—in order to foster, as Chris Patten put it, "cooperation at grass-root levels."

On April 2, 2003, Patten met a group of journalists from three Arab Middle Eastern countries that were participating in the latest fact-finding visit of the MEDA-funded Euromed Visitors' Programme in Brussels from March 29 to April 5, 2003.[31] The group included print media, news agencies, and TV journalists from Lebanon, Jordan, and Syria. This program aims at making journalists and NGO representatives from Mediterranean Partners more familiar with EU institutions, policies, and programs—with a particular focus on the Barcelona Process, the Middle East Peace Process and the MEDA Programme. It facilitates coordination of European and Arab media opinions, as well as NGOs concerning Israel, America, and the opposition to the war in Iraq.

Meanwhile, in Europe, some Israeli tourists were refused rooms in hotels. Jews were attacked in streets and shops. Synagogues were torched. Two persons in Paris were even victims of Muslim ritual murders, their throats slit—a jihadist ritual practice. Community buildings, cemeteries, and schools were targeted. All the while, the media daily disgorged Palestinian propaganda. Historian Robert Wistrich calls it: "the unending ideological and media war against the Jewish state."[32]

In France's school playgrounds, Jewish children were insulted as "dirty Jews" and frequently attacked. Like in Arab countries, they had to keep a low profile, while Muslims assumed a domineering attitude. If they were recognized as Jews in the streets and public transportation, they risked being lynched. In some schools, it became impossible to educate pupils about the Holocaust. Male doctors were attacked in some hospitals for treating Muslim women. In France, the basic rights of Jewish children to education, and of Jews in general to dignity and security, were scorned and violated on a daily basis.[33]

Books favorable to Israel, or critical of Arabs and Palestinians, have become increasingly difficult to publish in the EU. They are also often refused by bookstores, due to the strong Euro-Arab Dialogue associative network of booksellers and librarians. Pressure is brought by some European universities on the European Union to stop the renewal of cooperation agreements with Israeli universities—another result of Euro-Arab academic collusion and the Palestinization of European universities.

This situation is linked to Patten's "raised visibility of the partnership." It has unleashed such a tremendous display of intense anti-Jewish aggression all over the EU and at the international level that, by its world expansion, its systematization and organization, it can only be defined as a war—an extension of *jihad*. Yet no EU government worried too much about this rise of antisemitism until it was highlighted by the American press. Then the EU ordered a report—which was immediately shelved, precisely because it implicated Arab Muslim and pro-Palestinian Leftist and extreme-right groups in the antisemitic wave.[34] According to the New York weekly Jewish *Forward*, in late July 2003, four American politicians (Rep. Robert Wexler, a Florida Democrat, Republican Ileana Ros-Lehtinen of Florida, and Democrats Tom Lantos of California and Gary Ackerman of New York) wrote to EU foreign policy chief Javier Solana, as well as to Romano Prodi and to Prime Minister Silvio Berlusconi of Italy, whose country then held the rotating presidency of the EU, asking for the release of the draft report.[35] Solana replied that the work would not be made public because "it did not meet the criteria of consistency and quality of data." Prodi endorsed Solana's conclusions in a separate letter dated August 12, 2003, arguing that the problem of antisemitism also applied to the United States, instead of acknowledging the situation in Europe. In an exchange of letters with Wexler, Prodi stressed the "importance of distinguishing between legitimate political expressions and criticisms of the policies of the government of Israel on the one hand, and antisemitism on the other. The European Union will not tolerate antisemitism, nor will it tolerate any insinuation that its policy towards the Middle East is driven by antisemitism."[36] It seems as if the torching of synagogues, the physical attacks and beating of schoolchildren by Arabs are, for Prodi, legitimate political criticism of Israel's policy. Did he ask himself what would be legitimate political criticism of oppressive Arab regimes, Palestinian terror, and Islamic *jihad* all over the world?

Moreover, it looks as if the EU has adopted the totalitarian mentality of its best friends and allies by affirming this intolerance to criticism. The prevailing dictatorial political culture of the Arab states plagues the EU at its highest levels. However, despite Eurabian Eurocrats, the existence of antisemitism was eventually acknowledged by President Chirac and especially his minister Nicolas Sarkozy, and conferences on this subject were organized in February 2004 in Brussels, in April 2004 in Berlin, and in the UN in New York in June 2004.

As mentioned before, EU policy requires that Israeli exports be labeled by their precise place of origin. This hostile move contrasts with the docility of the EU's compliance with the Arab request for an increased accommodation of Islam and Arab culture in Europe—a demand that President Chirac gladly met in December 2003 at the Louvre Museum, where he proudly presided over the opening of an entire department devoted to the glory of Arab civilization—already well represented there as well as at the Institut du Monde Arabe, opposite Paris' Notre Dame Cathedral.

Significantly in the same Louvre, in the section "Levant—Oriental Antiquities" (Levant—Antiquités Orientales), in Room D, "Palestine and Transjordan, from the origins to the Iron Age," which covers the biblical period, the historical descriptions on the walls mention neither Hebrews, Israelites, nor Jews—with one exception. The stele of Mesha, king of Moab from the ninth century BCE (discovered in 1868) mentions Omri, king of Israel, although no reference is provided to the biblical reference in 2 Kings 3:4–5. The Aramaeans are remembered, as are the building and artistic competence of the Phoenicians and their kingdoms; in contrast, the contemporary kingdoms of Israel and Judea are omitted. The close alliance mentioned in the Bible between Hiram, king of Tyre, and Solomon, king of Israel—especially in building the Temple in Jerusalem—is totally ignored. It is surprising that a letter from a local ruler (Shuvardata) in central Canaan to the Egyptian Pharaoh Akhenaton (fourteenth century BCE) is described as coming from a "Palestinian prince" (prince palestinien), whereas the event took place more than a century before the Philistines— coming from the Greek islands—invaded the southern coast of Canaan, in the region of Gaza. Nowhere is there mention of biblical history and there is no relation between Philistines and Arab Palestinians.

Still, the policy of the EU must be sharply distinguished from the attitude of the majority of Europeans, who are neither antisemitic nor anti-Zionist. Indignation has flared up here and there on an individual level, although pro-Israeli and protest letters have frequently been ignored. Richard Ingrams, a columnist at the *Observer* in London, openly admitted that he had a general practice: he simply did not read letters written by Jews or defending Israel.[37] The pro-Israel opposition was disorganized. It was a series of personal and moral responses, in contrast to the carefully honed policy of the Euro-Arab accords. Thus, it was no match for the strongly entrenched Arab influence in EU trade unions, media, economy, and universities, operating through functionaries and the EAD network. Resistance was scattered, timid, and regarded with contempt by triumphant Eurabians. Individuals, Jews and Christians alike, felt trapped and paralyzed by a premeditated, planned and inflexible political straitjacket that had suddenly emerged in full force, embracing the whole EU. It seemed as if the Nazi and fascist years of totalitarianism were coming back with all their vulgar coarseness, their cynical contempt for truth and humanity, and their perversion of speech, whereby terrorists were absolved of their crimes and victims scorned and blamed for defending themselves.

The dread of terrorism has prevented various Muslim, Christian, and Jewish groups from expressing solidarity with Jews, Israel, and even with America. In addition, the economic threats and intellectual terrorism of the Arab Muslim states has reproduced in Europe the harassment and fear inherent to the *dhimmi* condition. However, this psychological warfare is not restricted to America, Israel, and the Jews. Ordinary Christians and liberal Muslims are also targeted.

As the mass of Europeans remain to this day totally ignorant of the EAD agreements, they did not perceive that the growing social insecurity, the erosion of their basic freedoms, and the unrelenting mutation of their societies resulted from the consciously chosen policies of their own leaders—concocted in the opacity of the European Commission decision center. The EU's various bodies, committees, and policies represent a complex supranational web that often escapes accountability and are impenetrable even to experienced people. Europeans have been unwittingly victims during thirty years of constant indoctrination, encouraged by state support—as evidenced in all the Euro-Arab agreements signed at the highest levels of government.

Thus, the majority of Europeans harbor no hate, but its culture is imposed on them through a policy planned and ordered at the top of Europe's political, cultural, and economic establishment. This European elite bears the responsibility for the transformation, in the European popular mind, of Israel into a "Nazi state" and of the Palestinian Islamikazes into its victims—as well as for the modernized version of the Jewish Peril threatening a peaceful world. The November 2003 issue of the Paris magazine *Observatoire du monde juif* is devoted to an analysis of the boycott of Israel on university campuses across Europe, Australia, Canada, and the USA.[38] The frenzy and unrelenting passion of the activities organized at national and international levels indicate that they emanate from a powerful center that has unlimited means at its disposal. The war against Israel is now fought throughout European institutions, in universities and schools, the media, in trade agreements, among NGOs, by churches and even in the streets where Jews have to hide their identity. Judaism and Zionism are fast becoming a crime, as they were in Nazi Europe and are today in the Arab world.

A striking and monotonous uniformity pervades the EU media, extinguishing independent thought. European magazines and newspapers prattle on about the archvillains Israel and America, while deploring Palestinian victimhood. Through NGO militantism, unilateral media reports, and EU-Arab funded projects, the Arab-Israeli conflict has gained in Europe the central status it has long enjoyed in the Arab-Muslim world. Much of Europe's media consistently place the alleged crimes of Israel above other human tragedies, whether caused by terrorism, tyranny, gender, and child abuse, or anything else. Europe's general indifference to the persecution and killings of Christians by Muslim terrorists tacitly acknowledges that non-Muslim life is cheap and can be shed without retribution—a basic tenet of *jihad* and dhimmitude. In his analysis of the situation of the Christians in Bethlehem at the end of 2003, Paul Marshall wrote,

> Like its parent, the Muslim Brotherhood, Hamas fights to reestablish an Islamic caliphate, and its founding covenant proclaims "the Koran is its constitution" and "the law governing the land of Palestine is the Islamic sharia."
>
> Islamization pressures now reach beyond Hamas, Islamic Jihad, and their kindred. The draft Palestinian constitution says, "Islam is the official religion in Palestine," and makes the "principles of the Islamic sharia" a "main source for legislation." Textbooks, PA television, and government-sponsored preachers now stress Islamist rather than nationalist themes. . . . Under this pressure, Christians throughout the Middle East are fleeing their homeland. . . . Their Christmas joy is also shadowed by pain and fear, since this is the peak season for anti-Christian attacks in Pakistan, India, Sudan, Nigeria, and beyond. The U.S. has issued terrorist warnings to westerners in Indonesia, but the likeliest targets are churches throughout the country—there were Christmas Eve church bombings in 18 cities three years ago, and terrorists arrested this year had maps of Christian meeting places.[39]

About all these human trials, the European media was strangely silent.

11

The New Euro-Arab Culture

Europe's pursuit of an all-embracing Euro-Mediterranean Partnership led to profound and enduring demographic and cultural changes. To fulfill in part the numerous requirements made by the Euro-Arab Dialogue for the expansion of Arab culture and language into Europe, the European Parliament on March 30, 1984 proposed the creation of a Euro-Arab University, as a joint project funded by the Arab League and the EEC. The university would be located in Spain, on land provided by the Spanish authorities. It would serve as a postgraduate institution, endowed with twenty-five to thirty professors and three hundred students. Since this project did not come to fruition, some universities created the Itinerant Euro-Arab University, with twice-yearly sessions alternating between Arab and European universities. In 1994, the EU Commission created a Euro-Arab School of Management in Granada, Spain. It was open to both European and Arab students and was funded for the first three years by the EU and Spain.[1]

The strengthening of Euro-Arab cultural links is both a permanent and unique feature of the Dialogue. It has taken place on a scale never before attempted with any other culture. Hence, the 1995 Barcelona Declaration (under "Partnership in Social, Cultural and Human Affairs: Developing Human Resources, Promoting Understanding between Cultures and Exchanges between Civil Societies") states:

> The participants recognize that the traditions of culture and civilization throughout the Mediterranean region, dialogue between these cultures and exchanges at human, scientific and technological level are an essential factor in bringing their people closer, promoting understanding between them and improving their perception of each other.

Such a Euro-Arab fellowship is based on the participants' belief "that dialogue and respect between cultures and religions are a necessary precondition for bringing the peoples closer. In this connection they stress the importance of the role the mass media can play in the reciprocal recognition and understanding of cultures as a source of mutual enrichment." This sentence elucidates the media subservience to the Euro-Arab coali-

tion's aims, its political correctness, and its pro-Arab bias. The Barcelona
Declaration proclaims the participants' intention

> to promote cultural exchanges and knowledge of other languages, respect-
> ing the cultural identity of each partner, and to implement a lasting policy
> of educational and cultural programmes; in this context the partners under-
> take to adopt measures to facilitate human exchanges, in particular by im-
> proving administrative procedures.[2]

This program has certainly been developed in Europe, where Arab culture, Islamic centers, and their political interests have become overwhelming, but no parallel endeavor appeared in the Arab countries, especially in
relation to Israel, a participant in the Barcelona Declaration. The participants agreed to invigorate and encourage exchanges among leaders of political and civil society, the cultural and religious world, universities, the
research communities, the media, the trade unions and organizations, and
private and public enterprises; to create programs to foster contacts and
exchanges between young people; and to support the rule of law and democracy. They emphasized the fight against racism, xenophobia, and intolerance—concepts which evidently were nothing more than euphemisms
for the suppression of any criticism that Muslims would find offensive,
since Judeophobia, Christianophobia, and anti-Americanism had never
been as flagrant in Europe as in the emerging Euro-Arab culture.

Section 4 of the annexed Work Program of the Barcelona Declaration,
"Partnership in Social, Cultural and Human Affairs: Developing Human
Resources, Promoting Understanding between Cultures and Exchanges between Civil Societies," covered cultural aspects of the exchange. It called
for regular dialogue on educational policies, focusing on vocational training, technology in education, the universities and other higher-education
establishments, and research. The program proposed meetings of policy
makers, academics, and educators, as well as representatives of universities
and higher-education establishments. Likewise, the conference decided
that the European Commission would strengthen the ongoing Med-Campus
program, another Euro-Arab cooperation project under the auspices of the
Euro-Arab Dialogue.

The subsection "*Dialogue between cultures and civilizations*" recommended
cultural exchanges and mutual knowledge of languages, concrete actions
to promote cultural and creative heritage, cultural and artistic events, co-
productions (theatre and cinema), translations, and other means of cultural dissemination. It stressed that understanding between the major
religions of the Euro-Mediterranean region would facilitate mutual tolerance. It pledged support for meetings of representatives of religions and
religious institutions, as well as for theologians, academics, and others who

would work against prejudice, ignorance, and fanaticism. The European Union would actively promote close interaction between the European and Arab media, in particular through the MED-Media program and annual meetings. It was to plan youth exchanges and other contacts between individuals—especially involving officials, scientists, academics, businessmen, students, and sportsmen. This Euro-Arab synergy contributed to the emergence of a totalitarian subculture.

At the Euro-Arab Parliamentary Dialogue in Damascus (July 11–13, 1998), the participants again stressed the need to pay greater attention to the cultural dimension in Euro-Arab relations, since this field reflected the historical and cultural dimension of the Euro-Arab relationship. They agreed to promote the following measures:

1. Establishing rules of behavior at the national and international level that ensure the preservation of cultural values;
2. Drawing up joint media plans whose aim is to rectify mistaken ideas prevailing in the countries of each side against the cultural and spiritual values of the other side;
3. Finding solutions for the problems of Arab workers and Arab immigrants and improving the conditions of their integration into the societies they live in, while respecting their rights in preserving their beliefs, traditions, and national culture;
4. Improving the facilities for teaching Arabic in Europe;
5. Supporting the Euro-Arab Business Management School, which was set up in Granada in 1994 as a potential basis for a real Euro-Arab university.

Parliamentary cooperation was also considered by the participants:

As regards cooperation between Arab and European Parliamentarians, the participants have expressed:
—their support for full membership of Palestine in the Inter-Parliamentary Union;
—their support for the setting up of a permanent Euro-Arab parliamentary committee whose task would be to follow up the development of the issue of peace in the Middle East.[3]

The Euro-Mediterranean Parliamentary Forum met three months later, in Brussels (October 1998). The participants called "for closer cultural ties to be established in the Mediterranean and for the European Union's exchange programs to be extended to include the Mediterranean partner countries."[4] In May 2000, funds from the European Commission and support from the Arab Inter-Parliamentary Union reactivated the European Institute for Research on Mediterranean and Euro-Arab Cooperation (MEDEA), which had been dormant for lack of funds. Its new chairman was Charles Ferdinand Nothomb, who had served as Belgium's minister of foreign affairs and minister of state. Nothomb reorganized MEDEA's European Parliament section—which comprised over one hundred members—while the other MEDEA sections in each parliament of the European countries continued their work. The MEDEA Institute, under Nothomb's leadership, issued regular press releases to opinion makers, intellectuals, and pressure groups. It had a major role in spreading Arab influence in Europe.

The Euro-Arab Parliamentary Dialogue met in Brussels on June 20, 2002, nine months after the 9/11 terror attack.[5] The conference was jointly organized by the Arab Inter-Parliamentary Union and the Parliamentary Association for Euro-Arab Cooperation.[6] Members of sixteen Arab parliaments and thirteen European national parliaments, as well as the European Parliament, participated. Representatives from the European Commission and from UNRWA attended as observers. The European Commission contributed to the funding of the conference.

The items on the agenda were political cooperation and economic and cultural cooperation. Participants first examined political cooperation in the Middle East peace process and the prospects for lifting the embargo imposed on Iraq. Then they considered the migrations and brain drain in the Euro-Arab zone and ways to improve agreements concerning economic and cultural cooperation between European and Arab countries. As usual, most of the interventions centered on the Middle East and nurtured the Euro-Arab anti-Israel obsession.

The Final Communiqué reaffirmed Arab conditions for a Middle East peace. It advocated the absolute primacy of improving the situation of the Palestinians and the elimination of Israeli political and military measures that allegedly fueled frustration, despair, and retaliation. The Euro-Arab Parliamentary Dialogue appealed to the relevant international bodies to bring political and economic pressure to bear on Israel, as well as to remove the sanctions against Iraq and Libya. On economic and cultural cooperation, the participants reaffirmed measures already recommended by previous meetings. They acknowledged the significance of cultural diversity as a basis for enriching human knowledge. They condemned any attempt to identify a linkage between Islam, Arabs, and terrorism.

In his report on the June 2002 meeting, the secretary-general of PAEAC summarized joint Euro-Arab activities that had taken place since the Damascus Dialogue of 1998, which was considered by the participants to have been particularly rich in political content and resolutions for the promotion of parliamentary diplomacy. Many anti–Israeli activities had begun after the Damascus Dialogue and continued on the European level in the press and information channels. The report recalled that a delegation of the Association had met with Austrian Minister of Foreign Affairs Wolfgang Schüssel in October 1998. PAEAC members had again reminded the minis-

ter of the importance of freezing the ratification of the EU-Israel partnership agreement, as had already been done by the Belgian and French
parliaments. The delegation had also raised the issue of extending the
Euro-Mediterranean Partnership to Libya and Mauritania.

After the delivery of their report, the Arab delegates to the 2002 Brussels
meeting strongly condemned American and British policy in Iraq. They referred to "the existence of an international public opinion including a European spectrum of wide representation gaining increasing impact in its
demand to lift the embargo imposed on Iraq." The subsequent mass demonstrations in European streets in favor of Saddam Hussein, amplified by
the media, reflected this coordinated Euro-Arab policy.

The other items of the 2002 Brussels meeting's Action Plan called for a
strengthening of Euro-Arab economic and financial partnership in various
fields, as well as a more genuine social, cultural, and human partnership,
respectful of cultural differences, essential for improving the dialogue. The
Plan recommended the creation of a special Foundation and the development of cultural and educational programs. The parliamentarians recalled
that the EAD had been active for over twenty-five years, and that such a
worthy institution needed continued financial support.

Over the years, contacts and collaboration between the Arab Inter-Parlia-
mentarian Union (AIPU) and PAEAC have been continuous. They involved the exchange of documents and statements on key developments in
the Middle East and the peace process. The two bodies had maintained
constant cooperation particularly through their General Secretariats.
Hence, from the start of the Palestinian terror campaign in October 2000,
the PAEAC has provided a powerful worldwide amplifier for Palestinian accusations, as, for example, of war crimes in Jenin after Israel had cleared
out the terrorist bases there in April 2002. It was also responsible for the
disinformation campaign concerning the Palestinian occupation of the Basilica of the Nativity in Bethlehem in Spring 2002. Through its numerous
contacts and networks, the PAEAC succeeded in arousing world opinion
against Israel, and provided regional and international support for the Palestinians. This was, of course, the first concern and main activity of its partner Arab Parliamentarians. The travesty of portraying Israelis as Nazis, and
the malicious post-9/11 campaign to forestall sympathy for Israel as a victim of the same jihadist terrorism, was a well-planned Euro-Arab campaign.
Indeed, this was alluded to at the June 2002 Brussels meeting. Hence, the
Parliamentary Association for Euro-Arab Cooperation constitutes a powerful Arab lobby within the European Union and its parliament, working with
the full consent of European statesmen, ministers, and politicians.

In 2002, France proposed the proclamation of a Palestinian state, an idea
supported by several EU member states. This measure would have bol-
stered the legitimacy of the Palestinian Authority and rewarded the Pales-

tinian terrorist war against Israel. However, the proposal was abandoned due to a lack of consensus within the EU. At the Brussels meetings of June 2002 the proposal to set up a permanent Euro-Arab Parliamentary committee, whose task would be to follow up on the development of peace in the Middle East, was reintroduced. The Arab delegation recalled that the

> settlement of the Arab-Israeli conflict is considered one of the main axes of the Euro-Arab relations and the Euro-Mediterranean Partnership (E.M.P.) because the establishment of peace in the M.E. [Middle East] and the Mediterranean basin constitutes a necessary priority for the success of the programs of economic, social and cultural cooperation among the states of the region and between these states and the European ones.[7]

Arafat's rejection of the Camp David II proposals amounted to a refusal of America's role and a turning to the EU. The Arab states needed Europe in order to break the American monopoly on the peace process and to impose Arab conditions on Israel. The Arabs made this clear at Brussels in June 2002:

> If we take into consideration the fact that Europe has increasingly become aware of the close connection between stable peace in the M.E. and the future of the Euro-Med partnership in which the Arab World constitutes the cornerstone, it is quite natural then to call Europe to find ways and means to activate its role in the M.E. This would serve our common objectives and would also serve international and regional peace and security.

On item 1 of the agenda, Political Cooperation, the Arab side presented its Paper entitled "Comprehensive Peace Process in the Middle East" where it laid down its conditions for peace. As we have seen, they included the imposition on Israel of the indefensible 1949 armistice lines, Jerusalem as the Arab Palestinian capital; and the resettlement in Israel of Arabs who had fled in the wake of the Arab aggressions against Israel and their military defeats of 1948–49 and 1967.

In the numerous joint declarations of the Euro-Arab meetings and those of the Euro-Arab Parliamentary Cooperation, some principal features stand out, as they were constantly repeated over the years. The Arabs remind the EU of its duty to pressure Israel into conforming to the Arab conditions that Europe had adopted, in order to secure her oil and trade with the Arab countries. This priority is reaffirmed in every discussion. The Arabs also constantly remind the Europeans that they have agreed to facilitate the spread and implementation of Arab language and culture across the EU, as if Arab culture was on a par with native European cultures, and not a modern, foreign importation. In fact, many European politicians have asserted that the Arabic language and Islam represent a component of European civilization, equal to any of the others. At the June 2002 Brussels meeting, the Arab working paper for the section "Improving the Agreements Concerning Economic and Cultural Cooperation Between European and Arab Countries" (item 2) emphasized that the cultural dimension was an important element of the Euro-Arab cooperation: "it expresses civilizational and historical continuation between Europe and the Arab World." The dialogue could not "be consolidated unless it was given a cultural dimension, through which the relationship between the people of the two regions would be deepened and enriched." In view of this, the Arab delegation put forth some recommendations:

> This situation raises the task of strengthening cultural exchange between the European and the Arab sides, and promoting cultural agreements signed between them with special stress on the following matters:
> 1. Each side would fight, within its society, the currents hostile to the other side. It has to be noted, in this respect, that the Arab side suffers more as a result of the rise of Islamophobia and Arabophobia, the rise of racism and xenophobia in Europe and attacks against Arab migrants in particular. These tendencies have increased after the events [*sic*] of 11 September [2001] in the U.S.A.
> 2. Working out carefully studied media plans aiming at correcting the wrong views spread in the countries of each side against the spiritual and cultural values of the other side. Such plans might include:
>   —The organization by both sides of symposiums or seminars on subjects of common interest;
>   —The conduction of dialogue through satellite channels where Arab and European intellectuals take part;
>   —The exchange of delegations, publications, artistic groups, films and cultural programs.
> 3. The revival of the project of the Euro-Arab University, and paying more attention to teaching Arabic in Europe.
> 4. The working out of a plan for translating Arabic books (especially those concerned with cultural heritage, novels and plays) to major European languages.

Another key feature of Europe's new symbiosis with the Arab world involved immigration, universities, cultural activities, and media. Migration had always been a thorny problem in the Euro-Arab Dialogue. The Arab side frequently complained about European restrictions on immigration; they requested special privileges, such as access to work opportunities for Arab immigrants in the EU on an equal basis with Europeans. Accordingly, host countries were exhorted to provide immigrants with vocational training, freedom of movement, suitable living conditions, and financial aid should they decide to return to their homeland.

The Euro-Arab collaboration was not to be only cultural. The Barcelona Declaration's signatories decided to step up exchanges in the scientific sectors, promote the transfer of technology, and to encourage the training of scientific and technical staff, by increasing participation in joint research projects. On the European side, the discourse was fundamentally irrational. As noted earlier, it was totally detached from the grim reality of the historical and religious culture and tradition of the Arab and Muslim world. In spite of the instability that prevailed in the Arab countries, the rapid expansion of radical Islam, and the fact that Islamist terrorists and ideologists came from educated and middle-class environments, the EAD's Eurocrats went ahead with plans to intensify scientific exchanges between Europe and the Arab countries.[8] Hence, at the June 2002 Brussels meeting, the European side proposed the establishment of scientific communication networks between Arab expatriates in Europe and the scientific communities in their Arab home countries, in order to ensure the transfer of European know-how. Again, the substantial EU funding, provided by the EU taxpayer, would simply add more subsidies, but would do nothing effective to improve living conditions in Arab countries.

Eurocrats appeared to anticipate Arab demands by making generous overtures. They took the initiative in offering projects intended to increase the dynamism of the Partnership. In most cases, they just endorsed Arab demands transmitted through PAEAC channels. The Action Plan proposed by the European Commission at the Brussels meeting could not have been more attractive for the Arab side. Its first suggestion was increased involvement of both the European Union and the Arab League in the Arab-Israeli conflict—which meant more pressure on Israel and a reduced role for America. Concretely, it led many European ministers to protect Arafat, thereby keeping the level of terrorism unabated and deflecting criticism onto the Israelis. The unofficial support that the EU lent to Marwan Barghouti, chief of the Fatah terrorist militias under Arafat's command, attests to the sinister side of this Euro-Palestinian solidarity.

Nevertheless, while the Europeans did all they could to please their Arab partners, none of the progressive policies the EAD promoted for the Arab world were accepted or applied. Indeed, the EAD trafficked in concepts that were largely foreign to the Arab world. What did freedom of conscience and religion, gender equality, and equality of dignity for all people really mean in societies that practiced segregation of women and infidels, death for apostasy, "honor" killings, female genital mutilation, and even the stoning of women, and which were riddled with the religious fanaticism and hate nurtured by the *jihad shari'a* values that persisted at the core of Arab/Muslim civilization? In his thoughtful book *Leaving Islam*, Ibn Warraq records the untold suffering of Muslim victims of intolerance.[9] Which Arab countries applied even one of the spurious exhortations of the Barcelona Declaration?

Europe's discriminatory and heavy-handed policy toward Israel contradicted its claim of impartiality. The presence of Israel in the Eurabian cultural agenda was clearly a nuisance. The EU decreed economic measures against Israel; five years before Barcelona, in January 1990, the EC Commission, under strong Arab pressure, had applied a partial freeze on scientific cooperation with Israel.[10] But despite the terrorist activities of the PA and its mass murder of Israeli civilians by *jihad* bombers, the EU maintained good relations with Arafat, even increasing its funding of the PA—as if the slaughter of civilians was of little importance as long as the slogans of the "peace process" were constantly reiterated. In 1998, the powerful Arab–Muslim lobby, acting through the Parliamentary Association for the Euro-Arab Cooperation, requested that Israel be suspended from the Euro-Mediterranean Partnership. Meanwhile, of course, normal relations continued unquestioned with Arafat, Syria, Egypt and other Arab countries where the rules of dhimmitude, mandatory under the *shari'a,* are still prominent features of the society.

Euro-Arab cooperation on the university level, meanwhile, has extended anti-Jewish racism on European campuses, as well as among the intelligentsia.[11] Throughout European universities, a campaign of hostility and abuse has targeted Israeli scholars. EU programs have been strongly pressured to boycott Israeli researchers and scientists, denying them the right to participate freely in academic life. Such decisions to exclude pro-Israeli Jews have revived the specter of Europe's darkest past, although the EU continues to pretend otherwise. As in earlier times, when Jews in Christendom—and Jews and Christians in Islamic lands—were denied access to universities and forced into intellectual isolation, so once again, under Arab/Muslim pressure a heinous exclusionism now prevails in some European academic circles and learning institutions against Israelis.

While the EU was strengthening its relations and fraternization with Arab scientific bodies, some of European universities and academics were deliberately insulting Israeli scholars. In December 2002, the governing council of the Pierre and Marie Curie University in Paris approved a pro-boycott statement against Israel. It was also endorsed by the universities of Grenoble and Montpellier.[12] A British biologist, Steven Rose, who with his wife spearheaded the boycott, justified it by claiming that "European Union science research is political in its own right, with its own criteria, own industrial goals and targets, and it's a fair target."[13]

At Oxford University, geneticist Andrew Wilkie rejected an Israeli student's application to work in his laboratory, because of the student's nationality.[14] Fortunately, the university ruled otherwise. Six months later, it suspended Wilkie from his academic duties for two months, without pay. Yet no one has ever barred Iraqi, Syrian, Palestinian, Egyptian, Sudanese, Saudi, Algerian, Iranian, or other Arab students from European universities—not to speak of students from non-Muslim dictatorships—because of their respective governments' policies, which discriminate against women and non-Muslims and approve terrorism.

The differences between the Barcelona principles of human rights, their call for the respect of other cultures, and the results of the implementation of these principles are nothing short of dazzling. An Arab culture of Judeo-phobia and anti-Americanism has swept over the EU into the media and all sectors of public life: political, economic, intellectual. The EU Amsterdam Treaty (1997), in section 1, "Freedom, Security and Justice," stipulates rules to be enforced by every EU state. It declares that the Union is founded on the principles of liberty, democracy, respect for human rights and fundamental freedoms, and the rule of law. It stresses the duty of the EU to fight discrimination based on sex, racial or ethnic origin, and religion or belief. How do these principles apply today to European Jews, who are targeted in their synagogues, their schools and community centers, and are daily victims of racist propaganda and defamation? Such laudable rules are not even enforced to defend the rights to security and the freedoms of EU citizens on EU territory. However, the EU governments, until early 2004, seemed to have no intention of redressing this situation. They simply dismissed the matter, except in particularly grave situations that were reported by politicians and the media.

In 2003, the approaching enlargement of the EU with the admission of ten Eastern European countries in May 2004 provoked resentment in the Arab Mediterranean region. Arab states, particularly those of North Africa, feared that this enlargement would work to their financial disadvantage. They primarily feared losing their status as Western Europe's privileged source of immigration. The European Union had to accommodate them with assurances of its determination to continue to improve relations. It reaffirmed once again its commitment to exploiting the potential of the Barcelona Process fully—whatever that formula means. In the words of a Euro-Mediterranean Study Commission (EuroMeSCo) paper in February 2003,

> The Union must also maintain an intensified presence in the Middle East as one of the principal promoters of peace in the region. Enlargement should therefore involve an intensification in economic and commercial relations between the European Union and its Southern [Arab][15] partners based on the exploitation of mutual interest.[16]

Regarding immigration, this study proposed that even if there were to be immigration from the countries of Central and Eastern Europe after the EU's Enlargement has taken place, "the principal sources of immigration into the European Union for the next two or three decades will be primarily provided by Turkey, a candidate member, the countries to the east of

Central and Eastern Europe, which are not candidates, and, above all, the Mediterranean Arab countries."

The EuroMeSCo study stated that it had deliberately avoided discussing the frontiers of Europe, whether geographic, cultural, historic, or geopolitical. Nonetheless, it said that one day the European leaders would have to decide how to fix those limits without creating a fortress. Such questions—this study reports—are increasingly asked by the Arab South Mediterranean region, which is worried by the EU Enlargement. In its typical and deliberately obscure terminology, the study comments, "In fact, the South Mediterranean countries have developed an irritating tendency to see the Eastern Enlargement of the Union as a new source of threat to trade, investment, European aid and even to migration."

However, the report's analysts assert that the free movement of people from the new EU countries will be limited. They "make it clear that the countries of Central and Eastern Europe will not be serious competitors to Mediterranean Arab countries which will continue to be the main sources of migrant inflows for the next two-to-three decades for two key reasons."

These reasons, according to the study, were: 1) growth perspectives in Central and Eastern Europe, major investment inflows, and gradual reduction of differences in living standards, as well as changes in demographic structures limiting migration flows; 2) the fact that immigration would come mainly from the Caucasus region. For those reasons:

> Southern Europe would then have every reason to make Mediterranean cooperation a priority and to reaffirm the importance of the Euro-Mediterranean Partnership as a strategic choice for the Union. Such a reaffirmation of the strategic value of European involvement in the Mediterranean, in the context of Eastern Enlargement, arises from the need to preserve institutional equilibrium within the European Union, restore regional security and strengthen the cultural dialogue, damaged by the discrimination practiced against Arabs and Muslims since the events of September 11, 2001. It is also based on the realistic yet generous vision of Europe as more than a European space but less than a European power. Everything that has been discussed above must lead to the conclusion that Enlargement must go hand-in-hand with the revival of the Euro-Mediterranean Partnership. This is what one great European, Jacques Delors, sought when he wrote, "It must not be the case that, because our attention is focused on making Enlargement a success . . . we forget the [Arab] South." On the contrary, the centrality of the Mediterranean must be emphasized, not by taking a rigid and unilateral Eurocentric vision, as the president of the European Commission, Romano Prodi, made clear at a conference at CERMAC on November 26, 2002, but ". . . by basing ourselves on a certain idea of co-ownership."

The paper thus recommends the reinforcement of the fateful policy that made the Euro-Mediterranean Partnership a strategic choice for the EU.

The strengthening of the cultural dialogue would imply the transfer of billions of euros to corrupt and unstable regimes. The so-called cultural dialogue had already proved itself a euphemism for a "cultural relativism" that whitewashed killings for blasphemy and "honor" killings, as well as jihadist ideology and terrorist practices in general. And describing the "events of September 11" simply as damaging to Muslims and evidence of a Western fault that must be redressed, while overlooking the indiscriminate terrorist crime against American and foreign civilians, can only be called a gross intellectual perversion on the part of the EuroMeSCo participants.

The spirit of the study appears clearly: Europe should become less European and more "generous"—or Eurabian. It should not adopt a rigid or unilateral Eurocentric vision. In other words, the study was trying to redress a problem: although the EU had deliberately dismissed Islamic terrorism, deflecting its causes on America and Israel, Europeans had become cautious toward the Arab world. To oppose this trend and calm Arab frustration, Eurocrat policy would balance the EU's expansion into Eastern Europe with an increase in Arab immigration. Once again, therefore, European policy has been dictated by Arab interests. Arab banks and funds invested in the EU countries weigh heavily on the European economy and on governments' policy.

The demand for increased immigration from the Southern Mediterranean was emphasized again by the French Institute for International Relations (Institut Français des Relations Internationales, IFRI) in its 2003 report to the EU Commission, *World Trade in the 21st Century*.[17] It predicted that the gloomy European future IFRI painted would only be brightened with increased Arab immigration.[18]

These reports, as well as other declarations, illustrate the enormous gap between Eurocrat theorists and the European population. In January 2003, David Blunkett, Britain's home secretary, warned that the social fabric of Britain could get out of control because of "the disintegration of community relations and social cohesion." Reporter Anthony Browne commented on the dangers of "[ignoring] the clear democratic will and [imposing] mass immigration on a people that really don't want it."[19] He asserted that the consequences of a policy promoting legal and illegal mass immigration would bring Britain to the verge of anarchy, and that covering up the mass illegal immigration for years had raised anger and frustration to a dangerous level. For some years the U.K. has become the center of Islamic radicalism against Jews, Christians, and Americans, as well as for propaganda literature. Preachers and militants like the Egyptian-born Abu Hamza al-Masri had links to al-Qaeda, with the radical group in Algeria, the GIA, and with terrorist cells in Italy. At America's request, he was jailed in 2004.

Far from being exceptional, Great Britain's situation illustrates the exasperation of the European majority. Many feel betrayed and misled by their own leaders. Not only do these Euro-Arab policies express Eurocrats' disdain for their own citizens; they also highlight their total blindness to facts contradicting their doctrine. Calls and *fatwa*s for *jihad* are widespread, and are issued by many preeminent and influential religious leaders in the Muslim world. What exactly is the meaning of Europe's obligation to become more "generous" and less "Eurocentric," when in the Muslim world incitements to *jihad* against the "Crusaders" and Jews are widespread?[20] Yet for Jacques Delors, the socialist finance minister of French President François Mitterrand, Islam is a component of Europe's value system, and this fact must be acknowledged in order to prevent the exclusion of Muslims.[21] Delors is no lone eccentric; he headed the European Commission from 1985 to 1994. But while the Eurocrats plan decades of Southern (Arab) migration, they are closing their internal Eastern borders.

Some clergymen and scholars promote the theory that Europe owes a debt of gratitude to the Arab-Muslim world that transmitted the Greek scientific heritage to it. Here again history has been distorted and is being used as a political tool. In fact, Greek civilization was taught in the Byzantine Empire, as well as in its Italian cities. The magnificence of Constantinople, Ravenna, and Venice testify to the greatness of this Byzantine and Latin art and civilization, which, in the early Middle Ages and later, superseded the budding Islamic culture that was flourishing among the people conquered by Islam. Fleeing the massacres and slavery brought on by *jihad* from the eleventh century on in Anatolia, and later on in the Balkans, Byzantine scholars took refuge westward. There they translated and taught the Greek classics in Latin. Byzantine influence is evident in Italian art and culture. Greek, Roman, and Judeo-Christian influences have molded European civilization. In light of this, it is strange that only the Islamic component is being promoted in Euro-Arab policy, as if it is the only relevant ancestor of modern European civilization. Moreover, this is being done by the very people who have the responsibility to teach and preserve the essential values of their culture, and especially to respect the historical truth.

Part IV
The Making of Eurabia

12

Arab and Muslim Unaccountability
as a Policy

The preceding chapters have explained the general structure of the encompassing political and cultural conception that has evolved into a nascent Eurabia. This section will examine how, over the years, life was injected into this ideological project, transforming it from an abstract design into a comprehensive set of attitudes and beliefs, inculcating in Europeans the corresponding intolerance of a new European Union cult. The translation of this theory into a quasi-religious faith, complete with doctrines, required the postulation of unshakeable axioms, the formulation of new canons delineating the guiding principles of the credo, and control over the mechanisms committed to propagation of the new faith. This transformation was accomplished by means of the multifarious activities of the EAD and was controlled and directed by the highest sources of authority and influence in the EC/EU.

Eurabian doctrine rests on five main pillars: 1) the creation of Euro-Arab human, economic, and political symbiosis motivated by European greed and fear; 2) a common goal of economic development as the source of human progress and achievement; 3) the firm belief that medieval Muslim Andalusia provides an exemplary model for the construction of Eurabia in the twenty-first century; 4) the vilification and demise of Israel as the key to Euro-Arab reconciliation; 5) hostility to America and obstruction of its influence in the Middle East.

As shown earlier, this evolution clearly resulted from the policy initiated by Charles de Gaulle in the late 1960s. The plan for a vast Euro-Arab geostrategic Mediterranean bloc, born after the independence of Algeria in 1962 and advanced through the mixture and interpenetration of populations from both shores (multiculturalism), has already been mentioned. Most French politicians—such as President Georges Pompidou; his minister Michel Jobert; Louis Terrenoire, a minister of de Gaulle and president of the Association de Solidarité France-Pays Arabes; Raoul Weexteen, adviser to socialist ministers from 1988 to 1993; Edgar Pisani, director of the

147

Institut du Monde Arabe; and Roland Dumas, minister of foreign affairs under Mitterrand—envisioned this bloc as the basis for a strategic and economic alliance, in which France would play the role of protector of Islam and the Palestinians against America and Israel. They hoped that a pro-French Islam would facilitate the quiet control of former colonies within the French orbit and spread French culture (the so-called Francophonia), associated with the benefits of an enormous market, across Muslim Africa.

The project for Euro-Arab integration was actually not so new in the 1960s. On October 25, 1941, Hitler had told Italian Foreign Minister Count Ciano that in the battle against America he envisioned "the common interests of a unified Europe within an economic zone completed by the African colonies."[1] In the international context, Muslim imperialism has always astutely profited from the religious, economic, and strategic rivalries of the West. Without going back to the alliance of Francis I with the Ottomans against the German-Spanish Empire of Charles V (1525), France was the first to play the Arab card against Great Britain in the nineteenth and twentieth centuries. Bonaparte, in Egypt (1798), portrayed himself a Muslim protector of Islam against the Turks and the British. Under the Restoration (1818–30) and following its conquest of Algeria in 1830, France dreamed of an Arab empire stretching from Algiers to Turkey—an ambition pursued by Napoleon III in the 1860s. The French historian Alain Boyer recalls that "France with its colonial empire declared itself a Muslim power, the protector of Islam, but with a paternalist attitude."[2]

Through its nineteenth-century foreign policy, France was pursuing the colonization of Algeria, while claiming in the Levant to be the protector of both the Eastern Christians and the Muslims against a "Jewish peril." It contrived this theme to serve its imperial designs after the 1840 Damascus blood libel was initiated by the French Consul Ratti-Menton as an anti-proto-Zionist strategy.[3] Endorsed by the papacy, this colonial policy sustained French prestige and Catholic control over Christian religious sites in the Holy Land against the ambitions of Russian Orthodoxy as well as British and German Protestantism. In 1838, Britain had obtained from the Ottoman sultan the authorization to open the first consulate in Jerusalem, whereby it afforded protection to *dhimmi* Jews in the Holy Land against the persecutions they suffered from both Muslims and *dhimmi* Christians—and especially the latin clergy and the French Catholic monks. It was then that the British, helped by indigenous Jews, resurrected Palestine in its biblical borders; under Muslim domination it had been an undifferentiated section of the caliphate, as was the case with all the other Islamized Christian countries.

British intrusion into the Holy Land aroused violent opposition from the French and the Vatican Curia. The campaign to demonize the Jews, agents of British influence, was disseminated via Church channels and intensified later in the century with the resurgence of a Jewish liberation movement in their homeland. France saw political Zionism as a threat to the exclusive protectorate that it had exercised for centuries over Christendom's Holy Places. Eastern Christians and their churches were thereby mobilized in a French-led anti-Jewish campaign for the Arabization of the Middle East under French patronage. In Algeria, some French colonists boasted that they were the protectors of the Arabs against the local Jewish *dhimmi* population, whom they portrayed as usurers and exploiters, even lynching some in several pogroms they triggered at the turn of the nineteenth century.

By the end of the nineteenth century, the concept of an Arab nation was beginning to be used to foster a Muslim-Christian alliance in the Levant against the Jews. Arabism embodied the nucleus of a Muslim-Christian symbiosis, bringing together the whole of Christendom and the Muslim world against Zionism and the Jews. In the mid-1890s, the draft of the *Protocols of the Elders of Zion* was being concocted in Paris and written in French in antisemitic circles linked to the Tsarist Okhrana police services. In a recent book, Pierre-André Taguieff identifies its author: Matthieu Golovinski.[4] He wrote the *Protocols* for the Tsarist secret police in France. In these circles, Christian Arabs and French antisemites worked together for a united Christian and Muslim Arab nation under a French protectorate. This nation, as they saw it, would seal the alliance of Islam and Christianity in their common battle against Zionism and Great Britain.

After World War I, North African and Middle Eastern countries were all French-, Italian-, or British-controlled colonies, protectorates, or mandates. These administrations conducted an appeasement policy toward the Muslim majorities. Anti-Zionism became an element of Euro-Arab policies, which were designed to achieve a Muslim-Christian symbiosis. It first involved the projection onto the Jews of the hostility of the Muslim peoples, colonized and humiliated by European powers; later, Nazi political and fascist movements coalesced in a Euro-Arab alliance and cooperation against Zionism. This current led during World War II to Arab collaboration in the extermination of the Jews. Haj Amin al-Husseini, the grand mufti of Jerusalem eagerly volunteered in this cause, which was supported by Palestinian Arabs. Emil Ghoury, a Christian Orthodox, was his private secretary and acting agent in Palestine. The anti-Zionist policy of the colonial administrations, with their executive offices in the imperial European capitals, followed a parallel Islamophile trend that was even more severe against the indigenous Christians, whose legitimate rights to autonomy and security were only answered with treacherous disdain.

After decolonization, France continued to pursue its Muslim colonial dream, which was both protective and paternalist. Thus, starting in 1964 France supported the most radical anti-Zionist ideologies and organizations that embodied the jihadist ideology. It favored Nasserism and Ba'ath-ism, which reformulated jihadist ideology in the then-current language of global "socialism," as well as the Libyan and Algerian military dictatorships and the PLO, choosing to overlook their neo-Nazi connections.[5]

Before the 1973 Yom Kippur war and the oil threat, European anti-Israeli associations representing various political and religious trends were already planning activities together with the Arab League. Petrodollars were spent in abundance for propaganda among a European public that was still largely hostile to such ideas. The Cairo International Conference in Support of the Arab Peoples in 1969 had stressed that it was the "incumbent moral and political duty of all participants to this conference to reveal the truth ["Israeli terrorism," "racial and religious discrimination," "apartheid," "intolerance," "illegitimacy," "imperialism," "unscrupulous propaganda," "threat to world peace," etc.] and spread it through the press, the radio, television, and via demonstrations, visits of delegation and the organization of seminars and conferences in the West and through all continents."[6]

Strong Euro-Arab bonds had been forged by the early 1970s, but without much effect on public opinion. Among their promoters were well-known Nazi collaborators and notorious antisemites.[7] Thus, by the time of the 1973 war, the Euro-Arab propaganda warfare against Israel had already been activated. The rapidity of the Franco-German submission to the Arab threat of an oil boycott arouses the suspicion that this threat represented a pretext for Europeans leaders to reverse previous EEC economic policy toward Israel and the Arab world. This seems all the more plausible since America had pledged to cover Europe's oil needs and had called the Arab states' bluff by demonstrating their total dependence on the West. The oil embargo offered France a long-awaited chance to drag the whole of a reluctant EEC into the Arab anti-Zionist political orbit. In fact, France did not even condemn the 1973 Yom Kippur attack by Egypt and Syria on Israel. State endorsement of the Arab perspective throughout Europe came with the initiation of the Dialogue as a consequence of the oil embargo. At that point, the gates of Europe were opened wide to an extensive anti-Israeli propaganda campaign in politics, the media and universities.

PLO terror increased the pressure on European governments through a series of murders and massacres: London, December 15, 1971; and in 1972, in Germany: Cologne on February 6, Hamburg on February 8 and 19, Munich on September 5 at the Olympic Games, and Frankfurt in October; in Brussels, May 9; in Israel, Lod airport, June 1; at Trieste, Italy, August 4; letter bombs to London, Paris, Brussels, Geneva, Vienna, Montreal, Ottawa, New York, Buenos Aires, and Kinshasa on September 20 and November 13, 1972, and finally, Thailand, December 28, 1972, and Khartoum, February 21, 1973, where a Belgian and two American diplomats were murdered.

The Munich terror attack targeted the Israeli Olympic athletes of which eleven were killed. The recent release in London of Public Record Office classified documents includes a letter of the then-British consul-general in Jerusalem, Gayford Woodrow, to the Foreign Office on September 12, 1972. Woodrow mitigates Palestinian terrorism and shifts the blame on Israel, urging understanding of the Munich massacre. A month later, Black September, the Palestinian terrorist organization that had carried out the Munich attack, hijacked a Lufthansa jet from Beirut to Frankfurt and forced the German authorities to release three of their terrorists captured during the Munich massacre. David Gore-Booth, the first secretary at the Foreign Office, urged restraint in condemning the hijacking and again shifted the blame on Israel's existence.[8]

It is worth recalling that the ninth resolution of the 1969 Cairo International Conference in Support of the Arab People stated that Arab "information" should specially target public opinion in countries where governments were pro-Israeli. Until the early 1970s, the Socialist International had been actively pro-Israel, pro-U.S., and pro-NATO. After Palestinian terrorism struck Austria (at the Vienna OPEC meeting on September 28, 1973), its Jewish-born socialist chancellor, Bruno Kreisky, adopted a pro-Palestinian policy. Kreisky, who was then president of the Socialist International, met Arafat several times from 1974 onward, courting him and proclaiming his trust in him. He worked unremittingly to enhance Arafat's position with the pro-Israeli European socialist parties. The chancellor's efforts on behalf of Arafat were linked to the economic prosperity of Austria. The Palestinian National Council in its session held from January 3 to 12, 1973, stated in point 9 of its Political Program: "The PLO will struggle to strengthen its solidarity with the socialist countries and the world forces of liberation and progress to foil all the Zionist, reactionary and imperialist schemes."[9]

By the mid 1970s, under the leadership of Kreisky, Willy Brandt—West Germany's socialist chancellor (1969–74)—and Olaf Palme, prime minister of Sweden (1969–76, 1982–86), the Socialist International's orientation had become anti-Israeli and anti-American. In 1977, it advocated the establishment of a Palestinian state and the recognition of the PLO as the sole representative for the Palestinians, in spite of the PLO's commitment to the annihilation of Israel. Although many socialists were reluctant to bow to the threats of a notorious international terrorist, Kreisky invited Arafat to Vienna on July 7, 1979 with all the honors due to a head of state. Willy Brandt, who by then was head of the Socialist International, welcomed him there.[10] The Declaration issued by the Eleventh Arab Summit Conference, held at Amman, Jordan, from November 25 to 27, 1980, stated:

> The Conference stressed the need for endeavours to ensure the continued support and backing of the group of socialist States for Arab [Palestinian]

rights and to strengthen co-operation with that group with a view to the promotion of joint interests and the furtherance and development of the support of those States for Arab rights in such a way as to increase Arab steadfastness capabilities. (See appendix 3)

It was during this period that Third World ideology developed in Latin America. Sustained by the Church's "Liberation theology," it swept over Europe and became a vehicle of Palestinianism. In its planning of a world anti-Zionist campaign, the Amman Arab Summit decided that

The Conference reviewed Arab relations with other countries throughout the world and stressed the need for closer ties and relations with the Islamic States and the Organization of the Islamic Conference, for a strengthening of the role of non-aligned movement and for co-operation with States members of that movement and with the group of Latin American States.

The conference also emphasized the need to promote solidarity with the Organization of African Unity and the states of the African continent, as well as to bolster Afro-Arab cooperation and consolidate ties and relations. In the 1980s, most of the non-Muslim Third World countries that had previously had fruitful economic and other contacts with Israel broke off their diplomatic relations under Soviet, Arab/Muslim, and French pressures. The Arab Summit was followed by the Third Islamic Summit Conference meeting in Mecca-Taif, held from January 25 to 28, 1981, which reaffirmed

that the Palestine Question is the core of the struggle against Zionism, and that Israel's continued refusal to withdraw from the occupied Palestinian and Arab territories and its flouting of the inalienable national rights of the Arab Palestinian people constitute a flagrant violation of the principles of the Islamic Conference Organization and UN Charter, the Universal Declaration of Human Rights and of the principles of International Law.

whereas in fact, the main principles of the Islamic Conference, which are based on *shari'a,* are totally opposed to the international secular instruments mentioned.

From the 1970s on, the policy of the European governments, particularly France and Austria, was determined by their arms sales to Arab countries and by their oil and energy requirements. By 1976—in spite of its campaign of assassination and abduction, its practice of air piracy and hostage-taking, and its policy of ethnic cleansing in Lebanon—European heads of state were actively courting the PLO. Thus, France became a protector of Palestinian rights, establishing close relations with the PLO and even opposed Egyptian President Sadat's visit to Jerusalem in November 1977 and the Israel-Egypt Camp David peace process that led to the peace treaty of January 1979.[11] Western countries simply followed the orders from the Arab and Islamic Summits. In Amman, the Arab leaders reaffirmed their rejection of the Camp David Accords, which, in their eyes, had lured the Egyptian leadership into the trap of plotting against the Arab nation. The Arab leaders emphasized their determination to defy those agreements, render them ineffective, and nullify them. The Mecca-Taif declaration "Strongly condemns the Egyptian government for proceeding to normalize relations with the Zionist entity and considers it a denial of the principles of Jihad and a danger to Islamic principles, ideals, heritage, culture and civilization; and decides to suspend Egypt's membership in the Non-alignment Movement."

Arab and EC declarations (1973, 1974, 1977, 1980, and many others) are strikingly similar concerning the PLO. At the Mecca-Taif Summit it was stated that the PLO is the sole legitimate representative of the Palestinian people and

is fully entitled to represent that people and to participate independently and on an equal footing in all Conferences, activities and international fora connected with the Palestinian cause and the Arab-Israeli conflict, with a view to achieving the inalienable national rights of the Palestinian people. No solution can be comprehensive, just and acceptable unless the PLO participates in its formulation and accepts it as an independent party and on an equal footing and parity with the rest of the parties concerned. No other party is entitled to claim the right to represent or negotiate on the question of Palestine, its people, its territory and its rights, otherwise it shall be considered null and void and by no means legally binding.

Since then—and until today—the EC/EU support for the PLO and Arafat has been unshakable and imposed on Israel with an iron fist by Europe. In fact, it has thwarted every possibility of peace. The EC reluctance to recognize the Camp David Accords obeyed the following Mecca Summit declaration

That no other party concerned should unilaterally seek a solution to the Palestine Question or to the Arab-Zionist conflict, that resistance to the Camp David Accords, should be pursued, their consequences, effects or any initiative emanating therefrom voided, moreover, material and moral assistance should be extended to the Arab Palestinian People in the occupied Palestinian territories, and their resistance against the autonomy conspiracy reinforced.

Article 5 of the Resolutions

Reaffirms its full and effective support to the Palestinian people in their legitimate struggle under the leadership of the Palestine Liberation Organization, their legitimate and sole representative inside and outside the occupied homeland, with a view to liberating it, restoring their inalienable national right in Palestine.

European governments have shown deference while being co-opted in the pursuit of these Islamic designs. The constant negative references to Israel by the present EU are the consequence of the centrality of Israel in the Arab League countries' foreign policies. From the beginning of the Dialogue, as we have seen, Israel was a permanent and prominent feature of the EC-Arab relationship. It should be noted that France's Arab policy in particular is constantly expressed in anti-Zionist overtones. This rhetoric throws doubt on the permanency and legitimacy of Israel, which was allegedly created by Jewish colonists on Arab Palestinian lands. On the subject of terrorism in France, French historian Jacques Frémeaux noted in 1995: "The French are almost totally spared the terrorism which attacks the nationals, the interests, or the supporters of Israel." After citing a few cases of this terrorism, he asks, "Is this relatively privileged situation the fruit of a more or less tacit entente with movements capable of organizing terrorist acts?"[12]

How should one understand this "privileged situation"? Frémeaux explains it as follows: "One must obviously also take into account France's Arab friendships with the PLO in particular, but also with the collection of states that support the most radical Palestinian movements." By supporting Khomeini's agents in 1978 and giving asylum to Khomeini himself, France even helped facilitate the emergence of the first twentieth-century radical Islamic state in Iran after the fall of the Shah, a former ally of America and Israel. Many of France's politicians and intellectuals were enamored with Khomeini and his brand of Islam. The most prestigious among them lined up to remove their shoes and pay their respects to the old man in his tent in Neauphle-le-Château, near Paris.

Arab antisemitism and anti-Zionism were implanted extensively in Europe through the conceptual framework set up by the Euro-Arab Dialogue, and its planning of "a movement of [public] opinion" to support the Arab anti-Israeli policy. Arab requests were backed by the Euro-Arab parliamentary associations—the powerful Arab/Muslim lobby—and were transmitted to the highest political, university, and religious authorities engaged in the EAD. There they were given practical application in the media, the universities, the trade unions, and a variety of political and cultural activities. This policy followed the Resolutions of the 1969 Cairo International Conference in support of the Arab Peoples. The Arab states contributed vast sums to universities, centers for Islamic studies, international communication agencies, and private and governmental organizations in order to win over world opinion.[13] This trend continued throughout the years; in 1980, the Amman Arab Summit declared that it decided to pursue its efforts on behalf of the Arab Palestinians within the framework of the United Nations, its specialized agencies and institutions and conferences of international organizations, to co-ordinate Arab positions and achieve co-operation in accordance with the principles and objectives of the joint Arab programme of action and the policies established by institutions of the League of Arab States.

This propaganda, an effective war machine, was labeled in Europe "the re-establishment of even-handed judgment." In fact, it was a *jihad,* as stated by the 1981 Third Islamic Summit Conference in its Mecca-Taif Resolution, "Declaration of Holy Jihad" (full text in Appendix 4, from UN document):

The Third Islamic Summit Conference . . . decided: to declare holy Jihad, as the duty of every Muslim, man or woman, ordained by the Shariah and glorious traditions of Islam; to call upon all Muslims, living inside or outside Islamic countries, to discharge this duty by contributing each according to his capacity in the cause of Allah Almighty, Islamic brotherhood, and righteousness.

In declaring Holy Jihad, Islamic states specified that they want to explain to the world that "Holy Jihad is an Islamic concept which may not be misinterpreted or misconstrued" and that it would be put into effect "by incessant consultations among Islamic states." European collaboration in this *jihad* was called "a just cause." American resistance to Muslim *fatwas* provoked Arab furor and European reprobation. The summit decided that every Islamic state would devote all its resources to "weakening the Israeli economy; stopping the political, economic and financial assistance received by Israel; endeavouring to turn national stands at the international level into friendly ones [to Arabs], and antagonistic or inimical stands into neutral or friendly ones."

The major themes of the Eurabian antisemitic culture were borrowed from the Arab world, where most had already been diffused since the 1950s. Mainly, they centered around: 1) denying the Holocaust; 2) claiming that Jews exploit the *Shoah* to blackmail Europe to Israel's benefit; 3) delegitimizing the State of Israel; 4) attributing Israel's ancient history to the Palestinian Arab Muslims; 5) promoting the destruction of Israel as a source of the world's redemption; 6) boycotting Israel culturally and isolating it on the international scene—a policy which recreated the status of the ghetto Jews in Christianity and of the *dhimmis* in Islam; 7) laying blame on Europe for the resurgence of Israel; 8) presenting Israel's resistance to a policy of elimination as a threat to world peace; 9) spreading a Christianophobia wrapped in anti-Americanism. Concerning Jerusalem, EU governments yielded to Islamic resolutions issued by the Arab and Islamic Summits in 1980 and 1981 (article 7), to all countries throughout the world to refrain from

• Signing any agreements in Al Quds [Jerusalem];

• Making official visits to Al Quds;

• Conducting official talks in Al Quds;

• Presenting the Credentials of Heads of Diplomatic missions in Al Quds;

Member states, meanwhile, were directed to use official, nonofficial, and other mass media outlets to mobilize their people psychologically for *jihad* to liberate Al Quds.

As Judaism was the target of Nazi ideology, so Israel's very existence is a central target of Euro-Arab policy. In the 1970s and 1980s, European public opinion, including that of intellectuals and many of the clergy, was still disinclined to Judeophobia and presented a solid obstacle to Arab goals. It is precisely this resistance that the Eurabians tried to overcome with their all-powerful network, financed by Arab and EU funds.

Already in the 1970s, the all-encompassing ideology of Euro-Arab symbiosis produced by the EAD inevitably led the EC to tolerate Palestinian activities, including terrorist acts, on its own territory. Later on it would provide a basis for the justification of Arab terror against Israel, passively legitimize the PLO terrorist infrastructure, and allow the inculcation of hatred in Palestinian and UNRWA schools. Some churches and their media networks became the most active agents of the legitimization of Palestinian terrorism. Political pressure and the promotion and funding of anti-Israeli clergy involved in the EAD swept away internal Christian opposition. A great number of Muslims who were wanted or even condemned in some Arab states for terrorist activities received political asylum in Germany, Britain, France, Italy, and other EC/EU countries. For instance, until 9/11 it was state policy in Germany that authorities should merely monitor, but do nothing to hinder, Islamist organizations and individuals based in the country—as long as they refrained from harming the Federal Republic. Abu Abbas, the Palestinian terrorist who hijacked the American cruise ship *Achille Lauro* in 1985 and threw an American invalid in his wheelchair overboard, was captured by an American force and held at its military base in Italy; the Italians released him rapidly. In a small but well-documented book, John Laffin details PLO connections with European leaders and the Christian religious hierarchy.[14]

After the European Parliament had honored Arafat in September 1988, the French, Italian, Greek, and Spanish governments were said to be seeking "an allusion to a necessary division of Palestine based on the 1947 UN Partition plan"[15]—that is to say, the dismembering of Israel. These anti-Israeli policies went hand in hand with massive business dealings with the

Arab world, including arms and military technology contracts involving substantial profits. The latter also accounted for the EEC's leniency toward the immigration into Europe of millions of Muslims, welcomed and protected by the various Churches, NGOs, and other organizations softened up by the EAD.

Unaccountability for terrorism began with the EC's blaming Israel for Palestinian terror in the 1970s–80s. The Barcelona process institutionalized this subversion of justice. The EU's war against Islamophobia and Arabophobia initiated the paradoxical indictment of the U.S. and Israel for Islamist terrorism. On October 14, 2003, the archbishop of Canterbury, Dr. Rowan Williams, lecturing at the London Royal Institute for International Affairs, urged America to recognize that terrorists can "have serious moral goals." He said that in its criticism of al-Qaeda, America ignored this point, along with the fact that terrorists pursued an aim both "intelligible and desirable." Thus, he said, America "loses the power of self-criticism and becomes trapped in a self-referential morality."[16]

In a strangely perverse quid pro quo, although Islamists invariably invoke the Qur'an and their religious texts to justify their war against the infidels and the Western seat of infidelity, the European Union brushes these justifications aside and instead identifies Israel as the cause of terrorism. In an April 1996 article in *Le Monde*, just before an official visit to Lebanon and Egypt, President Jacques Chirac—expressing the opinion of the European Union—was quoted as stating that "the slowness of the peace process and the Palestinian people's frustration" were the cause of Islamic terrorism.[17] French politicians constantly repeated this view to the media. Thus, in an interview with a leading Swiss newspaper in July 2003, Pascal Boniface, the socialist director of the French Institute of International and Strategic Relations, declared that the Israeli-Palestinian conflict was at the core of the problems between the Muslim and Western worlds.[18] Such a remark wittingly ignored the countless Qur'an verses, *hadiths*, and Muslim religious jurisprudence, inciting the faithful to wage war against infidels, including Christians, and the history of Christendom's constant defeats and retreats in the face of a millennium of *jihad* conquests and territorial advances in Europe and elsewhere.

Boniface's opinion was reminiscent of Nazi theory, which focused a multitude of problems on one central cause: Judaism and Jews. He evidently wished his hearers to believe that a country populated barely by six and a half million Jews, Christians, Muslims, Druzes, and Bedouins was at the core of the conflict between two billion Christians and well over a billion Muslims, who shared between them the greater part of the globe. Such opinions were also expressed by many European politicians. But Islamist terrorism, which has developed on all continents—even recently in Thailand—is grounded in Islamic policies emanating from doctrines that justify them and that pre-date—by a thousand years and more—the restoration of the State of Israel in 1948. If Israel is indeed at the center, it is as a scapegoat—or a decoy. Writing in 1982, Laffin noticed that the major propaganda victory for the PLO was the "propagation of the idea that the 'Palestinian issue' is the major threat to peace in the Middle East. Linked with this is the secondary notion that the Palestinian affair is closely bounded up with the 'oil issue.' If the first problem could be solved, PLO propaganda has insisted, a solution to the second must follow. This presentation is so insistently preached that politicians in many countries have come to produce it as their own idea." He recalled that the Palestinian and oil issues were linked in speeches made by Chancellor Kreisky, EEC leaders, as well as in the Venice Declaration, which referred to the Palestinian issue as the principal threat to Middle East peace.[19]

Elaine Sciolino illustrated this thinking well in an article: "Both Chirac and Villepin have long defined the Israeli-Palestinian war, rather than Iraq or terrorism, as the most serious of all global crises."[20] In March 2003, Prime Minister Tony Blair of Britain and other Europeans won a pledge from Bush to pursue the Road Map before the end of the Iraqi war, as a gesture of appeasement toward Arabs and Eurabians. In fact, this Arab requirement has been reiterated continuously by EU politicians, including Tony Blair even in his speech to the U.S. Congress on July 17, 2003.

In the same article, Sciolino quotes French Foreign Minister Dominique de Villepin spicing his French with an Arabic expression: "Because it is the mother of all crises, because it is fed by a profound feeling of injustice, we will only be able to build a durable peace that is built on justice." These words could easily have come from Arafat or Saddam Hussein. Two weeks before this, Chris Patten, the EU commissioner for external relations, also asserted that the lack of peace in the Middle East produced terrorism.[21]

In the second issue of *The Voice of Jihad*, the new biweekly online magazine identified with Al-Qaeda, Sheikh Nasser Al-Najdi wrote,

> Islam is an all-encompassing religion. It is a religion for people and for regimes. . . . At a time when people are given the choice [of believing] in Islam or paying Jizya [a poll tax paid by non-Muslims living under Muslim rule], Islam is the only alternative for the countries [of the world]. . . . Therefore, the crime of the tyrants in infidel [i.e., non-Muslim] countries, who do not rule according to Allah's law, is an enormous sin . . . and we are obliged to fight them and initiate until they convert to Islam, or until Muslims rule the country and he who does not convert to Islam pays Jizya. . . . That is the religious ruling with regard to infidel countries and all the more so with regard to those who rule Muslim countries by way of the cursed law [i.e., a man-made law].[22]

In an interview in October 2003, Abd Al-'Aziz bin 'Issa bin Abd Al-Mohsen, known as Abu Hajjer and a high-ranking al-Qaeda member, stated that his goal was to wave the banner of monotheism . . . and expel the enemies of Allah—the Jews and the Crusaders—from the land of the two holy places, to conquer the Muslim nations and restore them to their previous state. And may Allah lengthen our days to allow us to infuriate the enemies of Allah, kill them, and strike them by the sword until they either join the religion of Allah or we kill every last one of them. Our model is [the Prophet] Mohammad, who said to the infidels of Qureish: "I have brought the slaughter upon you."[23]

Abu Hajjer concluded the interview with this message to the youth he trained: "You must do something, you must fight the enemies of Allah, the Crusaders and the Jews, and become a bone in their throats and hearts." Such declarations have been repeated endlessly since the seventh and eighth centuries. They are not provoked by circumstantial modern events; they belong to a civilization created by and based on *jihad, jizya* for infidels, and dhimmitude.

With the upsurge of Arab vilification during the operations in Iraq, the foreign ministers of France and Britain stressed the urgent need for the Bush administration to get more involved in the Middle East peace process—in other words, to pressure Israel to appease the Arabs. British Foreign Secretary Jack Straw and his French colleague Dominique de Villepin agreed that the suppression of violence in the Middle East was the only way to bring stability to the world. One can hardly imagine that the Chechen, Kosovo, Macedonian, Kurdish, Iraqi, Sudanese, Nigerian, Algerian, Kashmir, Indonesian, Philippines, and Thai conflicts would cease because of a change in Israel's policy. Hostage taking, ritual throat slitting, the killing of infidels and Muslim apostates are lawful, carefully described, and highly praised *jihad* tactics recorded, over the centuries, in countless legal treaties on *jihad*. Yet Straw and de Villepin declared to the press that the Arab and Islamic world were angered by the injustice felt by the Palestinians, and that this was the most important issue in the world and in Euro-Arab relations.[24] During a rally in Paris against the Iraqi war, French Arab teenagers chanted slogans and pledged war and martyrdom in the name of Palestinians and Iraq and against Israel, shouting "*Allahu Akhbar!* God is more powerful than the United States."[25]

The March 2003 war in Iraq has provided another conspiracy theory for some Europeans: that Israel controls America. The accusation that Israelis control American policy is a well-entrenched belief in Muslim countries and now, it seems, is shared by French politicians. Pierre Lellouche, deputy and vice-president of NATO's Parliamentary Assembly, reported that French Minister de Villepin told his NATO delegation two weeks before the Coalition war against Iraq in March 2003 that "the hawks in the American administration have been totally co-opted by Sharon," the Israeli prime minister.[26] This remake of the *Protocols* is spreading from its French source throughout the world. Professor Matthias Küntzel reported in an address he delivered at Yale University on April 11, 2003 that Muhammad Atta and his accomplices believed that Jews were controlling America. Such a declaration was made by the leading core of the Hamburg al-Qaeda cell at their trial in Hamburg. The accused were convinced "that German and French policy always got along with the Arab countries." Villepin here was in good company.[27] On April 14, 2003, on the Channel 2 French television program, the former French socialist minister of defense, Jean-Pierre Chevènement, declared that Christian fundamentalists together with the "partisans of Great Israel control the American government." Richard Perle, then a Pentagon adviser to the Defense Policy Board, was one of those invited via satellite on the program. Chevènement had been the president of the France-Iraq association.

The continuous symmetry between the statements of the European ministers and those of their Muslim colleagues is stunning. The Libyan leader Muammar al-Qaddafi affirmed in a televised interview that Jewish groups controlled Washington's foreign policy—the same charge that Chevènement made. Qaddafi also alleged that America's policy provoked September 11.[28] Marwan Bishara, a teacher of international relations at the American University of Paris, expressed the same Muslim refusal to be held accountable for the crimes of Muslims. He judged America and Israel responsible for the carrying out of suicide attacks by Palestinians and Muslims of the Middle East.[29] This view conforms to *jihad* ideology, which can never be criticized, being a war to extend Allah's dominion. At the opening of the Organization of the Islamic Conference (OIC) summit in Malaysia on October 16, 2003, Malaysian Prime Minister Mahathir Mohamad urged Muslims to unite against Jews who, he alleged, rule the world by proxy and get others to fight and die for them. He received a standing ovation from all delegates (full text in Appendix 8).[30]

In recent years, the Islamist concept of *jihad* against the infidel has filtered through to the public, despite obfuscation in the Western press. From Indonesia to the Philippines, from Chechmiya and Afghanistan to Sudan, from Egypt to Algeria, and from Gaza to New York, London, and Paris, calls to *jihad* repeat the same themes and are integrated into the same ideological structure. Such homogeneity cannot be improvised. Nor is it the result of circumstantial external factors. On the contrary, it is integrated into a permanent historical trend that is based on doctrinal, legal and cultural foundations.

Today, diverse conflicts are tearing Muslim countries apart. Islamist movements develop on different fronts and at a variety of levels. Strategies of territorial reconquest of the *dar al-harb* are being developed in Kashmir, Indonesia, the Philippines, on different Balkan fronts, in the Caucasus, Spain, in Israel, Lebanon, Sudan, Nigeria, and elsewhere. In the West, the

Islamists are fighting for the in-depth Islamization of millions of Muslim immigrants who have supposedly been contaminated by the civilization of the infidels (*kufr*). Their efforts to convert Christians are having considerable success in pro-Palestinian and anti-Jewish Christian circles. Since the Islamic doctrine regards the whole world as Allah's patrimony entrusted to the *umma*, from an Islamic viewpoint the right to immigrate and settle in foreign countries is also theologically justified. Muslims invoke the rights of Christians in Islamic lands in order to demand the establishment of the *shari'a* in the EU. But the equation is invalid. Arabs expelled Jews and Christians from Arabia, the cradle of the Arabs and of Islam. Christian immigrant workers residing there over the last decades have suffered from severe discrimination. All over the Islamic world, indigenous non-Muslim minorities have been consigned to the status of *dhimmis* in their own countries. They were **not** foreign immigrants. Hence, the historical and legal condition of *dhimmi* communities is not the same as that of the millions of Muslim new immigrants in Europe and the Americas. For a proper comparison, the huge Muslim immigration to Europe should be compared to a hypothetical Western immigration in modern times into Muslim countries—including Arabia—on the same demographic scale, and with rights equal to those of Muslims.

The EC/EU's immigration policy promoted the Islamic goal of an Islamized Europe and provided it with very solid foundations. The real figures of this immigration were concealed from the public—as if it constituted a state secret. The agreements between the EC/EU and the Arab League facilitated the exportation of the immigrants' culture to the host countries as an inalienable right of the immigrants. It has created an obstacle to their integration—all the more so as the bonds with the countries of emigration were encouraged and supported to the utmost by cultural, political, and economic agreements between European and Arab governments, along with collaboration and exchanges at the university and international level. The EAD's European agents accused its adversaries of racism, in a cynical attempt to foreclose any discussion on the criminality and religious fanaticism of certain sections of a population that refused to integrate into Western society.

Since the EU, aware of the opposition of the Arab League, did not plan an integration policy for the millions of Muslim immigrants, the host population was asked to make the effort to harmonize with the immigrant. The policy imposed by the EAD apparatus, endorsed by the highest authorities of each country of the EU, revolved around six main themes: 1) the Andalusian utopia; 2) the alleged Islamic cultural superiority over Europe, and hence the inferiority of the latter; 3) the creation of a Western Palestinian cult, (Palestinocracy); 4) European self-guilt; 5) anti-Zionism/antisemitism; 6) anti-Americanism and Christianophobia.

Even if, in the early 1970s, the Islamist resurgence was somewhat obscured by an apparent secular and socialist Arab discourse, Europe had thirteen centuries of *jihad* experience on its lands, at its frontiers and in its cities. The French project for uniting the two shores of the Mediterranean, inspired by fear as much as by greed and misplaced ambition, led to the surrender of the EC/EU to Arab policies. The hope that it would guarantee security through tribute, support to terrorist states and groups, and anti-Zionism, has proved to be a grave miscalculation. Islam's entrenchment in Europe, reinforced by numerous European converts coming from antisemitic, anti-Western, communist, and post-Christian backgrounds, has exacerbated Europe's dangerous societal, tectonic drift. Provided with generous funds, EAD activists have established a trans-European network of Islamic associations—as planned by the EAD program, with state encouragement—thereby confusing real, peaceful multiculturalism with an illusory respite from an endless *jihad*.

Faced with Islamic militancy, the hopes for a "peaceful multiculturalism" are dwindling. One cannot suspect the conceivers of EAD policy of gross ignorance. All European participants in the Dialogue were specialists of the Arab/Muslim world. Diplomats, politicians, academics, journalists, Christian theologians engaged in Qur'anic studies—they all had strong affinities with, and often long professional contacts or jobs, in Arab countries. This knowledge of Islam might explain the European governments' reluctance to insist that the millions of Muslim migrants should be integrated into the host societies. Simply put, Muslims are traditionally forbidden by their religion to adopt the laws of non-Muslims; hence, Arab governments negotiated special arrangements through the EAD for the preservation of the migrants' separateness, particularisms, and for maintaining them under their own jurisdiction.[31]

13

The Andalusian Utopia

The Euro-Arab policy planned by numerous Euro-Arab organizations strove to legitimize the growing Muslim settlement in Europe by invoking the centuries of Muslim presence in European countries. Muslim domination—whether in the Iberian Peninsula or the Balkans—was depicted as benign and enlightened governance. Islam, in this view, had a historic legitimacy in Europe; it was not a foreign hostile intruder imposed by war and conquest. It belonged to Europe, and Europe was its rightful homeland. It was therefore only just to grant to Arab and Muslim countries a privileged status as sources of immigration to Europe.

Apologists for Muslim immigration invoked the invaluable historic contribution that Muslims had made to European civilization and the alleged tolerance of the Arab Andalusian caliphate. The peaceful coexistence over centuries of Muslims, Christians and Jews in the Iberian Peninsula under benign Islamic rule became a compulsory nostalgic illusion. This "golden age" of blissful Andalusian dhimmitude for the Christian Spanish majority and the Jews in the Middle Ages would provide a model for the social and political projects of Euro-Arab fusion in the twenty-first century. This plan for the future, which was conceived mainly in French academic laboratories of Islamology, was rooted in the dogma of an idyllic past of peaceful Christian-Jewish-Muslim coexistence that had only been marred by the Crusades waged from 1096 by Christian fanaticism and, in the modern period, by Zionism that was allegedly supported by Europe. This dogma, embedded in misleading economic and geostrategic interests, was strongly defended by doctrinaire Eurabians and seemed irrefutable. Yet it was similar to the communist paradise in that it was an object of faith, not of objective demonstration.

The myth of Islamic tolerance was born in France during the seventeenth and eighteenth centuries, and exerted an influence on political thinkers of the Enlightenment. In the nineteenth century, the myth fulfilled an ideological and political function, serving the colonial ambitions of France in the Middle East and Great Britain's interest in preserving the Ottoman Empire as a bulwark against Russian and French expansionism.

This policy served also to contain the Balkan pan-Slavic upsurge, as well as Greek Panhellenism and Hapsburg expansionism in the Turkish European provinces. As a political and ideological weapon, it justified the defense of the territorial integrity of the Ottoman Empire's European possessions—a defense which Britain undertook on condition that the Ottoman Empire modernize its institutions and emancipate its non-Muslim subjects.[1] During the twentieth century, the tolerance myth continued to be employed in support of the pro-Muslim policies of European statesmen.

France, meanwhile, adopted an Arab version of the tolerance theme to serve its own colonial ambitions in the Ottoman Arab territories. After World War I and the genocide of the Armenians, which was fueled by Islamic *jihad* ideology and accompanied by massacres of Assyrian Christians, the myth of "Ottoman tolerance" was replaced by that of the "peaceful coexistence under the first Arab caliphs." Like its predecessor, this slogan served the political interests of the European powers in their Arab and Muslim colonies and protectorates.

In fact, there are no historical proofs of the first Arab caliphs' tolerance in the Christian lands conquered by *jihad*. It is well known that in the first century of Arab colonization, the situation was chaotic. The indigenous population of the Middle East at that time was Christian and Jewish, with Zoroastrians predominant in Persia. The Muslims represented an army of occupation, formed from numerous tribes gathered from all Arabia and expanded by the constant flow of Arab colonists settling in the conquered lands. Arab caliphs used Christian notables and patriarchs to impose despotic rule over their overwhelmingly Christian *dhimmi* populations.

Nonetheless, the theme of seventh-century Arab tolerance formed the cornerstone of modern Muslim-Christian Arab nationalism in Palestine, and an ideological weapon against any claims to independence by Jews and Christian *dhimmi* peoples. In the 1970s, this theme was integrated into the larger framework of Eurabian doctrine, promoted by the EEC's foreign ministers, politicians, and intellectuals involved in the EAD as a device facilitate the demographic and cultural Arabization of Europe.

European economic interests in the Arab world required a lax and complacent policy toward the Muslim immigrants streaming into Europe. They were welcomed as builders of the future Euro-Arab alliance: "Eurabia." The EAD's cultural sections devised two main themes for imposing the absorption of millions of foreign Muslim immigrants on a reluctant European population, often afflicted with economic recession, insecurity, and terrorism. The Andalusian myth overshadowed the debate on immigration, while the theme of Christian and Western guilt smothered attempts to discuss the problems concretely.[2] That of Andalusia provided Eurabia's proponents with abundant arguments to check the growth of anti-immigration movements that could have poisoned Euro-Arab economic exchanges and obstructed the emergence of a future Euro-Arab entity. The myth of Andalusia introduced into Europe the same historical amnesia that had long formed an important part of the protective mechanisms employed by Eastern Christian *dhimmi* communities.

Iberia, with Portugal, was conquered in 710–716 CE by Arab tribes originating in northern, central, and south Arabia. Massive Berber and Arab immigration and colonization of the peninsula followed the conquest. Most churches were converted into mosques. Although the conquest had been planned and conducted in conjunction with a powerful Iberian Christian dissident royal faction, including a bishop, it proceeded along the lines of a classic *jihad*—with massive pillaging, slavery, deportations, and killings.[3] Toledo, which had only submitted to the Arabs in 711 or 712, revolted in 713. The town was punished by pillage; all its notables had their throats cut. In 730, the Cerdagne (in Septimania, near Barcelona) was ravaged and a bishop was burned alive. By the end of the eighth century, the rulers of North Africa and Andalusia had introduced Malikism, one of the most rigorous schools of Sunni Muslim jurisprudence. Subsequently they repressed other currents of opinion in the Islamic faith. In the mid-twentieth century, before Eurabian political correctness began to dominate historical publications, the distinguished French scholar on Andalusia, Evariste Lévy-Provençal, could write: "The Muslim Andalusian state thus appears from its earliest origins as the defender and champion of a jealous orthodoxy, more and more ossified in a blind respect for a rigid doctrine, suspecting and condemning in advance the least effort of rational speculation."[4]

In regions under stable Islamic control, Jews and Christians were tolerated as *dhimmis*—as they were elsewhere in other Islamic lands. Thus, they were forbidden by Islamic law to build new churches or synagogues or restore old ones. Segregated in special quarters, they had to wear distinctive clothing that easily marked them out for discrimination. Subjected to the *jizya* tax mandated by Islamic law (Qur'an 9:29) and other heavy ransoms, the Christian peasantry formed a servile class attached to the Arab domains. Many abandoned their land and fled to the towns. Harsh reprisals accompanied by mutilations and crucifixions prevented the Mozarabs (Christian *dhimmis*) from calling for help from the Christian kings of Europe. Moreover, if one *dhimmi* harmed a Muslim, the whole community would lose its status of protection—leaving it open to pillage, enslavement, and arbitrary killing.[5]

The humiliating status imposed on the *dhimmis* and the confiscation of their land [6] provoked many revolts, punished by massacres, as in Toledo (761, 784–86, 797). After another Toledan revolt in 806, seven hundred inhabitants were executed. Insurrections erupted in Saragossa from 781 to 881, Cordova (805), Merida (805–13, 828 and the following years, and later in 868), and yet again in Toledo (811–19). The insurgents were crucified, as prescribed in the Qur'an (5:37), a punishment still applied in the Sudan today. The revolt in Cordova of 818 was crushed by three days of massacres and pillage, with three hundred notables crucified and twenty thousand families expelled.[7]

Feuding was endemic in Andalusian cities between different sectors of the population—Arab and Berber colonizers, Iberian Muslim converts (*muwalladun*) and Christian *dhimmis* (Mozarabs). There were rarely periods of peace in the Amirate of Cordova (756–912), nor later.

Contrary to the prevailing myth, *Al-Andalus* represented the land of *jihad* par excellence. Every year, and sometimes twice a year, the Muslim rulers sent raiding expeditions to ravage the Christian Spanish kingdoms to the north, the Basque regions, or France and the Rhone valley, bringing back booty and slaves. Andalusian corsairs attacked and invaded along the Sicilian and Italian coasts. They journeyed even as far as the Aegean Islands, looting and burning as they went. Thousands of people were deported to slavery in Andalusia, where the caliph kept a militia of tens of thousand of Christian slaves brought from all parts of Christian Europe (the *Saqaliba*) and a harem filled with captured Christian women. Society was sharply divided along ethnic and religious lines, with the Arab tribes at the top of the hierarchy, followed by the Berbers who were never recognized as equals, despite their Islamization. Lower on the ladder came the *muwalladun* converts and, at the very bottom, the *dhimmi* Christians and Jews.

The Andalusian jurist Ibn Abdun (d. 1134) wrote in his legal treatise, which was used by authorities in Seville, that Jews and Christians, being Satan's party (Qur'an 58:20), should be detested and avoided. To be recognized, they should be obliged to wear a distinctive sign, as a disgrace for them. Ibn Abdun forbade the sale of scientific books to them under the pretext that they translated them and attributed them to their coreligionists and bishops.[8] In fact, plagiarism is difficult to prove, since entire Jewish and Christian libraries in synagogues, churches, and monasteries were looted and destroyed all over the Islamic empire. Another renowned eleventh-century Andalusian jurist, Ibn Hazm, wrote that Allah established the infidels' ownership of their property merely to provide booty for Muslims.[9]

Despite brilliant cultural achievements and occasional periods of tolerance in the tenth and eleventh centuries, Andalusian history is one of cruelty, war, and slavery. Charles-Emmanuel Dufourcq (d. 1982)—a professor of medieval history at Paris's Nanterre University and a scholar and specialist on Muslim-Christian-Jewish relations in the Maghreb, Spain, and Sicily—described its society in somber colors. Nevertheless, the EAD integrated the Andalusian myth into its dogma as a support for its political actions.

Obviously, the belief in peaceful coexistence under the *shari'a* law strengthens Islamic doctrine. It confirms the perfection of the *shari'a*, even in one of its most severe versions, Malikism, which was applied in the Maghreb and in Andalusia. It should be remembered that the *shari'a* was the only legislation governing the *dar al-Islam* until European rule, influence, and pressure for modernization was exerted in the nineteenth century.

Today, the slightest criticism of the *dhimmi* status is rejected, as it undermines the doctrine of the perfection of Islamic law and government. In the past, praise of the tolerance and justice of Islamic government, expressed with all due gratitude, constituted an integral part of the *dhimmi*'s obligations. The *dhimma* treaties concerning the "protection" accorded to *dhimmi* peoples subjugated by *jihad* specified that criticism of Islamic law constituted a serious offense, associated in some cases with blasphemy.[10]

Currently, Jewish and Christian *dhimmi* networks spread all over the Western world the theme of a happy, peaceful, millennial coexistence under Islamic law. Those taken over by the Turks vaunt Ottomanism; others, sponsored by the Arab League, glorify the Muslim-Christian religious symbiosis of the Arab Empire. A fertile soil for the blossoming of historical negationism, this theme has become the cornerstone on which a multicultural Eurabia is being built. In *La Vie Quotidienne*, published in 1978, Dufourcq addressed the ambiguity of words that prepare the way for historical revisionism, affirming that one might "even think that our closing 20th century encourages us to wonder whether the upheaval carried out on our continent by Islamic penetration more than a thousand years ago is not likely to recur tomorrow, with other methods."[11]

In his book on Islamic totalitarianism, Alexandre Del Valle examines the symbolism of the Andalusian myth that is used to support Muslim political claims on Europe. The myth particularly inspires the anti-Christian "Association for the Return of Andalusia to Islam," which was founded by Christian converts to Islam, communists and neo-Nazis from all over Europe.[12] Del Valle describes the activities of people affiliated with the Vatican and other Christian bodies in adopting, engineering, and extending a European Islamophile culture. The American writer on Islamic *jihad*, Robert Spencer, has detected the same endorsement of Islam by the Church in North America.[13] We now know that the EAD agreements between universities, cultural centers, publishers, and Churches instigated this cultural and media subversion of history targeting Western societies.

Islamic Cultural Superiority over Europe

The tendency to overestimate the debt owed by Western civilization to the grandeur of medieval Islam, despite archaeological and historical evidence to the contrary, first came to the fore in resolutions and recommendations issued in the Arab world in September 1968. Shortly after the Arab

defeat in the Six–Day War, the Fourth Conference of the Academy of Islamic Research of al-Azhar University in Cairo—comprising seventy-seven
prominent *ulemas* and guests—raised this debt in resounding terms. One
of its resolutions stated:

> The conference recommends the publication of a detailed book in diverse
> tongues, to be circulated on a large scale, pointing out the viewpoint of Is-
> lamic civilization regarding the Rights of Man and drawing a comparison
> between it and that of Western Civilization.
>
> The conference recommends the preparation of a historical and scientific
> study explaining the impact of Muslim civilization and teachings on the
> movements of political, social, and religious reform in the West, since the
> age of European Renaissance.[14]

Heeding this call—whether knowingly or motivated by other factors—a
spate of works written since the 1970s by distinguished Western Arabists
has magnified the Islamic contribution to European civilization.[15] This endeavor, as we have seen, was promoted and monitored by the EAD. Few
other opinions could be published.

In September 1991, the Parliamentary Assembly of the Council of Europe held an assembly debate on the contribution of Islamic civilization
to European culture deferring to the al-Azhar connoisseurs of European
civilization.[16] Speakers recalled that this was simply a follow-up to a previous
Resolution on the Jewish contribution to European culture in 1987.[17] After
a colloquy conducted by the Committee on Culture and Education in Paris,
the Parliamentary Assembly issued some pertinent recommendations:

1. The colloquy showed that, in addition to Christianity and Judaism, Islam
   in its different forms has over the centuries had an influence on European civilisation and everyday life, and not only in countries with a Muslim population such as Turkey.
6. Islam has, however, suffered and is still suffering from misrepresentation,
   for example through hostile or oriental stereotypes, and there is very little
   awareness in Europe either of the importance of Islam's past contribution
   or of Islam's potentially positive role in European society today. Historical
   errors, educational eclecticism and the over-simplified approach of the
   media are responsible for this situation.
9. The Assembly is aware of this situation, of the need for a better knowledge of the past so as better to understand the present and prepare the
   future, and of the valuable contribution that Islamic values can make to
   the quality of life through a renewed European approach on an overall
   basis to the cultural, economic, scientific and social fields.[18]

In the next paragraph, the assembly stressed that greater attention
should be given to cooperation with the Islamic world: "The Council of
Europe has already done a considerable amount of work on intercultural

understanding and this should be further developed with specific reference to Islamic culture." It directed the council to seek more avenues of
cooperation with nongovernmental institutions. The assembly recommended that the Committee of Ministers of the EC give more importance
to the Islamic world in the intergovernmental program of activities of the
Council of Europe and in its recommendations to the governments of
member states (article 11). This recommendation clearly indicates that the
Islamophile trend in the EC was initiated by directives given through each
EC member government. As before, this policy is perfectly in line with the
overriding EAD principles.

In relation to education, the assembly recommended that the history of
Islam should be included in education curricula and textbooks along the
lines of the international research project "Islam in textbooks," with a balanced and objective approach. It directed that the teaching of Arabic as a
modern language in European schools be extended, as well as scientific
research on Islamic matters. It advised that the number of Arabic and Islamic professorships in universities likewise be increased, so that Islam
could be included in mainstream studies—for example in the history and
philosophy departments with sections on Islamic history and philosophy,
with Islamic law in law departments, and so on. The assembly stated that
cooperation between universities in Europe and the Islamic world should
be expanded, along the lines of an earlier recommendation that a Euro-
Arab University be created.[19] It also called for increased student and
teacher exchanges.

The assembly, moreover, considered that places of Muslim cultural and
intellectual expression were needed for immigrants from the Islamic
world—although the preservation of their own culture should not entail
their isolation from the society and culture of the host country. It proposed
that "cultural itineraries of the Islamic world inside or outside Europe and
cultural exchanges, exhibitions, conferences and publications in the fields
of art, music and history should be encouraged." As museums had an important role to play in this respect, Muslim sections should be enlarged. To
gain better understanding for Muslims in Western society, the translation
and publication of Islamic works, classic and modern, were to be greatly
increased.

Regarding the media, the assembly decided that "[t]he production, co-
production and broadcasting of radio and television programmes on Islamic culture are to be encouraged." It called for a real effort to continue
the dialogue between Europe and the Islamic world, with a view to reinforcing and developing democratic and pluralistic tendencies. Particular attention was given to direct cooperation with the Arab countries around the
Mediterranean, as well as with immigrant communities within Europe.

The Assembly also asks the Committee of Ministers [of the EC] to invite interested countries of the Islamic world to make similar initiatives on a reciprocal basis and, wherever appropriate, to accede to Council of Europe conventions and open partial agreements, with a view to harmonising legislation and developing intercultural understanding.

The Muslim and European scholars who participated in this assembly debate stressed the superiority of Islamic civilization and the humanism of the Andalusian "golden age" over Europe's obscurantism. This affirmation is noteworthy since, as we have seen, the *shari'a* was the only law applied during this "golden age": the Islam that was being praised by the assembly was decidedly not a modernized or Westernized version of the faith.

In his Explanatory Memorandum, the Spanish socialist rapporteur Lluis Maria de Puig stated that

both the reports and our discussion re-affirmed the Islamic civilisation's enormous influence on West European culture. It is an established fact that—in a wide variety of philosophy, science, art, architecture, town-planning, medicine, language, everyday life and lastly, culture—we cannot explain the history of Europe without taking into account all that is of Islamic origin.[20]

The rapporteur deplored the conflicts caused by the Crusades, the Inquisition, European imperialism and colonialism, and Europe's paternalism and ambiguity concerning the Israeli-Palestinian problem.[21] Thus, de Puig explicitly situated Israel within the context of the Euro-Arab relationship on a par with the Crusades and Inquisition. In his paper presented at the colloquy, Omar Khalifa el-Hamdi, secretary-general of the National Council for Arab Culture, Morocco, stressed this historical linkage by saying that it was

necessary to lay bare the reasons that have prompted the concealment of the Arab role in the building of contemporary civilisation. The real reasons why the Arabs have been subjected over the centuries to calumnies, aggression and attempts to obscure their identity must be identified.

The importance of such a revision of historical concepts and outlook will escape none of the participants in this colloquy, for the contacts between the Muslims and Europe have in the past engendered events of the gravest kind, such as the Crusades, European colonialism, the foundation of the State of Israel and, lastly, the Gulf War.[22]

The same tactic of invoking Israel in a Euro-Arab context was played out again and again. It seemed as if Europeans and Muslims could not meet without primarily condemning Israel, whatever the subject, and as if the four thousand years of Jewish history had to be reduced to the Arab population's flight from the State of Israel, as a consequence of Arab wars to destroy it. Jihadist wars against infidels for over a millennium were not mentioned.

Italian Gaetano Adinolfi, deputy secretary-general of the Council of Europe, declared in his Opening Statement to the Assembly that the arts, languages, law, philosophy, sciences, music, and even gastronomy highlighted the influence of the Islamic civilization in European culture from the twelfth century to our day. According to Adinolfi, this was an indication of the immense debt owed by Europeans to Islamic civilization and culture. He made no mention of the legacy of the Greek, Roman, and Byzantine empires—as if a void had engulfed Europe at the dawn of Islamic influence in the twelfth century. Adinolfi even mentioned the contribution of Arabs in the agricultural domain.[23] In fact, Arabs did not engage in agriculture: Jewish or Christian farmers cultivated the Arabian oases. The Prophet Muhammad's dislike for agricultural work is recorded in several *hadiths*. Once, when he saw a plough, he said, "This will not enter any people's house without God causing ignominy to enter it."[24] Whatever Arabs knew about agriculture, they learned from the people they had conquered, who were neither Arabs nor Muslims.

The Italian Roberto Barzanti, chairman of the Committee on Youth, Culture, Education, Sports and Media of the European Parliament, also participated in the colloquy. After emphasizing Islam's cultural superiority over Europe, he expressed his great admiration for "the system of Madrasah." For him the *madrassa* (Islamic religious school) should serve as the model for the special Erasmus teaching program launched by the European Community. He showed no sign of being aware of the Pakistani *madrassa* school system, or the Saudi international network of *madrassas* from which, in the mid-1990s, the Taliban movement emerged. Instead, he praised the tuition courses on Ibn Malik, the *Risala* of Ibn Abi Zyad [al-Qarawani] and the *Muwatta* of Malik Ibn Anas that were given in the *madrassas*. These scholars belonged to the Maliki school of Islamic law, created in Medina by Malik b. Anas (d. 795), which—as we have seen—imposes the most severe restrictions upon non-Muslims. Barzanti quoted the Islamic jurist an-Nawawi (1233–77) admiringly. However, if he had really read his works, he seems to have overlooked the section on *jihad*, which calls for the killing of unbelievers and the enslaving of their women and children. He, likewise, seems to have missed the section on institutionalized discrimination against Jews and Christians. Barzanti preferred to call for solidarity and fraternity— "which should overlap with the value of sharing which is central to the Islam of these young people and would also be seen as part of our own cultural heritage."[25]

The participants emphasized "the debt that Europeans owed to the cultural heritage of Islam." Hence, the Parliamentary Assembly of the Council of Europe adopted numerous recommendations concerning the development of Arabic and Islamic studies in different fields, such as education, media, and culture.

For their part, the Muslim representatives asked for the opening of European universities to Muslim students and the transfer of Western technology to their countries. They considered these perfectly reasonable demands in light of the fact, taken for granted by everyone, that European culture had an Arab-Muslim origin. These requests were integrated into the Barcelona Declaration (1995), which directed that the study of the Arab Islamic source of European civilization be included in European school textbooks.

On July 10, 2003, the opening ceremony of the Great Mosque of Granada took place. It was attended by Spanish officials and the Qur'an students of the *madrassa* of Majorca. Its builders saw it as a symbol of the revival of Islam in Europe and of Spain's "glorious Islamic heritage." However, reports indicated that for that very reason many Spaniards were quietly unhappy. "Everybody is opposed to it, but they know it's politically impossible to voice their objections," said one local journalist.[26] Two days after the mosque opened, it hosted lectures that were attended by about two thousand Muslims. Amir Abu Bakr Rieger of Germany said that Islam could only be practiced in Europe in a traditional way, not in one adapted to European values and structures. Umar Ibrahim Vadillo, the Rais (head) of the Murabitun World Da'wa Movement, called on all followers of Islam to stop using Western currencies such as the dollar, the euro, or the pound, and instead to adopt the gold dinar. Such a measure, he declared, would unify the Muslim world and totally destroy Western capitalism.[27] *Murabitun* is a name for the Almoravids, an extremely fanatical and puritanical Berber sect of jihadist warriors in the early eleventh century. They conquered North Africa and crossed to Spain in 1086, where they fought Christian armies and expelled Mozarabs (Christian *dhimmis*) and Jews from Andalusia.

Faithful to the 1991 colloquy of the Council of Europe's Parliamentary Assembly, British Foreign Secretary Robin Cook, speaking at the Ismaili Center in London on October 8, 1998, stated, "It is the most wonderful reminder in the very heart of London that the roots of our culture are not just Greek or Roman in origin, but Islamic as well. Islamic art, science and philosophy have helped to shape who we are and how we think." After stressing "the debt our culture owes to Islam," he added, "Islam laid the intellectual foundations for large portions of Western civilization."[28]

Such assertions are obviously motivated by electoral and economic interests, but they may also be viewed as political ploys to facilitate the integration of millions of Muslim immigrants into a European culture that allegedly has Islamic roots. Islamic doctrine forbids Muslims to accept the influence of infidel cultures. It requires the acknowledgment of Islamic prestige and superiority, and European ministers have shown themselves glad to oblige with proclamation of the Islamic origin of, or predominant contribution to, Western civilization's science and arts. Some of these proclamations are so florid they suggest that without Arab science, Europeans today would be a mass of illiterates, for Europe owes its civilization and culture to Islam.

However, Cook's assertions were in fact groundless. Islam actually inherited most of its knowledge from Greece, Rome, and the Judeo-Christian, Armenian, Persian, and Hindu civilizations that Muslims conquered and colonized and upon which they built their own contributions. During the Middle Ages, Byzantine science, literature, and arts flourished in Anatolia and the Balkan region, reaching to Italy and Armenia with a brilliance that Abbasid and Andalusian Arab caliphs envied, as is clear from Muslim contemporary writings.

Yet, since the inferiority of the infidel is a dogma enshrined in the Qur'an and in so many Islamic religious dictums, the obsequious declarations of Eurabian ministers, politicians and intellectuals are reminiscent, as we have seen, of the obligatory acknowledgement of Islam's superiority under dhimmitude. *Dhimmi* submissiveness, with its crawling behavior, emerges from a study of historical records and can be analyzed in populations reduced to an almost hostage condition.[29] The great enigma of our time consists in its adoption by so-called free Western nations. Legitimate acknowledgement of mutual cultural borrowing between peoples, which allows for transformation, assimilation and improvement, is different from uncritical and self-serving adulation.

This adulation was designed to undermine Europe's Judeo-Christian roots. The principle of a Judeo-Christian civilization in Europe was belittled by producing and constantly propagating the Islamic origin of European civilization. Hamadi Essid, head of the Arab League Mission at Paris and its permanent delegate to UNESCO, told a meeting as early as 1970, "For some time there has been a catch-phrase: 'Judeo-Christian values.' This slogan is directed against the Arabs."[30] Arabs reject the term "Judeo-Christian civilization" and replace it with "Abrahamic civilization" because, as Abraham was a Muslim (according to the Qur'an), it follows that Western civilization not only *includes* the Islamic dimension, but *is* Islamic in its essence through Abraham, the Muslim prophet.

"Abrahamism" is a notion that totally denies the historical identity and origin of Judaism and Christianity, since it reduces them to falsifications of Islam, the true religion of Abraham.[31] Today, any reference to Europe's Christian sources—not to mention its Judeo-Christian roots—has been omitted from the EU Constitution on "secular" grounds, but mainly so as not to offend Muslim immigrants.

Moreover, Judaism and Israel tend to generate such hate that many European politicians have gladly rallied to Abrahamism. By this reasoning Christianity is no longer related to Judaism but to Islam, the first religion of mankind which antedates, in the Islamic view, the other two monotheistic religions. The biblical personages depicted in European churches and artwork are Jewish, and there is a direct filiation of Christianity from Judaism. However, this is not so according to Islamic doctrine. Islam teaches that the whole biblical story is a history of Muslim prophets—including Jesus, his family and the apostles, who all preached and practiced Islam. Church iconography and stained glass windows are thus considered to recall in a distorted way a sacred history that is properly Qur'anic. Christianity is not linked to Judaism but to Islam. Since Adam and Eve, Abraham, Moses, David and Solomon, and all the prophets of Israel down to Jesus, are seen to be Muslims, Islam becomes the first monotheist religion, preceding Judaism and Christianity.

This clarifies why the Judeo-Christian and sometimes biblical language of President Bush so exasperates the Islamized Eurabian politicians. Linked as they are with Judaism and Israel, quotations from the Bible are treated with contempt and derision, and the Bible itself provokes acrimonious debates. Derisive words and hostile insinuations are voiced even by high-ranking officials, who rarely express in public any embarrassment with Islamic totalitarian principles or the Qur'an.[32]

The EAD's cultural infrastructure has thus made it possible to import into Europe the traditional cultural baggage of Islamic anti-Christian and anti-Jewish prejudices against the West and Israel, conceived by the same religious community that created and promoted a jihadist civilization for over a millennium. The hostile nature of this baggage was not even discussed; it was simply overlooked as if nonexistent. If it was admitted at all, it was explained away as a reaction to Israel's existence or American arrogance.

Immigrant groups became vehicles to spread these prejudices throughout Europe, with the active collusion of academics, politicians, and the whole of the EAD's cultural apparatus. The debasement of the "infidel" Judeo-Christian culture was engineered through the affirmation of the superiority of Islamic civilization from which, so it is said, European sages had humbly drawn inspiration. Neither the centers of learning scattered over Latin and Byzantine Europe during the Middle Ages; nor the creation of printing, essential for the diffusion of knowledge, in the following centuries; nor the Industrial Revolution, women's emancipation, the scientific discoveries of European scholars and their technological applications; nor the innovative evolution of Western legal and political institutions, humanitarian organizations, and the welfare state; nor the artistic and cultural wealth—so evident everywhere in Europe—could undermine the axiom of the inferiority of Europe's culture to that of Arab Muslims, the alleged creators of science and the arts.

This absurdity, slavishly repeated by so many European politicians, constitutes, as we have seen, a religious principle of the Muslim world that acknowledges no superiority on the part of any infidel civilization.

At the 10th OIC Summit in Malaysia in October 2003, Malaysian Prime Minister Mahathir Muhammad declared in his farewell speech, after having defamed the Jews:

> The early Muslims produced great mathematicians and scientists, scholars, physicians and astronomers etc. and they excelled in all the fields of knowledge of their times, besides studying and practising their own religion of Islam. As a result the Muslims were able to develop and extract wealth from their lands and through their world trade, able to strengthen their defences, protect their people and give them the Islamic way of life, Addin, as prescribed by Islam. At the time the Europeans of the Middle Ages were still superstitious and backward, the enlightened Muslims had already built a great Muslim civilisation, respected and powerful, more than able to compete with the rest of the world and able to protect the ummah from foreign aggression. The Europeans had to kneel at the feet of Muslim scholars in order to access their own scholastic heritage. [See appendix 7.]

Such preposterous insults illustrate the dhimmitude that has been deliberately chosen as a way of thinking and acting by European leaders motivated by greed, fear, and cowardice.

The September 1991 debate held by the Parliamentary Assembly of the Council of Europe thus represents a major step forward in the Euro-Arab symbiosis and the process of the cultural Islamization of Europe. It has consolidated two trends: the confirmation of Islamic superiority over Christianity (a basic Qur'anic assertion) and the expansion throughout the EU of a network intended to spread Arab/Islamic influence through schools, universities, and cultural institutions.

Such a network, linked to the Arab League and the OIC and implemented by the institutions and cogs of the EU, is a unique phenomenon enjoyed by no other culture. It is worth recalling that the Parliamentary Assembly of the Council of Europe stated that the Colloquy in Paris of May 1991 was held in a similar spirit to the one on the Jewish contribution to European culture. Judaic influence, with the Bible, radiates through Western thought and culture; it is intrinsic to Western identity. The policy of replacing it with a Muslim identity, on the basis of a shallow impulse of multicultural equivalence, has paved the way for Europe's Islamization.

14

Palestinianism: A New Eurabian Cult

As shown in chapter 3, support for the Palestinian Liberation Organization (PLO) was integrated from the beginning into the whole political structure of the Euro-Arab Dialogue. The Third World and the international networks of Arab Churches advocated this policy. As early as 1974, at the Lahore Summit of the Organization of the Islamic Conference, Secretary-General al-Tohami commended the efforts undertaken by the Churches in the Arab countries and worldwide on behalf of the Palestinians, and praised their backing for Arab sovereignty over Jerusalem. His address, quoted on page 112, conformed to the Qur'anic dogma of Islam's precedence over Judaism and Christianity and the Islamization of biblical history. He referred to Jesus as a Muslim prophet, together with other biblical persons mentioned in the Qur'an. The Muslim interpretation of Jewish and Christian Holy Scriptures negates the links between Judaism and Christianity and rejects them as opposed to Islamic doctrine.

A full-blown "Palestinian replacement theology" was created and spread throughout Europe, encouraged by EAD pro-PLO indoctrination. The new Arab Jesus unites in his Palestinianism both Muslims and Christians against Israel. This holy synthesis sanctified the Palestinian Arab cause against a demonized and isolated Jewish state. Palestinians are thus endowed with the divine mission to remove Israel from Arab Palestine, thereby upholding the honor and truthfulness of Christianity and Islam.[1] "Palestinianism," the new Eurabian cult, thus conferred a theological value upon Palestinian sufferings. Palestinian victimology—the Jewish victimization of innocent Palestinians—was drummed into the European political conscience through the church institutions, the media, and Eurabian networks. Arab Palestine came to symbolize the crucifixion of Jesus by Jewish evilness. Such was the thesis preached by Kenneth Cragg, the assistant Anglican bishop in Jerusalem from 1970 to 1973. Till 1985 he continued to hold that post in an honorary capacity.[2] Yet Cragg wastes no charity on the Christian Maronites, who were victims of the Palestinians' murderous war in Lebanon.[3]

The cult of Palestinianism often exploits the theme of the Crucifixion. Although the Qur'an actually denies the Crucifixion altogether (4:157),

Muslims and the Islamized and Eurabian Churches identify the Crucifixion with Palestine or the Arabs of Palestine. In a lecture in Paris on June 2, 1970, Mgr. Georges Khodr, Metropolitan of Byblos and Mt. Lebanon, stressed, "It is not for me to tell the Muslims what force the evangelical ferment would contribute to the Arab cause." In his conclusion, he declared to have chosen Arabness because, on the June 5, 1967, "I saw that Jesus of Nazareth had become a Palestinian refugee."[4] The Arab Palestinian poet Mahmud Darwish, much praised in Europe, identified in his verse Arab Palestine with Christ crucified by Israel. Such abuse of Christian symbols to incite hatred of Jews has been strongly condemned by many Christians as blasphemy.[5] Nonetheless, Arab/Muslim acts of aggression against French Jews in 2003 were widely explained away on the pretext of Palestinian suffering. In a lecture given to the London Society of Jews and Christians on April 29, 2004, British journalist Melanie Phillips declared that leaders, periodicals, and aid agencies within the Protestant churches are viscerally hostile to Israel.

Palestinianism has been conceptualized and spread by Christian theologians—Protestant and Catholic[6]—despite strong opposition from some Protestant circles and the Vatican's repeated and clear rejection of replacement theology.[7] This conception holds that the New Covenant replaced the First totally. Palestinianism provides the moral justification for the elimination of the State of Israel. It revives in a political and religious framework the traditional Christian demonization of the Jews, officially rejected by the Catholic Church at the Second Vatican Council in 1962–65. Conceived by theologians, Palestinianism relies heavily on ancient anti-Jewish religious texts and myths that had inculcated behavior patterns leading to the *shoah*. Some scholars revived ancient Christian writings that held that Jews had lost all rights to their land because of the Crucifixion.[8] Biblical history that legitimized Israel became ever more contemptible and discredited, unless purified of its Jewish interpretation by Palestinian Liberation Theology. Its conceiver, canon Naim Ateek, is revered in European Protestant churches. Theologians aligned on Ateek's interpretation called for a new Christian reading of the Bible, in line with the Qur'an, that would expel Israel from its biblical identity as well as its patrimony.[9] These Christians believe that they would thereby obey God's will by helping to destroy Israel by whatever means. Such views fostered acceptance of Palestinian terrorism against Israel. In her lecture, Phillips mentioned that Canon Andrew White, the Archbishop of Canterbury's envoy in the Middle East, told her that Palestinian politics and Christian theology have become inextricably intertwined. Hence, the same motivations that a century ago, in the time of Theodore Herzl, led to the *shoah* are still very potent today under the disguise of Palestinianism. It is in this traditional European antisemitism that Palestinianism or Palestinolatry could flourish as a modern Eurabian cult.

Although Palestinianism, within the theology of Palestinian Liberation, purports to unite Christian and Muslim theological concepts, it is not a marriage of equals, despite its tactical rapprochement with Christianity, the Islamic component condemns Christians as well as Jews and other infidels, as dictated by classical *jihad* theory and rooted in the Qur'anic interpretations (9:29–30). Thus, the denial of Jewish history and rights in Israel entails similar consequences for other peoples whose rights and history Islamists contest. Supported by Muslim countries and the EU, Palestinian Arabs are waging a *jihad* against Israel in order to reimpose on the infidels the *shari'a* laws that dispossessed, decimated, and exiled the Jewish people from its homeland. The same applies to Christians in their Islamized lands, i.e., the whole of the Middle East, while former Islamic conquests in Europe are targeted for Islamization. As the PLO's structure, functioning, and ideology embody all aspects of *jihad,* it also targets Christians, in spite of the EU's billions of euros paid to the PA. Thus, the future of the few remaining Christians looks bleak in the forthcoming Palestinian state. Every sign points to a radical jihadist mentality, which already imposes the subservient and fearful *dhimmi* status mandated by the *shari'a.*

On the day he was sentenced for his role in the Islamist mass killings in Bali on October 12, 2002, the smiling jihadist Amrozi shouted in the courtroom, "Jews, remember Khaybar! The army of Muhammad is coming back to defeat you!" In pre-Islamic times, Khaybar was an Arabian oasis owned and cultivated by Jews. The Prophet Muhammad attacked them unexpectedly in 628 while they were going out to their fields. He defeated them and took their property, but allowed them to stay on their land on the condition that they would give him half of their harvest for as long as Allah would allow it. Muslim jurisprudence has taken the conquest of Khaybar, but also the treatment of Arabian Jews in Medina by Muhammad, as the setting for the Islamic jihadist rules against Jews, Christians, and other non-Muslims. In Arabia, the Christians were given the same pact of protection (*dhimma*) as the Jews in Khaybar. In 640, all of them—Jews and Christians alike—were expelled from the Hijaz by the caliph Umar b. al-Khattab. Victims of the same religious cleansing policy, they lost their houses, lands, synagogues, and churches. Amrozi, who participated in the massacre of nearly 200 Christians, Buddhists, and Hindus in Bali in October 2002, thus reminded the world that Muhammad's *jihad* against the Jews of Arabia is a war waged against all non-Muslims.[10]

Nowadays, in the budding Eurabia, many church publications, when soliciting funds and prayers, recount Arab Palestinian martyrology. Israelis butchered by Palestinians receive scant attention. An EAD project called "Sharing Stories" began in September 2000 at the inception of the renewal of Palestinian terrorist war against Israel, after Arafat's rejection of the Peace Process at Camp David II. The project, included in the EAD web, came as an initiative of the Inter-Church Peace Council (IKV)—the main project holder—in cooperation with Pax Christi Netherlands and Muslim immigrants in the Netherlands. Mgr. Michel Sabbah, the Latin patriarch of Jerusalem and a close collaborator of Arafat, had then just been elected president of Pax Christi International, a major position that lent him a prominent role in Church policy on an international level. The project emerged from a number of seminars organized by the EAD in the PA's territories and in Egypt, where the participants met. According to its website the project was initiated after the first Gulf War of 1990–91[11]

> as a response to growing tensions between the Arab world and Europe, the "Clash of Civilisations." The projects aim [*sic*] is to develop a positive response to this clash of civilisations through dialogue, co-operation and exchange between people in both societies. The Project focuses particularly on contacts between the Netherlands, Palestine, Morocco, Egypt and Tunisia. Its main target groups are youth, education and municipalities. In the "Sharing Stories" project, EAd co-operates with the Arab Educational Institute in Bethlehem and the Catholic Pedagogical Centre (KPC) in Den Bosch (Netherlands).

"Sharing Stories" was part of a Euro-Arab education exchange between schools in the Arab territories and the Netherlands. It recounted the life of Palestinian youth in the manner of Anne Frank, the Jewish Dutch adolescent deported and killed with her family and other Jews by the Nazis and their Dutch collaborators. It was modeled on the Jewish experience during the *shoah* in Europe, which was now transferred to the Palestinian situation with the Israelis playing the role of Nazis. These articles spoke about the isolation of the Palestinians and their abandonment by the world, but of course made no mention of Palestinian terrorism against Israelis. They were circulated through e-mail and the Internet but in fact were largely propagated throughout the main European media by the EAD network. "Sharing Stories" illustrates perfectly the functioning of Eurabia, which brings together European leaders and ministers, EC delegates, highest Church personalities, and the media, all joining their efforts in a media war against Israel to soothe Euro-Arab tension and the "Clash of Civilizations." However, the "shared story" is in fact the shared hatred of European anti-semites and Arab Palestinians during World War II, which now continues against Israelis, murdered by Palestinians, supported by Europe. A "shared story" bonding Israelis to the extermination of European Jewry.

On November 15, 2002, Sabbah received the title of doctor *honoris causa* from the Faculty of Theology at Fribourg University in Switzerland. He lamented over the Israeli "occupation" as well as the Netanyahu and Sharon governments—but said nothing about the terrorism of Hamas and Islamic Jihad. In reality, towns and villages of "Arab Palestine" have Hebrew, not

Arabic names. They are linked to Jewish, not Arabic history. The Qur'an mentions not one Palestinian province, city, or village, not even Jerusalem—merely "the furthermost mosque," which could have referred to Mecca or to the Holy Sepulcher, and not necessarily to the Temple in Jerusalem whose ruins were still covered with garbage at the time of Muhammad. Hence, Israel's delegitimization can only be justified by Christian and Muslim replacement theologies, with the latter replacing not just Judaism but Christianity as well. Only on these grounds can Muslims claim the Holy Land and confer on both its Jewish and Christian peoples a *dhimmi* status.

Sabbah stigmatized the European Churches for abandoning the Palestinian Christians, who he proclaimed, do not suffer from Muslims—thereby implying that they suffer from Israel.[12] However, the facts show otherwise. In July 2003, a Muslim convert to Christianity went into hiding in the territories controlled by the PA; ten days later his body was returned to his family, butchered, and quartered by Palestinian Islamists. He had run afoul of the death sentence prescribed in Islamic law for those who leave Islam. Other Christians were harassed; many took refuge in Israel.[13] At present, the only "protection" that European Christians offer Christians living under the Palestinian Authority—1% of the Arab population—and in the Arab/Muslim world is their contribution to the demise of Israel through the Euro-Arab symbiosis policy, and by the weakening of the U.S.A. It is noteworthy that over 125,000 local Christians living in Israel as citizens remain, but the few under Arafat's Palestinian Authority began emigrating as soon as Israel left the territories, and have continued to do so.

Through the EAD's obsessive demonization of Israel, the victimization of Palestinians overshadowed any other tragedy in the world. It became the crucial subject, constantly recalled and commented upon in the mass media and taken up by the solidarity rallies. Several times a day, television, radio, and newspapers focus the European mind on an obsessive and ritual veneration of Palestinianism. Everything derives from it; everything goes back to it. A grieving Arab Palestine constantly calls on the distressed compassion of Europeans, provoking frustrated hatred against Israel, which is mentioned only in negative terms: occupation, injustice, apartheid, Nazism. Israel's population, which had liberated from dhimmitude a tiny corner from the vast Christian, Buddhist, and Hindu regions colonized by Arabs, appears to have been expelled to another galaxy. It seems as if Israel has neither arts nor science, nor history worth mentioning. In 1998, the European press passed over in silence the concerts and festivities in Israel commemorating Jerusalem's three thousand years since David was anointed king there. Israel has no right to Jerusalem or the Holy Land, which, according to Palestinianism, belongs only to Christianity and Islam—a position reinforced by the word "occupation" hammered in by Palestinian and Eurabian Churches.

The Palestinian Authority's allegation of a massacre at Jenin in April 2002 was hysterically publicized in Eurabia without verification. Palestinian leaders claimed there had been more than five hundred innocent deaths, mainly women and children. In fact, Israeli soldiers blew up booby-trapped terrorist houses, during which fifty-two Arab terrorists and twenty-three Israeli soldiers were killed. A year later in Geneva, the serious newspaper *Le Temps*, advertised the film "Jenin . . . Jenin" by Mohammed Bakri as "realized in 2002 during the massacre perpetrated by the Israeli army in the Jenin camp."[14] From the beginning of the Palestinian war against Israel in 2000, European newspapers published lengthy articles nearly every day on the suffering of the Palestinians "under occupation." This propaganda war, which focused mainly on Arab children and adolescents, covered the whole EU; television filming was coordinated to show only children stone-throwers, carefully avoiding the gunmen behind them.[15] *Jihad* rules allow the enrollment of adolescents; it was applied in the Iran-Iraq war by Khomeini's forces and in the current *jihad* carried out by the Islamic regime in Sudan.

The conception and practice of Palestinianism as a hate cult against Israel has had a profound impact on European society. Even if not everyone adheres to it, many absorb its noxiousness unconsciously, since it is constantly distilled by the EU mainstream media, by the political apparatus of the Euro-Arab Partnership and by the third pillar of the Barcelona process (see chapter 10). It is difficult to assess the resistance to this propaganda, since the EAD press network has silenced most protests against it for years. With the exception of a vigorous rebuttal from the Protestant International Christian Embassy in Jerusalem, there has been practically no consistent opposition, nor any strong denunciation from other organizations of this return to the old indoctrination of hate—and certainly not from NGOs.

In this heavy silence, the voices of some non-Jewish European intellectuals, like Pierre-André Taguieff,[16] Guy Millière, and Alexandre Del Valle,[17] in France, and Abbé Alain René Arbez in Switzerland, and many others, as well as the impassioned writings of Oriana Fallaci,[18] have resounded loud and clear. All received threats and insults. They were stigmatized by other intellectuals, the media and politically influential circles for saying in Eurabia that Palestinianism is the return of the Euro-Arab Nazism of the 1930–40s.

Palestinianism pits Christians against Christians. In May 2002, Christian religious leaders in Arab countries and in the Palestinian-controlled territories viciously attacked the West in most aggressive terms.[19] During the Muslim occupation and profanation of the Basilica of the Nativity in Bethlehem at that time, some Arab Christian clerics proffered hateful declarations against Christians in Europe and America, as well as against Jews and Israel. The Arab media gave full publicity to these statements, probably as a device to protect Christians in a hostile Muslim environment. Resorting to such vilification for self-protection testifies to the degree of terror under which Christians live in Arab countries. It also raises questions about the veracity of similar historical statements given over the centuries by clerics who sided with their Muslim oppressors and glorified magnanimous Islamic tolerance.

On June 19, 2002, the day that the grand sheik of al-Azhar Muhammad Tantawi approved the "Islamikaze" bombers in Israel,[20] the spokesman of the Orthodox Church of Jerusalem and the Holy Land, Atta Allah Hanna, did likewise. Commendably, two weeks later, the Greek Orthodox patriarchate strongly condemned Hanna's declaration and dismissed him from his post.[21]

Among the tragedies of the second half of the twentieth century, historians will recall Europe's silence and its cynical indifference toward Christianity's demise in Arab and most Muslim countries—a tragedy paralleled by that of nearly a million Jewish refugees expelled from Arab countries through indiscriminate terror, confiscations, expulsion, and insecurity—with indifference from all international bodies.[22]

Christian distress and isolation were vividly illustrated by the Lebanese war and European support for the PLO. Lebanese Christians were the first indirect victims of the EAD agreements of the 1970s that endorsed European political advocacy for the PLO, which was already the most deadly of terrorist organizations and today still competes with Hamas and al-Qaeda. Lebanon was forced by its Arab "friends" to host the PLO. While the PLO and its allies preyed on the Lebanese Christians, wiping out whole villages, desecrating and burning churches, murdering, and mutilating corpses (as at Damur in 1976), Europe was supporting Arafat.

The agony of Lebanon holds many important lessons for Europe, particularly since the EAD has prepared the conditions for the EU's future Lebanonization. When the civil war erupted in Lebanon in April 1976, there were twelve thousand regular Syrian troops in the country. Soon this increased to twenty-five thousand, with a Syrian workforce of three hundred thousand. The large Palestinian civil population, with its innumerable groups and factions, impeded the functioning of the state.[23] The PLO received help and training from Arab and Communist countries, as well as from Nasserite, Ba'athist, and communist organizations in the region. Factional divisions and pusillanimity weakened the Christian camp, which was blinded by profits from Arab oil and financial contracts.

The Lebanese war was butchery, conducted with the outmost violence. With public attention focused on Palestinian martyrdom, the PLO inflicted mass murder, abductions, untold suffering, and destruction on over a hundred thousand Christians in Lebanon. This was one of the bloodiest phases of the Palestinian *jihad* since it had initiated international terrorism and indiscriminate murder of civilians with the first hijacking of an El Al airplane to Algiers in 1968.

Yet the valiant Christian resistance was demonized by a European press that sided with the PLO—the *jihad* camp that believes (as is expressed today in widespread graffiti in PA areas) that after the "Saturday people"—the Jews—comes the turn of the "Sunday people"—the Christians. Europe's indifference to the long and bloody agony of the Christian resistance against the world's then most powerful terrorist organization, which it was supporting, was the first sign of the subversion of its values and the perversion of its language, a process that would progressively poison it. Today, when Eurabians remember the Lebanese war at all it is only to lament the massacre at Sabra and Chatila, which was committed by Christian Maronites in retaliation for PLO massacres, and inevitably blamed on Ariel Sharon. That of Damur, which preceded it and was personally supervised by Arafat, is conveniently ignored.[24] An eyewitness gave an account of the massacre of 582 Christians in Damur by the PLO and its Muslim allies on January 22, 1976: "The attack took place from the mountain behind. It was an apocalypse. They were coming, thousands and thousands, shouting 'Allahu Akhbar! God is great! Let us attack them for the Arabs, let us offer a holocaust to Mohammad!' And they were slaughtering everyone in their path, men, women and children."[25]

In East Timor, a Muslim *jihad* against Christians has led to genocide. In Sudan, the rebellion of the non-Muslim South against Islamization imposed by the Muslim North was crushed by a *jihad* in which two million people died; up to two hundred thousand were abducted and enslaved over the years; and four and half million have suffered displacement and famine. *Jihad*, in Africa, Pakistan, Kashmir, Indonesia, and the Philippines, targets Christians and Hindus without distinction. In Egypt, discrimination against the Copts is rampant, and girls are abducted.

In Indonesia, over five hundred churches were attacked or destroyed between 1996 and 2002. By the end of 2000, half a million Christians had been internally displaced, more than five thousand killed, and as many as seven thousand forcibly converted to Islam.[26] The town of Poso in Central Sulawesi used to have a population of forty thousand, mostly Christians; by the end of 2002, it had been reduced to an exclusively Muslim population of five thousand, with all of its churches destroyed. In Ambon and Sulawesi, villages were looted, burnt, and razed to the ground. The Laskar Jihad included fighters from Afghanistan, Pakistan, the Philippines and Saudi Arabia. Mark Durie, a distinguished Australian scholar and Anglican minister, stresses that

> The label "sectarian violence," used so irresponsibly by the media for all this terror, has served to conceal and minimize the overall impact of the radical

jihad groups' activities within Indonesia. The world has allowed destabiliza-
tion, terror and displacement to advance a very great way already.[27]

In the Ivory Coast, the fighting that started in September 2002 between
Christians and Muslims caused hundred of deaths and a million internal
refugees within four months. Christian homes were looted and burnt;
churches and mosques were razed. In 2002 in Kaduna, Nigeria, Muslim
youths slaughtered scores of Christians and injured hundreds. Muslim religious leaders instigated the riot. The reverse happened in May 2004.

Yet Palestinian victimology has eclipsed this picture of global violence
and persecution.[28] These terrible human sufferings receive little coverage
in the Western press, which nonetheless reports incessantly on the Palestinians. It is difficult to believe that peace in the Middle East will convince
Islamists throughout the world to renounce *jihad* and the *shari'a,* the two
essential components of their religion that trigger the violence against
Christians and other non-Muslims.

The EAD has made Palestine and the Palestinians the crux of its Eurabian policy, thus generating a culture of "Palestinolatry" in Europe. Palestinianism has become the principal characteristic of Eurabia, the main
drive of its politics; it is constantly referred to as the panacea to all world
conflicts. On March 3, 2004, EU foreign policy chief Javier Solana, when
asked about U.S. proposals to implement democratic reforms in Arab
states, declared:

> The peace process always has to be at the center of whatever initiative is in
> the field. . . . Any idea about (reform of) nations would have to be in parallel
> with putting a priority on the resolution of the peace process, otherwise it
> will be very difficult to have success.[29]

Solana just repeated the opinion of Egyptian President Hosni Mubarak
after his meeting with him. This opinion was shared by the Arab League
Secretary-General Amr Moussa, who refused to consider any reforms in
Arab countries before the settlement of the Arab-Palestinian conflict. Since
Arab conditions for a settlement conform to Islamic jihadist principles that
would lead to Israel's dismantlement, any democratization and change of
Arab societies demanded by the West are thus linked by the Arabs with Europe's participation in Israel's demise. This link was rejected by Senior U.S.
State Department official Marc Grossman when visiting Cairo on March 2,
2004. He said that the democracy plan should not depend on a settlement
of the Middle East conflict. But Egypt's foreign minister, Ahmed Maher,
answered, "Egypt's position is that one of the basic obstacles to the reform
process is the continuation of Israeli aggression against the Palestinian people and the Arab people."

These words overlook Palestinian jihadist terrorism. According to Reuters, Amr Moussa, speaking at the opening session of a regular ministerial meeting, declared: "The Palestinian cause . . . is the key to stability or instability in the region, and this issue will continue to influence in all its elements the development of the Arab region until a just solution is reached."

Mary Robinson, former President of the Irish Republic and former UN High Commissioner for Human Rights, repeated this European credo on the commemoration of the Swedish foreign minister Anna Lindh's murder (September 11, 2003). At this occasion the newly created Euro-Med Anna Lindh Foundation had invited personalities to a symposium in Stockholm on the fight against terrorism. Mary Robinson stressed that the solution of the Arab-Israeli conflict was as indispensable instrument for the world's pacification and especially in the Arab world. It is a central issue, she affirmed, while deploring Washington's lack of action. This coded language means that Israel is not being pressured enough to obey Eurabian requirements.[30]

Eurabian notables—whether Chirac, Solana, Prodi, de Villepin, Mary Robinson or others—have continuously stressed the centrality of the Palestinian cause for world peace, as if more European vilification of Israel would change anything in the global *jihad* waged from Africa to Chechnya and in Asia. In such a view, Israel's very existence, not this genocidal jihadist drive, is a threat to peace. In fact, most Arab governments are hostile to Western reform, as is shown by the total failure of the Barcelona process. The Euro-Arab linkage of Arab/Islamic reforms to Israel's demise is spurious and only demonstrates, once again, Europe's subservience to Arab policy. Moreover, we have seen how numerous Arab and Islamic summits imposed over the world the centrality of the Palestinian policy and requested that all political problems should be subordinated to it. European leaders are just merely performing their obedient *dhimmi* service by complying.

One of these services was their unremitting effort to align America on the Arab policy. But despite the February 2004 rapprochement between German Chancellor Gerhard Schröder and George W. Bush, the American president made it clear "We must not neglect a basic Middle East problem—the conflict between Israelis and Palestinians—and we must not allow this conflict to close off or interfere with other perspectives."[31]

Senior *IHT* correspondent John Vinocur stressed that such a statement was in line with American policy for an overall solution for the region, provoking irritation in Brussels within the EU and on the part of France. It is true that in a speech in early February 2004, Germany's foreign minister, Joschka Fischer—as if discovering the wheel—"described 'jihadist terrorism' as a 'new totalitarianism' that was the world's greatest security threat."[32]

Nothing represents the new Eurabian dogma and the Euro-Arab symbiosis more than Palestinianism, the most popular and cherished cause of Eurabians. Its religious dimension has allowed Christian traditional antisemitism to be revived in the form of a Palestinian replacement theology that buys Muslim favor for the Eastern and Western Churches. It is an inextinguishable fountain of anti-Americanism, anti-Christianity and antisemitism, and a source of visceral and acrimonious hatred posing as a virtue —especially since it is linked to a European moral rehabilitation regarding the *shoah* and Europe's past attitudes to Jews.

Manipulation of Jewish History

Before the early 1970s and the spread of deadly Arab propaganda against Israel through EAD channels, the general feeling in Europe toward Israel was positive. Antisemitism, although it still existed, was much reduced and controlled. The Jewish-Christian rapprochement initiated by Vatican II was widely accepted and enthusiastically pursued by fervent Christians. This trend, of course, later contradicted the EAD policy to impose Euro-Arab solidarity against Israel. When, in the 1960s, European Christian theologians were engaged in a painful process of self-criticism and moral reassessment through the examination of Christian antisemitism, the Arab Churches were pursuing a Muslim-Christian dialogue intended to reassure the Muslim world and counterbalance the Jewish-Christian rapprochement.

The Arab states exploited their *dhimmi* Church leaders to impede this timid rapprochement. Eastern Christian communities were blackmailed and threatened. Any criticism of the pejorative characteristics attributed to Jews by the church fathers—especially those of St. Augustine and St. Chrysostom[33]—was considered blasphemous by Muslims, since they are echoed in the Qur'an. Publications by Western historians and intellectuals on the sources and history of Christian antisemitism created a mirror Arabophile Western literature that duplicated Jewish history, but in an Islamic version that transferred victimhood to Muslims. Countless books were written to prove Europe's anti-Muslim racism and its culpability. Norman Daniel,[34] a serious scholar, and Edward Said were the pioneers and champions of this trend beginning in the 1970s. Christian antisemitism reappeared in recastings of Muslim-Christian relations that endeavored to explain away the *jihad* ideology and regulations that had led to a millennium of Islamic conquests of Christian lands and the subjection of Christian populations on three continents. Since there was no Jewish expansion on Christian territories comparable to the Muslim war, the Muslim expansion was omitted altogether in order to establish a false parity between Judaism and Islam in relation to Christianity. Similarly, the whole Muslim anti-Christian theological, juridical, and historical system of dhimmitude, which also had no equivalent in Judaism, was ignored. Without these elements, the focus could shift entirely to the sins of Christians against Muslims. Not only was Western history falsified, but also a new principle was introduced into Christian-Muslim relations: the European guilt complex toward Muslims.

The guilt syndrome

On March 21, 1970, at a demonstration of solidarity with the Palestinians in Brussels, Bernard Schreiner, the representative of the "Christian Witness" groups and former president of the French National Union of Students, declared that the Church's favorable attitude toward the Jews was conditioned by its remorse.[35]

With considerable success, the Arab League used the same argument of remorse to explain to Muslims the spontaneous, popular Christian sympathy for Israel. During an International Conference on the Palestine Question, held in Geneva on August 29, 1984, the secretary-general of the Arab League, Chedli Klibi, stated:

> Zionism has turned the persecution of the Jews into a bargaining matter with European states and peoples. It has implanted a guilt complex in these states and peoples and in order to wipe out the West's responsibility for the crimes committed in the West against the Jews, Zionism requires the Western conscience to wipe out the crimes perpetrated by the Zionists against the Arabs, as well as those they are counting on perpetrating to complete the achievement of their expansionist and aggressive ambitions in the region.[36]

This remorse, according to Klibi, prevented Westerners from dealing severely with Israel. The idea that Israel was born of the guilt of the Western states and continued to live off this guilt was a primary motivating factor in the campaign to blame the West vis-à-vis the Muslims, and particularly the Palestinians. Eurabia, the UN, and lobbies worldwide exploited this theme to deny the *shoah*, regarded as anti-Palestinian political blackmail; they seek to compensate it by the request for a symmetrical European guilt vis-à-vis the Palestinians and Muslims and by the transfer of Jewish history to the Palestinian Arabs.

Consequently, a Muslim-Christian replica counterbalanced the Judeo-Christian dialogue although there is not the slightest resemblance between the history of the Jews in Christendom and the history of the Islamic *jihad* and expropriation of conquered Christian lands. The denunciation of the Crusades, the Inquisition, imperialism, and European colonialism, like the accusation that Europe had collaborated in the creation of Israel, tended to imply that Europe owed a moral debt to the Arab Palestinians and to the Muslim world. Yet no one ever suggested that the Muslim *jihad* expansion that had purged huge areas from their ethnic population and culture, starting in Arabia, incurred for the Muslims any moral debt whatsoever.

By accusing the Jews of using the *shoah* as blackmail, Muslims and their allies belittled the Christian desire for atonement to the Jews, along with the entire Jewish/Christian reconciliation process. Using EAD mechanisms, European governments counterbalanced acknowledgment of the genocide of the Jews by accusing Israel of conducting the same policy against the Arab Palestinians, portraying Palestinians, as we have seen, as victims of the Israeli Nazis. Hence, using false-mirror tactics, the Arabs and the Palestinians benefited from the *shoah*.

The European guilt complex was exploited on two levels by the EAD: 1) European guilt induced by the *shoah* was used to equate Europe's refusal to receive European Jews fleeing extermination with concerns about the Muslim immigration into Europe; 2) Western history was subverted by Muslim concepts postulating that *jihad* against non-Muslims is a "defensive" war and that non-Muslim resistance constitutes aggression against the *umma*.

As to the first trend, EAD propaganda skillfully exploited the history of European antisemitism to castigate a Western public opinion concerned about mass Muslim immigration from Arab states. It deliberately created confusion between anti-Judaism and the opposition to uncontrolled immigration. Eurabian clergymen and politicians manipulated the *shoah*, aggravating antisemitism and transforming Jewish history into a Trojan horse for immigration. With the utmost cynicism, Jewish history was used to camouflage unpopular policies and exploit the guilt of public opinion over the extermination of the Jews during the war. Linking xenophobia to the extermination of European Jewry not only concealed the history of two thousand years of anti-Judaism; it also reduced the *shoah* to a problem comparable to the illegal economic immigration of Muslims to Europe and jihadist European cells.

This transfer and appropriation of European guilt by Muslim newcomers and their advocates was not only cynical and dangerous; it also brought no solution to the immigrants' specific problems, or to those of the host populations. Europe's subservience established complex asymmetrical relations between North and South. The self-inculpation of the erstwhile colonial powers was matched by the moral irreproachability felt by an Islam that was now spreading rapidly in European countries.

Today, the EAD anti-Israeli propaganda machine continues to project its own European history of Nazism, colonialism, and apartheid onto Israel. It evokes the ancient practice of Christians, when Byzantium ruled the Holy Land, who threw their heaps of garbage on the ruins of the Temple Mount.[37] The EU poses as the savior of Palestine, trusting Arafat to protect Christianity against Israel. Arafat, the instigator of so much indiscriminate mass killing, safeguards the Arab Christians from Islamists and preserves Europe from terrorists, while in exchange the EU supports the Palestinian usurpation of Israeli identity, history, and rights.

The second trend—rewriting the history books—was alluded to by the Parliamentarian Assembly of the Council of Europe in September 1991 regarding the "historical errors" and the "hostile oriental stereotypes" responsible for the negative European image of Islam. Its recommendations strengthened the historical current that began in the 1970s with Edward Said, which adopted the Islamic view of European history to alleviate Muslim rancor. Earlier works of distinguished scholars were set aside or overlooked. *Jihad* wars were recast as simple interfaith interactions; the dhimmitude system was praised as a model of tolerance to be emulated in the twenty-first century.[38]

Some politicians suggested that Europe needed Islamic spiritual values for its own moral regeneration. Wars were blamed on Europe's resistance to Islam in the past. These views were defended most convincingly by certain clergyman, such as Anglican Bishop Cragg—who criticized the European kings and the popes for not having cooperated with the invading Muslim armies, a surrender which would have amounted to collaboration in their own demise. An Islamophile and apologetic literature developed, funded by the EAD network of joint Arab and European scholars working on the reinterpretation of history. This trend, based on the Muslim view of history that incriminates the West for every historical evil, uses the same thinking that condemns Israel, since the *dar al-harb* is the source of evil. The permanency of a *dar-al harb* assimilated to theological evil also explains the total lack of gratitude from Muslim people toward the West, in spite of continuous humanitarian, medical, and economic aid. This attitude perpetuates the haughty and contemptuous behavior toward *dhimmis,* who had to buy back their existence by their services to the *umma*.

The uncritical adoption by the EAD of the Muslim historical conception and values led to the present Islamization of European thought and civilization. The EAD apparatus has succeeded in transforming the European continent demographically and culturally. In 2004, thirty years after the first EAD agreements, it is necessary to assess the results of this deliberate policy of Europe's political leaders.

15

Conditioning Minds

The term "dhimmitude" does not refer just to isolated incidents. The *dhimma* system was a key component of an entire civilization, encompassing thirteen centuries of Jewish, Christian, and Muslim interaction on three continents. One should also include the entire Hindu history under Muslim rulers in this dhimmitude civilization. In 1930 Arthur Stanley Tritton published a critical study on the caliph's non-Muslim subjects;[1] Lebanese Antoine Fattal's pioneering and extensive research followed in 1958.[2] However, by the 1970s and 1980s, studies in academia had become diluted by omissions, sycophancy, or politically correct bias.

Dhimmitude studies and Eurabian conceptions of history and present-day relations between Muslims and non-Muslims, of course, present two diametrically opposite historical and philosophical visions. Dhimmitude studies, for their part, examine the laws, practices and history of *jihad*, which culminates in the Muslim conquest and domination of huge territories populated by non-Muslim populations of various faiths, ethnicities, and cultures. Muslim jurisprudence prescribes specific laws to govern the vanquished populations who refused to convert. As we have seen, this discrimination determined a specific status for the subjected native peoples. Jews and Christians, considered jointly as belonging to the People of the Book, were placed in the same legal category, while other faiths suffered harsher treatment.

Dhimmis' lives and properties were protected as long as they remained within the framework of their debased condition; hence, they were called "protected people," *dhimmis*, a word derived from the "pact of protection," or *dhimma*. Rebellions entailed enslavement, deportation, or death. The *dhimmi* status was applied only in former non-Muslim lands conquered by *jihad*. In contrast, by 640, the *Hijaz*—the Islamic/Arab heartland—had been cleansed of all pagan cults and religions, as well as of Judaism and Christianity. In a unanimous consensus, Muslim jurisprudence imposes special rules in Arabia, which today are often mistakenly understood to be merely inventions of the Saudi Wahhabi sect.

The term "dhimmitude" refers to the study of the Islamic jurisprudence applied to the *dhimmis*; the examination of its origin and the ways in which its application, as mandated by theology and law, determines relationships between Muslims and non-Muslims. It includes the reactions of *dhimmis* and their adaptation to this status, according to the geographical location and history of each group with the complex and evolving interactions between them. Research should encompass the impact on the condition of the *dhimmis* of the relentless *jihad* waged against Christendom for over a millennium and the influence upon *dhimmi* history of European rivalries, ambitions, and manipulations. History not being an abstract record of facts only, but duration as materialized in humanity, it is a potent receptacle of fervor, tragedy, hope, pusillanimity, desperation, and faith. Such is the texture of dhimmitude, darkened by a hapless resignation to oppression. While dhimmitude embraces other religions also, the aspects relating to its Jewish and Christian victims are deeply rooted in their biblical values and perception.

The concept of Eurabia, on the other hand, springs from the Andalusian political myth examined in chapter 12. It is a fundamentally pleasant and optimistic concept, since to Eurabians "Andalusia" represents the paradisiacal life of Jews and Christians living under the *shari'a* in the Moorish caliphate of the early Middle Ages. According to Eurabian thinking, Jews and Christians were grateful to be protected and to learn from the achievements of Muslim scholars; and neither *jihad* nor dhimmitude existed, except on rare occasions and only in defense of Islam. Any such grudging acknowledgments of mistreatment of *dhimmis* are usually compensated with the deceitful allegation that Muslims suffered as much. This vision propagates and imposes the theory that only in Islamic lands did science, art, and civilization flourish, while Christendom was still immersed in barbarism and illiteracy. On February 1, 2002, Sheikh Abd al-Rahman al-Sudayyis, imam of the al-Haraam mosque in Mecca, told his worshippers: "The noblest civilization ever known to mankind is our Islamic civilization. Today, Western civilization is nothing more than the product of its encounter with our Islamic civilization in Andalusia and other places."[3] Eurabia is immersed in the Islamic conception of history, which sees Islam as liberation from unbelief, superior as a religion and a civilization to Christianity and to all other infidel creeds.

The history of dhimmitude has profoundly influenced the *dhimmi* nations. Through centuries of oppression, they developed a particular mentality, as well as modes of political and social behavior essential to their survival. This pattern can be studied in its historical manifestations, but it can also be observed today among non-Muslims who live in Muslim countries governed in whole or part by the *shari'a*, as well as among those in the West who replicate, as if by instinct, the behavior transmitted by generations of *dhimmis*.

A brief summary of the *dhimmi* cultural pattern that has determined Jewish and Christian relations toward the Muslim dominant groups, as well as toward one another, will serve to clarify certain modern aspects of European dhimmitude. The core element pertains to the premise of Muslim superiority over all other religious groups. This point is a matter of Islamic faith stated throughout the Qur'an, which traditional Muslim theology deems to be the exact uncreated words of Allah.

In Muslim lands governed by the *shari'a,* Jews and Christians had to acknowledge the superiority of Islam at all times. Criticism of *shari'a* law drew severe punishment. *Dhimmis* adopted a servile language and obsequious demeanor for fear of retaliation and for their self-preservation. Specific laws ordained permanent inferiority and humiliation for the *dhimmis.* Their lives were valued at considerably less than that of a Muslim, usually one half, and half again for *dhimmi* women. The penalty for murder was much lighter if a *dhimmi* was the victim. Likewise, penalties for offenses were unequal between Muslims and non-Muslims. A *dhimmi* was forbidden to possess arms and to defend himself if he was physically assaulted by a Muslim; he could only beg for mercy. He was deprived of two fundamental rights: the right of self-defense against physical aggression and the right to defend himself in an Islamic law court, which refused *dhimmi* testimony in relation to a Muslim. *Dhimmis* could be judged under the provisions of their own legislation. However, *dhimmi* legislation was not recognized in Muslim courts, whose judgments superseded *dhimmi* legal decisions.

Dhimmis were forbidden to have authority over Muslims, to own or buy land, to marry Muslim women, or to have Muslim slaves or servants. In the social domain, they had to be recognizable by their clothes, the shape, color, and texture of which were prescribed from head to foot; the color and size, as well as the location, of their homes was also strictly regulated. Riding a horse or a camel was prohibited to *dhimmis,* as these animals were too noble for them. A donkey could be ridden but only astride, and only packsaddles were allowed; when sighting a Muslim, the *dhimmi* had to dismount. A *dhimmi* had to hurry through the streets, always passing to the left (impure) side of a Muslim, who was expected to force him to the narrow side or into the gutter. He had to walk humbly with lowered eyes, to accept insults without replying, to remain standing in a meek and respectful attitude in the presence of a Muslim and to leave him the best place. If he was admitted to a public bath—forbidden in many regions such as Morocco—he had to wear bells to signal his presence. Stoning Jews and Christians was not unusual in Muslim domains, especially Arab-populated regions—likewise disdain, insults, and disrespectful attitudes toward them were customary. Some regional rules represent an aggravation of this pattern: in Morocco and Yemen, Jews were forbidden any footwear outside their segregated quarter. In Iran, Jews and Christians, considered impure, could not go out in the street on rainy days.

These laws are the basic regulations set down in the classical texts on *dhimmis*. They had to be enforced throughout the lands of Islam/dhimmitude. Muslim jurists, including Andalusian authorities, strongly condemned any alleviation of these measures whenever it occurred. Its various elements were imposed with lesser or greater severity depending on the circumstances, whether in the Levant—including Egypt, Palestine, Syria, in Mesopotamia, Persia, Yemen, and the Maghreb—or in Anatolia or the Balkans.

Today, many aspects of dhimmitude remain active or potential political forces in modern states where the *shari'a* is applied or constitutes the source of the laws, as in Egypt, Iran, Sudan, Nigeria, Pakistan, and, until recently, in Afghanistan. The condition of Christians in some modern Muslim states is inspired by the traditional rules of dhimmitude relating to the laws of blasphemy, mixed marriage, and apostasy, or those concerning the building and repairing of churches, and religious processions. Discrimination in employment and in education, as well as in penal and civil law, also occurs.

Anglican Canon Patrick Sookhdeo examines the condition known in Pakistan as "bonded labor."[4] This is of particular interest to the historian of dhimmitude because it was the condition of Jewish and Christian peasantries, often referred to in their own chronicles from the eighth to the nineteenth centuries. It illustrates the subservience perpetuated by fiscal exploitation and indebtedness that inevitably led to expropriation and a system of slavery. The same fiscal oppression and the ransoming for security were observed in the nineteenth century for Christians and Jews in Syria, the Holy Land, and Lebanon,[5] as well as Mesopotamia, Armenia, and Kurdistan, and some European provinces of the Ottoman Empire. It was reported by Edouard Engelhardt, French plenipotentiary minister in Turkey in the middle of the nineteenth century.[6] Some decades later, an Anglo-French and Russian Commission of Enquiry noted a similar situation relating to Armenians in the Sassun region, after the massacres of 1894–95.[7]

Likewise, Sookhdeo demonstrates how the inferior status of the non-Muslim can validate an abuse that is in theory forbidden by law and make it irreversible—for example the abduction of Christian women or a false accusation of blasphemy. The former crime, still perpetrated in Egypt today and elsewhere, has been a consistently recurring feature of dhimmitude.

To summarize: the main features of dhimmitude display an acceptance and internalization of self-degradation, as can be observed with slaves, hostages, or populations subject to discrimination. Dhimmitude's submission is due to insecurity, vulnerability, abasement, and the principle of purchasing one's life through tribute and excessive taxation. Deprived of their history, *dhimmi* societies tend to become amnesic collections of individuals who seek their survival by flattering their oppressors.

The Signs of Dhimmitude

The destruction of the self

The main feature of dhimmitude culture stems from a denial of the difference and identity of the "Other." The belief expressed by al-Faruqi that Islamic dogma sees Judaism and Christianity as just an outdated expression of Islam ultimately negates the respective intrinsic essence of both of those religions. Deprived of a sense of historical belonging to their own roots, Jews and Christians fall prey to manipulation by those who appropriate their history to justify their policy. Such tactics undermine the core of both religions, and in particular weakens Christian awareness of the Jewish origins of Christianity. The Islamic denial of the Jewish roots of Christianity and continual attacks against the Judeo-Christian rapprochement increases the tendency of some Christians to drift toward Islamization and grow estranged from their religious origins.

Eurabian anti-Zionist culture shares the Islamic conception of Israel's historical illegitimacy and the Arab/Muslim appropriation of Israel's past. It induces the repudiation of and contempt for the First Testament.[8] It propagates a Christian Gnosticism or Marcionism adapted to Islamic expectations of Christianity and of Europe. This aspect will be examined in the next chapter.

The elimination of history

Jihad has been a devastating and genocidal war throughout history. Millions of people have been massacred, abducted, enslaved, deported, and dispossessed of their land and countries. The ensuing colonization of conquered territories is an endless and agonizing history, chronicled by its contemporaries, victims, and perpetrators. There is no lack of reliable testimony on the advance of *jihad* and dhimmitude over the continents, through the centuries, and today. Muslim authors, who recorded the sufferings of infidels as a divine retribution for their stubbornness in sin, provide detailed descriptions. Yet despite massive evidence of atrocities recorded by Muslims themselves, Muslim scholars continue to maintain the ethical perfection of *jihad*. Such opinions manifest a profound racism toward the vanquished and dehumanized populations, whose own history is also suppressed to suit the Muslim conception of ethics.

Ismail Raji al-Faruqi asserted: "Compared with the histories of other religions, the history of Islam is categorically white as far as toleration of other religions is concerned."[9] Since the 1970s, books, speeches, and documentaries by scholars, politicians, and journalists, vaunting the great Islamic civilization, have flooded Europe.[10] Muslims there teach that Islam has spread only by peaceful means. Al-Faruqi wrote in 1978, "Nothing is farther from the truth and more inimical to Muslim–non-Muslim relations than the claim that Islam spread by the sword. Nothing could have been and still is more condemnable to the Muslim than to coerce a non-Muslim into Islam."[11] This is a half-truth: Islamic law does indeed condemn forcible conversion, although this law has been frequently contravened in practice throughout Islamic history. The laws of *jihad* that require the Islamic community to wage war in order to establish the hegemony of Islamic rule, and those of *shari'a*, which lay such a heavy burden of discrimination and harassment upon the *dhimmi* communities, are potent tools to impose conversion.

The Muslim version of history is now being taught and accepted in Europe and America, while more accurate treatments such as historian Paul Fregosi's book *Jihad in the West* faced a wall of opposition.[12] Mainstream views of *jihad* gloss over its fanaticism and such practices as enslavement and massacre. The responsibility for the *jihad* wars' atrocities is attributed to Christian resistance to Islamization and to the iniquitous Crusades—but not to the concepts of *jihad* and *dar al-harb*, the land of war where the infidels must be subdued. Today, many priests, bishops, and historians lament the Crusades, the expulsion of the Moors from Spain, or the victory of Lepanto in 1572 that saved Europe from the Turkish armies and from Islamization. European victories over Muslim armies are deemed regrettable.[13] There is no doubt that this chorus of tearful contrition helps to strengthen the Muslim opinion that Islamic *jihad* is a liberating and peaceful favor granted to the infidels.

On June 6, 2002, at Harvard University, a Muslim biomedical engineering student named Zayed Yasin delivered a lecture at a prestigious annual ceremony to a public of professors and students. In it, he condemned the misuse of the Arabic term "*jihad*". The twenty-two-year-old Yasin defined *jihad* as "the determination to do right, to do justice even against your own interest" and as "an individual struggle for moral behavior." Yasin, a former president of the Harvard Islamic Society, received support from Harvard President Lawrence H. Summers. Such wishful thinking ignores the rivers of blood that characterize the historical reality of *jihad* as described in countless Muslims and *dhimmi* chronicles. In academia, noble words and dreamy inconsistencies have replaced the hard moral discipline of confronting historical truths. In his insightful comment, Daniel Pipes, a scholar on Islam—later member of the U.S. Institute for Peace—refers to this academic current which he calls "Apologizing for militant Islam":

> Hiding jihad's awful legacy is standard operating procedure at Harvard. A professor of Islamic history portrays jihad as a "struggle without arms." The Harvard Islamic Society's faculty adviser defines true jihad as no more fearsome than "to do good in society."[14]

Suppression of the history of *jihad* and praise of the Islamic conquest of Christian countries[15] continue to inspire the anti-Western, apologist *dhimmis* of the school of Edward Said. This Muslim-sanitized view is now taught by Professor Rashid Khalidi of the Middle East Arts, Language and Culture faculty (MEALC) at Columbia University. Christian academics who conform to the *dhimmi* mentality manifest a servility whereby oppressive ideology is praised by its victims, who unconsciously adopt a self-accusing complex to vindicate their oppressors and appease them. In Europe, this trend conforms to EAD directives concerning university teaching, which were reinforced by the EU's 1991 resolutions at Strasbourg.

Acknowledgment of European inferiority

On May 2, 2003, Sheik Jamal Shakir Al-Nazzal declared in his Friday sermon at the Great Mosque in Falouja, Iraq:

> Brothers, before we begin with the matter of the destruction that has struck large and small in this country, I would like to say that it was the Islamic State that established the beacon of science for all humanity in the spheres of engineering and law. The era of the Islamic State became a golden age, at a time when Europe was living a life of ignorance, like beasts, without [its people] knowing law, human rights, or women's rights. In France there was [even] debate regarding whether women were considered human.
>
> Islam arrived and illuminated the minds of man. Andalusia is testimony to this. The king of Britain, France, Austria, and Norway, which were then a single state, wrote to the emir of the believers in Andalusia and requested [permission] to send his children to study sciences with the Muslims at the University of Cordoba in Andalusia. He told him—and the letter still exists— "I am sending you my children, the fruit of my loins, to study science with you." He signed the letter, "Your servant, George."
>
> Let all hear—the Muslims, George, and George's supporters: This same Islamic culture, that enlightened the land, takes precedence over Europe. Europe and its forces must treat the Muslim lands with sanctity, primarily Baghdad, the capital of [Haroun] Al-Rashid which gave the Europeans the sciences, the clock, and gifts, out of friendship.[16]

Such statements abound not only from sheikhs, but also in speeches and books by Europeans who have adopted today's new "enlightened" views.

European politicians continually harp upon the Islamic superiority over Christendom in art, science, civilization, and religious tolerance. As we have seen, in September 1991, the Parliamentary Assembly of the Council of Europe adopted numerous recommendations concerning the development of Arabic and Islamic studies in education, media, and culture in the EU. No other foreign culture enjoys such prestige in Europe; nor is any other so strongly supported and imposed upon the population through an elaborate network including universities, the media, and governmental institutions, directly connected to the foreign ministries of each member state of the European Union and the European Commission.

Self-guilt and self-abasement

In Europe, the politics of dhimmitude manifest themselves today in the decades-long silence on violations of human rights in Muslim countries, or tolerance of it on the grounds of "cultural relativism." This look-the-other-way policy of Europe, while claiming to defend human rights, obeys a fundamental law of dhimmitude: *dhimmis* are forbidden on pain of death to appeal for help to outsiders, or to propagate ideas considered hostile to Islam. They may not denigrate or misquote the Qur'an, nor criticize the Prophet, nor the Muslim religion.[17] *Dhimmis* who request help from Christian countries are deprived of all the rights and privileges they had obtained through the protection pact, and "of the right of immunity of life and property."[18] Christians facing persecution and discrimination in Islamic countries are forced, by a system that prohibits victims from testifying against their Muslim tormentors, to withdraw into an isolation conducive to their own destruction.

Europe's silence on this anti-Christian oppression amounts to implicit submission to the *shari'a* prohibitions of blasphemy. The *dhimmi* attitude that has developed among European intellectuals, politicians, and the clergy gives rise to flagellatory stances that serve to incriminate the West—and particularly Israel. These spokesmen repeat the usual anti-Western Islamic recriminations, thereby accrediting and justifying them.[19] It puts the Western public sphere in the position of conforming to one of the basic rules of dhimmitude: the express prohibition of Christians and Jews to criticize Islamic history and doctrine.

Qadi 'Iyad (d. 1149), the famous Imam and prolific author and scholar of Andalusian origin, studied in Andalusia and was *qadi* in Granada and in Ceuta. He described explicitly the various types of blasphemy which deserve death: "all who curse Muhammad . . . , or blame him or attribute imperfection to him in his person, his lineage, his '*deen*' [religion] or any of his qualities, or alludes to that or its like by any means whatsoever, whether in the form of a curse or contempt or belittling him or detracting of him or finding fault with him or maligning him," these persons should be killed.[20] In the case that "someone intentionally calls the Prophet a liar in what he said or brought or denies and rejects his prophethood or his message and its existence or disbelieves in it," this person is treated like an unbeliever and must be killed.[21] The Imam can choose to cut off the head, burn, or crucify someone who curses or disparages the Prophet. Repentance cannot remove the sanction. If *dhimmis* curse the Prophet or minimize his message, they should be killed—unless they become Muslims.

> When they do what neither the treaty nor their *dhimma* status allows them, then they violate their *dhimma* status and fall into the category of unbelievers and people with whom the Muslims are at war [*dar al-harb*]. So they are killed for their disbelief. Furthermore, *dhimma* status does not remove any other of the *hudud* [specific penalties ordained by *shari'a*] of Islam from them, such as cutting off the hand for theft or executing someone for a murder committed by one of them, even if that is permissible by their own deen.[22]

Any Jew or Christian who reviles the Prophet is to be beheaded or burned, unless he converts. This threat might explain much of the Eurabian and *dhimmi* glorification of Islam and their demonization of the West. Edward Said's apologetic works on behalf of Islamic culture, received as a new gospel in Europe, is illustrated by his constant criticism of the supposed "Us vs. Them" divide between Westerners and Muslims—a divide he attributes to the White Man's ethnocentrism. His criticism would have gained credibility if he had included an analysis of the Islamic theory of *dar al-Islam* (we Muslims) and *dar al-harb* (they, the non-Muslim enemy), and the whole system of social and international relations it generated through *jihad* and dhimmitude. Said never seemed to notice that this is a theological system of separation and discrimination that is still valid in the Islamic world today.

The unilateral self-inculpation by Western pro-Arab lobbies accords with the traditional Islamic demonization of the *dar al-harb*. With support from the highest political and religious levels in Europe, this self-hatred is now assumed, internalized, and propagated by Western academics and writers. The rejection of the Bible and Europe's self-denigration in relation to Islam are developing into a form of anti-Christianity, combined with anti-Zionism—typical of the interreligious conflicts provoked within the venomous context of dhimmitude.

Asymmetry

What image of Europe and Israel, of Christianity and Judaism—the twin *dhimmi* religions—do Muslim scholars and thinkers living in Europe, Asia, and the Arab countries project? Is there a courteous reciprocity through recognition of past mistakes, or an effort to suppress the prejudices that are contained within the Islamic religious tradition? Muslim opinion takes as unquestionable truth Europe's inferiority to Islam, its evilness, its spiritual bankruptcy, the fanaticism of the Crusades. As for Israel, Arab defamation and demonization have surpassed even the Nazi production. In short, except in Turkey, the general Muslim reaction to Europe's charm offensive was a vociferous eschewing of recriminations, claims, and pretensions to a monolithic superiority.

The classical Islamic view of the *dar al-harb* was expressed by modern Islamists like the Egyptian Hasan al-Banna, founder of the Muslim Brotherhood in the 1920s; Sayed Qutb, the major Muslim Brotherhood theorist; the Sudanese spiritual leader Hassan al-Turabi, and the Pakistani Abu Ala Mawdudi. In spite of Europe's conciliatory efforts—and funds—the Islamist sensibility that inspires the bin Laden discourses is able to capitalize on popular Muslim feeling because it expresses traditional patterns of contempt toward *dhimmis* and infidels.[23] Europe's negation of the sources of Islamist rage, by attributing them to circumstantial situations like "poverty," "under-development," "humiliation," or "frustration"—for which the West and Israel bore responsibility—manifests the *dhimmi*'s obsequiousness as a response to offensive behavior.

Dhimmis are accustomed to this asymmetry. The inferiority of infidels is a fundamental principle of Islamic law, inscribed in every aspect of their status: "And Allah will never give the disbelievers a way against the believers" (Qur'an, 4:140) and in the *hadith*: "Islam surmounts, [it is] not surmounted." Medieval Arab cartographers, like al-Idrisi, and others, placed the North (Europe), below and the South (the Maghreb) above. Because Jews, Christians, and other infidels are, by nature, inferior to Muslims, the *shari'a* rules their exclusion from any post giving them authority over Muslims. Nowadays in Nigeria, Indonesia, Pakistan, Morocco, Yemen, Egypt, and the Palestinian territories, Jewish and Christian blood—of both *dhimmis* and tourists—is often shed with evident impunity, despite government efforts to restrain the Islamists.

Asymmetry also characterizes the rights of Muslim immigrants to the West, as compared to those of European immigrants and even indigenous *dhimmi* Christians in Muslim countries. The latter are subjected to the Islamic blasphemy law and the prohibition to proselytize, among many other restrictions.[24] The particular conditions for non-Muslims in Saudi Arabia have no parallel in the West.

An article by Günther Grass in the *International Herald Tribune* illustrates the loss of balance and judgment that results: confusion and false equivalence between a great democracy and a terrorist movement.[25] Grass wrote, "Religious fundamentalism leads both sides [America and the terrorists] to abuse what belongs to all religions, taking the notion of God hostage in accordance with their own fanatical understanding." He speaks of the pope, "who knows how lasting and devastating the disasters wrought by the mentality and actions of Christian crusaders have been." Grass opines that the "moral decline of America" and its "organized madness" will be the "[m]otivation for more terrorism."

For years, Europeans played with the equivalence of aggressors and victims, often as a pretext to escape from guilt and transform the victim into an aggressor—as if there were no strict moral premises to judge crime. The equivalence of all religions, as professed by Grass, belongs to the modern Eurabian cultural trend in which, all values being the same, none is good or bad. This simplistic thinking from the pen of a reputable German writer provides the pretext for exhibiting a skeptical indifference to evade action and often to side either passively or actively with evil, since evil and good are the same. Grass's focus upon what he calls the moral decline of America in its war against international Islamic terrorism, points up "old Europe's" moral debacle in its alliances with—and effectual surrender to—terrorist states. His explanation that fighting terror will breed more terror implies that security entails surrender to *jihad,* and not resistance to it.

A tributary continent

Tabari, the great Muslim scholar and author of a monumental historical work on the seventh and eighth centuries' Arab-Muslim conquests, describes the Islamic conquest of Basra (Iraq) in 636. Iraq was then a province of Sassanid Persia, where Jews and Christians formed the majority of the population. Tabari reports that Umar b. al-Khattab, the second caliph, instructed the commander of the troops that he sent to al-Basra as follows:

> Summon the people to God; those who respond to your call [meaning they convert], accept it from them, but those who refuse must pay the poll tax out of humiliation and lowliness [Qur'an 9:29]. If they refuse this, it is the sword without leniency. Fear God with regard to what you have been entrusted.[26]

This is the pattern of the *jihad* war. Tabari died in 923. By then the Muslim empire had expanded from Portugal to India. After Tabari's death, the Muslim conquests continued in Asia, as well as in Christian eastern European lands. The Christian kingdoms of Armenia, Byzantium, Bulgaria, Serbia, Bosnia, Herzegovina, Croatia, Albania, and parts of Poland and Hungary were conquered. The Muslim armies were only stopped at the gates of Vienna in 1683. The jihadist conquest lasted over a millennium; dhimmitude, and the colonizing system it implemented, endures today in many regions.

The *dhimmis,* the conquered infidels of all those territories, were protected from the *jihad* rules only by paying countless taxes and ransoms extorted by threat and torture, whether legally or not.[27] Their lives and belongings were spared on payment of the poll tax, the *jizya*. Payment for security is the foundation of dhimmitude. It is instructive that a 1997 book on Islamic jurisprudence by Abbasali Amid Zanjani bears the title *Minority Rights according to the Law of the Tribute Agreement.*

The multibillion loans from the EU countries to Arab states, and the Palestinian Authority's corrupt terror infrastructure, have already been briefly mentioned. The EU's huge investments in Arab countries provide the EU with an immense political leverage that could have been used to suppress Arab terror and racism. However, the EU never blocked any agreements with Syria, the terror-backed occupier of Lebanon, nor with Egypt, Algeria, or other Arab dictatorships. Despite his ties to terrorism, whether Hezbollah or PLO, Syrian President Bashir al-Assad is treated with all the deference ordinarily accorded world leaders: he was received by Queen Elizabeth II in an official visit to London in 2002, and in October 2003 he hosted the Spanish royal couple in Damascus.

Romano Prodi, the president of the European Commission, visited Algeria on March 30, 2003, and Tunisia on the two following days. In both countries, he restated the EU's readiness to work with the Maghreb countries as partners within the Euro-Mediterranean context. Prodi's program was presented as a "Wider Europe–Neighborhood initiative." He invited those countries to make full use of the Association Agreements. The fact that all North African countries have dictatorial regimes, and that in Algeria a civil war has claimed about 150,000 lives, gave him no anxiety. Nor did the fact that civilians—sometimes whole villages—were being routinely butchered, Europeans are abducted, and that religious Islamic fanaticism has become a tool of terror. None of this has impinged upon the EU's policies toward its Arab partners.

The meeting of the EU-Mashrak Partnership in Damascus on October 23–25, 2003 brought together business representatives from Syria, Jordan, Lebanon, and the EU. In stark contrast, the EU continues to pursue a discriminatory policy toward Israel, freezing economic agreements for political reasons.[28] But the EU is unconcerned that Syria is listed by Washington as a terrorist state for harboring and supplying terror organizations: Hezbollah, Islamic Jihad and Hamas—three groups responsible for hundreds of civilian deaths in Israel.

The Policy Dialogue and Co-ordination Committee of the "Facility for Euro-Mediterranean Investment and Partnership" (FEMIP), at its second meeting in Istanbul (April 3, 2003), noted that some €1.5 billion had been approved by the European Investment Bank (EIB) for investment in Arab countries. FEMIP would facilitate access to finance by private sector firms, increase provisions for long-term credit, promote financial leases and guarantee funds for development of new products for equity and quasi-equity financing, and provide technical assistance to the banking sector. Participants represented all twelve Mediterranean Partners, including Israel, the fifteen EU Member States, the European Commission, the World Bank, the African Development Bank, and the European Central Bank. On November 11, 2003, on its third meeting at Naples, FEMIP announced that the Bank had extended over €1.8 billion of new loans and approved another €1.8 billion of new investment operations in the Muslim world.[29]

The EU financing plan for 2003 included several projects in the West Bank, Gaza, and Arab countries, which, like Syria, Egypt, and the Palestinian Authority, are breeding grounds of anti-Western Islamic fanaticism. Without Europe's financial aid and know-how, those countries would hardly be able to feed their own growing populations. Europe could easily compel them to abandon their racist culture, instead of vindicating it.

Money collected from European taxpayers is generously distributed to Arab dictatorships as a modern "poll tax" to buy Europe's security; no gratitude may be expected from the beneficiaries. The relationship between the *umma* and the exploited *dhimmis* has developed on a transcontinental level. Yet despite their financial and other contributions to Muslim societies, European travelers are again targets for Islamists. It looks as if we have returned to the former practices, abolished in the late nineteenth century, when infidel travelers in Islamic lands had to be protected by Muslim soldiers and an *aman*, an Islamic recognition of protection, or else risk being taken hostage, ransomed or killed.

Even if we assume that the majority of Muslims disapprove of the violence and terror directed against foreigners in their countries, the increased aggression demonstrates the ascendancy of the *jihad* ideological conception of how Islamic states deal with both non-Muslim individuals and governments.

On December 9, 2003, Prime Minister José Maria Aznar of Spain announced in Morocco the largest financial package Madrid has ever granted to any nation, in order to slow illegal immigration. The deal includes $478 million (390 million) of soft loans and debt swaps intended to create jobs in Morocco to diminish the flow of illegal immigrants to Europe.[30]

A frightened continent

In his book on daily life in Andalusia, Charles-Emmanuel Dufourcq describes what he calls *"Une grande Peur"* (A great Fear): the terror of the European population targeted by jihadist war incursions.[31] On the Eastern side of the Mediterranean, Greek and Slavic chroniclers record the same flight of terrorized people away from the Turkish advance.[32] The Serbian geographer of the early twentieth century, Jovan Cvijic, wrote in his very informative book on the Serbs that for centuries the *dhimmi* population lived in constant fear.[33]

From the beginning of the EAD transactions, the European public was fed fears of upsetting the Arabs. Preventing the humiliation of the Arabs became a primary concern in political and cultural French circles. Jacques Berque, the influential French Arabist scholar, born in Algeria, recommended prudence toward the Arab world on more than one occasion. As France prepared for the Gulf war in August 1990, Berque declared, "[The Arabs] weigh heavily on the flanks of Europe, even in its very heart, with the immigrants. The humiliation of the Arab world is a luxury which we cannot afford."[34]

The respectful reverence shown to everything Arab is linked to this European anxiety. However, a greater alarm agitated Europe's leading circles with the development over the last thirty years of PLO, Hamas and Hezbollah terrorism and radical political Islamism. Long before Spain's antiterror resistance collapsed in the face of the Madrid terror bombing of March 11, 2004—when nearly two hundred civilian passengers were killed—fear of provoking Islamic terror panicked European ministers and prevailed in political decisions. It was this concern that drove them into the lion's jaws with an appeasement policy and a servile vassalage to the PLO. In March–April 2003, the threat of Islamic terror and of the dreaded clash of civilizations was constantly cited by Europeans who filled the streets, shouting anti-American slogans. French Foreign Minister Dominique de Villepin told U.S. Secretary of State Colin Powell that the war in Iraq and fears of further hostilities had sparked a "feeling of worry and humiliation" in the Arab world.[35]

For "old Europe," America is a danger because it fights a war against terrorism, and proudly asserts its values and its freedom. Journalist Barry James reported that the spokesperson for President Chirac's party in Paris, Renaud Donnedieu de Vabres, said that the French government "continues to think, as paradoxical as it might sound, that we are the best allies of the Americans, because we are preoccupied by the same reality—terrorism."[36] There's no doubt about the shared preoccupation. The difference is that America fights terrorism, while France goes along with it. Terrorist groups like Hezbollah or Islamic Jihad were not identified as such by the EU until September 2003. After the terrorist group Hamas had killed hundreds of innocent civilians in Israel, members of the European Union finally agreed to blacklist Hamas on September 6, 2003. Even then, however, France and Germany still refused to recognize Hamas as a terrorist entity—although it claimed responsibility for most of the 104 jihadist bombings in three years of warlike acts.[37]

In his rich and dense book on the religious ideology and political literature of the *Islamikazes*, Raphael Israeli, former Professor of Chinese and

Islamic and Middle Eastern Studies at the Hebrew University, Jerusalem, details the countless justifications for terrorism against the West which are widely popular in the Muslim world.[38] In England, a spokesman for the radical Islamic group al-Muhajirun, Salim Abd-al-Rahman, announced that because of the British attacks on Afghanistan after 9/11,

> government buildings in Britain, military installations, and N° 10 Downing Street have become legitimate targets. If any Muslims want to kill him [Prime Minister Tony Blair] or get rid of him, I would not shed a tear for him. In the Islamic view, such a man would not be punished for his deeds, but would be praised.[39]

Eurocrats pretend to fight terrorism, yet they pamper it in attributing its causes to poverty and injustice, allegedly provoked by America and Israel. In this way, the fight against Islamic international terror is conveniently diverted to a more comfortable fight against America and Israel, while Europe strengthens its alliances with the Arab dictators that sponsor it. The most illustrative example is the European backing and funding of Yasser Arafat, the "godfather of terrorism," well protected by the EU, his erstwhile victim.

Europe is rapidly assuming the role that *dhimmis* held in traditional Muslim societies. *Dhimmis* had to walk to the left side of the Muslims, in the gutter, and accept insult and blows without responding, so as to avoid humiliating their Muslim lords. Forbidden to carry or possess arms, their weakness humbled them before the armed Muslims. With services, money and humility, they begged forgiveness for their existence.

In history—and in Europe today—*dhimmis* do not fight. Dhimmitude is based on peaceful surrender, subjection, tribute, and praise.

A culture of hate

Jihad ideology embodies the concept of perpetual war. Therefore, it requires perpetual enemies, which the *umma* is obliged by religion to fight and subject. Its joint concept of *dar al-harb*, the land of war that must be conquered by the *dar al-Islam*, incites constant hostility against the infidels, leading to razzias or war on their territory. Al-Wansharishi, a fifteenth century Morocco mufti, wrote in one of his *fatwas*:

> God Almighty, the One, the All-Conquering, has created abasement to be inflicted on the accursed unbelievers, fetters and chains for them to drag from one place to the next as a demonstration of his power and of the superiority of Islam, and to honor his chosen Prophet . . . and what is required from the believers is faith in God, in the last day, and an effort to distance oneself from the enemies of God.[40]

In his book exploring the ideology supporting global terrorism, *Hatred's Kingdom*, Dore Gold—Middle East expert and former Israeli ambassador to the United Nations in New York—exposes the deeply ingrained hatred feeding the *jihad*. He quotes Sheikh Abdul Aziz bin Baz, vice chancellor of the Islamic University of Medina: "According to the Koran, the Sunnah, and the consensus of Muslims it is a requirement of the Muslims to be hostile to the Jews and the Christians and other *mushrikun* [polytheists]." Bin Baz added that various verses in the Qur'an prove "with absolute clarity that there is a religious requirement to despise the infidel Jews and Christians and the other *mushrikun*." In 1974, Sheikh bin Baz was appointed president of the Directorate of Religious Research, Islamic Legal Rulings, Islamic Propagation and Guidance, an important Saudi legal and religious governmental body.[41]

In late 2002, Sheikh Muhammad bin Abdul Rahman al-Arifi, the imam of the mosque of King Fahd Defense Academy, wrote, "We will control the land of the Vatican; we will control Rome and introduce Islam in it. Yes, the Christians who carve crosses on the breasts of the Muslims in Kosovo—and before then in Bosnia—and before then in many places in the world—will pay us *Jiziya*, in humiliation, or they will convert to Islam."[42] The linkage between hatred, war, and humiliation is evident.

The numerous and varied signs of degradation attached to *dhimmi* existence created in the *dar al-Islam* a constant focus for hatred of the *dhimmis*, who were only tolerated as long as their inferiority was maintained. The dominant religion's language of contempt and abuse could freely develop in the silent and humble world of dhimmitude. The perpetuation of this hate cult today in relation to Israel was condemned by British Prime Minister Tony Blair in his speech at the United States Congress on July 17, 2003. "The state of Israel should be recognized by the entire Arab world, and the vile propaganda used to indoctrinate children not just against Israel but against Jews must cease. You cannot teach people hate and then ask them to practice peace."

The unbounded hate speech against infidels, so prevalent in Arab societies, has overflowed into Europe—imported by EAD channels throughout the European Union. Jihadist hate has rekindled latent Nazi and fascist vitriol in the concoction of Eurabian culture. As a former vice-prime minister of Sweden, Per Ahlmark, put it in his strong protest against antisemitism,

Constantly singling out Israel as the enemy of humanity is part of the campaign directed against the Jewish people. . . . Attacks on synagogues have been triggered by defamatory language about the conflict in the Middle East. . . . It is to the shame of all of Europe that so many French Jews today cannot send their children to school without profound anxiety about their security. Many Christians in various countries are still influenced by the legacy of anti-Jewish theology. They must be exposed and resisted when they, for religious reasons, express their hostility against Israel![43]

In a brilliant article, "The Modern *Hep! Hep! Hep!*," American novelist Cynthia Ozick quotes George Orwell: "Political language is designed to make lies sound truthful and murder respectable, and to give the appearance of solidity to pure wind." She adds: "In our time, the Big Lie (or Big Lies, there are so many) is disseminated everywhere, and not merely by the ignorant, but with malice aforethought by the intellectual classes, the governing elites, the most prestigious elements of the press in all the capitals of Europe, and by the university professor and the diplomats."[44]

Robert Spencer has examined, in his well-documented recent book *Onward Muslim Soldiers*, the modern, global, jihadist culture in Muslim countries and in Europe—and its violent manifestations.[45] As an NGO representative for nearly twenty years at the UN Commission on Human Rights and its Sub-Commission, historian David Littman has denounced this jihadist ideology and the general indifference of the "international community"—what he called "Islamism grows stronger at the UN."[46]

Years ago, Eurabians had already established the essential points of their anti-American and anti-Israeli propaganda. The powerful EAD lobbies integrated them into Europe's economic and security apparatuses, within their strategic Euro-Arab alliances. The compromises of some European governments with the PLO in the 1970s, as we have seen, neutralized terrorism on European soil in exchange for an anti-Israel strategy, which effectively renewed traditional antisemitism. Moreover, the immigration within two or three decades of several million Muslims, principally from Arab countries and Asia, imported to Europe the conflicts stemming from dhimmitude.

The agents

The *dhimmi* policies of submission, humiliation, and services, blended with antisemitism and anti-Americanism, have given Eurabian dhimmitude its complex fabric. It follows the historical jihadist pattern by fomenting animosity between *dhimmi* groups and division between infidel nations. It is not surprising that some clerics, being the most efficient purveyors of religious prejudices, became also the best agents of dhimmitude in Europe. The condemnation of Bush for impiety by some European Protestants and Catholics fits this pattern: negative comments on his evangelical Protestant religiosity from clergymen and others of the Protestant and Catholic Churches in Europe illustrate the resentment his antiterror efforts have aroused in some Islamophile Christian circles. An anathema against Bush as "a false Christian" has spread within the church institutions in tandem with EU anti-American feelings. Islamophile *dhimmi* Churches condemn Bush as a fanatic and, paradoxically for clerics, disdain his invocations to God[47]—unaware apparently that the expulsion of God from European public speech frees the vacuum for Allah. Americans are proud of their Judeo-Christian values; Europeans dissimulate about theirs like *dhimmis*.

Such feelings are much stronger in the Arab Churches. The exhibition of animosity toward the West was for centuries the ransom they had to pay for their survival. Vehicles of Arab policy, in line with the long tradition of dhimmitude, they chose to speak of the Palestinian problem rather than their own plight as Christian *dhimmis*. In July 2003, Palestinian church leaders declared that American Christians who support Israel's right to the Holy Land based on biblical grounds have no connection to true Christianity[48]—thereby suggesting that replacement theology and deicidal accusations are entrenched. Today, the *dhimmi* Churches strive conscientiously to weave Western society's fabric of dhimmitude.

Flattery and servility, anti-Americanism and anti-Zionism, coupled with a tremendous fear of Islamic terrorism, dominate current European media and political discourse. Lord Dubs, chairman of the now subsumed Broadcasting Standards Commission (BSC), the ethics supervisory body for the British audio-visual media, acknowledged that British scriptwriters are cautious: "In portraying Muslims they have held back, they have censored themselves, they are timid. . . . I have seen them pour scorn on Christianity more than on other religions. Christianity is an easier and more acceptable target, followed to a lesser extent by Jews and Hindus."[49] Monstrous anti-Americanism and antisemitic rallies are the tribute humbly paid by a Europe with little courage left to fight for its own security. The indignity is so profoundly internalized that it is barely conscious; and when felt, it is gloated upon and even praised.

Clerics and leftists join forces in their gravitation toward the Qur'an. In February 2003 a French politician and leftist intellectual, Régis Debray—formerly an ally and a fan of Che Guevera—published a virulent attack against America in the *New York Times*.[50] Among his numerous charges, he denounced the biblical self-assurance of the United States: a puritanism that keeps "America hostage to a sacred morality." Indictment of the Bible, linked to the hatred of Israel, is a current trend in the culture of Eurabia. Debray's comment, "Our suburbs, after all, pray to Allah," indicates to what extent France has become a satellite of the Arab world. It explains, perhaps, his blindness to the Arab *jihad* while denouncing the American "crusade."

The contribution of Arab Christian politicians and intellectuals to *dhimmi* militancy in the Islamic cause, following the banner of Edward Said, has been overwhelming in Europe and America. Middle Eastern Christians in America, as well as Greek, Serbian, and other Slavic historians, have often denounced the type of Christian collaboration that reproduces the permanent pattern of *dhimmi* behavior customary under Muslim colonization. In spite of their tenacity and courage, Lebanese, Coptic, and Assyrian refugees from Arab countries could hardly compete with the "Arabists," their brother-enemies, who are generously funded and protected by powerful lobbies—and whom they consider as traitors.[51]

For thirty years now, Europeans have been subjected to a permanent campaign of disinformation through the Euro-Arab Parliamentary Association and the multifarious lobbying networks of the Dialogue, sprawling through its committees and subcommittees into business and finance, media and publications, academia and church, throughout the EU. Eurabian functionaries populate the centers of decision; EU anti-Zionist and anti-American policy orientations have been adopted across the political spectrum, buttressed by internal guidance right down to the grassroots, in the pursuance of EAD's twin purpose: the emergence of Euro-Arab unity as a pole of power rivaling America, and a way to secure oil supplies.

The current Palestinian terrorist war, started in October 2000, and the EU alliance with Arafat and the PA, gave the opportunity for a uniform media campaign throughout Europe based on the Euro-Arab partnership regarding cultural and human affairs, as stated in the Barcelona Declaration. Articles, photographs, and testimonies on Palestinian sufferings inundated the media. It inoculated the public with gigantic doses of hatred against Israelis—even as they were dying in the streets, restaurants, shops, and buses. Aggressiveness against Jews was sustained by a libelous and harping media. The culture of anathema in the EU was not dissimilar to that spread in the Arab countries, and it proceeded in the same way. Apparently, it went unnoticed by many church leaders, politicians, intellectuals, and journalists, who were so prompt to denounce racism and Islamophobia in mass demonstrations. Some even welcomed the renewed antisemitism with delight, as if a deep and resentful rage had finally resurfaced. Verbal violence, cynical and unwarranted coarseness against Jews and Israel, reminiscent of the Nazi viciousness, are now common and proudly exposed in European media and universities contaminated by the shameless language of abhorrence pervasive in Palestinian and Arab societies.

Yet Europeans in their majority are still hostile to this phenomenon, which is after all an institutionalized policy imposed by the Eurabians—and in which they feel imprisoned and debased, powerless to fight what has become an Israelophobic culture.

Part V
Dialogue on Trial

16

The Islamization of Christianity

Interfaith dialogues are one of those generous and positive initiatives that have emanated from the Western Christian world since the mid-twentieth century. They were a follow up to the World's Parliament of Religions, which was held at the Columbian Exposition of 1893 in Chicago. Conducted with praiseworthy intentions, interfaith meetings aimed at suppressing prejudices and building mutual esteem instead of focusing upon differences. In the 1940s Christian-Muslim dialogue—which preceded the Jewish-Christian dialogue—prompted feverish excitement in Europe among the clergy, European Arabist political agents such as the French scholar Louis Massignon, in Orientalist circles, and among antisemitic activists.

Ismail R. al-Faruqi (1921–86)—a Palestinian Muslim professor in the Department of Religion at Temple University, Philadelphia—was a forceful exponent of Islam's identification with Judaism and Christianity. He was much admired by his former student, John L. Esposito, Professor of Religion and International Affairs at Georgetown University and Director of the Center for Muslim and Christian Understanding. Esposito wrote an admiring foreword to a posthumously published volume of al-Faruqi's essays, *Islam and Other Faiths* (1998).

In his lectures and writings, al-Faruqi asserted that Islam views Judaism and Christianity not as "other religions" but as its very self. It recognizes their God as its God, their Prophets as Muslim Prophets. Muslims are committed by their faith to bring the divine invitation to the People of the Book (both Jews and Christians), to cooperate with them and live together as a first step toward religious unity, i.e. toward their Islamization. Many Christians gladly interpreted such calls as invitations to harmonious cooperation and dialogue.

Yet Michel Hayek, a Lebanese priest and a knowledgeable Arabist, sounded a warning note by clarifying Jesus's actual place in Islam—an aspect that had been overlooked or misinterpreted.[1] He pointed out that the Qur'an and the *hadith* express negative views of non-Muslim faiths, including Judaism and Christianity, the latter spoken of as associationism or idolatry.[2] Some verses, of course, do speak favorably of the People of the Book; others that praise Jews and Christians seem to refer, according to some exegeses, to those who have seen the light and have converted to Islam. The principle of abrogation—mentioned twice in the Qur'an[3]—adds an additional difficulty for interpretation: some earlier verses mentioning Jews and Christians are thus believed to have been abrogated and replaced later by others, without specifying which verses were in fact abrogated.

Today, some European Muslims—including Bassam Tibi, professor at Georg-August University in Göttingen, Rachid Kaci in France, as well as the Egyptian jurist Muhammad Said al-Ashmawi—try to contextualize the Qur'an's negative assertions about Jews and Christians by relating them to specific past situations. However, such views are considered marginal in the Islamic world: traditional prejudice remains the norm.

Muslims, however, deny that the portrayal of Jews and Christians given in the Qur'an is negative. To suggest that such a portrayal is pejorative would imply that their Holy Book, considered the word of Allah, provides an inaccurate description of non-Muslims. Hence, the accusations leveled against them are believed to be the truth.

In numerous Qur'anic verses, Allah exhorts Jews and Christians to obey the rules given by Muhammad to humanity, otherwise they will be damned for eternity (2:155). The oneness of Muhammad's revelation with those of the Hebrew patriarchs, prophets and Jesus is a fundamental assertion of the Qur'an: "Abraham was not a Jew, nor was he a Christian but he was a Hanif, a Moslem, and he was not one of the Polytheists" (3:60), and "Say: 'We have believed in Allah, and what has been sent down to us, and what has been sent down to Abraham and Ishmael and Isaac and Jacob and the Patriarchs, and what was given to Moses and Jesus and the prophets from their Lord; we make no distinction between them, and we to Him do surrender'" (3:78).[4]

This predication is one of the many reasons why some Christian theologians deny the prevalent view that the God of the Bible is identical to the Allah of the Qur'an. For if they were the same, then Jews and Christians, as true believers, should immediately obey Allah's injunction and convert to Islam. This would imply the endorsement of the literal words of God as materialized in the Qur'an and recited by Muhammad, the last of the prophets sent to the whole of humanity and whose laws and exemplary life all should emulate.

The indictment of Jews and Christians as apostates and betrayers of their own Islamic faith is precisely one of Islam's gravest accusations against them. Yet over the last decades, Jewish and Christian theologians have often proclaimed this Muslim version of the same deity: Allah/God. For instance, during the Iraq war, in spring 2003, representatives of the three monotheistic faiths in Europe reiterated official proclamations in which they confessed their common faith in One God and in the message of the Prophets of their Holy Scriptures. It is noteworthy that those peaceful statements are made in Europe while calls for a worldwide *jihad* against infidels and support for terrorism increase among the Muslim population worldwide—in the name of Allah.

Another important point in these controversies concerns Abraham. The Qur'anic Ibrahim is not the same as the biblical Abraham, and Muslims do not accord any validity to the Bible. So when Jews and Christians speak of Islam as an Abrahamic faith like Judaism and Christianity, to which Abraham do they refer? The Qur'anic one, Ibrahim, who is a Muslim prophet, allegedly preaching Islam, ready to sacrifice his son Ishmael with whom, later, he built the Kaaba—or the biblical Hebrew patriarch Abraham, who offered his youngest son, Isaac?

According to Islam, the Abrahamic unity of Judaism, Christianity, and Islam is based on Ibrahim's *Hanifi* religion, which is the Islamic creed. This *Hanifi* religion is *din al-fitrah*, i.e., Islam, the first religion common to the whole of humanity. Muslims, says al-Faruqi, believe in and will continue to strive for this unification of world religions until there is only one religion prevailing in the world, which is Islam.[5]

In line with this thinking, some Muslims objected to the Christian dialogue with Judaism that began in the 1960s, after the Vatican II Council. They asserted that Christianity was just a deformation of the Islamic faith and as such was not free to conduct a rapprochement independently with Judaism. Muslim leaders argued that in view of Christianity's relation to Islam, the Vatican should have consulted it first before adopting any liturgical or other changes concerning the Jews. Hence, al-Faruqi writes, "In brief, it should be said that Christians may not settle their relations with the Jews alone in isolation from the Muslims. The Muslim's view is relevant and must be taken into account."[6] As strange as it might seem, this position was shared by the Arab Christian clergy and many in Europe and elsewhere.

Palestinianism: Christianity's Flight to Marcionism

The Christian policy that would eliminate the Jewish source of Christianity by suppressing the link between the Hebrew Bible and the Gospels represents an old and lingering trend, always opposed by the Church. It was first formulated by Marcion, a second-century Byzantine priest of pagan background who was strongly influenced by Gnosticism. Today, Palestinian Marcionism (Palestinianism) paves the way for the Islamization of the Church as it prepares mentalities for an Islamic replacement theology. It is, perhaps, the strongest trend in European churches, and encompasses the whole paraphernalia of traditional antisemitism.

Although the Vatican stresses the Jewish roots of Christianity, Palestinianism flourishes in the Catholic as well as Protestant European and Arab Churches. It presses for the removal of the Gospels from their Judaic matrix and their grafting onto Arab Palestinianism, thus bringing them closer to Islam. Integrated into the Interfaith Dialogue of the EAD, the movement benefits from the EU's Arabophile and pro-Palestinian policy. The process of Islamization of Christianity is rooted precisely in this separation from Judaism and the Arabization and Palestinization of the Jewish Jesus.

Palestinian replacement theology, or Palestinianism, was analyzed recently by an Italian Jesuit, Francesco Rossi de Gasperis, in an article with the evocative title "The Spiritual Shoah Actualized by the Arab Christian," and published in the Vatican journal, *Chiesa*.[7] De Gasperis is a distinguished biblical exegete and scholar residing in Jerusalem. He recalls the fundamental theological reorientation of the Catholic Church since Vatican II and its determination to rediscover its Jewish roots and spiritual values under the guidance of Pope John Paul II. He deplores the total opposition of the Arabized Middle Eastern patriarchs and bishops to this policy and their tremendous fear of Muslim reprisals caused by Arab resentment of Jewish-Christian rapprochement. According to him, Eastern clerics had even to apologize to Muslims and explain the new trend as a European guilt complex.

The Palestinian position scandalizes de Gasperis. He considers it a manifestation of traditional Christian anti-Judaism based on replacement theology. He recalls that in early Christianity, anti-Judaism sprang from the Eastern churches and developed there, later influencing the Muslims.[8] De Gasperis deplores the fact that many Christian Palestinians, like Muslims, do not admit to any historical or theological link between the biblical Israel, the Jewish people, and the modern State of Israel. They view the latter as a temporary foreign entity, without any spiritual or historical connotations or roots in the Holy Land, and consider its very existence to be an injustice to Christians and Muslims. It is this intransigent denial of the identity and the history of the Jews and of Israel—negationism—that de Gasperis calls a spiritual and cultural *Shoah*.

De Gasperis explains that Palestinian Christians interpret the Bible as being only a Christian revelation, with no roots in Judaism. Their liturgical and pastoral perspectives spring from the conviction that Christianity was a totally new religion, which replaces Judaism in the divine history of salvation. The Church is the New Israel, the other Israel, and has no connection whatsoever with the Jews. For the Palestinians—both Muslims and Christians—Israel is thus just a symbolic name devoid of concrete reference to history and cultural reality. Furthermore, Palestinian Christians have been convinced that they had always lived happily with the Muslims until the restoration of the State of Israel.

De Gasperis emphasizes that the Catholic Church repudiated replacement theology with Vatican II. Numerous statements by the Pope and distinguished theologians affirmed the Jewish roots of Christianity, Jesus, and the apostles, and the indissoluble link between the two religions. However, replacement theology, fed by the Palestinian Arab Churches, spreads today among Catholics as well as Protestants—and incorporates the theological and political components of modern European anti-Zionism.

Palestinian Marcionism

The search for a Muslim-Christian common ground has led since the middle of the twentieth century to a "de-biblicizing" of the Bible. In line with the Massignon school and one of its most active defenders, the late Abbé Youakim Moubarak, the Bible was reinterpreted from the viewpoint of the Qur'an. Some Arab Palestinian clergy are currently campaigning to induce the Church to forego the First Testament altogether, as well as its spiritual links with Judaism. They recommend retaining only the Gospels, interpreted in line with Qur'anic assertions. They hope to suppress the Judeo-Christian connection in order to attach the Gospels to the Qur'an, in particular through the adoption of the Qur'anic interpretations of the Palestinian Arab (Muslim) Jesus.

The *dhimmi* Churches' Arabized interpretation of the Gospels combines traditional anti-Judaism with the psychological conditioning of dhimmitude. Jesus, his mother Mary, and the Apostles are all assimilated with the local Arabs and lose their Jewish historical and cultural identity. This Islamization of the Jewish sources of Christianity, disseminated through European Islamophile church networks, plays into the hands of Muslims eager to co-opt Christianity and instrumentalize Christians as partners in their struggle against Israel. It is aggravating the disintegration of Christian identity, compounding the *dhimmi*'s cultural amnesia with falsification of the Christian faith's foundations.

Some theologians recommend the reading of the First Testament with an exclusively Christian understanding—amounting to an expulsion of the Jews from their own Scriptures. In Britain, an evangelical Anglican, the Rev. Dr. Steve Motyer, who promotes this view, calls it "a broadly 'replacementist' position" and pleads that Christians must interpret the Old Testament from the perspective of the New.[9]

The Arab *dhimmi* Churches—especially the Syro-Palestinian ones—have elaborated an entire theology of the non-Jewish, Arab roots of Christianity: Palestinian Liberation Theology. According to this trend, Christianity was born in an Arab tent and with a Palestinian identity. This new Arab-Palestinian sui generis embodiment of Christianity evidently also denies any historical rights to the modern State of Israel in its Hebrew-Israelite birthplace.

The rooting of Christianity in Arab Palestinianism involves the mechanism of the *perversa imitatio*: the perverse imitation, i.e., the duplication of Jewish history in an Arab-Palestinian context.[10] This device is a rehash of traditional anti-Judaism that has repeatedly been condemned since Vatican II, as well as by several Christian scholars and clergymen, but it has become the root of the Palestinian theology that is flourishing in Western Churches. Thus, Palestinians describe the flight of Muslims and Christians to neighboring Arab countries in 1948 following the Arab war against Israel as the exodus of the Hebrews from Egypt, with the Israeli leaders representing pharaoh. But for the Israelis, their defensive war against five Arab armies represents their liberation from the "gallut," the exile and suffering imposed upon them by Christian and Muslim rulers. In other mythical Arab appropriations, Israel symbolizes Herod, "killer of the Innocents," or the Roman oppressors in Judea—the Muslim Palestinians being the oppressed Jews.

The Arab Palestinians, heirs and symbol of the Arab Palestinian Jesus, replace the fallen deicide Jewish people, whose sins, in this view, have deprived them of their history and rights to their own land. Palestinianism cements the sacred Islamo-Christian fusion in Jesus as symbolized by a Palestine crucified by Israel—a concept and image constantly propagated during the Muslim/Christian Palestinian war against the Jews. The suffering of the Palestinians in their struggle to destroy Israel evokes Christ's passion, his suffering on the cross to save the world. Moreover, like Jesus, the mission of Palestinian Liberation Theology is to liberate the world from Israel's evil by unveiling its diabolic character, and cement through Palestinianism a worldwide Muslim-Christian alliance.

This Palestinian reading of the Bible and of Jewish history allows for the confiscation of Israel's biblical history, so as to delegitimize Israel. It thus conforms to the Qur'an, which Islamizes the entire biblical narrative—including the Gospels. "Justice" and "peace" will prevail through the restoration of the "old order," brought about through Christian replacement theology and Islamic *jihad,* both working together to efface Jewish identity, history, and nationhood and to revive a demonic interpretation of Israel.

For anti-Zionist Christians, the repeated references to "settlers," "colonizers," and "occupiers," referring to the Israelis in their own ancestral homeland, implies that any historical right to the land has been revoked and transferred to the non-Jewish Arabs, according to the theological principle of the "fall and substitution" which was condemned by Vatican II in 1965. In this view, Israel's rebirth on its land violates the fundamental religious principle of the "fall" and thus represents an injustice of cosmic proportions. Muslims and Christians, united in the same sacred mission, should redress this injustice.

As de Gasperis and Habib Malik,[11] another distinguished Christian scholar, have noted with alarm, the pseudotheology of Palestinianism is rooted in the Marcionist heresy. Its "divine mission" amounts to little more than the demonization of Israel and the exaltation of Arab suffering and victimhood. EAD media channels and moral support coming from some countries of Eurabia to the Palestinian terrorist war from October 2000 amplified this deceptive indoctrination into transcontinental and worldwide dimensions.

The Christian attitude of self-mutilation—and rejection of the very essence of Judeo-Christian spirituality—represent the final stage of dhimmitude preceding conversion to Islam. However, even this denial of the self, which is the inevitable consequence of Arab-Christian anti-Judaism combined with dhimmitude, will be insufficient to improve the situation of Christians in the Arab-Muslim world. Muslims do not oppress them because they believe in a Jewish Jesus and in the Gospel written by his Jewish disciples; rather, Christians are oppressed as falsifiers of the Islamic message of the Muslim Jesus—the Muslim prophet who, according to a *hadith*, will come back at the end of time to suppress Christianity. The revival of an ancient heresy or Christian hatred of Israel and the West will not satisfy the Islamists. Only full Christian adherence to the Qur'an will change the condition of Christian *dhimmis*. The discrimination and humiliation they endure are prescribed for Christians per se by the *shari'a*; they are unrelated to the existence of Israel, having been established through Islamic law in the seventh and eighth centuries.

Palestinian clerics often express rancorous grievances against Israel. They request apologies for its very existence, alleging that it causes them great distress. Yet Christian Palestinians have suffered much more from their alliance with the *jihad* forces and their many failed wars to suppress Israel. It is not Israel's restoration that has caused them trouble, but the Arab wars and terrorism aimed at destroying it. Before the British mandate over the whole area of Palestine—today's Jordan, Israel, and the disputed territories—Christians in Ottoman Palestine had the status of an oppressed *dhimmi* minority. Their sparse demography only increased in the second half of the nineteenth century under European protection and through the massive immigration of refugees fleeing massacres in Syria, Lebanon, Iraq, and Turkey.

Echoing Judeo-Christian conflicts of the second century, some Syrian clerics have stated that past Muslim massacres of the Jews gave Christians revenge for earlier Jewish defamations of the Virgin Mary. Such accusations fed religious polemics throughout the centuries. Thus, Michel Hayek, writing in 1959, sees in the killings of the Medina Jews by Muhammad in 628 a

Christian victory.[12] Yoakim Moubarak, a Syrian Catholic priest influential in Europe in the 1970–80s, expressed the same ideas in virulent terms.[13] There can be little doubt that the image of Arafat and Islam as protectors of Christians against a demonized Israel also sprang from this view. Actually, the history of both Christianity and Islam in the Holy Land is a sad record of the persecution of Jews over the centuries.

The Christian service to Islam

In the Christian lands that were conquered by *jihad*, *dhimmi* populations were tolerated because of the services they performed in helping the Muslim military minority consolidate its power. Mandatory service by the conquered *dhimmi* population was specified from the beginning of the Islamic conquest; it is mentioned by the earliest Muslim chroniclers and the founders of Islamic jurisprudence. The tribute (*jizya*) was one such service; it was assessed and collected from the Christians by their leaders—usually their patriarchs—for the Muslim authorities. Churchmen, financiers, and notables managed the caliph's treasury and supplied him with political advisers and scholars. Through the services provided to the Muslim community (*umma*), a class of clerics and civil servants arose. In the new Arab Empire, Christian leaders administered the Christian *dhimmi* majority to the advantage of the Muslim minority. The *dhimmi* Jews performed the same services as the Christians.

Christian consciousness in Muslim lands retains through its historical memory the experiences of persecution, vulnerability, and genocide. Anxiety increased in the twentieth century and aggravated the fissures between the Middle Eastern Christians, manipulated by the divergent ambitions of the colonial European powers and the Muslim world. Some Syro-Palestinian Christians, linked since the nineteenth century with powerful European antisemitic forces, exploited this anxiety as they strove to cement the Muslim-Christian alliance against Zionism.

Since the emergence of Palestinianism in the 1970s, the Arab *dhimmi* churches have striven for a united front against Israel by identifying totally with the Arab Palestinian cause. They saw their service to Islam as bringing together the whole Christian world in solidarity with the Palestinians and promoting an anti-Israel campaign in the West.

The Christian service to Islam thus consists primarily in its worldwide support for the Muslim *jihad* against Israel. It has also included spreading Islamic propaganda through Western religious channels, encouraging and giving practical or moral succor to anti-Israel terrorism by blaming it on Israel, demonizing Israel and America, vindicating Islam, and, above all, concealing the Islamization and religious "purification" of Arab societies—including the discriminatory and humiliating restrictions imposed on native Christians. These tendencies, implicitly enunciated in the January 1969 Cairo International Conference in support of the Arab peoples, were prevalent in the EAD. They fostered the foundation of a European and church "Muslim policy." The criminalization of Zionism in the West, which the Arab countries made an essential condition for Muslim-Christian rapprochement,[14] reinforced the elimination of the Jewish state as a common priority.

Church activism in Europe also operates in the service of Muslim immigration. Church leaders have preached the abolition of frontiers and of "chauvinist" nationalisms in order to merge both shores of the Mediterranean. The EAD policy of mass Muslim immigration into Europe is often backed by a generous clergy who strenuously advocated an open immigration, matched with full political rights. This is motivated not only by the imperative of human rights, but in the hope—often voiced—of obtaining equivalent rights in Muslim countries for indigenous Christian communities. However, this reasoning is based on the principle of reciprocity between equals, a principle denied by the *shari'a* legislation applied to varying degrees in most Muslim countries, despite the Partnership agreements.

Muslim leaders are aware that churches and clergymen have always been their strongest allies. Thus, citing the evidence of history, the Iranian jurist Abbasali Zanjani suggests that Muslims should favor exchanges with Christian priests, clergymen, and theologians, since they have always encouraged the propagation and the supremacy of Islam.[15] Such Christian advocacy in the service of Islam has given the Arab Christian clergy a political voice that is of strategic advantage to Arab governments. As has already been noted, at the Lahore Islamic Conference in 1974, Secretary-General Hassan Al-Tohami expressed his appreciation of the efforts undertaken by Christian Churches all over the world to explain to international public opinion the Arab/Muslim rights to the Holy Land, particularly to Jerusalem. At the Fez Islamic Conference (1980), this praise was reiterated toward the World Council of Churches.

Yet this supine attitude has not worked to the advantage of Christians in the Holy Land and the Middle East in general. The appeasement policy that blames on Israel and America the deterioration of their condition to evade any criticism of Muslim intolerance, highlights the dangers inherent in Christian *dhimmi* life. However, within the Vatican it appears that this unwillingness to confront the real situation is now being contested. On October 18, 2003, the semiofficial periodical *Civiltà Cattolica* published a strikingly severe article on the mistreatment of Christians in Muslim countries. *Chiesa* (The Church), which gave some extracts, reported: "The central thesis of the article is that 'in all of its history, Islam has shown a warlike and conquering face'; that 'for almost a thousand years, Europe lived under its constant threat'; and that what remains of the Christian population in Is-

lamic countries is still subjected to 'perpetual discrimination,' with episodes of bloody persecution."[16]

Muslim replacement theology

Not surprisingly, alongside Christian Palestine Liberation theology runs
a parallel Muslim thinking. In fact, it is so difficult to disentangle them that
it looks as if Muslim and Christian theologians collaborated on their positions, as the two sides express themselves in much the same terms and employ similar reasoning. In his Muslim replacement theology, al-Faruqi
adopts the Christian Marcionist position. He denies any links between Judaism and Christianity, using arguments similar to those of Palestinian Liberation theology. He discerns in the First Testament two currents: a
"nationalist particularist" stream and a "monotheic universalist" strain,
within which he detects the existence of "Palestine" even before Abraham.[17] This latter strain allegedly belonged to the Aramaean kingdoms,
particularly to the Arabs migrating from the Arabian Peninsula. It was
"brought to the apex of revolution by Jesus." Al-Faruqi's "Old Testament"
analysis induces him "to sift its material into that which is Hebraic or Ju-
dahic [sic]—which can never be Christian in any sense—and that which is
universal, monotheic, ethical and Christian."[18] In other words, he anchors
Christianity in an explicitly anti-Jewish context. Al-Faruqi's interpretation
of the First Testament employs the usual caricatured features of classical
Christian anti-Judaism, earning him great admiration in some Christian mi-
lieux, especially from his former student John Esposito.

Just as he calls the biblical land of four thousand years ago "Palestine,"
al-Faruqi also affirms that the Old Testament is not just Hebrew or Christian Scripture, but also Islamic Scripture—inasmuch as it is a partial record
of the history of prophecy, and hence of divine revelation. Jews therefore
have no right to claim that the Old Testament is their heritage; in fact, he
describes their using Scripture for their own purposes as racist ethnocentrism. However, he concedes that Christians and Muslims cannot "make
total abstraction of the Hebrew understanding because the Old Testament
is, after all, a Hebrew scripture written in Hebrew by the Hebrews and for
the Hebrews."[19] Yet since its content is not only Hebrew but also has Semitic themes, it belongs to all Semites. Islam, he asserts, which is a Semitic
religion, born in Arabia—the cradle of all things Semitic—brings to this
material another and allegedly older Qur'anic perspective. Just as Christianity is "a new Israel," Islam is "another Israel," with its own understanding of First Testament material.

In his introduction to al-Faruqi's book, editor Ataullah Siddiqui praises
al-Faruqi's discovery that elements of Jesus's teaching were already present
in Judaic traditions and in Hanifism in particular. Hanifism, as we have

seen, is, in the Muslim view, Islam: the primal religion of humanity before the coming of Muhammad. For al-Faruqi, Hanifism "incorporates every noble thought in the Old Testament . . . from which sprang Christianity, the religion of the spirit," which he disentangles from Judaism by "a virgin birth"—in direct opposition to Jewish ethnocentrism.[20]

For al-Faruqi, Islam *is* Christianity, inasmuch as Islam is contained in the development of Judaism and Christianity, in a similar way as Christianity developed within Judaism. That is why Islam rejects neither Hebrew prophets nor Jesus, but differs from Jewish and Christian views concerning them. Accordingly, Islam is both Christianity and Judaism. It represents a Muslim revolution from within, just as Christianity was a revolution against Judaism. The Arabic Qur'an expresses the universal brotherhood under the moral law and universalizes, in Islam, the opposition of the Muslim Jesus to Judaic particularism.

This interpretation leads al-Faruqi to affirm: "Islam was the first 'reformation' of Judaism and Christianity, the first 'Protestantism.' Equally, Islam gave birth to biblical criticism. The Qur'an was the first piece of textual criticism."[21] He feels that it is repugnant to Muslim ears to hear the claim of Western scholars that the discipline of comparative study of religions is a Western innovation born out of the European Enlightenment, or that the coming together of the world religions was first initiated by the Chicago Congress in 1893. In al-Faruqi's view, this is the result of ignorance and of a superiority complex that blinds Western scholars to the achievements of non-Westerners. The truth is, he states, that Islamic scholarship on religions is a millennium older and had already been expounded in the Qur'an. Hence, Islam also provides regulations for each religion, worthy of emulation by the whole world.

Islam holds that there is only one religion in the world to which every child is born: Islam. Muslims and non-Muslims alike possess the natural religion (*din al-fitrah*) by birth. Islam teaches that the historical religions are outgrowths of the primal *din al-fitrah*. In this view, Islam precedes Judaism and Christianity and was present at humanity's birth. Islam recognizes the Hebrew and Christian "prophets," but only as Muslim prophets: "It regards them all as Muslims and their revelations as one and the same as its own."[22] The religious truth of Judaism and Christianity is Islam. The sameness of the Divinity in the three religions leads to the sameness of the revelations and the religions—an Islamic uniformity. For this reason, the Christian belief that Jesus, the apostles, Jesus' disciples and Christianity itself are related to Judaism is—according to al-Faruqi—a monumental error. Jesus rebelled against Judaism precisely to restore Islam, his religion. Christianity is an outgrowth of Islam; the Hebrew prophets, Jesus, his mother, his disciples, and apostles were all Muslims who preached Islam.

Hence, because Christians belong to the Muslim creed, they cannot settle their relations with the Jews apart from the Muslims.

However strange it may seem, these assertions have been constantly affirmed and proclaimed by the *dhimmi* Arab Churches and supported in Europe and America by the anti-Zionist trend in the Church and in academia. The Palestinian Arab clergy repeatedly refuses to be considered as a religious minority. It proclaims itself an inseparable part of the Muslim majority—an opinion that vindicates the belief that Islam encompasses Christianity. Hence Father Raed Awad Abusahlia, the then chancellor of the Latin Patriarchate of Jerusalem, explained in his *Olive Branch* of October 9, 2000 that Christians are so inseparable from Muslims that they should not even be called a minority: "Here I would like to comment on a dominant mentality, which must be resisted, the tendency to call the Christians in the Orient 'a minority' within a majority which is not Christian. I repeat the call for the cancellation of these words from the dictionary of our relations." He justifies his position by saying that Christians were neither persecuted nor weak, characters that are associated with other negative elements of the minority's pattern.[23]

In an article published in *Seminar of the Islamic-Christian Dialogue* in 1981, al-Faruqi clarifies the basic ground of the Dialogue.[24] "There can be no cooperative endeavor [between Christians and Muslims] without consciousness of the common base and shared purpose," he wrote. "This should not be restricted to the elite, if it is to bear fruit for history, but must become common heritage to all ranks of Christians and Muslims." He called for a Muslim-Christian dialogue that would mobilize Christians and Muslims around the world. A moral imperative should develop from the general awareness among Muslims and Christians of their common roots. In the author's view, the theme of the common essence of Islam and Christianity should be promoted, defended and elaborated through the mass media and in learned publications. Above all, al-Faruqi warns that Christian voices allied to Zionism must be silenced forthwith. He accuses these spokesmen of enticing Christians to side with Israel, to reform Christian beliefs and attitudes, and to reinterpret Christianity itself within the Zionist interpretation of "Palestine's" history. As he puts it, Muslims and Christians both believe in the God-like mission given to Jesus—namely to liberate man from the chains of Judaism.[25]

The religious interpretation and policy developed, taught and propagated in American academia by al-Faruqi conforms to the EAD line. In Europe, the Arabized Jesus and apostles in iconography and in teaching fit into the EAD indoctrination of "sameness." The Arabization of Jesus in "Palestine"—a land that, during his lifetime, and for over a hundred years after his death, was still called Judea, as all ancient authors and the Gospels attest—also implies the Arabization of his ancestry. Thus, Palestinianism confirms the Islamic theory that Moses, Jesus, the Hebrew patriarchs, prophets and Israelite kings were Muslims, the terms "Arab," "Semite," and "Muslim" all being synonymous as in al-Faruqi's interpretation of history.

From the 1970s on, this Muslim current was strengthened by the EAD pro-Palestinian policy and was fundamental to the development of a European Palestinian cult that would redeem Christianity from the State of Israel. Churches with a Marcionist or Islamic-Christian syncretic tendency in the West supported *dhimmi* and Islamic alterations and interpolations in Christian doctrine and worship. These views aggravated the divisions at the very heart of the Church. Christian Judeophobia—generating hatred of its own theological roots, bound together with Islamophilia—opens the surest way for the Islamization of the Church. Islamic supersessionism does not tolerate a Jewish-Christian history outside Islam, nor before Islam. It refutes differences and diversity and brings them into a singular and exclusive mould: Islam, which embraces all of them in its unique truth. *Jihad* and *da'wa*—the call to Islam—are seen as the compulsory and legitimate fight to bring back to Islam its recalcitrant "lost members." The common biblical figures in the Bible and in the Qur'an—especially Abraham, whom many have believed since the 1950s might provide a ground for rapprochement—represent in fact the greatest source of contention.[26]

In a lecture given at the Conference of Christian Colleges and Universities in Washington on February 2, 2003 Habib Malik, chairman of the Charles Malik Foundation, examined the philosophy of dialogue.[27] He denounced the band of myopic apologists in certain academic circles who have romanticized the Middle East.

> Western apologist academics, ecclesiastical wishful thinkers, reaching out to conduct religious dialogue, or embarrassed policy planners attempting to soften the image of some brutal allies in the name of a vague multiculturalism—these are the ones who, out of ignorance or design, continue to push for dialogue with this mirage of moderation.

Malik stressed the importance of defining the parameters of dialogue to avoid the asymmetry of dhimmitude and the distortion and corruption of words. He also emphasized the need for reciprocity from Muslim states. He deplored the syncretism and moral and cultural relativism that obscured the difference between wrong and right and reduced the dialogue to prattle.

In November 2002, a report on the representation of Christianity in Egyptian school textbooks was published. It was part of a larger project on the representation of Christianity in school textbooks in predominantly Muslim countries.[28] The survey indicates that the Christian West is seen as

the archenemy of Arab-Muslim culture, as an inferior culture and an imperialist aggressor against the Muslim East. The Islamic conquests of Christian lands are described as a liberation. The books reproduce the
stereotyped vision of a barbaric Europe against a tolerant Islam. They highlight that religious fanaticism and ignorance submerged Europe, while
Islam had developed a bright and tolerant civilization where human rights
had been applied since the time of Prophet Muhammad. Europe has simply taken its culture from the Muslim East. Yet, for internal political peace,
the books taught a very positive view of the Copts, as an indigenous part of
the Egyptian nation.

17
Eurabia Against America

The Franco-German plan to build a unified Europe linked to the Arab world—and as a rival to America—led to a strategic, economic and political Euro-Arab alliance. For Arab and Muslim states, this new cooperation was intended to weaken Europe's alliance with America and bring Europe into line with the Arab League's policy toward Israel, while making Europe the new ground for preaching Islam (*da'wa*) with full state and Church approval. France's obsessive dreams of grandeur and nostalgia for its lost Arab empire induced successive governments to champion Arab League goals, and to whitewash PLO terrorism. Under French leadership—as confirmed by Arab commentators—the EEC adopted this plan, which was articulated in several declarations dating from 1973. The European Community's haste, after the October 1973 war, to accept the Arab League's conditions for rapprochement suggests a previous entente between the parties. The oil embargo appears to have been just a pretext for a political reversal already planned by France and Germany.[1]

Although it had pivotal importance for the Arabs, thwarting Israel was not the main element of this French policy; it was merely a tool to suppress Arab anti-French resentment stemming from France's earlier colonization of vast Arab territories and its bloody Algerian war (1954–62). There was also the fear of a growing terrorist threat, as the Algerian-born French scholar Jacques Frémeaux noted in his book on the Arab world and the security of France, *Le Monde Arabe et la Sécurité de la France*. The preceding chapters have described the stages of this Mediterranean policy, which made Israel hostage to France's ambitions, fears and latent anti-Americanism.

French President Jacques Chirac reaffirmed the main contours of this policy in his address at Cairo University on April 8, 1996.[2] He solemnly stated that France's stance toward the Arab world must be a cornerstone of its foreign policy. France, he declared, would endeavor to include all of Europe in the building of a Euro-Arab partnership of equals. Chirac asserted that common interests linked the Arab and European destinies. To their cultural and economic association, he emphasized, the two sides should also add a grand political ambition that would bond them together. He saw the development of powerful political links between Europe and the Arab countries as a means to strengthen their relations. Chirac reaffirmed that the Middle East peace process was a priority for France, as well as for all of Europe and the Arab countries. He also underlined the major role played by the European Union in this process through its massive financial contribution to the Palestinian Authority, which amounted to no less than half of the PA's budget.

Chirac also revealed another French grand design: the creation of a Euro-Arab Mediterranean community, allowing for the free movement of people and goods. He reminded his audience that, on France's initiative, Europe had convened the Euro-Mediterranean Conference in Barcelona, which laid the groundwork for this partnership in the industrial and financial fields. Cultural cooperation would bring together the universities and encourage student exchanges. European and Arab teachers should write their books jointly, he said, especially history books, and common film projects should be increased. French and Arabic would each become a lingua franca of the Mediterranean world.

This address displayed the tendencies that contributed in subsequent years to: a) the Euro-American rift; b) Chirac's pretension to define EU foreign and security policy; and c) the unleashing throughout Europe of a newly invigorated, concerted and violent anti-American, anti-Israeli, and anti-Jewish campaign.

Continual French obstruction to American policy is intrinsic to the Euro-Arab partnership. It determined France's adamant refusal to recognize the roots of Islamic terrorism, which French officials generally blame on America. For France, U.S. policy, rather than Islamic terror, has to be contained. Euro-Arab collaboration with NGOs resulted in the shameful exhibition of racism and hate at Durban in September 2001 (see chapter 10).

While maintaining steady opposition to the United States, the EU was able, under the mantle of the Dialogue, to develop good relations with such champions of human rights as Egypt, Syria, Algeria, Morocco, Tunisia, Libya, Iraq, Sudan, and Saudi Arabia. The development of these relationships, indeed, was the primary goal of the Euro-Arab Dialogue, largely established by France and Germany and imposed willy-nilly upon the other countries of the EU. Nevertheless, despite the European taxpayers' contribution of billions to Arab regimes to provide them with services and to improve their economy and skills, anti-Western hostility only increased among their population, fed by the frustration of their failed and totally dependent societies, as confirmed in the UN Human Development Reports of 2003 and 2004.

This edifice, constructed upon billions of petro-dollar profits, was suddenly threatened by the 2003 war against Saddam Hussein. Although this was an occasion to flaunt Europe's Arab alliances and demonstrate its readiness to serve the Arab cause—as well as to further Israel's demonization and isolation—America's war against Islamist terrorism alarmed the EU. The effect of America's unmasking of Islamist terrorism, which Europe had officially denied and tried to deflect onto Israel, was profound. The Iraqi war brought to the surface the anti-Americanism that had been simmering for years among European Arabophiles, neo-Nazis, Communists, and leftists in general. Much of this hostility is a by-product of the EAD. As the war loomed closer, France, Germany, and Belgium continued to invoke "multipolarity" and "multilateralism," as they had for years, to support their alignment with regimes that sponsored terror, including that of Saddam Hussein. But the terms "soft diplomacy," "soft power," and "multilateral actions" concealed a policy of collusion and surrender.

Eurabians today pretend that they are not anti-American, but only opposed to President George W. Bush and his government. In conjunction with this, they virulently reproach America's attachment to a Bible culture and its stand for Western values of freedom. From 2003, they hoped for the fall of the Republican Party, thinking that the Democrats would be more amenable to their policy. Europe pretends that its political "sophistication" and engagement in dialogue and trade with dictatorial states sponsoring terrorism and hate will create a secure world regulated by international law. In fact, the EU is implicitly abetting a worldwide subversion of Western values and freedoms, while attempting to protect itself from Islamic terrorism by denying that it even exists, or blaming it on scapegoats. In 2003, throughout Europe, demonstrators against the Iraq war, hostile to America and Israel, affirmed EU solidarity with the Arab world, and particularly with Arafat. At his September 2003 trial in Jerusalem, Marwan Barghouti, the head of the Al-Aqsa Martyrs' Brigades (an offshoot of Arafat's Fatah movement), was cheered by European parliamentarians. Thus, by their support of such terrorists, these parliamentarians bear a direct moral responsibility for the scores of Israeli civilians murdered and mutilated by jihadist bombers.[3]

The fundamental difference between America and the EU is apparent in their respective policies toward the Islamist drive for world domination. While America, like Israel and India, confronts Islamic terrorism, Europeans have chosen deliberately to circumvent and deny it. Hence, the great importance given in Europe to catchwords like "despair," "poverty," and "injustice," and the spending of billions in Arab lands to purchase immunity from societies brought up on fanaticism and frustration. In the words of the American columnist William Pfaff, an effusive admirer of the European line, Europe "deploys much more economic influence, diplomatic and developmental experience, skills in nation-building and peacekeeping, and cultural attractiveness than the United States does."[4]

Yet, considering the security measures constraining Europeans for decades before 9/11, the results of these tactics are deceiving. Many analysts in the media praised Europe for choosing the path of international law and a strategy based on negotiations, diplomacy, and trade before the start of the second Iraqi war in March 2003. However, the United Nations that is considered the foremost exponent of international legality is constituted in great part by dictatorial regimes, whose criminal leaders violate the very principles that the UN is supposed to uphold.

Moreover, we have seen with the Barcelona Declaration, and with other agreements, how the EU has created a meaningless legal smokescreen to allow it to conduct normal political and business relations with totalitarian states, some of whom sponsor international terrorism. With Syria, for example, a dictatorship that, as noted previously, shelters terrorist training camps and maintains twenty thousand troops in Lebanon, the EU promotes closer political and economic ties through the Barcelona Association Agreement. Syria has provided continuous support for radical Palestinian factions and for Hezbollah in Lebanon. As indicated, the EU refused to call these groups "terrorists" in order to maintain its good relation with Damascus and to protect its complex web of economic and political agreements with the Arab countries. The EU assisted Syria against America by promoting the corrupt PLO leaders and covering up for Hezbollah. Chirac entertained excellent relations with Hafez el-Assad and with his son Bashar who succeeded him. The recent anti-American and antisemitic wave in Europe and the Arab countries coincided with the tightening of cultural Franco-Syrian cooperation in 2001, increasing French influence.

In October 2003, a subcommittee of the U.S. Congress put forth the Syria Accountability Act for final approval to the Congress, and called for a wide-ranging boycott. On October 9, 2003, the EU denounced the U.S. move to impose diplomatic and economic sanctions on Syria, declaring that instead it would continue to seek closer cooperation with Damascus. The spokeswoman for EU Commissioner Chris Patten stated that the EU was in the process of negotiating a political-economic association agreement with Syria. Another EU spokesman, Diego de Ojeda, acknowledged that it would not be easy to compel Syria to respect human rights and reject terrorism, but said that the EU hoped to get positive results by offering financial rewards.[5]

In America, however, President Bush signed the Syria Accountability and Lebanon Sovereignty Restoration Act in December 2003. It accused Syria of sheltering terrorist groups such as Hamas, Hezbollah, and Islamic Jihad. Europe's complacency has borne bitter fruit: since 2002, Palestinians have carried out more than one hundred jihadist bombings; Hamas has been responsible for more attacks and more Israeli deaths than any other terrorist group.[6] Nor were only Israeli Jews targeted: the majority of the twenty-one victims killed by the Islamikazes in a Haifa restaurant on October 4, 2003 were Lebanese Christian refugees who had settled in Israel. As researcher Rachel Ehrenfeld wrote, "Maybe it's time to hold European donors legally accountable for the return on their investment."[7]

Pursuing relationships with dictatorial Arab regimes and promoting anti-Americanism, while paying lip service to human rights, is by no means the EU's only manifestation of Eurabian dhimmitude. Its repeated invocations of international law ring hollow when bribery, pressure, and threats win votes. It deliberately ignored that for most of the fifty-six Muslim states of the OIC only the *shari'a* is ultimately binding and has primacy over UN international covenants. This point has been emphasized by the secretary-general of the 1974 Lahore Islamic Conference, Mohammed al-Tohami, and others since; it was underlined in the 1990 Cairo Declaration of Human Rights in Islam and has been repeatedly affirmed by Muslim leaders.

This calls into question the definition of legitimacy itself. The words "legality," "rule of law," "justice," can be repeated ad infinitum, but they are often an exercise in equivocation. International agreements, no matter how numerous or admirable, are meaningless in the Muslim world if they contradict *shari'a* rule. These worthy principles, however nobly they are worded, are thus divorced from reality not only in Muslim lands, but in Europe as well. The West's high-minded principles have been repeatedly and flagrantly contradicted by the EAD-dictated media campaign targeting Israel and by governmental indifference to Judeophobia in Europe until late in 2003.

The EU countries, which have denied *jihad* and dhimmitude as historical and ideological components of Islam's relations with non-Muslims, cannot and do not want to perceive the threat of global *jihad*. Having based their policies on this obfuscation, they prefer to consider as a danger those countries like Israel and America that, by fighting *jihad,* expose its reality. The Spanish capitulation after the March 2004 Madrid bombings is perhaps the most notorious example of state submission to Islamic terror.

This denial forms the very core of the Euro-Arab Partnership against America. Europe's close alliance with Arab regimes and the corrupt PA infrastructure prevents it from disavowing allies to whom it has entrusted its security and its future. The EU would rather challenge America in order to strengthen the Euro-Arab Partnership and achieve its political goal of full Euro-Arab integration.

Yet, however forceful the denials of the European political establishment, the reality of militant *jihad* and Islamism are only too well known to every European government. It is precisely Europe's trauma that has sealed an alliance with the Arab world, which is cajoled by soft diplomacy, flattery, and assistance. Euro-Arab rapprochement resulted from the 1973 oil crisis, but as American policy during that crisis proved, there never was an oil threat: the desert sheikdoms were too dependent on the industrial countries to eliminate their only source of revenue.

Since it was formulated in hopes of competing with America, France's drive to dominate the EU obviously tended to bring it closer to the Arab anti-American and anti-Israeli position. France's ongoing maneuvers to implement its Eurabian anti-American policy were revealed during the diplomatic crisis that preceded the 2003 war in Iraq. On February 16 and 17, 2003, at an EU summit in Brussels, French President Jacques Chirac threatened to block EU membership to Central European candidate countries because of their trans-Atlanticist inclination. He also launched a project to build a European military "inner core," with France, Germany, and Belgium posing as a counterweight to the U.S. The Franco-German-Belgian axis represented those states most adamantly opposed to the war against Saddam Hussein. These were also the three countries most involved in the Euro-Arab Dialogue.

The obstructions the French placed in the way of the removal of Saddam Hussein were not only dictated by France's links to his criminal regime—and the large debts in the form of credits—but also by Iraq's pivotal role as a leader of the Arab anti-American policy. It was well known that Saddam Hussein was also funding Palestinian terrorism: each Palestinian Islamikaze family received $25,000, and $10,000 was paid for each Palestinian killed in attacking Israel.

The EU Proximity Policy

In EU internal policy the Commission's most important task and responsibility is to advise the foreign ministers and set the program for discussions. Its president and his collaborators have a pivotal role in shaping European policy, as the Commission selects the different subjects of discussion and directives. On October 13, 2003 in Alexandria, the President of the European Commission, Romano Prodi, delivered a speech entitled "Sharing Stability and Prosperity" at the Tempus Meda Regional Conference Bibliotheca Alexandrina.[8] In his opening remarks, he stated, "**The peoples of Europe do not believe in any clash of civilisations.** European public opinion is united in its rejection of that myth. We Europeans want peace and dialogue" (bold in the published text). Europe's vision—said Prodi—was a Proximity Policy: "To build security with our neighbors—not by building walls or installing missile shields, but through trade, exchange and dialogue." This Proximity Policy, explained President Prodi, involved the establishment, "more clearly than in the past," of a Euro-Mediterranean partnership on an equal footing. The term "equal footing" which was also pronounced by President Chirac in his Cairo speech of 1996, is not clear. For Prodi, the Proximity Policy prepares the ground for lasting stability and security. It "creates the conditions for cooperation and understanding. This is what we call 'soft security.' " And here Prodi seems to apologize: "But this is not as 'defensive' as the term may suggest." And again, later, he apologizes for Europe's enlargement: "**This enlargement is a great opportunity, not a threat.** . . . When the Berlin Wall fell, we in Europe decided we did not want to erect new walls. Because we have learned that **security does not come with higher walls or deadlier weapons,** but with stronger, more stable relations based on peace and prosperity—the 'soft security' I mentioned. Stronger, peaceful relations and exchanges are the only form of security that is ultimately sustainable. We in Europe have turned our backs on extremism in politics" (bold in the published text).

The dhimmitude of Europe, so well illustrated by Prodi's preening about exchanging trade and services for security, led him to insult two democracies, America and Israel, for resisting jihadist wars. He offered it as a form of flattery to the host country, Egypt, a dictatorship that oppresses its Christians and spreads a most vile culture of hatred. Furthermore, Prodi announced that Europe was ready to help the Arab world, as the Proximity Policy would offer greater opportunities—in terms of markets, growth, and trade. He promised that it would extend the area of freedom for free circulation of goods, capital, services and people, and that it would enhance cooperation in the fight against common threats. Prodi affirmed his belief that the Proximity Policy "will strengthen good governance, respect for human rights and individual freedoms, the rule of law and participatory institutions." And then he declared, "Ladies and gentlemen, **This is the substance of our political offer. We are willing to help**" (bold in the text).

President Prodi claimed that the building of a new Europe would involve a strong Euro-Mediterranean partnership on an equal footing, ruling out a "Eurocentric" approach. But he failed to clarify whether Arabocentrism would also be ruled out. He announced the establishment of a High-Level Advisory Group on Dialogue between Peoples and Cultures, "[b]ecause I felt we needed to foster such a dialogue, based on respect for the other, equality, freedom of conscience, solidarity and knowledge." He promised yet another future Euro-Mediterranean Foundation for intercultural dialogue that "will be one crucial instrument for an active, operational dialogue. It will provide the first practical illustration of our equal partnership and a place where we can work together, plan and carry out common projects."

He recalled that at its June 2002 meeting in Brussels (see chapter 11), the Euro-Arab Parliamentary Dialogue had requested the creation of another foundation for the development of joint cultural and educational programs. However, this new foundation, explained Prodi, would add the principle of "co-ownership":

> As the Union's first joint structure with its partners, the Foundation will fulfil the desire to give concrete form to the principle of co-ownership, of the feeling of belonging. . . . The personalities of regional civil society to act as advisers to the Foundation will provide fresh, dynamic input for its activities, and will offer real added value to what is already being done in the cultural field. The Foundation will promote exchanges between cultural and intellectual players. It will involve opinion formers in both northern [European] and southern [Arab] countries who are already engaged in the dialogue. And in particular it will seek to take the dialogue further and open it up to the wider public. This means the Foundation will need to set in motion an ongoing cultural debate, in particular using multi-media techniques. Special attention needs to be paid to focus groups, such as journalists and young people.

On 15 October 2003, two days after Prodi's speech, the Commission sent a message to the Council and the European Parliament, in preparation for the Sixth Meeting of Euro-Mediterranean Ministers of Foreign Affairs. This meeting took place in Naples on December 2 and 3, 2003 as part of the Barcelona Process, because of its lineage from the first Euro-Mediterranean Conference, held in Barcelona on November 27–28, 1995 (see chapter 9).[9] The Commission's paper on the forthcoming Naples meeting advised the Ministers "to send a message of common interests, shared values and **solidarity** between Europe and its Southern [Arab] neighbours; to reaffirm their joint interests in reinforcing security and stability in the region; and to ensure that extreme fundamentalism and terrorism are not allowed to get in the way of progress in political and economic reform" (bold in the text).

Several issues were to be examined, including migration, economic aid, free trade, financial partnership, investments, cultural and human partnership, and education. It proposed the establishment of a Euro-Mediterranean Parliamentary Assembly; a Euro-Mediterranean Bank lending Facility for Euro-Mediterranean Investment; and Prodi's dream: a Euro-Mediterranean Foundation for the Dialogue of Cultures. It declared that the Ministers should welcome the following ongoing programs in their respective countries: Euromed Heritage, Euromed Audio-visual, Euromed Youth, and Euromed Youth Platform.

The Commission advised the European ministers to finalize the establishment of the Euro-Mediterranean Foundation for the Dialogue of Cultures, which would promote intercultural dialogue and understanding between civilizations. It directed that the Foundation's "organization, as a network of networks [sic] with a light administrative structure, will allow a regular dialogue, notably between cultural circles outside official diplomatic and cultural forums." The Commission also called for substantial financial contributions "to guarantee the successful launch" of the Euromed Foundation.

The Euro-Mediterranean Foundation for the Dialogue of Cultures

In October 2003 at Brussels, the High-Level Advisory Group, which was established at the initiative of the president of the European Commission, issued its report: "Dialogue Between Peoples and Cultures in the Euro-Mediterranean Area."[10] It laid down the aims and functions of the Foundation. A note on the first page specified: "This Report represents the opinion of the High-Level Advisory Group only and does not necessarily reflect the views of the European Commission." However, there are many similarities between its analysis and Prodi's declaration in Alexandria.

The introduction explained that the report intended to answer two questions asked by Romano Prodi after September 11: 1) How to contribute to the emergence of "a society of peoples and cultures" in the Euro-Mediterranean area? 2) What shape should a dialogue between cultures take, "conducted primarily among the peoples who inherit and pass on those cultures"?

Prodi charged the Advisory Group with making proposals for the Euro-Mediterranean area under a neighborhood policy intended to create "a zone of prosperity and a friendly neighbourhood—a 'ring of friends'—with whom the European Union enjoys close, peaceful and co-operative relations."

In point 1.2, the report reassures the southern side of the Mediterranean, the Arab—designated also as "so-called southern countries"—by showing that the enlargement of the EU to include Eastern European countries would work to the advantage of the Arab countries through this EU "neighborhood policy." In other words, the EU's Arab policy would compensate the Arab countries for its Eastern enlargement. And indeed, the European Commission recently gave way to Arab states' irritation at the enlargement by announcing that, for the first time, the EU had decided to consider its Mediterranean partners on a par with its neighbors in Eastern Europe. Moreover, nine of the fifteen EU member states planned to restrict Eastern European citizens' access to jobs in their countries in order to fulfill promises made to their Southern neighbors, i.e., the Arab countries.

The report also argued that the new EU Member States could themselves become open lands for Southern Muslim immigration—a main concern for Arab states eager to keep Europe as an outlet for their rapid demographic growth. The report predicted optimistically that the Muslim population of Bulgaria, the Balkans, and Turkey, combined with the population of Turkish origin in Germany and Austria, would join with Arab Muslims in the diversification of European Islam.[11] "These two future developments [Muslim immigration in the new EU countries and the increase of European Muslims] will have a number of positive effects on the prospects for immigration and on the place of Islam in Europe. First of all they will show that a European Islam has come into being, thus dispelling the image of a rampant Islamisation of Europe."[12]

The report saw a "balanced North-South/South-North partnership" as one of the numerous preconditions for the success of the dialogue. The emergence of the Arab South as a coherent partner was considered a vital element of the dialogue. Here Israel was blamed for the lack of progress in the Middle East peace process, and for not contributing to democratization in the Mediterranean region. Perceived as a conveyor of American influence in the Mediterranean (a major sin for the hegemonic EU policy in the region), Israel's policy could only be seen in a negative light. Yet the report notes that over "the last fifty years, the Arab population has grown from 80 to 320 million inhabitants, 50% of whom are aged under 20" (italics and underlined in the text).[13] Could Israel really prevent 320 million people from establishing their own democracy if they want it?

The report set a policy for the EU in relation to enlargement, its identity and its "neighborhood," another euphemism for the Arab countries:

> The neighbourhood policy is the creative expression of the vision of making the Union one element in good neighbourly relations—as well as being specifically responsible for providing the neighbourhood with a stable core— and therefore ensuring that it maintains closer links with its immediate "ring of friends."[14]

For the uninitiated, this is just gibberish. In plain words, it is a policy of controlling the Mediterranean, i.e., the Arab countries, and reinforcing Europe's associations with the ring of Arab friends. These neighbors, says the report, are exposed to outside threats that would prevent their unification; their interests should direct them to create a large Mediterranean unit with the EU. To neutralize the external threat—whatever that might be—the Report recommends development of a sense of co-ownership among all the Mediterranean countries. This policy would unfold in continuity with longstanding initiatives, like increased teaching of Arabic[15] and special structures for the integration of Muslims into European society. These requests reiterate calls made by the 1974 EAD meeting in Damascus and subsequent ones since then. The report gives the impression that the Mediterranean is not just a region of the globe, but a controlled area from which "outsiders" are to be kept out.

This concept of exclusionary co-ownership of regions and cultures means barring others and explains the row in the EU when the Eastern European countries affirmed their Atlanticist orientation in Spring 2004, as opposed to the EU-Arab anti-American partnership. Nothing could have been more detrimental to the great Mediterranean political project announced by Chirac in 1996 in Cairo, and Prodi in October 2003 in Alexandria, than the support that the 2003 Coalition war in Iraq gained among the applicant EU Member States.

The report only makes clear after thirteen pages that the "neighbors," South and North (which are the only terms for Arabs and Europeans that appear in the entire report), represent specific human groups and not just vague geographical orientations. This effacement of countries works according to the same principle that suppressed biblical geography, so that the West Bank (of what?) replaced the Judea and Samaria of world and Jewish history. The report's awkward terminology for defining Europe as the "North" emerged also from Edward Said's accusatory interpretation of "us and them." The choice for such vague denomination is explained:

> The temptation to look at the project of intercultural dialogue in the Mediterranean on a North-South/South-North axis only would therefore be dangerous if it was restricted to that alone. The problem is quite simply much more comprehensive and much more general: there has been a failure to grasp the impact of culture on historical developments in the North, the South, and even one might be tempted to say, between the North and the South—though such provocative suggestions should ring warning bells because from North/South it is a short step to Europe/Africa, Europeans/Arabs, Christians/Muslims, Christianity/Islam, them/us or us/them.
>
> However, the reality that needs to be taken into account is quite different: it is simply Us; an Us which begins with each person for themself and extends to all the neighbours, in this case the Euro-Mediterranean area, but potentially extending to the universal. We are citizens of here and the world, and hence of everything that falls between the two, and not first individuals of X ethnicity or groups of Y country belonging to Z region—all of which define themselves by opposition to others. In other words, feelings of belonging now work as intersecting circles, and no longer as concentric or juxtaposed circles.[16]

As in the former Soviet Union or a virtual Communist empire, identities are to be destroyed in order to dissolve diversity into a uniform anonymous humanity. Because intolerance hates the freedom of genuine diversity, differences are submerged into a collective Us.

Would this insistence on co-ownership and solidarity of the Mediterranean countries allow for the numerous non-Mediterranean Christian and Jewish diasporas that fled the persecution of Muslim Mediterranean countries to be recognized as part of this partnership? Would they have the right to speak about their own history, despite living now in America, Australia, Canada, Japan and elsewhere? This is not a rhetorical question.

In the next chapter, we shall see that the Foundation has planned to retain exclusive and totalitarian control on everything written and taught about the Mediterranean area in EU schools and universities. The report outlines a program to control the intellectual life, thoughts and activities of the whole Partnership area through guidelines given to the press, the schools, the universities and NGOs; through the arts, films, publications, and political pressure; and through the expurgation of history, reworking of school syllabi and other means—all in order to create a new mankind according to the Dialogue's standards "in the spirit of and in support of the EU's neighbourhood policy."[17]

It is unlikely, therefore, that these diaspora communities would be given a voice; instead, this control would enforce the teaching of the myth of Andalusia and Edward Said's demonization of the West. In this view, there is no clash of civilizations. Indeed, that idea is abhorrent to the drafters of the report. They see differences between Europe and the Islamic world as a mere remnant resulting from the destruction caused by crusading, colonizing Europe. These differences would be effaced by "cross-fertilization," a "good neigborhood," and a "ring of friends."

The political section of the report deals with funding and projects to be monitored by an institutional structure. The much decried "Fortress Europe," with its visa limitations "and the increasingly restrictive immigration policies of the Member States have relegated the partnership to a virtual reality by barring the [European] territory to the other [Arab] half of the partners, thus sapping it [the partnership] of credibility even further."[18]

The report proposed a new structure composed of three bodies: 1) a Euro-Med Council for culture and education; 2) a Euro-Med Parliamentary Assembly, with a powerful committee on the dialogue between peoples and cultures; 3) the Foundation, which would work together with the Parliamentary Assembly on violations of the fundamental principles. These principles which will direct the whole European and Arab policy are: respect for the Other; equality at all levels between states, peoples, cultures, individuals, genders; freedom of conscience; solidarity of every kind and in every field; knowledge of the Other. The report stressed that these fundamental principles of the "good neighborhood policy" must "provide active support and real sustenance to all those—from heads of state to local associations and groups of citizens, parliamentary assemblies, trade-unions, nongovernmental organizations—responsible for building the Euro-Mediterranean area."[19]

The Foundation's council would work out a "program of priorities" and would assess cultural programs and the cultural impact of other measures in the economic field or on visa, immigration policy, and prevention of discrimination.[20] Civil authorities, organized along geographical or thematic lines (drawn by whom?), would have access to each of these joint institutions. This support would not be all in one direction—at least on paper. The High-Level Advisory Group on Dialogue between Peoples and Cultures called for reciprocal treatment in the Southern (that is, Muslim) countries for Jews and Christians,[21] but this is an empty provision: there are virtually no more Jewish communities in the Arab countries—less than one half of 1% of the former population—and Christians are constantly fleeing. Moreover, immigration of non-Muslim Europeans to these countries, especially Saudi Arabia, on the scale of recent Muslim immigration to Europe—would never be tolerated.

Section 3 of the report, "Immediate Need to Engage in Renewed Dialogue," conveys a sense of urgency to act. This is probably due to the impact of 9/11, the war on terror and the war in Iraq, as well as the threat to Arab leaders who sponsored terror—principally Arafat and Assad of Syria, who are both precious allies for the Euro-Arab Partnership leaders. Moreover, the U.S. Greater Middle East project, which envisions reforms and democratization in the Arab countries, was seen as threatening Euro-Arab dominions.

The funding of the Euro-Mediterranean Foundation had to be commensurate with the hopes invested in it: according to the report, it was to aim at "nothing else than peace itself." [22] Such an exalted mission required that "the Foundation must enjoy both financial and administrative independence and intellectual independence."[23]

The Foundation seems to be designed to condition the minds of Europeans and mold them according to guidelines imposed by the Euro-Arab network. Its programs engage the EU population in numerous ways. The Foundation craved for political control over visa and immigration policies, as well as over the foreign policy of each EU state. In fact, the Foundation is the European Commission's instrument to do nothing less than control, dictate, and conduct the foreign policy of the member states.

Here again, however, its ambition cannot cross to the Southern shore of the Mediterranean. It is wholly ineffective and powerless in the "Southern neighborhood" where, despite European concessions, Islamism, fanaticism, and terror have only heightened with each passing year. Euro-Arab agreements have imposed political censorship upon EU media, cost journalists their jobs, and brought pressure upon universities and publishing houses. In Arab countries, meanwhile, including the Palestinian-controlled territories, incitement to hate and kill Jews and Christians, their designation as pigs and monkeys in religious sermons broadcast on TV, and violent aggression against Christians are all increasing.

"Enlargement of Minds"

From November 13 to 16, 2003, the European Cultural Foundation (ECF) held a seminar in Toledo on "Enlargement of Minds" in cooperation with the School of Translations in Toledo, Castilla-La Mancha University.[24] Pat Cox, president of the European parliament and the patron of the ECF's "Enlargement of Minds" action-line, launched this initiative to tackle the issue of the cultural consequences of the enlargement of the European Union.

The workshop team, Gonzalo Fernandez Parilla, Malika Embarek, Odile Chenal, Isabelle Schwarz, and Selma Mutal, explained in the seminar publication the project and aims of "Beyond Enlargement." First, they deplored "fortress Europe" and worried that Europe's southern borders would become even more rigid. The aim of their project was twofold: it was intended to create a place for debate on the impact on the Arab-Muslim countries of Europe's enlargement, and to strengthen cultural cooperation with them through new tools, schemes and possible partnerships involving cultural organizations (EU, national governments, NGOs, and foundations). "Beyond Enlargement" aimed at policy and action developments at various levels and was to propose advocacy strategies through a select group of artists, writers, and journalists from the Arab countries—"experts and professionals involved in cultural policy and activity in Europe and the [Arab] South Mediterranean (including representatives of migrant communities); representatives from the EU, the council of Europe, other private and public European organizations, and national governments (foreign and cultural affairs); journalists as experts but also as 'opinion shapers.'" The aim of these Euro-Arab activities was to propose policies, programs, and partnerships that would include the South Mediterranean Arab countries in a larger European cultural space. It would also study strategies for advocating the Euro-Mediterranean cultural relationship. The project would furnish "Documentation on conference results supporting these initiatives, including publication in the series Enlargement of Minds, publications on-line and in the cultural supplements of several newspapers."

The foreword of the seminar publication explains: "The action-line consists of research and publications, artistic initiatives, partnership with the media, as well as three workshops." The last seminar, "Beyond Enlargement," aimed at ensuring action, cultural cooperation, political and operational proposals "to those organisations at various levels—from intergovernmental and national organisations to the level of foundations and associations—which strive to develop Euro-Mediterranean cooperation." The word Mediterranean was misleading, as Israel was represented only in connection with Palestine. The background information indicated that the dialogue between cultures only concerns the Arab countries and Turkey.

It is clear that the EU was creating a gigantic machinery involving politics and culture in order to condition European minds. The seminar publication opens with a quotation from Edward Said, who was the chief promoter and principal agent of the West's cultural dhimmitude. In the spirit of Said, the European contributors to the publication adopt a self-accusatory style, while the Arabs do not evidence any remorse for their thirteen centuries of *jihad* and dhimmitude policies.

The seminar expressed virulent anti-American and anti-Israeli rhetoric by European and Arab participants and revealed the stereotypical prejudices of many key European Union leaders. There are numerous complaints of Arab humiliation, suffering, and victimization. In an open letter to Europe, a certain Radwa Ashour sees the "United States of America attempting to dominate the world and consolidate its status as an omnipotent empire, monopolising the legal and moral criteria governing life on the planet." Its thirst for domination sustains its arrogant and disdainful view of the world and of Europe.

Ashour laments the "enormous anxiety caused by the material and psychological violence to which we Arabs are daily subjected: the bombing of cities, the sieges and incursions, the humiliation of the people, destruction of homes and uprooting of trees; all those future generations wounded by war, all the disabled, the victims of pernicious diseases; the media portraying the dead as executioner, the victim as beast. All this is happening to us at this moment in Palestine and Iraq. . . . For centuries we have been the 'invisible man,' the servant whose masters recognise only servitude and the knowledge necessary to keep us enslaved. Invisibility is violence and also evil. It carries with it a despotic negation of the humanity of the other." Here Ashour confuses the history of Arab Muslim conquerors in language that describes the fate of Jewish, Christian, Zoastrian, Hindu, Buddhist, and other *dhimmis* enslaved in dhimmitude, forbidden by Islamic law to testify in court, and condemned to silence.

Radwa Ashour's letter was accompanied by a supporting, equally incriminatory, "answering" essay from Gonzalo Fernández Parrilla, director of the School of Translations in Toledo, Spain. He entitled it "Orphans of Edward W. Said." A lengthy, nostalgic eulogy of Said,[25] this essay contains reminiscences of Said's *Orientalism* where "repatriation" of illegal immigrants is confused with "deportation," although the word "repatriation" is linked to the country of origin. Parilla's Manichean and simplistic vision of the world laments only the Crusades, European colonialism, the devastation of seven thousand years of Iraqi history, and Bush's ignorance. He combines this pseudohistorical narrative with charges of Arabophobia, Islamophobia, and praise for the great humanitarian views of the Palestinian writer Murid Barghouti.

The other texts of the seminar publication fantasize along the same lines. They include an attack by José Maria Ridao against the antiterror security measures adopted in Europe. In the light of the later Madrid bombing and its victims, this type of discourse published under the auspices of the president of the European Parliament, Pat Cox, demonstrates incompetence and irresponsibility.

In his book *Eight Years of Government*, published eight weeks after he lost power, the former Prime Minister José Maria Aznar recognizes that the Islamist threat was not detected. He writes, " I must acknowledge, however, that Spanish public opinion was perhaps not sufficiently aware, until March 11, of the extent of the threat of Islamic terrorism, or at least not as much as it was about the threat of ETA terrorism." With an honesty rarely found in politicians, he comments, "If that is the case, the government undoubtedly has to bear the responsibility."[26] The Madrid bombing has obliged European leaders to wake up to the sociopolitical tensions emerging within each European country confronted with this reality. From a report on industrial British cities like Luton, Crawley, Birmingham, and Manchester—as well as in other cities in France, Germany, Italy, Holland—a majority of Muslims of Pakistani, Arab, Turkish, or other origin see terrorism as a justifiable means to impose Islamic control over international policy.[27] In February 2004, as already mentioned, German Foreign Minister Joschka Fisher had declared in a Munich statement that the danger was "destructive jihadist terrorism with its totalitarian ideology."

At the Sixth Euro-Mediterranean Conference of Foreign Affairs Ministers, held in Naples on December 2–3, 2003, the political and economic prospects for the region were discussed in the context of the EU's Wider Europe policy. European officials reaffirmed Europe's solidarity with its Mediterranean partners, who were considered of geostrategic importance, especially in connection with security, environmental and energy issues, and South-North migratory flows. They reasserted their commitment to reinforcing even further the Euro-Mediterranean Partnership—that is, the process begun in 1995 in Barcelona.[28]

Also manifest in Naples was the Commission's propensity to multiply foundations, committees, and subcommittees for dialogue like metastatic bodies, while downplaying the real threat of terrorism and the lack of tangible results from the Euro-Arab Dialogue itself in matters of democracy and rights in the Arab partner countries. Proposals repeated at Naples and ultimately adopted included the establishment of the long-discussed Euro-Mediterranean Foundation for the Dialogue of Cultures, as well as a Euro-Mediterranean Parliamentary Assembly and a fully fledged subsidiary of the European Investment Bank (EIB), which would build on the existing Facility for Euro-Mediterranean Investment & Partnership (FEMIP).

It goes without saying that this proliferation of organizations increases EU budgets, as well as the influence and power of Euro-Arab initiatives. On February 10, 2004, the European Commission asked for a spending increase of €38 billion ($45 billion), or 32 percent over seven years. Romano Prodi introduced the proposal, justifying the increased expenses as being necessary for research, development, international aid and "intercultural dialogue."[29]

But what can ordinary Europeans make of all these years of Euro-Med dialogues, dialogues of civilizations, intercultural dialogues, and MEDEA dialogues, all financed by their taxes? All those endless meetings involved travel, hotel, and organizational expenses for the numerous people involved. European taxpayers also fund the countless ongoing Eurabian cultural projects and associations.

The culture of hate that flourishes today in Arab/Muslim countries has now contaminated Europe through these dialogues. To this culture of hate, Europe had contributed its *Protocols of the Elders of Zion* and the "ritual crimes of Damascus," now part of the cultural creations of its privileged partner-countries—Egypt and Syria—from where they are beamed to the whole Arab-Muslim world.

European anti-Americanism, the rejection of its Judeo-Christian identity, the growing Judeophobic culture of its universities and its media, and the totalitarian censorship and control of its intellectual life are the foremost result of these dialogues. This was manifested in the late 2003 polls, conducted by the European Commission and featuring biased questions, that identified Israel as the biggest threat to world peace. An opinion so contrary to reality could only have been obtained after years of Euro-Arab symbiosis and dialogue.

Economic stagnation, the lack of political reforms and democracy, and the spread of Islamism in the Arab countries—as mentioned in the 2002 and 2003 United Nations Reports on Arab Human Development—all point to the failure of the Barcelona Process.[30] Nevertheless, Commissioner Chris Patten declared in 2004 that the Barcelona Process remains crucial to Europe's needs and aspirations and the best chance to address instability and diversity in the Mediterranean at a multilateral level.

European Anti-Americanism

Today's anti-American passion in Europe results in great part from Europe's Mediterranean policy, and from the Arab and Palestinian cult that grips it. Fear of retaliation has prompted Eurabians to distance themselves from America—as was evident from Prodi's speech. George Bush's June

2004 visit in Ireland provoked hostile demonstrations. According to the *Irish Examiner,* the mayor of Shannon said that "the town's residents were being made into potential targets for a terrorist attack."[31] François Heisbourg, director of the Paris Foundation for Strategic Research announced a future catastrophe with al-Qaeda soon gaining access to weapons of massive destruction, the extensive support it enjoys in the Arab world, and the lack of preparedness in the targeted countries. He advises that Europe dissociate itself from America.[32] Are we to understand by this that Europe, unable to fight terror, should seek protection by siding with al-Qaeda? It rings old bells . . .

Another factor contributing to European anti-Americanism—more psychological than political—is the profound resentment that cowardly or impotent societies, which have chosen surrender through fear of conflict, have toward those who stand strong. Constant anti-American propaganda in Europe gives Europeans, even as they submit to the Islamic political agenda, a sense of moral superiority.

Yet for all their caustic jokes about America, while sneering at the war on terror, Europeans have themselves been forced to implement antiterrorist measures since the 1970s. In spite of its multifaceted partnership with rogue states, Europe's airports and sensitive areas, including embassies are guarded. Security precautions were particularly stringent during Christmas 2003 at the Vatican, when reports suggested that St. Peter's Church might be a target of terror attacks.

At a NATO summit in Istanbul in June 2004, U.S. President George W. Bush blamed the autocratic rulers in the Arab world and beyond for fostering a culture of extremism and resentment of the West. He declared: "In the last sixty years, many in the West have added to this distrust by excusing tyranny in the region, hoping to purchase stability at the price of liberty." The president commented: "But it did not serve the people of the Middle East to betray their hope of freedom and it has not made Western nations more secure to ignore the cycle of dictatorship and extremism."[33] Such declarations could not have hurt some Europeans more. Chirac announced that Foreign Minister Michel Barnier would pay his first official visit to Arafat in Ramallah, where he spent the night (29 June 2004).

Anti-Americanism is, in short, an intellectual totalitarianism disguised as a virtue for states which have entrusted their security to those who threaten them. Despite being imposed by the EU's upper echelons, anti-Americanism only floats on the surface of European culture and has triggered internal opposition. French journalist Alain Hertoghe is among those authors and intellectuals who have strongly protested anti-American bias in the European press. For this, however, he was fired from his post as deputy editor at the web site of *La Croix,* a respected Roman Catholic daily newspaper. In the new Eurabian totalitarian culture, basic freedoms seem to be dispensable.[34]

18

The Backlash of the Partnership

The preceding chapters have clarified how the EAD constructed a political doctrine and managed to impose it on the European population through various legal, cultural and political frameworks. In the beginning, its main objectives were to secure a regular oil and energy supply to Europe from the producing countries and to build a strong, united Euro-Arab alliance through the Mediterranean Partnership as an international political rival to America, of equal or even greater strength. France was the initiator and guiding force behind this policy. Within the European Community, it acted on behalf of Arab interests, using the common need for a stable energy source as a tool for European integration—that is, a uniform foreign policy for all member states, implemented by a supranational European body, the European Commission.

On the eve of the 1973 oil crisis, Western Europe imported 45 percent of its oil from the Middle East. In the following years, energy sources and production were diversified; reliance on Middle Eastern oil diminished considerably. Moreover, Arab countries were totally dependent on the sale of their oil and natural gas, the main resource of state revenue for many of them. This economic dependence was, in fact, a severe constraint for the Arab producing countries, whose development relied greatly on the West, which provided them vital imports, as well as industrial and technological training, especially for the oil industry. The EEC, therefore, could have kept its political autonomy. However, despite its favorable position in relation to the Arab League countries, the EEC chose to build a foreign policy aligned on Arab League goals.

Notwithstanding Western Europe's diminished reliance on Arab oil, EU support for an Arab/Palestinian policy grew stronger over the years. This situation indicates that legitimate oil needs were secondary to political objectives, that is the emergence of a Euro-counterweight to America and support for Arab policy related to Israel. Those were the primary and determinative motives behind the EEC/EU's Arab-Muslim policy. The threat of international Palestinian terrorism, concurrent with a flow of petro-dollars and trade, prevailed in shaping its strategy.

243

The policy of partnership initiated by the EEC was not restricted to the Arab region; it encompassed many other regional groups of nations—including the African, Caribbean and Pacific countries (EC-ACP) the Latin America Free Trade Area (FTA), with which it entered into a trading partnership; the ASEM (Asia-Europe Meeting); and the EC-ASEAN Economic and Commercial Cooperation Agreement. As with the EAD, three principal bodies regulated each of these partnerships: the Council of Ministers; the Committee of Ambassadors; and the joint Consultation Assembly. Each side was represented equally in each body and invested with specific powers and functions. Priorities focused on regional and global security, trade, agricultural and industrial development, investments, educational exchanges, and collaboration in international forums.[1] This collaborative network disseminated the principles of the Euro-Arab Dialogue throughout the world, above all the stigmatization of Israel and anti-Americanism. Thus, Israel is increasingly isolated and routinely condemned in international forums, while the gross human rights abuses of Muslim and other dictatorships in Asia and Africa are glossed over.

For each regional groups, an institutional framework for dialogue, similar to the EAD, was built on three pillars: economic, political, and cultural. This ensured the interdependence of development policy, external relations, and foreign policy. With its partner countries, the EU promoted the rule of law, the independence of the judiciary, legal redress, equality before the law, the accountability of the executive, and general human rights. Of course, none of these goals has been attained in the African, Middle East, and Asian dictatorships. Moreover, none of these multilateral partnerships has ever realized, in other regions, the structural demographic, religious, political, and cultural changes wrought in Europe by the EAD.

Through the Euro-Mediterranean Partnership, Europe expected that industrialization and modernization would prevail in the Arab countries. Instead, it has imported to its own territory the quagmire that plagues the Arab world. Having now embarked upon what has proven to be a dangerous path, the EU—seemingly incapable of extricating itself—continues to compound past errors. On December 12, 2003, EU High Representative Javier Solana and the European Commission presented to the European Council two papers: *Strengthening the European Partnership with the Arab World* and *A Secure Europe in a Better World.* The first one states:

> Problems of terrorism and WMD [weapons of mass destruction] originating there have a direct impact in Europe. In this context, the solution of the Arab-Israeli conflict is essential. There will be little chance of dealing fully with other problems in the Middle East until this conflict is resolved; such a resolution is therefore a strategic priority for the EU.[2]

Here again the council expresses the myopic view of political Islam that has set Europe on the road to concessions and impotence—as if this "solution" will resolve "problems of terrorism and WMD". Such statements, often echoed in the media, have conditioned European public opinion to believe that Israel is the major threat to regional, even world peace. The paper stresses that European action for development in the Arab world should be coordinated with increased relations across the Wider Middle East. Its authors repeat the same redundant recommendations on good governance, democratization, gender equality, promotion of human rights, economic reform, and the much-touted religious and cultural dialogue—the latter being merely disingenuous apologetics for the spread of *da'wa* (Islamic proselytism) in Europe. The paper affirms the EU commitment to fight

> all manifestations of racism and discrimination in all its forms. Full respect for the rights of immigrants in Europe is a consistent policy throughout Europe. Its implementation should be improved further and co-operation in the framework of existing agreements should be enhanced to take into account the concerns of Arab partners.

Among other worthy recommendations, it states that translations between Arabic and European languages should be actively encouraged, and that the EU should ensure "balanced coverage in European media of issues related to the Arab world." There was no reciprocal mention of the need to ensure balanced coverage of the West in the Arab media.

The paper also mentioned "the development of civil society actors in the region," an initiative limited to the financing of the "Geneva Peace Initiative" which sidetracked Israeli democracy. It illustrates the EU's long-standing policy of eroding Israel's internal cohesion, while strengthening—with its Arab allies and its irrevocable support for Arafat—EU influence in the Middle East at the expense of America.

On December 12, 2003 in Brussels, the European Council adopted a number of conclusions related to the Euro-Mediterranean Partnership, including statements on Interfaith Dialogue and the Middle East Peace Process.[3] The European Council, made up of EU heads of state or government, thus reaffirmed "the strategic importance of the Mediterranean for the European Union," and confirmed "its resolute determination to reinforce co-operation significantly with the Mediterranean Partners."

On the Middle East Peace Process, the European Council again called "on both parties, Israel and the Palestinian Authority, to immediately and simultaneously fulfil their obligations and responsibilities under the Road Map." The European Council also stressed "the importance of establishing a credible and effective monitoring mechanism including all members of the Quartet" and welcomed "initiatives from civil societies on both sides, including the Geneva Peace Initiative." The council expressed the ministers' commitment to two states: "Israel and a viable and democratic Palestinian State,"[4] viability, though, is not mentioned for Israel. On relations with the Arab world, the European Council welcomed the report drawn up by Javier Solana and the European Commission. On interfaith dialogue, it encouraged "the relevant Ministers to support a sustained, open and transparent dialogue with the different religions and philosophical communities as an instrument of peace and social cohesion in Europe and at its borders." They reaffirmed "the EU's firm commitment to oppose any form of extremism, intolerance and xenophobia."

The EU claims that it promotes democracy, the rule of law, respect for human rights, and fundamental freedoms with the Arab countries through the Barcelona process. In view of this, the Commission adopted a communication entitled *Reinvigorating European Union actions on Human Rights and democratisation with Mediterranean partners*[5] within the framework of MEDA, which describes itself as "the principal financial instrument of the European Union for the implementation of the Euro-Mediterranean Partnership." The commission announced that MEDA funding would be increased to provide a deeper and more operational focus for political dialogue on human rights and democratization at all levels. It also earmarked additional funds for the development of national and regional action plans on human rights and democracy issues with those MEDA partners willing to engage in such an exercise. Between 1995 and 1999, some 86 percent of the resources allocated to MEDA were channeled to the Mediterranean partners of Europe: Algeria, Egypt, Jordan, Lebanon, Morocco, Syria, Tunisia, Turkey, and the Palestinian Authority. On December 6, 2003, the European Commission Representation in Jerusalem announced the signing by the European Commission and the Palestinian Authority of Financing Agreements for three MEDA-funded cooperation programs totaling €32 million ($40 million).

By the end of 2003, the consequences of the EAD policy initiated thirty years ago, and later enlarged in the Euro-Mediterranean Partnership, were well entrenched in international and domestic European policies regarding Euro-American relations, Euro-Arab relations, and Euro-Israeli relations. In December 2003 the European Constitution failed to gain a consensus which would have enhanced the Commission's power and given more opacity to a body that ultimately determines the governing of Europe. It was finally approved in 2004, after much tension, but has still to be ratified by all twenty-five member states of the EU.

Euro-American Relations

Anti-Americanism—one of the EAD pillars—permeates great segments of European society. This became clear, as we have seen, during the mass anti-American demonstrations of 2003. These demonstrations, like the antisemitic wave that accompanied them, raised the visibility of the Euro-Arab partnership. The combined danger of international Islamist terrorism and the threat posed by some European Muslim groups led the EU to strengthen its relations with the Arab world. At the Naples Forum in 2003, it made recommendations for setting up a Euro-Mediterranean Parliamentary Assembly. The EU passion to incorporate the Arab countries into the Wider Europe project and to create a European-dominated Mediterranean area was fueled by a desire to exclude and supersede America.

A superficial observer might conclude that the war against terror could have been avoided altogether if America had adopted Europe's policy of accommodating terrorism. In fact, nothing is further from the truth. The current conflict stems from much deeper problems, which the EU tries to conceal or engages superficially through empty interfaith and cultural dialogues. According to an international survey by the Pew Global Attitudes Project, conducted from late February to early March 2004, attitudes expressed by the population in Morocco reflect a clear trend toward religious intolerance and very wide support for the Islamikazes. Among the Moroccans, 45 percent favored Osama bin Laden; 60 percent approve the suicide attacks against Westerners and Americans in Iraq; and 73 percent harbor negative opinions of Christians, while only 2 percent have a somewhat favorable one. Negative sentiments regarding Jews are exhibited by 92 percent, with only 1 percent having positive feelings for them.[6]

Supported explicitly or implicitly by the majority of the Muslim world, jihadists and Islamikazes are carrying on their *jihad* war against the free world, as announced by Osama bin Laden on February 23, 1998 in his "Declaration of Jihad against the Crusaders and the Jews."[7] They aim to impose upon Western and other countries their own vision of Islamic supremacy and international politics. The EAD model, applied so successfully in getting Europe to bow to Arab demands on Israel, is becoming the worldwide strategy of extremist Islam. Europe, a co-creator of the EAD, has fallen into its pit, torn between submission or resistance.

As we have seen again and again, the relationship of the EU with the Arab states is all-encompassing. It even embraces organizations sponsoring terrorism, making the EU an accomplice to their policies. Some EU's member states, fearing that their alliances with the most repressive and sanguinary Arab regimes were threatened, opposed the Iraq war. The EU pressured and hectored Washington, attempting to justify its association with corrupt and criminal regimes under the guise of "international legality." While the EU, and particularly France, maintained excellent relations with Syria, the Bush administration approved the Syria Accountability and Lebanese Sovereignty Act, which imposes economic sanctions against Syria. Likewise, Eurabian policymakers would certainly be scandalized by the submission of Republican Senator Rick Santorum (PA) to the U.S. Senate of Resolution 325, in April 2004, concerning refugee populations in the Middle East, North Africa, and the Persian Gulf region. Santorum recalled that the national existence of Jews in the Middle East and the surrounding regions preceded by a millennium—and for Christians and others, by centuries—the Arabization and Islamization of those lands. The resolution stated:

> Whereas the discussion of refugees in the Middle East generally centers on Palestinian refugees, even though estimates indicate that, as a result of the 1948 war in which numerous Arab armies attacked the newly-founded State of Israel, more Jews (approximately 850,000) were displaced from Arab countries than were Palestinians (approximately 726,000).

The resolution cites Presidents Jimmy Carter and Bill Clinton who both acknowledged that

> Whereas the United States has demonstrated interest and concern about the mistreatment, violation of rights, forced expulsion, and expropriation of assets of minority populations in general, and in particular, former Jewish refugees displaced from Arab countries, as evidenced, inter alia, by the following actions:
>
> (1) A Memorandum of Understanding signed by President Jimmy Carter and Israeli Foreign Minister Moshe Dayan on October 4, 1977, states that "[a] solution of the problem of Arab refugees and Jewish refugees will be discussed in accordance with rules which should be agreed."
>
> (2) After negotiating the Camp David Accords, the Framework for Peace in the Middle East, President Jimmy Carter stated in a press conference on October 27, 1977 that "Palestinians have rights. . . . obviously there are Jewish refugees. . . . they have the same rights as others do."
>
> (3) In an interview with Israeli television immediately after the issue of the rights of Jews displaced from Arab lands was discussed at Camp David II in July 2000, President Clinton stated clearly that "[t]here will have to be some sort of international fund set up for the refugees. There is, I think, some interest, interestingly enough, on both sides, in also having a fund which compensates the Israelis who were made refugees by the war, which occurred after the birth of the State of Israel. Israel is full of people, Jewish people, who lived in predominantly Arab countries who came to Israel because they were made refugees in their own land."

The resolution instructs the United States representative to the United Nations and all United States representatives in bilateral and multilateral forums that, when the United States considers or addresses resolutions that allude to the issue of Middle East refugees, its delegation should ensure that the relevant texts refer to the fact that multiple refugee populations have been created by the Arab wars against Israel in 1947, 1967, and 1973.

It adds that any explicit reference to the required resolution of the Palestinian refugee issue must be matched by a similarly explicit reference to the resolution of the issue of Jewish refugees from Arab countries. In modern times, the United States has often voiced its concern about the mistreatment of minorities and continues to play a pivotal role in seeking an end to the Middle East conflict and the promotion of a peace that will benefit all the people of the region. Such a statement—which does not preclude the creation of a Palestinian state alongside Israel—runs opposite to Eurabian Middle East policy.

After 9/11, Bush insisted "there is no neutral ground—no neutral ground—in the fight between civilization and terror. There can be no separate peace with the terrorist enemy. Any sign of weakness or retreat simply validates terrorist violence and invites more violence for all nations." This declaration was countered by the French minister for foreign affairs, Dominique de Villepin, who asserted that the Iraq war increased terror. Although Saddam Hussein paid "bounties" to Palestinian jihadist murderers and their families, in addition to terrorizing and committing mass murder against his own people, as well as neighboring populations, de Villepin, as if on another planet, affirmed, "Terrorism didn't exist in Iraq before."[8]

In an insightful article published on January 20, 2004, John Vinocur examined European rage against America. He detected efforts among European politicians to bring America into line with European subservience to the Islamic threat: to solve the problem by pretending that it does not exist.[9] Now that the rift between Europe and America simmers, the Arab pressure which exploits it will only increase as Arab immigration into Europe continues. Furthermore, the EU political establishment currently lacks the courageous resolve and the foresight to extract Europe from the quicksand of dhimmitude.

Europe and the Arab-Muslim World: The Partnership

Has Europe succeeded in bringing democracy, the rule of law, and respect for other religions to the Muslim world? Has the Partnership made Europe safer? Have the billions of euros from European taxpayers resulted in the economic, political, and social reforms that are essential for the modernization of the Muslim world? Is the Muslim world ready to forgo its concept of the infidel *dar al-harb* and to accept legitimate criticism? Do Muslims admit that *jihad* is not "a war of liberation," but rather a war for world dominion? Are the Palestinians and the Arab world ready to recognize Israel's historic and political legitimacy on land colonized and emptied of its indigenous Jewish population by the Arabs? Have the Palestinian Arabs established a basis for democracy in their autonomous areas?

Alas, today's hero among the Muslim population of Europe, as well as of the Islamic world, appears—from all the polls so far—to be Osama bin Laden. Poverty, illiteracy, corruption, unemployment, terrorism, and fanaticism destabilize Arab countries. Liberal Muslims, notably in Egypt and Pakistan, risk death as apostates; Christians are victimized by murderous pogroms in Kosovo, Egypt, Sudan, Nigeria, Pakistan, and Indonesia, and suffer from incessant discrimination, including false accusations (such as blasphemy allegations carrying a death penalty) that—under *shari'a*-based criminal codes—cannot be refuted in fair trials. The Palestinian towns look like *ribat*, a sprawl of traditional jihadist city-camps formerly on Christendom's borders, breeding grounds of mortal hatred. The PA's Islamic character causes Christians to flee from PA-administered areas. Rat poison laces Islamikazes' bombs, to compound suffering and ensure death. Killers suffering from AIDS, hepatitis, or other diseases infect the tissue of their victims as they explode their bombs. Israeli doctors have seen x-rays of victims with nuts, bolts, and nails lodged in brains, hearts, muscles, and other vital organs, which cannot be removed surgically. These facts were hardly ever reported in the mass media of the Euro-Arab partnership. There is little European compassion or humanitarian aid for Israeli victims of Palestinian terrorism, as there was for the nightmare in Belsan, Russia in September 2004.[10]

Arab Judeophobia has risen to a hysterical level. In Egypt, a serialized version of *The Protocols of the Elders of Zion* was aired on television in late 2002 during Ramadan. In the Alexandria Library partly funded by UNESCO and Italian taxpayers, its director placed, next to the Bible, an Arabic translation of the *Protocols of the Elders of Zion* in Autumn 2003. Although Egypt is a major country of the partnership, its media is suffused with vile and genocidal Judeophobic hatred. A culture of popular fanaticism permeates Egypt. Innocent Christians are killed and girls abducted in shops for conversion. On March 17, 2004, the Coptic Pope Shenouda III called for them to be returned to their families. He mentioned that youths travelling in the country have been arrested and jailed for fifteen days, for carrying a Bible.[11] As in the rest of the Arab world, Egypt's intellectuals strive to revive Christian anti-Jewish accusations about the death of Jesus. When the pope visited Syria in May 2001, he was publicly insulted as seen on world TV when President Bashar Assad criticized the absolving of the Jews for the Crucifixion. Muslim leaders continue to reproach the Vatican vehemently over the prohibition of the deicide accusation, as well as for the Judeo-Christian rapprochement movement. Cardinal Tucci, the director of Vatican Radio, declared on November 6, 2003:

> I would like to say that a Muslim antisemitism exists also. Now in the whole Muslim world, in the media, the radio, television, in schools, a whole system

inciting to antisemitism exists. It is the worst antisemitism that can be imagined after Nazi antisemitism, if not its equal.[12]

He stated that no criticism is expressed in the Muslim world against government policy, but instead "an antisemitism of the worst type prevails."

With the culture of *jihad* prevalent among the populace, European hostility toward America and Israel can secure only a conditional peace for Europe but not ultimate freedom from Islam's jihadist intentions. Spain has pursued policies hostile toward Israel, only recognizing its legitimacy as late as 1984, while issuing multiple pro-Palestinian and Arabophile declarations. Nevertheless, Spain, Portugal, Greece, Sicily and many other Eastern European lands remain in the same Islamic legal category as Israel. Traditional Muslims believe that these former Islamic lands must one day return to the *umma*. After the March 11, 2004 bombings in Madrid that killed 190 and wounded about two thousand, the new Prime Minister Jose Luis Rodriguez Zapatero adopted an appeasement policy toward Islamic terrorist groups. Endorsing the complacent Eurabian policy, he immediately declared in the vision of Prodi and Solana, "Combating terrorism with bombs, with operations of shock and awe, with Tomahawk missiles, is not the way to beat terrorism. Not like that. It is a way to generating more radicalism, more people who can wind up being tempted by using violence." This epitomizes *dhimmi* submission to a deadly jihadist attack. "Our allegiance will be for peace," he said, "against war, no more deaths for oil." He hoped for a dialogue with John Kerry, George W. Bush's Democrat rival in the U.S. elections. According to his aide, Julian Lacalle, Zapatero said that the three men who planned the Iraq war, Bush, former Spain's Prime Minister Jose Maria Aznar, and British Prime Minister Tony Blair, would lose upcoming elections.[13]

Nevertheless, Zapatero's appeasement of terrorists almost immediately proved itself a failure. Three weeks after March 11, another bomb was found on the railway of the Madrid-Seville line. The explosive's similarity to the previous one seemed to indicate the same source. A radical Muslim group issued a statement warning of more bombs if Spain did not submit to additional demands.[14] Romano Prodi, the president of the European Commission, followed Zapatero's example. He declared that if the Olive Tree, a coalition of centrist and leftist political parties that he headed, came to power in Italy, Italian troops in Iraq would return home.[15] Sardinia, Corsica, and the southern cities of Italy were savagely raided by jihadists from the ninth century on; Malta was captured in 868 and Sicily conquered by 878, remaining an Arab colony until the eleventh century. Did fear of the past, when cities and parts of the countryside were emptied of their population—massacred or deported, as recorded by Muslim chroniclers—motivate Prodi's appeasement policy?

The willful blindness of EU leaders has thus brought the jihadist threat to the heart of Europe. While European authorities deny the existence of a radical Islamic terrorist war on their Continent, police and soldiers have to patrol its cities, train stations, and airports. This reality, plus the anxiety of the public, points to the opposite conclusion: that, in fact, Europe is in a war she does not wish to recognize or to fight—preferring to maintain the illusion of peace. Because the history of *jihad* and dhimmitude have been denied, and replaced by mythical narrative, we see the re-emergence in the twenty-first century of the millennial struggles between *dhimmi* collaborationists and the free leaders within the *dar al-harb*, which is threatened by *jihad*. The future of civilization depends of the outcome of this conflict.

Furthermore the impact of 9/11 and the greater awareness of Europeans to Islamic terror could hold up or even undermine the Euro-Arab integrative project, built on the assumption that Islam is less dangerous inside Europe than outside. The failure or the abandonment of a policy conducted systematically for three decades could unleash chaos throughout Europe of an uncontrollable magnitude. The indictment of Bush and Sharon, and Putin recently, by politicians and a complacent media—or the conspiracy theories accusing Jews and Christians (Americans) for 9/11—rehabilitated a more and more unpopular Arabophile policy. 9/11 hit America brutally but in Europe the aftermath could be even more devastating.

Eurabia

The foremost consequence of the EAD has been a rampant transformation of the European continent engineered with EU leaders' approval. The Mediterranean Partnership has increased the influx of Muslim immigrants into Europe from Arab and Muslim countries, and ensured their status as the preferred source of immigration to Europe. This policy, as we have seen, will continue. The EEC, and then the EU, never planned to integrate so many millions of Muslim immigrants into European society (multiculturalism); instead, the countries from which they came expected the European host countries to adapt themselves to the immigrants' cultural and religious customs. And indeed, any reluctance or hesitation from Europe about immigration is labeled racism by the EAD's agents and executives. These Eurocrats avoid any discussion about the insecurity, criminality, and religious intolerance of certain significant sections of this immigrant population that is hostile to Western secularism and its Judeo-Christian mores, culture, and history. Such Islamists provoke racist reactions that threaten the well-being and security of the many Muslims immigrants who have successfully integrated into Western societies. According to an interview in the

London *New Statesman*, Tariq Ramadan, a collaborator of Prodi on the Foundation for the Dialogue of Cultures, does not see Islam adapting to local conditions, but "as an extension of the 'house of Islam' into the lands of the unbelievers."[16]

As the Madrid attacks of March 11, 2004 reveal, EAD policy has made the entire continent of Europe hostage to Islamist networks linked to countries where anti-Western prejudices and jihadist religious imperialism have been entrenched for thirteen centuries. The culture of concessions is now so internalized in Europe that in France a new law reaffirming secularism in schools is considered a provocation. Sheikh Muhammad Hussein Fadlallah, leader of Hezbollah, sent a letter to President Chirac in spring 2004 threatening French interests if Muslim girls were forbidden to wear the *hijab* in schools and forced to comply with French school regulations. Muslim anti-French demonstrations and threats expanded in the Middle East and Asia. George Carey, the former Archbishop of Canterbury and head of the Anglican Church, incensed Muslims in Britain by his criticism of Arab authoritarian regimes in a lecture he gave in Rome on March 25, 2004. He regretted the insufficient condemnation by moderate Muslim leaders of suicide bombers and acknowledged the decline of Islamic critical scholarship over the last five hundred years. Iqbal Sacranie, the secretary-general of the Muslim Council of Britain, as well as other Muslim representatives, reacted angrily to these observations.[17]

After the April 2004 arrest in Britain of a terrorist cell with connections in Belgium and Italy, the Muslim Council of Britain issued, for the first time, a text asking Muslims in Britain to condemn and fight terrorism, clearly and unequivocally. However, some groups put conditions upon any Muslim collaboration with the government. Among these were demands that the British government pursue hostile policies toward the U.S. and Israel.[18]

The War Against Western Culture

The EAD monitored the development and implementation of the Euro-Arab symbiosis on all levels. The obsequiousness and prejudices of many academic institutions corroded the norms, criteria and discipline necessary for objective academic study. Their submission to a political power dominated entirely by economic materialism and policy recalls the autocensorship and control over academia exerted by National Socialism and Communism.

Education inspired by Islamization also permeates European textbooks. A chief instrument of this policy is the International Institute of Islamic Thought (IIIT) founded by Ismail Raji al-Faruqi. It was created in 1981 to challenge Western philosophy and education, which were considered a threat to the *umma,* the universal Muslim nation. The institute and its branches, which are now spread over Europe, Canada, and America, conducted research and teaching programs that introduced a new concept: the Islamization of Knowledge.[19] This view asserts that the Revealed Knowledge (Islam) is the source of all knowledge, and that its messenger, Muhammad, was entrusted to provide guidance to all humanity. Historically, according to this view, the Islamization of knowledge allowed sciences, arts, and medicine to flourish in Muslim lands, ensuring a millennium of Muslim domination over the world. Western knowledge simply borrowed from Muslim science. In this optic, the resumption of the Islamization of knowledge in modern times would restore to Muslims their own patrimony, which had been taken over by the West.

The IIIT's program for the re-Islamization of Western science was proposed by Ismail Raji al-Faruqi. He saw no hope for the revival of the *umma* unless the dualism in Muslim education that separates Islamic and secular aspects be abolished once and for all.[20] He and other Muslim academics that succeeded him have endeavored to introduce the Islamization of Knowledge, an integral part of the Islamic Renaissance, in Europe and America to fill the vacuum created when Western civilization will finally collapse.[21]

Significantly, in October 1982, al-Faruqi complained in the preface to his book about the *umma*: "If it has made any contributions to the historical battle of humanity against disease, poverty, ignorance, hostility, immorality and impiety in modern times, it has been negligible." He proposed "to take the youth further on the road of genuine self-reform, bring up-to-date as it were, the early ideational insights of the great reformers of the Salafiyah movement, Muhammad ibn 'Abd al Wahhab, Muhammad Idris al Sanusi, Hasan al Banna and others."

For al-Faruqi, the word *umma* is not translatable, it is not synonymous with "the people," or "the nation," or the "state."

> Its territory is not only the whole earth, but all of creation. Neither is the *ummah* restricted to any race. . . . The *ummah* is a sort of "United Nations" with one strong and comprehensive ideology, a world-government and a world-army to enforce its decisions. The *ummah* is the social order of Islam; and the movement which pursues it, or seeks to actualize its goals, its ummatism.

A few pages later, he described the universal mission of the *umma:*

> It exists solely as an instrument of the divine will which seeks, through the ummah, to find concretization in space and time. It constitutes the matrix of God's definitive revelation, the instrument of His will, and the point at

which the divine meets the cosmos, and here the cosmos is launched on its infinite march toward fulfillment of the divine purpose. As the Qur'an has put it eloquently, the ummah exists so that "the word of God may be supreme."[22]

The principles of the Islamization of knowledge have been developed in European schools, especially those with a majority of Muslim pupils. In England, the Muslim Educational Trust asked for specific arrangements based on Islamic rules for Muslim children in schools, and a revision of the content of the curriculum considered as un-Islamic. Muslims demand that teachers from the Arab countries be brought to teach Arabic to their children and that Arabic be taught in Europe like any another European language.[23]

In America, schoolteachers were initiated to Islamic education through *Strategies and Structures for Presenting World History*, published by the Council on Islamic Education (CIE) in 1994.[24] Its author, Susan Douglass, was assisted by a group of historians affiliated with CIE. Ten years ago, this book called for scrupulous examination of textbooks in order to make sure they conform to the Islamic view of world history. *Strategies and Structures* labels Western historians and scientists as domineering, triumphalist, and closed-minded; it asserts that Western teaching victimizes immigrants and espouses an elitist worldview that inculcates a myopic view of other societies, thus spreading old ideas—"old assumptions, old approaches, old sequencing and old facts"[25]—based on superficial research and leading to shallowness and cultural prejudice. New textbooks should eliminate this narrow, egocentric Western perspective, correcting it with an Islamic worldview and knowledge.

The contemptuous denigration of Western culture by the book's author reflects and promotes Edward Said's disparaging view of the West, most notoriously expressed in his spurious 1978 attack on Orientalism, as well as al-Faruqi's depiction of Islam as the matrix of Judaism and Christianity, and the source of all prophecy. Said, a Christian—who grew up in Egypt and later reinvented himself as a Palestinian refugee—declared "that every European, in what he could say about the Orient, was consequently a racist, an imperialist, and almost totally ethnocentric."[26] This became the prevailing view in America and is disseminated widely in Eurabia as well. *Strategies and Structures* conveys exactly this opinion. The book expounds at length the Western debt to Islamic culture in virtually every aspect of human endeavor, including music and science and even textiles and agriculture—as if humanity before the Arab-Islamic invasion and colonization of a large portion of the civilized world was naked, and the earth barren. In other words, the book assumes that Western culture *is* Islamic and that its alleged Muslim origin is deliberately ignored only out of anti-Islamic prejudice.

This charge reiterates the traditional Islamic accusation against Jews and Christians that they are assumed to know the superiority of Muhammad's religion and deny it only out of jealousy.

The book also explains how to influence the West by changing Western perceptions of Islam and Muslims. One point directs that in photographic representations, Muslims should be shown dressed as Americans. The book gives the impression of a self-consciously inferior Islamic culture reacting to the pervasive frustration and humiliation that were born of its encounter with Western culture. It also manifests a determination to dominate and appropriate Western civilization, by simply declaring it Islamic.

Since the 1970s a great many history texts and schoolbooks have been rewritten to accord with the Islamic view of history. This tendency gained momentum in the 1990s after the European Community decisions of 1991, which were reaffirmed by French President Chirac in his Cairo University address in 1996. Now, the Islamic view of history and the Islamization of knowledge permeate the entire European cultural spectrum.[27] In March 2002, heavily armed federal agents raided a cluster of more than one hundred Muslim charities and companies based in and around Herndon (Virginia), which then flourished after the establishment there of the International Institute of Islamic Thought (IIIT), founded by its guru, Ismail Raji al-Faruqi. The raid was motivated by alleged ties with Palestinian and other terrorist organizations, and their funding.[28]

Many Muslim reformers have been indoctrinated by this Islamization of Knowledge theory which teaches the application of *ijtihad*—the principle of legal interpretation and change—but in a circular movement whereby the Qur'anic precepts are modernized. Western thinking and sciences are integrated in an Islamic interpretation.[29] This movement, very close to the Wahhabi and Salafiyah trends, reproduces in modern times a parallel and similar system that had induced in the Qur'an the Islamization of Judaism and Christianity. The mixture of modern openness (*ijtihad*) linked to the traditional set of values confers to its followers an ambiguity suspicious to Muslim modernists. In fact the whole movement was already planned and explained by al-Tohami at the Lahore 1974 OIC meeting.

It may seem of no consequence to a postreligious Europe whether Jesus[30] was a Muslim prophet who preached Islam or a Jew inspired by the Bible, but on this question depends the core of Christian belief—as well as the fundamental values of the Judeo-Christian civilization, and their survival. Besides the theological aspect, which does not interest Churches that have already accepted dhimmitude, the idea that Islam actually precedes Judaism and Christianity runs counter to the West's logical chronology and rationalism, the very foundations of its scientific achievements.

The omission of a clear reference to the Judeo-Christian roots of European civilization in the preamble to the still unratified European Constitution amounts to a repudiation of its past, as was underlined by a long analysis in the Vatican's *Civiltà Cattolica*, published on September 20, 2003. The obliteration of Europe's historical memory, to suit the Arab-Islamic concept of history, makes possible the diffusion of a sort of negationist and guilt-inducing pseudoculture, in which veneration of the Andalusian myth and the Palestinian cult replaces knowledge of the reality of *jihad* and dhimmitude in Muslim Spain and elsewhere. Thus, the rejection of the Judeo-Christian character of European civilization does in fact address the need to integrate a massive Muslim population.

Europe and Judeophobia

In conjunction with Europe's Islamization, another grave development of the EAD unfolded: Europe's Judeophobia. The two are connected. Is antisemitism the face of the future Muslim-Christian Eurabia? How does the Charter of Fundamental Rights of the European Union, proclaimed at Nice on December 7, 2000, apply to European Jews today? The human rights that the EU boasts of promoting are flouted on its own territory when rights to safety and education are eroded, synagogues are torched, cemeteries desecrated, and doctors attacked in hospitals by Muslim traditionalists who refuse unisex European medical care for their women. European Jews are today continually assailed with libelous accusations and by an inquisitorial media.[31] Freedom of religion and opinion are compromised when Jewish centers are attacked and expressions of Zionism provoke threats and insults. In 2003, after an uproar over European antisemitism in the American press and Bush's ironic reminder of Europe's past, the EU ordered an inquiry into antisemitism—but the European Commission suppressed the results through fear of revealing the identity of the perpetrators: Muslim immigrants to Europe and the pro-Palestinian Left.

France's energetic Interior Minister Nicholas Sarkozy, who inherited a deplorable situation, vigorously condemned antisemitism in France and on a visit to the U.S. In late 2003, a report by the politician and immigration expert Bernard Stasi included a description, based on the testimony of schoolteachers and representatives of civil society, on the rise of antisemitic intimidation and violence that were generating hate and fear in everyday life.[32] It finally prompted a firm reaction from President Jacques Chirac, who declared in an address on December 17, 2003 that France would fight xenophobia, racism and, in particular, antisemitism. Yet on March 8, 2004, the Jerusalem Center of Public Affairs had to announce that a fundraising event featuring Israel's Defense Minister Shaul Mofaz would be postponed after organizers and owners of the Palais des Congrès, one of Paris's largest halls, received death threats from local Palestinians.

Some high-ranking Catholic clergymen have condemned the current wave of Judeophobia. Cardinal Roger Etchegaray declared in an interview with the Italian newspaper *La Stampa* on December 20, 2003 that the rise of antisemitism in Europe required constant vigilance. "Not to recognize it, not to call it by its name is an unwitting way of accepting it." As we have said, Judeophobia and Israelophobia are not common among ordinary Europeans. It is rather a general climate created by the politicians, intellectuals, and journalists involved in the Partnership network that now permeates the entire EU. For example, the Euro-Mediterranean Conference of Ministers of Foreign Affairs, held in Naples on December 2 and 3, 2003, points to Israel's duties but asks comparably little from the Palestinians. While the ministers call on the Palestinian Authority to demonstrate its determination in the fight against extremist violence, they urge the Israeli government, "in exercising its right to protect its citizens, to exert maximum effort to avoid civilian casualties and take all necessary actions to ease the humanitarian and economic plight of the Palestinian people and facilitate the relief work of international donors. Israel should refrain from any action that violates international law."[33]

The EU here follows what we have seen to be a well-established pattern by showing no interest in calling on the Palestinians to refrain from killing Israeli civilians and demonstrating no sympathy for the humanitarian and economic plight of Israelis suffering from terrorism. The EU Ministers in Naples expressed concern over the humanitarian situation in the West Bank and Gaza, but not in Israel—where so many families grieve for the victims of terror. Their statement underlines the "intolerable life" of the Palestinians and approves the international community's measures to improve it, but it does not commiserate about the suffering of the Israelis and the country's economic recession as a result of Arafat's launching the October 2000 *jihad* three years earlier. It reiterates how the Barcelona process and the Middle East Peace Process are complementary, but does not mention the violation of fundamental human rights in the Arab countries, including the PA-controlled territories, as incompatible with the principles of the Barcelona Process.

A Declaration of the American and European Catholic Bishops, issued on January 21, 2004, expresses the same imbalance. It condemns the building of a security fence called a "wall of separation," without acknowledging that Palestinian terrorism has made it necessary. The problems for Palestinians caused by the restriction of their movement and especially of their access to Israeli territory are much lamented, but there is no regret for Israeli citizens: Jews, Christians, Druzes, and foreigners blown up in buses, streets, restaurants, or universities by Palestinians. By any reasonable standard, time delays in moving from one place to another and indiscriminate killing of civilians does not involve suffering of comparable magnitude. This point apparently escaped the bishops who signed the declaration. The Latin patriarch of Jerusalem, Michel Sabbah, who met the Israeli President Moshe Katsav on January 14, 2004, legitimized genocidal jihadist terrorism by equating it with the Israeli "occupation" of Judea.[34] Following these various declarations, and particularly the EU Presidency's Conclusion, the British Parliament's Select Committee on International Development published a report on February 5, 2004 urging "the UK Government to propose to the EU Council of Trade Ministers that Israel's preferential terms of trade with the EU be suspended until it lifts the movement restrictions which it has placed on Palestinian trade."[35] The damage to Israel's economy inflicted by Palestinian terrorism is not mentioned.

At the initiative of the European deputy François Zimeray, a team of inspectors from OLAF, the European Union Fraud Office, arrived in Jerusalem at the end of January 2004 to investigate whether EU funds had been misdirected by the Palestinian Authority. According to the BBC, former Palestinian cabinet minister Abdel Fattah Hamayel admitted paying $40,000 per month in "living expenses" to gunmen of the Al-Aqsa Martyrs' Brigades. Between 1995 and 2000, according to the IMF, 900 million (over $1 billion) were diverted in corrupt practices. Javier Solana, the EU commissar for foreign policy and security, declared that Europe's duty was to help the Palestinian Authority, adding, "If it didn't exist we would have to invent it!"[36] In fact, the Palestinian Authority *is* Europe's creation, as was Arafat's international status as PLO leader for 30 years.

In the preceding chapter, we saw how the European Cultural Foundation was manufacturing a Euro-Arab cultural space by financing a network of associations of artists, writers, comedians, actors, film, theater and video producers, journalists, NGOs, intergovernmental organizations, and national cultural operatives such as museum curators and exhibition directors, in the service of its political design of Cross Mediterranean Cultural Cooperation. This cross cultural Euro-Arab fertilization was illustrated in Sweden at the Stockholm International Forum, which was held from January 17 to February 7, 2004. There, a composition was exhibited honoring a jihadist woman who murdered twenty-one Israelis at a restaurant in Haifa. Her picture was posted in twenty-six subway stations throughout Stockholm—evidently celebrating the murder of Israelis.[37] It was labeled a work of art and therefore deemed untouchable. Thomas Nordanstad, the Swedish museum official in charge of the exhibition at the Museum of National Antiquities, refused to remove it, but agreed to take down the giant posters from the subway stations in Stockholm. Israeli ambassador Zvi Mazel showed his contempt for this glorification of a criminal ideology that has massacred thousands: he unplugged the light illuminating the exhibit—an act that much scandalized the enlightened Eurabian media and the artists, one of whom was a former Israeli.

Meanwhile, hideous antisemitic cartoons flourished in European newspapers. One drawn by Dave Brown in the *Independent* even won the UK "Political Cartoon of the Year Award for 2003" from the Political Cartoon Society.[38] The award was presented to the winner on November 25, 2003, by Claire Short, Labor MP and former minister for overseas aid. A virulent opponent of Blair's alliance with the U.S., she resigned during the Iraqi war.

Such encouragement inspired others to show their talents in a similar way. In December 2003, another artistic pro-Palestinian Nazi-style performance was played by the French comedian M'Bala M'Bala Dieudonné, who protested that he was simply expressing his art. Other poets and writers followed, expressing through "art" the vociferous Israelophobia fed by the Mediterranean Partnership and the European Cultural Foundation. As in the days of the Nazis, art became the vehicle of European anti-Israel hatred. Probably Europeans will never know how many millions, if not billions, of euros they have spent to create a poisonous pseudoculture that now permeates every stratum of the European Union's societies, albeit constantly denied.

These events illustrate the EU policy of Euro-Arab association in art, films, documentaries, media, audio-visual productions, and universities. The EU is spending millions to back anti-Israeli denunciations by Jews and Israelis, and encouraging what it calls the will of "civil society" outside the usual political or diplomatic channels. Ilka Schröder, an independent German member of the European Parliament, noted:

> The relationship between the EU's actions and the open expression of anti-Semitism is among the last things responsible EU officials would like to be discussed publicly. Yet they know that this open expression is the logical result of their efforts for "peace and understanding" in the Middle East. . . . Hardly any European politician could be interested in having the EU support of the war against Israel become an issue in the European elections. Conservatives, Socialists, Liberals, Greens, and Leftists were involved in downplaying, hushing up, and denying the mortal effects of the European peace policy. The collective hope is that nobody will be interested in the scandal after June 2004. . . .
>
> But even if Europe adopts a more moderate tone in the coming months, the dream of German blue helmets on patrol in east Jerusalem will still be alive. The strategy may change, but the aim will be the same: to use the Middle East as a playing field for Europe's ambitions to become an independent and dominant superpower in world politics.[39]

This was the original aim of the Euro-Arab Dialogue. But today the Partnership has turned it into a tremendous enterprise to buy off terrorist threats. The EU now spends almost €1 billion annually in the "South," promoting reform and development through the MEDA program.[40]

The Utopian Society

The advisory group established by Prodi (see chapter 17) claimed that in the next half-century the two parts of the Euro-Mediterranean (European and Arab) area would have integrated their day-to-day life. Consequently, it declared that the relationship with the South—that is the Arab countries—should be made a priority. Its task was to prepare the ground for this, as "It is a historic and hence politically crucial task, and it is as urgent."[41] The new EU policy plans to establish the Euro-Mediterranean Foundation in order to create a culture that will end "the discriminations from which European citizens of immigrant origin still too often suffer and the persistent situation of injustice, violence and insecurity in the Middle East in implementing educational programmes."[42]

Since the EU cannot bring cultural and social changes to the Arab countries, the Foundation's worthy goal to eliminate prejudice will operate only in the EU, on behalf of Arab/Muslim immigrants, while indigenous Arab xenophobia will not be addressed. In his well-documented book, *Islamikazes*, Raphael Israeli writes:[43]

> [T]here is a vast silent portion of Muslims who sympathize, if not with militant Islam, then at least with its horrendous acts of terror, as the profuse statements and demonstration of jubilation among Muslim intellectuals, professionals, columnists and the masses attested to in the aftermath of 11 September, and, on a daily basis, following every horrendous Islamikaze act which leaves Israeli civilians ripped apart, killed or maimed for life.

The Foundation will endeavor to consolidate a Mediterranean cultural unity "which holds together and makes sense." To this end, the dialogue must be "cemented by mutual awareness and understanding" between societies and peoples who develop a perception and feeling of "shared destiny."[44] The group deplores the Arab-Israeli conflict, "which every day casts doubt . . . and causes great bitterness and a profound sense of double standards"—allegedly favoring Israel. The project conducted by the Foundation should achieve a convergence of interests, values and political priorities; it should foster "a will to live together" and a necessary solidarity.[45] The policies and actions that contribute to this dialogue will "combat all forms of discrimination, disinformation, ignorance, violations of human dignity, and unequal relations between states, between populations, between men and women and between individuals."

The advisory group repeats that no culture can claim any kind of superiority. The two Mediterranean entities "must be aware that, within them, as also between the two entities that they form, the cultural dimension of our unfolding history will now be crucial" (underlined in the text). The group asserts that such a vision responds to Europe's determination to enrich its own identity through its neighbor's culture. "It responds to the desire of the peoples of the Mediterranean to see their contribution to global civilisation acknowledged. It also responds to the need to create links between Europe and the other Mediterranean countries on the basis of understanding."[46]

The group recommends giving priority to education, so that the dialogue "suffuses civil society and permeates the social fabric."[47] It also calls for promotion of the learning of Arabic among schoolchildren of the North—that is, Europe.

> This sort of encouragement and commitment to giving the younger generations of Europeans a taste for these languages [of the southern shores of the Mediterranean, i.e., Arab] and a desire to learn them will be a decisive step in the direction of renewed dialogue between the two shores of the Mediterranean and a crucial element in the internal dialogue within Europe between the local populations [European] and the new Europeans who are descendants from migrants.[48]

It also directs that travel should be greatly encouraged, as an important means for the mixing of populations through youth exchanges and the sharing of experience at all levels of society. The group calls on the EU to fund a huge mobility program for schools, with special emphasis on ten- to twelve-year-olds and the funding of travel and of accommodation costs. The alignment of the educational content of the different school systems would lay down the foundations of a "common knowledge" in the humanities and social sciences, whose disciplines would be redefined. It would allow for "the re-examination in depth of the history of the Mediterranean region, looking at the anthropological, legal, cultural, religious, economic and social dimensions in such a way as to identify and weed out all the tendentious interpretations, misleading ambiguities of language or vocabulary, all the false truths, all the distorted images of the Other, all the marks of mutual defiance and the ways these are exploited politically and ideologically."[49]

States will have to undertake a re-examination of schoolbooks dealing with the history of the region. Study centers and networks of scholars will assume the control of publications and the diffusion of the knowledge of the history of the Euro-Mediterranean region. Cultural dialogues would also include dialogue between the arts and artists, creators and authors. "The Foundation will have to create an active network of artists and writers and organise meetings and events" to stimulate the dialogue.[50] It will make the media a vital instrument of its policy.

Specific action will be needed to support the guidelines, aimed at the emergence of an enlightened dialogue. The group calls on public authorities to encourage programs in the worlds of film, television and publishing.

It demands support from the European Commission for audiovisual channels in the "countries of the South and to encourage the creation of 'neighborhood channels' that can help to reinforce the bridging role played by Europe's immigrant population with their native country in the South."

The Foundation's design is thus nothing less than complete Euro-Arab integration under its guidance, with control over European intellectual life and education. On February 19, 2004, French Foreign Minister Dominique de Villepin gave an interview to *Le Figaro* describing the Partnership which "should take into consideration all the political, economic, social, cultural and educational dimensions" in association with the Arab countries "for peace and progress." Solutions should not be imposed from outside. For de Villepin "nothing would be worse than to activate a feeling of confrontation between our countries and the Arab world, between the West and Islam." The *dhimmi* mentality has prevented European leaders from acknowledging jihadist Islamic confrontation. The Partnership epitomizes the complacency of *dhimmi* policy. De Villepin insisted on Europe's dedication to peace in the Arab-Israel conflict, but the EU has failed to stop its funding and support for PLO terrorist activities.

This intercultural dialogue thus requires that the Europeans reinvent their identity and history in order to integrate the Southern (Arab) migrant populations. The EU keeps the doors of immigration open for the Southern Partnership while closing them for the Eastern European countries, even though the latter are now members of the EU.[51]

The group does not explain how it will implement reciprocal policies in the South (the Arab world). Moreover, the future projects concern abstract, faceless, and amorphous entities: "North," "South," "Neighborhood," "Us." Such language blurs the realities of Arab-Muslim and European societies, as if dealing with phantom peoples. The readiness to relinquish one's own identity, culture, and history reflects the *dhimmi* tendency toward self-negation. The Foundation enterprise continues the utopian Barcelona Process, which has failed so far to bring about democracy or freedom in any Arab-Muslim country.

Euro-Mediterranean foreign ministers met on May 5–6, 2004, in Dublin and agreed on the creation of the Foundation under the name Anna Lindh Foundation for the Dialogue of Cultures whose headquarters will be in Alexandria, Egypt. Anna Lindh, of the Social Democrat Party, was the Swedish foreign minister stabbed to death by a mentally disturbed person in September 2002. On the Middle East and America, she promoted support for Arafat's tactics and announced a personal boycott of Israeli products; she urged the EU to suspend its relations with Israel, and condemned Bush's Middle East policy.[52] Naming the Foundation after her indicates its policy. Egypt was selected by the EU to harbor the Foundation for the dialogue of civilizations, in spite of a November 2002 report on the negative views on Christianity and Europe in recent Egyptian government textbooks used in schools.[53]

In March 2004, the Center for Monitoring the Impact of Peace (CMIP) published a comprehensive report on 139 Egyptian school textbooks in both the state and religious systems. While acknowledging the positive elements in the state system, like the favorable view of the Copts, the report noted the resilience of negative stereotypes of non-Muslims. Textbooks teach the traditional view that Islam is the only religion, which the Bible has distorted. Israel, by name, is not recognized as a sovereign state—the expression "Jewish state" is mentioned only twice—and peace is conditional to Arab demands. Europe is demonized under the label "Crusaders" and "imperialism", and its history much neglected. Middle East archeology and history—before the appearance of Islam and the Arab conquests of the seventh century—are Arabized and Islamized. The textbooks of the religious system continue to teach *jihad*, with the traditional beheading of infidels described in religious al-Azhar education, and the mandatory rules of dhimmitude. This was described by David G. Littman in an oral and written statement to the UN Sub-Commission on Human Rights on August 10, 2004, enlarged for a lecture to the First International Symposium on "Egyptian Copts: A Minority under Siege" on September 24, 2004, in Zurich and published.[54]

As a visual symbolic of Europe's future, the first page of the report establishing the aims, funding, and functioning of the Anna Lindh Foundation was adorned with a thirteenth-century map of the Mediterranean area (North and South). But it is an unusual map, turned upside down: it shows the Arab Islamic world at the top in the North, above the European countries below in the South. An explanatory line indicates that the orientation of the map corresponds to the world view of the Arab cartographers of the Middle Ages.

Conclusion

Dialogue on Trial

Viewed with thirty years' hindsight, can one argue that the initial Franco-Arab plan has evolved successfully? Some would probably affirm it, but others would disagree. Europe has become overtly anti-American and anti-Israeli; the Atlantic alliance is threatened. Europe is weakened by its own divisions, while the Muslim world becomes ever more united under an Islamist anti-Western ideology. Europe has been neutralized from within by EAD policy and by internal Islamist terror, which has also silenced and intimidated Muslim reformists. Many of the latter have denounced their own European government's laxism and felt the danger threatening their whole community. The September 2004 Belsan massacre (Northern Ossetia), its exposure throughout the international media, triggered a sudden realism and self-criticism from Arabs and Muslims as never before. In London and Paris, more and more Muslims have vehemently condemned Islamic terrorism and threats to Europe.

Firmly ensconced at the summit of each EU state, with a determining influence at ministerial and governmental levels, the EAD and the Euro-Arab Partnership apparatuses have conditioned Europeans to dhimmitude—that is to say, to passive submission to intellectual censorship, insecurity, internal violence, and even terrorism. These plagues are simply gainsaid by governments elected to uphold the rule of law in their countries. Massive European funding to Arab states is accompanied by European self-guilt, while lauding the greatness and tolerance of Arab-Islamic civilization. This is called "maintaining peace" and "cultivating friendly relations." No one dares imagine the consequences of the EU closing its borders or diminishing its payments. The recent declaration of the Spanish prime minister, Jose Luis Rodriguez Zapatero—in a statement at the UN General Assembly on September 23, 2004—calling for "an alliance of cultures" between "the so-called Western world" and the Arab and Muslim countries confirms the mixture of fear and subservience characteristic of dhimmitude. Zapatero was elected after the Madrid March 11, 2004 bombings, and he represents the jihadists' victory. Zapatero asked UN Secretary General Kofi Annan to set up a high-level group to study the creation of an alliance of civilizations, to discuss on political and cultural issues, joint peacekeeping missions, and interfaith dialogue—one more group of dialogue. He added the usual Eurabian *dhimmi* servile pledge by calling on the international community to combat terrorism, whose roots he alleged are in the Israeli-Palestinian conflict—and through economic development. Hence more funding for the jihadist ideology.[1]

Today it can be acknowledged that the EAD has served as a vehicle for the policy decided at the 1974 Lahore Islamic Conference, the 1980 Islamic Conference at Fez, the 1980 Arab Summit Conference at Amman, and the Islamic Summit at Mecca-Taif in 1981. It has carried out the missions of each of these conferences in the European and international levels. The United Nations has been transformed into an international antisemitic tribunal, seeking to impose on Israel the Islamic condition of dhimmitude: denial of its identity, usurpation of its history, isolation and vilification.

Till this day, dhimmitude is studied outside of Western academia. It is banned from Middle East departments of universities wherever the Saidist Palestinian cult dominates. Though dhimmitude is based on an ideology, a well-established legal sector, an immense wealth of historical source-materials and concerns the history of hundred of millions of human beings from Spain to India, this subject is still denied.

The Franco-German duo that engendered the EAD has revived a sinister alliance, this time built upon the oil market, financial agreements, the demise of Israel, and anti-Americanism, as well as Islamic threats. Europe is sinking to the status of a *dhimmi* continent fighting for Islamic jihadist causes that it argues disingenuously are its own. European opposition to the war against Iraq and to America was concerted throughout Europe by the EAD's vast apparatus—the Euro-Arab Parliamentarian Co-operation and the Mediterranean Partnership. Their networks and NGO collaboration reach into all the political parties, the churches, the universities, the intelligentsia, media, banking, and into financial and industrial circles. Currently, the entire European political, intellectual, and religious establishment envisages, as we have seen, a Euro-Arab conglomerate with a faceless European population called "Us." One of the architects of this new humanity, Tariq Ramadan, a first generation Swiss citizen, was invited in 2004 to the prestigious Catholic Notre Dame University in Indiana, to lecture on religion, conflict, and the promotion of peace. He would have promoted in America the *Dialogue Between Peoples and Cultures* established by the High-Level Advisory Group to the European Commission, of which he was a member—nominated by the then European Commission President Romano Prodi, had his American visa not been refused in September 2004.

Tariq Ramadan—whose father, Said Ramadan, was given asylum in Switzerland when he fled Nasser's Egypt—is the grandson of Hasan al-Banna, founder of the first modern jihadist group, the Muslim Brotherhood, and is a controversial figure in European politics. He recently wrote an anti-semitic pamphlet[2] and declared in the Moroccan monthly magazine *Version Homme*, "the great trickery is to let Europe believe that it is of Judeo-Christian tradition. It is an absolute lie."[3] This utterance epitomizes the Muslim view that a Judeo-Christian spiritual tradition and civilization have no legitimate existence, as both Judaism and Christianity are late deformations of Islam. Ramadan's statement merely echoes the understandings expressed in November 2003 by President Jacques Chirac to Philippe de Villiers, president of the French rightist party Mouvement pour la France when he declared: "Europe's roots are as much Muslim as Christian."[4] Engaged in interfaith dialogue, the Churches collaborated with Islam at different levels, promoting a culture of conviviality and dialogue. They undertook the integration of the Muslim immigrants through numerous humanitarian and social actions. Christianity, Eurabian leaders taught, would be enriched by contact with Islam. The struggle for such common goals as Palestinianism and Israel's withering away built a dynamic of Muslim-Christian rapprochement as a means of Muslim integration into Europe. A fraternal struggle for "justice and peace" for Palestinians was seen as fulfilling the truth of both religions in relation to Israel. A growing blindness and hatred has prevented the clergy from seeing that Palestinian justice is *jihad* justice against the infidels and that their stand is *dhimmi* subservience to Islam. Muslim records and texts testify to the usefulness of the Churches' collaboration in the anti-Israeli policy. Now, terrified by Islamism, the Churches seek their security by advocating openly an anti-Israeli policy.[5] The jihadist interpretation of "justice and peace," having been lauded as a solution for Israel, is now threatening Europe itself.

It is rather pitiful to see Jews and Israelis believing naively that the Judeophobic culture now flourishing in the EU comes from simple ignorance, and that it would vanish if only they apologize and engage in endless self-justification for their mere existence. As if they had learned nothing from the lessons of antisemitism, they do not perceive the whole edifice of lies and defamation willfully built over the years to conduct this very policy leading to their elimination. They are not dealing here with a matter of justice or truth, but with a visceral hate that pursues the destruction of Israel. Could Jews discuss with the Nazis and persuaded them of the falsity of their lies? Clearly, the Nazis knew they were lies because they themselves had invented them. The Palestinian cult that now poisons Europe was fabricated in the European capitals that championed Arafat—as Chirac still does, when sending him his minister of foreign affairs, Michel Barnier in June 2004.

Like Judeophobia, anti-Americanism is a planned policy, whose masterminds are determined to maintain it as long as America does not comply with the Islamic world order. Even if thirty years ago anti-Americanism represented an option among others, today it is imposed by the demographic Muslim pressure from within, combined with the terrorist threat from without—unless Europeans themselves reassert a new consciousness of their own identity and destiny, highly improbable today after three decades of debilitating indoctrination.

Meanwhile, Islamism has entrenched itself in Europe's strategic nerve centers, engineering the irreversible process of Europe's dhimmitude: its respectful obedience to *shari'a* rules relating to social and political behavior, teaching, and gender. This signifies the definitive affiliation of an aging, confused, and timorous Europe with an assertive, demographically booming, Arab-Muslim world. The EU policy of impotence was planned, proclaimed, and implemented over the years by Europe's democratically elected leaders and its spiritual guides. It has engendered dialogue after dialogue, or what Habib Malik calls "the dialogue industry." A flight from reality displaced real threats onto scapegoats, allowing cowardice to flourish in a culture of vilification. Responsibility lies at the level of the European Commission, which set the political agenda, organized the funding, wielded the influence, and had the leverage to impose this agenda throughout the EU's political, economic, cultural, religious, and social sectors.

At this point, it is legitimate to ask: Who were the creators of Europe's passive *dhimmi* surrender? Who were the consultants, the advisors, the lobby groups? The main strategists of this policy from the 1970s were civil servants, some of them nostalgic for the French Arab colonial empire, imbued with a mixture of rabid Drumont-type antisemitism, anti-Americanism and an idealized passion for all things Arab and Islamic—stimulated, perhaps paradoxically, by a visceral fear of Islam.

Today's situation is the realization of the program set by the twenty-three resolutions voted at the January 1969 Second International Conference in Support of the Arab Peoples in Cairo, and at the May 1970 first World Conference of Christians for Palestine in Beirut, both under the leadership of Georges Montaron, the French director of *Témoignage Chrétien*. (See chapter 3) The EAD and its network implemented those resolutions at the European level. At the 1975 Strasbourg meeting, the delegates of the PAEAC were fully aware of the links between politics and culture and pointed them out to the Arab delegates, as an important factor of the new Euro-Arab culture they were created. (see p. 66) The PAEAC has been the European executive instrument for implementing *da'wa* in Europe.

Till this day the Euro-Arab Dialogue is totally unknown to Europeans, even though its occult machinery has engineered Europe's irreversible transformation through hidden channels. European tax-payers do not realize that they are funding the numerous foundations of the Dialogue, its complex bodies which are working under their own national parliament, the European parliament, the Commission, academia, press, media, and politicians—all weaving the web that conditions them to acclaim a system that has raised as virtues the denial of the Islamic threats and the renunciation of self-defense.

However, this combination of Middle-Eastern Christian *dhimmis* serving pan-Islamic interests, Judeophobic Europeans expelled from former Arab colonies, and a transnational coalition of neo-Nazis, communists, and Muslim activists could not have brought about Europe's transformation without the complete approval and unofficial support of successive European leaders. The Franco-German-Belgian team used the energy policy to shape the *da'wa* mindset in the institutions of the EEC and to monitor it through a network of committees. The strengthened EU framework has institutionalized a symbiotic Euro-Arab partnership, preparing a Kafkaesque cultural and political totalitarianism, wherein Islamist jihadist values subvert the whole European conception of knowledge, human rights, and fundamental individual liberties.

Decisions made years ago have had a snowball effect that may be irreversible. Today Europe is the hotbed of a virulent combination of anti-Jewish, anti-Christian and anti-American animosity that exudes from every sector of activity covered by the EAD. This result could only be achieved because it was institutionalized by an EU supranational policy: it was not out of Europeans' free choice. The war against jihadist terrorism in Europe was already lost in 1973 with the formation of a Euro-Arab coalition, through which both parties have pursued their own specific goal. Europe is pleading for the peace and security of dhimmitude, an Andalusian "Golden Age," long desired, now offered on the horizon as a future "Eurabia"—all too present.

It is too early in October 2004 to evaluate the long term consequences of the Coalition's war against Saddam Hussein. As a first result, it destroyed a regime which terrorized its own people for thirty years and was linked to international terrorism by its public funding of the Palestinian terror network. The future will tell whether the Iraqi people will finally seize the opportunity offered them with the blood of the Coalition soldiers to become a beacon for democratic reform and modernization in the Middle East—or if they will join the destroyers of civilization.

Integrated in Bush's declared war against terrorism, the Iraqi conflict has debunked Europe's complacency and collusion. Furthermore, President George W. Bush has unveiled the lethal danger of Islamist terrorism and placed it on the international world stage, dethroning the "Palestinian cause," and thus revolting many Europeans by weakening the Euro-Arab struggle against Israel. The political polarization of the West between the American resolve and the Chirac/Prodi-like complacency, has crystallized within European societies an awareness and resistance to a policy of dhimmitude. One may hope that America's resolute policy has opened new perspectives and new opportunities for the world to eschew a former order of political connivance with hate and crime. Yet nothing is sure—for it is human beings who are the creators and actors of history.

Appendix 1:
Venice Euro-Arab Seminar, 1977

Euro-Arab Seminar on "Means and Forms of Cooperation for the Diffusion in Europe of the Knowledge of Arabic Language and Literary Civilization"

Venice, 28–30 March 1977. University of Venice, Cà Dolfin
Fondazione Giorgio Cini, Isola San Giorgio Maggiore
A report by Giovanni Oman*

*The Recommendations***

The reports presented to the Seminar of the Euro-Arab Dialogue held in Venice from the 28th to the 30th of March 1977 on the subject : "Means and forms of cooperation for the diffusion in Europe of the knowledge of Arabic language and literary civilization" clearly demonstrate the growing interest of the members states of the European Community in the Arab countries and in Arabic-Islamic studies.

Therefore the participants in this Seminar unanimously forward the following *recommendations* for consideration by the governments of the member states of the European Community and the League of Arab States.

1. Coordination of the efforts made by the Arab countries to spread the Arabic language and culture in Europe and to find the appropriate form of cooperation among the Arab Institutions that operate in this field.

2. Creation of joint Euro-Arab Cultural Centres in European capitals which will undertake the diffusion of the Arabic language and culture.

3. Encouragement of European institutions either at university level or at other levels that are concerned with the teachings of the Arabic language and the diffusion of Arabic and Islamic culture.

*Source: *Euro-Arab Dialogue. The Relations between the two cultures. Act of the Hamburg symposium April 11th to 15th 1983*. English version edited by Derek Hopwood, (London: Croom Helm, 1983) 317–23. Extracts.
**Italics in the text.

4. Support of joint projects for cooperation between European and Arab institutions in the field of linguistic research and the teaching of the Arabic language to Europeans.

5. Emphasis on a simplified and efficient method of teaching standard Arabic (fasiha) which is the language of culture that binds together the people of the Arab countries.

6. Necessity of paying attention to the teaching of Arabic at pre-university levels and to the extension of this teaching within the framework of existing educational systems in European countries.

7. Preparation of sufficient numbers of teachers specialized in the teaching of the Arabic language to Europeans.

8. Necessity of supplying European institutions and universities with Arab teachers specialized in teaching Arabic to Europeans.

9. Coordination of research of relevance to the spreading of the teaching of Arabic and Arab culture which is being carried out in Europe and in the Arab countries, and supplying it with funds. These researches should include the following themes:

   a) basic research on the Arabic language, making use among other things of the computer and other technical aids . . .

   c) applied research aiming at simplifying the teachings of Arabic to Europeans . . .

10. In teaching Arabic emphasis must be laid on different linguistic skills; the teaching of Arabic must be linked with Arab-Islamic culture and contemporary Arab issues.

11. Necessity of cooperation between European and Arab specialists in order to present an objective picture of Arab-Islamic civilization and contemporary Arab issues to students and to the educated public in Europe which could attract Europeans to Arabic studies.

12. Necessity of preparing a comprehensive study of translations from Arabic into European languages in order to elucidate the difficulties which such translation faces and to define the methods which will achieve the desired effect of spreading Arab culture in Europe.

13. Necessity of cooperation between Arab and European universities in training European teachers of Arabic, offering them the opportunity of studying in Arab universities and institutions specializing in Arabic language and of organizing programmes for them.

14. Necessity of exchange visits of all kinds between university teachers, specialists and researchers, including the organization of annual seminars to exchange views in all fields connected with the problems raised in these proposals.

15. Encouragement of Arab and European academic institutions to offer scholarships to European students specializing in Arabic and

Arab culture to enable them to study in Arab universities and institutes.

16. Necessity of establishing a centre for the distribution in Europe of Arabic periodicals, books and teaching materials in order to enable the European reader of Arabic to keep up with what is published in the Arab countries. The European group should agree on a location in Europe for this proposed centre and ALECSO will be the responsible organization on the Arab side.

17. Necessity of holding similar seminars to study the means and methods of spreading the knowledge of European languages and culture in the Arab countries, in order to further mutual understanding and joint efforts for the benefit of mankind.

18. European Governments participating in the Euro-Arab Dialogue are urged:

    a) to support institutes in European universities with funds for the realization of the tasks entrusted to them in teaching the Arabic language as well as Arab and Islamic studies,

    b) not to decrease the numbers of the teaching and research staffs in Arab countries,

    c) to exempt the above mentioned institutes from cuts in their funds.

19. In order to achieve the above, the participants consider it necessary as a result of this Seminar to establish a permanent committee of Arab and European experts to follow up the recommendations for disseminating Arabic and Arab culture in Europe; this to be within the framework of the Euro-Arab Dialogue.

Euro-Arab Symposium, Paris, 1977: Final Resolution*

At the initiative of the Association of Franco-Arab Solidarity (ASFA) and the European Committee and Coordination of Friendship Associations with the Arab world (EURABIA), a Euro-Arab symposium was held in Paris from September 20–22, 1977 with representatives of twelve European countries (Federal Republic of Germany, Great Britain, Belgium, Luxembourg, Holland, France, Switzerland, Portugal, Italy, Sweden, Ireland, Spain), as well as European and American personalities from the political, economic, academic, and journalistic fields.

Point 5. The symposium demands that the Conference of the so-called "Euro-Arab Dialogue" should welcome, without restrictions and with realism, the political problems—while following the implementation and development of cooperative economic and cultural goals.

---

*Bulletin d'information N° 74, October 1, 1977. Groupe d'étude sur le Moyen-Orient, Geneva, 14. For the affiliation of this Group with ASFA (Gaullist Group. President: former Gaullist minister of information, Louis Terrenoire) and EURABIA, see above p. 63 and note 1.

Appendix 2:
Fez Islamic Conference, 1980

Third Extraordinary Session of the Islamic
Conference of Foreign Ministers

Al Quds Al Sharif Session*
Fez 9–11 Zul Ke'da 1400 H.—18–20 September 1980

The Third Extraordinary Session of The Islamic Conference of Foreign Ministers convened in Fez, Kingdom of Morocco, from 9–11 Zul Ke'da 1400 H. (18–20 September, 1980) at the recommendation of Al Quds (Jerusalem) Committee, which had met in Casablanca, Kingdom of Morocco from 5–7 Shawal, 1400 H. (16–18 August, 1980) and at the request of the Palestine Liberation Organization.

The Extraordinary Session was attended by The General Secretariat of the Organization of the Islamic Conference, People's Democratic Republic of Algeria, State of Bahrain, People's Republic of Bangladesh, United Republic of Cameroun, Republic of Chad, Federal Islamic Republic of Comoro, Republic of Djibouti, Republic of Gabon, Republic of the Gambia, Popular Revolutionary Republic of Guinea, Republic of Guinea Bissau, Republic of Indonesia, Islamic Republic of Iran, Republic of Iraq, Hashemite Kingdom of Jordan, State of Kuwait, Republic of Lebanon, Socialist People's Libyan Arab Jamahiriya, Malaysia, Republic of Maldives, Republic of Mali, Islamic Republic of Mauritania, Kingdom of Morocco, Republic of Niger, Sultanate of Oman, Islamic Republic of Pakistan, Palestine (P.L.O.), State of Qatar, Kingdom of Saudi Arabia, Republic of Senegal, Democratic Republic of Somalia, Democratic Republic of Sudan, Syrian Arab Republic, Republic of Tunisia, Republic of Turkey, Republic of Uganda, State of United Arab Emirates, Republic of Upper Volta, Yemen Arab Republic, Yemen People's Democratic Republic.

Leader of the Muslim Turkish Community in Kibris [Cyprus] H.E. Raouf Denktash attended as Observer.

H.E. President Al Haj Ahmed Sekou Toure, in an important address, outlined the dangerous circumstances, in which the Extraordinary Session was

*Organization of the Islamic Conference (OIC) http://www.oic-oci.org/english/fm/All%20Download/frmex3.htm. Extracts.

convening, with regard to the question of Al Quds (Jerusalem) and Palestine. He declared that Israel's decision to annex Al Quds (Jerusalem) was a challenge to the whole of mankind, and emphasized that the Holy City could never become the property of Israel.

President Sekou Toure then projected the power of Islam which depended, not on the force of arms, but on its inherent qualities as an ideology, intellect, behaviour and morals. He called for upholding these divine principles which would ensure victory and the recovery of Al Quds Al Sharif.

He also delved in the Islamic principles that guarantee for every Muslim, wherever he may be, his personality and creative talents, making him an integral part of his community that cannot break away or be cast off. . . .

President Leopold Senghor, in his address, said his country had been quick to recognize the Palestine Liberation Organisation, following the resolution of the Arab Summit in Rabat considering the PLO as the sole legitimate representative of the Palestinian people.

President Senghor denounced Israel's decision of annexing Al Quds Al Sharif, emphasising that Al Quds was a Holy City not only to Jews but to Muslims and Christians alike; and that two billion Muslims and Christians—i.e. half the population of the world—were today protesting against the challenge Israel had thrown at them.

He said it would be better for the Conference to depend on the legal and moral reasons that he mentioned to demand—in the United Nations—the restoration of Al Quds to its pre-1967 status.

His Majesty King Hassan II of Morocco, in his address, said the significance of Jihad, in Islam, did not lie in religious wars or crusades. Rather, it was strategic political and military action, and psychological warfare, which, if employed by the Islamic Umma, would ensure victory over the enemy.

He said that Islam was subject only to God Almighty, and to reason, and that the recent Zionist decision had greatly affected the Islamic world; for Islam, and the noble ethics of the Prophet, had taught us to curb our wrath unless Allah's sanctities were desecrated, and was there a greater desecration than that against Al Quds Al Sharif the First Qibla and Third Haram.

His Majesty, in the name of the Islamic Group, emphasized to the Palestinian brethren that they alone were not the only ones to suffer the loss of Al Quds: the whole Islamic world has suffered the loss also, and will restore the Holy City with them; for Al Quds was not a trust to the Palestinians alone, but a trust to every single Muslim, man or woman.

His Majesty was convinced that the forthcoming Islamic Summit, to be held in Mecca Al Mokarramah, in the Kingdom of Saudi Arabia, will, once and for all, unify Muslim ranks and will purge the Arab arena from all hatred. His Majesty called for further intensification of efforts, organisation of ranks, and exploitation of the enemy's errors. He emphasized that col-

lective action was more useful than individual effort, and that sound careful planning, on the collective level, was the best method to bring the target
nearer.

H.E. Habib Chatti, the Secretary General of the Organisation of the Islamic Conference, in his address, dealt with the latest developments of the
question of Al Quds since the Tenth Islamic Conference of Foreign Ministers, in Islamabad, and the action undertaken at the Arab, Islamic and international levels.

He said this Extraordinary Session must define the areas of mobilising
all the potentials of the Islamic Umma so that Jihad would enter its practical phase in a manner much more effective than at present, and the will of
the people will bear fruit, especially that we had won over to our side world
public opinion through the serious positions we adopted and our determination to pursue our confrontation with Israel, the expansionist entity that
has usurped the rights of the Islamic Umma.

In conclusion, the Secretary General pointed to efforts of His Majesty
King Hassan II, in his capacity as Chairman of Al Quds Committee, and
who, as we all know, is motivated by a strong Islamic spirit and zealously
upholds the values and ideals of our Divine Religion.

Pakistan Foreign Minister, Mr. Agha Shahi, in his capacity as current
Chairman of the Islamic Conference of Foreign Ministers then addressed
the meeting. He said that Al Quds Committee, in its last meeting in Casablanca, had approved a comprehensive plan to be implemented by the Islamic states on both the national and international levels, and in the
United Nations, to prevent Israel from using force and suppression to complete the annexation of Al Quds and continue obliterating its Muslim and
Christian features.

He affirmed that the Palestinian question had reached a very critical
stage and was on the verge of an explosion, which necessitated the adoption of a responsible and positive action by the Islamic Conference. He said
there was a change in favour of the Palestine issue: the abstention by the
European countries from voting at the Special General Assembly Session
on the resolution on Palestine; the resolution on Al Quds submitted by the
European countries to the Security Council; the condemnation of Israel's
policy [by] prominent re[l]igious bodies, such as the World Church Council, were indications pointing to an increasing recognition of our just position on the issue.

The Conference, in its plenary sessions, [h]eard statements by a number
of delegation heads, who expressed their countries' views on Al Quds Al
Sharif and Palestine issues in general. There was a unanimous call that the
Islamic Conference attains its objectives of liberating Al Quds Al Sharif
from the clutches of vicious Zionism, and of achieving the legitimate rights
of the Palestinian people to repatriation, to self-determination without out-

side interference, and to establish their independent state on their national territory.

There was also unanimity on the necessity of going further than the adoption of resolutions denouncing Israel's subversive positions and actions to the adoption of resolutions defining bold, specific and practical steps to confront the Zionist enemy, and to ensure the intensified mobilisation of the potentials of Islamic states in this field . . .

In expression of the determination of the Islamic states to confront the Israeli challenge and liberate Al Quds Al Sharif and recover the occupied Palestinian and Arab territories, the Conference adopted a resolution, the most important items of which are:

The Islamic Conference of Foreign Ministers, meeting in Extraordinary Session, at the recommendation of Al Quds (Jerusalem) Committee, in Fez, 9–11 Zul Ke'da 1400H, 18–20 September, 1980, examined the grave development in the cause of Al Quds (Jerusalem) and the Palestine Question, following the Israeli Knesset's decision to annex Al Quds Al Sharif and consider it as the "unified eternal capital" of the Zionist entity. The Conference considered this action a blatant challenge to the sentiments of Muslims, and a hostile act against the Islamic countries, as well as a confirmation of Israel's refusal to abide by the recent Security Council Resolution 478, stipulating that all Israel's legislative and administrative measures, as well as all other action, to alter the identity and status of Al Quds (Jerusalem), are null and void, and must be rescinded immediately.

The Islamic states committed:

—to meet this challenge and liberate Al Quds Al Sharif (Jerusalem);
—to uphold Arab-Islamic sovereignty over the Holy City;
—to confirm their support to the Palestinian people;
—to counter the Israeli aggression with their power and potential;
—to sustain support for the heroic struggle of the Palestinian people until the liberation of Al Quds (Jerusalem) and the restoration, by the Palestinian people, of their inalienable rights, including their right to repatriation, self-determination and the establishment of their own independent state on their territory:

Proceeding from the spirit of Islamic solidarity;
The Conference decides:

1. TO ADOPT the recommendations and resolutions of Al Quds (Jerusalem) Committee in its Extraordinary Meeting, held from 16–18 August, 1980, in Casablanca, and to declare that all Islamic countries are committed to their implementation;
2. TO REAFFIRM the commitment of Islamic countries to mobilize all

their political, financial, petroleum and military potentials to counter the Israeli decision of annexing Al Quds (Jerusalem), and to approve the application of political and economic boycott against any country that recognizes Israel's decision, or contributes to its enforcement, or establishes an embassy in Al Quds Al Sharif (Jerusalem);

3. TO REQUEST all the countries of the world to refrain from dealing with Israeli authorities in any way that could be exploited by these authorities as an acceptance of the fait accompli in Al Quds (Jerusalem) and in all other occupied Palestinian and Arab territories; else they would be liable to boycott measures;

4. TO WELCOME Security Council Resolution 478, on August 20, 1980, and calls upon the Council to adopt military and economic sanctions against Israel as provided by the UN Charter;

5. TO EXPRESS FULL SATISFACTION at the response of the countries that have transferred their embassies from Al Quds Al Sharif (Jerusalem) in recognition that Israel's decision is illegitimate, null and void; and notes that the response of these countries to the appeal of the Islamic states by transferring their embassies from Al Quds (Jerusalem) underlines the unanimous opposition of the international community to the Israeli measure of annexing Al Quds (Jerusalem) and declaring it the capital of the Zionist entity;

6. TO NOTE WITH SATISFACTION the position of the Federal Government of Switzerland reflected by refraining from concluding agreement with Israel in Al Quds (Jerusalem) and hopes that all countries would follow suit;

7. TO RECONFIRM all forms of support extended by Islamic countries to the PLO to counter the war of aggression launched by Israel to annihilate the Palestinian people in occupied Palestine and Southern Lebanon, and calls upon the Member States to enable the Lebanese Government to put an end to these aggressions;

8. TO EXTEND material and political support to the Arab Palestinian people, inside and outside their occupied homeland, and to enhance their capability to combat the devious designs of the autonomy conspiracy, and the Israeli occupation and racist practices;

9. TO CALL UPON member states of the Islamic Conference which recognised Israel to withdraw such recognition and to sever all political and economic relations with it;

10. TO SUSTAIN its repudiation of the Camp David Accords, and the like, and secure the total defeat of such Accords and any consequences thereof;

11. TO RECONFIRM its condemnation of the United States' policy that supports the Israeli occupation authorities in their settlement prac-

tices, and repeated desecration of Islamic holy places in the occupied Palestinian and Arab territories; and also CONDEMNS the position adopted by the United States in international fora, in favour of Israel and against the Palestinian right, in a manner contradicting with the UN Charter, the General Assembly's resolutions and the provisions of the Universal Declaration on Human Rights; and DECLARES that any support extended to the Zionist entity to sustain its illegitimate occupation and desecration of holy places, be it direct or indirect, overt or covert, constitutes a challenge to the Islamic world;

12. TO REJECT any political settlement of the Palestine Question, and the Arab-Israeli conflict, under the disruption of the balance of power caused by the conclusion of the Camp David Accords and Washington Treaty (Egyptian-Israeli Treaty), together with the Israeli practices, and TO DECLARE that Security Council Resolution 242 incompatible with Arab and Islamic rights, nor does it constitute a sound basis for resolving the Middle East crisis, especially the Palestine Question; and TO FIRMLY CALL FOR the implementation of UN resolutions, particularly General Assembly Resolution 1, adopted at its Extraordinary Emergency Session; and TO REJECT any initiative inconsistent with these resolutions;

13. TO INITIATE political action, at the UN, with the Big Powers, notably the European Community, with a view to enlisting further support to the Palestine Question and to tightening Israel's isolation;

14. TO WORK for the adoption, by the current session of UN General Assembly, of a resolution seeking the counsel of the International Court of Justice on Israeli practices and measures violating the national inalienable rights of the Palestinian People, as well as the acts of aggression perpetrated by the Israeli authorities against the Palestinian people inside occupied Palestine and Arab territories, on condition that such a procedure would not prejudice the national inalienable rights of the Palestinian people, and that it be endorsed by the Palestine Liberation Organization as the sole legitimate representative of the Palestinian people;

15. TO CALL UPON the UN General Assembly not to accept the credentials of the Israeli delegate to the UN since he represents a government that has violated international law and has declared Al Quds (Jerusalem) its capital;

16. TO REQUEST the Big Powers and international organisations to assume their responsibilities and counter the Israeli challenge by applying the sanctions provided in the UN Charter against Israel;

17. TO CALL UPON all the countries of the world to curb Jewish immigration to the occupied Palestinian and Arab territories, in view of

the Zionist settlement policy in these territories, and Israel's persistent denial of the Palestinian people's right to repatriation, to the exercise of self-determination and sovereignty, and to the establishment of their own independent state on their national territory;

18. TO INTENSIFY contacts with the Holy See and Christian circles with a view to expounding the position of Islamic states towards the recent Israeli decision, and to requesting their support to the inalienable rights of the Palestinian people, as well as extending recognition to the Palestine Liberation Organization;

19. TO INITIATE a wide-scale information campaign denouncing the Israeli decision, and to seek the implementation of the information plan for countering the Israeli challenge;

20. TO REQUEST member states to withhold loans and contributions to the International Monetary Fund and the World Bank should they fail to grant the Palestine Liberation Organization Observer-status;

21. TO ESTABLISH an Islamic Office for the boycott of Israel pursuant to the Islamic Conference resolutions in this respect, and provided that it coordinate action with the Head Office for the Boycott of Israel, affiliated to the General Secretariat of the League of Arab States;

22. TO COVER the capital of Al Quds (Jerusalem) Fund, and the Fund's Waqf;

23. TO DECLARE the commitment of the Islamic states to holy "Jihad," with its wide-ranging humanitarian dimensions, as it constitutes steadfastness in the face of the Zionist enemy on all military, political, economic, information and cultural fronts;

24. TO ENTRUST Al Quds (Jerusalem) Committee with the task of formulating an over-all strategy to mobilize all the potential of Islamic countries to counter the Israeli aggressiveness, and to draw the attention of Al Quds (Jerusalem) Committee to the contents of the Palestinian-Syrian Working Paper on economic, military and political issues, and submitting this strategy to the forthcoming Islamic Summit Conference due to be held in the Kingdom of Saudi Arabia.

Appendix 3:
Amman Arab Summit Conference, 1980

Complete text of the Final Declaration of the Eleventh Arab Summit Conference, held at Amman from 25 to 27 November 1980*

In accordance with the sixth resolution of the Tenth Arab Summit Conference held at Tunis between Dhu al-Hijjah 1399 A.H. and the 2 Muharram 1400 A.H., corresponding to 20–22 Tishrin al-thani (November) 1979, His Majesty King Hussein bin Talal, King of the Hashemite Kingdom of Jordan, invited the Eleventh Arab Summit Conference to meet at Amman, the capital of the Hashemit Kingdom of Jordan, from 18–20 Murharram 1401 A.H., corresponding to 25–27 Tishrin al-thani (November) 1980.

Basing themselves upon their commitment to national responsibility, to the necessity of pursuing joint and earnest inter-Arab action in confronting the dangers and threats to which the Arab nation is exposed, and believing that an effective and efficient confrontation can only come about on the basis of unanimity, the transcending of differences and the elimination of divisive factors in arriving at unity in the Arab ranks, the Arab leaders, meeting in Amman, worked together to study the present Arab situation and those political, military and economic developments which have taken place in the Arab world and in the international arena since the convening of the Tenth Arab Summit Conference in Tunis, examined the Arab-Zionist conflict, and reviewed it latest developments and have adopted political, military and economic resolutions aimed at building up Arab capacities and strengths in all of those areas.

The Arab leaders reaffirmed their adherence to the resolutions of the Summit Conferences of Baghdad and Tunis and particularly to those dealing with the Palestinian question, considering the fact that it constitutes the essence of the Arab struggle with the Israeli enemy and national responsibility with regard to it make it incumbent upon all Arabs to act and struggle in order to repulse the Zionist danger which threaten the existence of the Arab nation.

---

*UNITED NATIONS General Assembly Security Council, A/35/719, S/14289, December 8, 1980. ENGLISH. Original: ARABIC/ENGLISH. Extracts.

The Conference also emphasized that the liberation of Arab Jerusalem was a national duty and a national obligation, proclaimed the rejection of all measures taken by Israel, requested all nations of the world to adopt clear and defined positions in opposition to the Israeli measures and resolved to break off all relations with any country recognizing Jerusalem as the capital of Israel or transferring its embassy there.

The Arab leaders have underlined their determination to continue their support for the Palestine Liberation Organization in its capacity as the sole legitimate representative of the Palestinian people for the purpose of the restitution of all its rights including the right to self-determination and the establishment of an independent State on its own territory, and, they also reiterated their support for the independence of the Organization and for its freedom of action. The Conference acclaimed the steadfastness of the Palestinian people in the occupied Palestinian territory, its heroic sacrifices and its fearless resistance in persistently opposing the Israeli occupation, giving proof time and again to the entire world of the staying power of that people and its determination to claim those rights which are its due.

The Conference reasserted the right of the Palestinian Arab people, as represented by the Palestinian Liberation Organization, its sole legitimate representative to return to its land, to determine its own destiny and to establish an independent Palestinian State on the soil of its homeland, while pointing out that it was the Palestine Liberation Organization which along has the right to take upon itself the responsibility for the future of the Palestinian people.

The Conference also emphasized that Security Council resolution 242 (1967) was not in keeping with Arab rights and did not constitute an appropriate basis for a solution to the Middle East crisis and particularly the Palestine question.

The Arab leaders reaffirmed their rejection of the Camp David accords, which had lured the Egyptian leadership into the trap of plotting against the Arab nation and its portentous cause and which had as their objective the destruction of Arab unity and solidarity and had removed the Egyptian régime from the Arab ranks and led it into negotiating with the Israeli enemy and into signing a separate peace treaty, thereby challenging the will of the Egyptian people and ignoring its national role and its deep-rooted Arab allegiance. The Arab leaders emphasized their determination to defy those agreements, to overthrow them, and to render them ineffective. They emphasized their support for boycott measures against the Egyptian régime in accordance with the provisions of the resolutions of the Summit Conferences of Baghdad and Tunis. The Conference sent greetings of solidarity to the fraternal Egyptian Arab people which formed an important part of the Arab nation and whose struggle was inseparable from that of the rest of the Arabs, and expressed the hope that it would be able to overcome the circumstances which has alienated it from its brothers and return to fraternal and constructive participation in the future of the Arab nation. . . .

The Conference expressed its thorough condemnation of the continuing Israeli aggression against the sister State of Lebanon, stigmatized that aggression as a challenge to the honour of the international community, declared its absolute solidarity with the people of the sister State of Lebanon and called upon all the parties in Lebanon to support the legitimate Government in order to preserve the sovereignty and territorial integrity of Lebanon. The Conference also reaffirmed the resolutions of the Tenth Summit at Tunis aimed at the reconstruction of Lebanon. . . .

The Conference affirmed the determination of the Arab States to pursue the Euro-Arab dialogue with a view to the promotion of joint interests and the achievement of greater understanding of the justice of Arab demands, particularly with regard to the question of Palestine.

The Conference stressed the need for endeavors to ensure the continued support and backing of the group of socialist States for Arab rights and to strengthen co-operation with that group a view to the promotion of joint interests and the furtherance and development of the support of those States for Arab rights in such a way as to increase Arab steadfastness capabilities.

The Conference decided to pursue its efforts, within the framework of the United Nations, its specialized agencies and institutions and conferences of international organizations, to co-ordinate Arab positions and achieve co-operation in accordance with the principles and objective of the joint Arab programme of action and the policies established by institutions of the League of Arab States.

The Conference stressed the need for the continuation of contacts with the Vatican and with other Christian religious organizations and institutions in order to ensure their support for the recovery of full Arab sovereignty over Jerusalem.

The Conference condemned the continuing political, military and economic support given by the Government of the United States of America to Israel and which had enabled the latter to perpetuate the occupation, to deny the legitimate rights of the Palestinian people, to disregard international resolutions and to continue its aggression, expansion and colonial settlement. The Conference also condemned the hostile attitude of the Government of the United States of America towards the Palestine Liberation Organization, the denial of the latter's right to represent the Palestinian Arab people and its designation as a terrorist organization. . . .

Appendix 4:
Mecca Islamic Summit Conference, 1981

Question of Palestine*

Political Resolutions Adopted at the
Third Islamic Summit Conference

"Palestine and Al-Quds Al-Sharif Session"
Held in Mecca From 25–28 January, 1981

Resolution No.1/3-P(IS) on the Islamic Programme
of Action Against the Zionist Enemy

The Third Islamic Summit Conference (Palestine and Al-Quds Session),
held in Mecca, Kingdom of Saudi Arabia, from 19 to 21 Rabi-ul-Awal 1401
A.H. corresponding to 25—28 January 1981,

Guided by the resolutions of the First Islamic Summit Conference in
Rabat and the Second Summit Conference in Lahore, and by all resolutions of Islamic Conferences of Foreign Ministers and of the Committee on
Al Quds as regards supporting the struggle and resistance of the Palestinian people, since this struggle is a struggle for liberation, from colonialism
and zionist racist occupation and is being waged in defence of the national
inalienable rights of the Palestinian people,

Stressing the determination of the Palestinian people to maintain their
eternal right to the Holy City of Al Quds as the capital of their homeland
Palestine and the insistence of Muslim Governments and peoples alike on
their eternal right to the Holy City of Al Quds, in view of the paramount
political, religious, cultural and historical importance of Al Quds to all
Muslims.

Recommends the following
    (1) Stressing that the Palestinian issue should be viewed as the para-
        mount issue of the Muslim nation and that no party may renounce
        this commitment,

---

*United Nations General Assembly, A/36/138, original: Arabic/English/French, Thirty-
sixth session. Extracts. Underlining in the text.

(2) Stressing the commitment to liberate all the Palestinian and Arab territories occupied since the 1967 aggression including Holy Al Quds Al Sharif and that there should be no renunciation or relinquishment of any part of these territories or impairment of the full national sovereignty over these territories.

(3) Rejecting any situation that would prejudice Arab sovereignty over Al Quds Al Sharif.

(4) Pledging to recover the national inalienable rights of the Palestinian Arab people, including their right to return to self-determination and to the establishment of an independent Palestinian state on their national soil, led by the Palestine Liberation Organisation, the sole legitimate representative of Palestinian people.

(5) Refusing to admit of a unilateral action by any one of the Arab or Islamic parties to reach any solution of the Palestinian issue in particular, and the Arab-zionist conflict in general, and the continuation of the resistance to the Camp David approach and accords and to any consequences thereof until they are eliminated and their sequels removed as well as resistance to any initiative stemming therefrom, extending material and moral support to the Palestinian Arab people in the occupied Palestinian territories, and enhancement of their resistance to the conspiracy of autonomy.

(6) Rejecting of any political settlement of the issue of Palestine and the Arab-Israeli conflict that does not ensure the realisation of the above mentioned principles.

(7) Viewing the Security Council Resolution 242 as inconsistent with the Palestinian and Arab rights, stressing that it does not constitute a sound basis for the solution of the Middle East crisis and the Palestinian issue.

(8) Ensuring continued support of the struggle and steadfastness of the Palestinian people inside and outside the occupied homeland under the leadership of the Palestine Liberation Organisation until they recover their national inalienable rights.

(9) Ensuring continued support of the Palestine Liberation Organisation and consolidating its independence.

(10) Confirming the commitment of Islamic States to make use of all their military, political, economic and natural resources, including oil, as an effective means of upholding the national inalienable rights of the Palestinian people and the Arab nation, and of confronting those countries that extend support to the zionist entity at military, economic, political and human resources levels.

(11) Intensifying of efforts to win further international support at both official and popular levels, especially in Europe, for the issue of Palestine, the liberation of the occupied Palestinian and Arab terri-

tories, to promote the status of the Palestine Liberation Organisation in the international arena, and extend the range of recognition of the Organisation as the sole legitimate representative of the Palestinian Arab people in accordance with the United Nations resolutions relating to the issue of Palestine and the representation of the Palestinian people, and particularly General Assembly resolutions 3236 and 3237 and its resolution 7/2 of 29 July 1980, resolution 3375 of 10 November 1975 and resolution 35/169 A, B, C, D of 15 December 1980.

(12) Pursuing the efforts of the Member States of the Organisation of the Islamic Conference within the United Nations and its specialised agencies to expose and isolate Israel with a view to:

a) Having a resolution adopted in the UN General Assembly soliciting an advisory ruling from the International Court of Justice on the Israeli practices and measures which violate the inalienable national rights of the Palestinian people, and on the acts of aggression perpetrated by the Israeli authorities against the Palestinian people in Palestine and the occupied Arab territories. This should be achieved with the consent of the Palestine Liberation Organisation, as it is the sole legitimate representative of the Palestinian people. Entrusting the Islamic Secretariat with the task of undertaking, upon agreement with the Bureau of the Committee on Al Quds, the legal and procedural studies necessary to ensure the success of such endeavour.

b) Inviting the UN General Assembly to reject the credentials of the Israeli delegation to the United Nations, as representative of a government that violates international legality and declares Al Quds its capital. Entrusting the Islamic Secretariat with the task of conducting, upon agreement with the bureau of the Committee on Al Quds, the relevant legal and procedural studies.

c) Calling on Member States of the United Nations and its Specialised Agencies to shoulder their responsibilities, contend with the continued Israeli refusal to implement the United Nations resolutions by adopting the necessary sanctions against Israel, in implementation of Chapter VII of the UN Charter, Assigning the Islamic Secretariat to conduct in agreement with the Bureau of the Committee on Al-Quds, the relevant legal and procedural studies.

d) Inviting the UN General Assembly to freeze the membership of Israel, in view of its failure to implement the UN resolutions, although such implementation was a condition set for its admission to the United Nations under the Lausanne Protocol.

Entrusting the Islamic Secretariat with the task of conducting, in agreement with the bureau of the Committee on Al Quds, the relevant legal and procedural studies.

(13) Calling on Member States of the Organisation of the Islamic Conference which have earlier recognized Israel to withdraw this recognition and to sever all diplomatic and economic relations with Israel.

(14) Consolidating relations between Islamic countries and Latin American countries in various fields, with a view to evolving the position of the latter countries in favour of the liberation of Al Quds and the occupied Palestinian and Arab territories, the restoration of the inalienable rights of the Palestinian people and the recognition of the Palestine Liberation Organisation.

(15) Maintaining contacts with the Vatican and the World Council of Churches as well as other Christian Institutions and foundations to ensure their support of the restoration of full Arab sovereignty over Al Quds, recognition of the Palestine Liberation Organisation as the sole legitimate representative of the Palestinian people, and support of the inalienable rights of the Palestinian people.

(16) Strengthening relations with Arab and Islamic Communities abroad and making full use of their capacities and potentialities to serve Arab and Islamic causes.

(17) Working for the establishment of associations similar to that of FRANCE—AL QUDS in the States of Western Europe and North and South America with a view to gaining increased support from public opinion for the cause of Al Quds.

(18) Viewing Jewish emigration to occupied Palestine as an act that consolidates the aggression of the zionist entity against the Palestinian people and their inalienable rights and calling on all countries to put an end to such emigration and to refrain from extending facilities to Jewish emigrants in view of the zionist settlement policy which is in violation of international law.

(19) Calling on the government of the United States of America to change its hostile attitude towards the issues of Palestine, the inalienable rights of the Palestinian people and the Palestine Liberation Organisation, the sole legitimate representative of the Palestinian people. The Islamic Conference stresses its condemnation of this policy and views the continued United States military, economic and political support of zionist entity as a hostile attitude towards the Islamic World and a challenge to Muslim feelings, which would negatively reflect on US interest and relations with the Islamic World.

(20) Concentrating activities within the circles of U.S. public opinion

on explaining the Palestinian issue, and the zionist aggression on the Arab and Islamic Ummah and highlighting further damage brought about by the pro-Israeli US policy to both the Arab and American people.

In Respect to Al Quds Al Sharif

(1) Confirming the commitment of the Islamic States to the Liberation of Arab Al Quds to become the capital of the independent Palestinian State, and the rejection of any situation that may prejudice full Arab sovereignty over the city.

(2) Confirming the commitment of Muslim States to utilize all their potentialities to oppose the Israeli decision to annex Al Quds, endorsement of the decision to impose a political and economic boycott on these States that recognise the Israeli decision, contribute to its implementation or set up embassies in Al Quds Al Sharif.

(3) Inviting all countries to respect international legitimacy by abstaining from dealing with the Israeli occupation authorities in any form that may be construed by these authorities as amounting to implicit recognition or acceptance of the status quo, imposed by their declaring Al Quds to be the unified and eternal capital of the zionist entity, and in particular, inviting all countries to refrain from:
   a) signing any agreements in Al Quds Al Sharif;
   b) paying any official visits to Al Quds;
   c) conducting any formal talks in Al Quds.

(4) Inviting Member States of the European Community to implement their pledge to refrain from extending the effect of their bilateral and multilateral economic agreements with Israel to the occupied Palestinian and Arab territories; exerting efforts to reach similar results with other countries that have such agreements with Israel.

(5) Stressing the need to cover the capital of Al Quds Fund, as well as its waqf (endowment) to meet all necessary and urgent requirements to support the resistance and struggle of the Palestinian people.

(6) The undertaking by all Islamic countries of psychological mobilization through their various official, semi-official, and popular mass media, of their peoples for Jihad to liberate Al-Quds.

IN THE ECONOMIC FIELD:

1. Utilising all Islamic economic potentialities and natural resources in a well-oriented and studied manner for the following objectives:
   a) weakening Israeli economy;

b) halting the political, economic and financial support to Israel;

c) enhancing the resistance of the front-line states and the Palestine Liberation Organisation in the various fields;

d) bringing about changes in the political positions of States in favour of the Palestinian cause and enabling the Palestinian people to recover their inalienable national rights;

e) exerting efforts to transform neutral international attitude into friendly ones, and transforming hostile attitudes into neutral and friendly ones.

2. Adopting measures to set up an Islamic Office for the boycott of Israel, pursuant to relevant resolutions of the Islamic Conference, and ensuring coordination between such an office and the main office for boycott of Israel within the General Secretariat of the League of Arab States.

3. Adopting a stiffer stand as regards legislation enacted in the United States and other countries to counteract the boycott of Israel, and stressing the legitimacy of this boycott, as well as dissuading other countries from adopting such legislation.

IN THE MILITARY FIELD:

1. Exerting efforts to ensure a strategic military balance with the Zionist enemy.

2. Ensuring military coordination among the front-line states and the Palestine Liberation Organisation, on the one hand, and the Islamic States on the other, to ensure full utilization of the potentialities of the Islamic States in the service of the military effort; and setting up a military office in the Islamic Secretariat to be responsible for such coordination, in agreement with the Committee on Al-Quds.

3. Meeting the needs of the Palestinian Liberation Organisation as regards military expertise and equipment, both qualitatively and quantitatively, and conducting bilateral contacts between the Palestinian Liberation Organization and all Islamic countries to ensure the implementation of the above.

Resolution No.2/3.P (IS) on the Cause of Palestine and the Middle East

The Third Islamic Summit Conference (Palestine and Al-Quds Session) meeting in Mecca, from 19 to 22 Rabi-ul-Awwal 1401 H (25–28 January, 1981); . . .

Seriously concerned over the deteriorating situation in the Middle East which could result in a new war thus endangering international peace and security, in view of Israel's persistence in its aggressive, colonialist and racist policy, and as a result of the collusion with the Egyptian regime and the United States,

Reaffirming that the Palestine Question is the core of the struggle against Zionism, and that Israel's continued refusal to withdraw from the occupied Palestinian and Arab territories and its flouting of the inalienable national rights of the Arab Palestinian people constitute a flagrant violation of the principles of the Islamic Conference Organization and UN Charter, the Universal Declaration of Human Rights and of the principles of International Law,

Noting with great concern the recent developments of the Middle East problem and the Palestine Question in the region, particularly the normalization by the Egyptian regime of its relations with the Zionist entity and its persistence in carrying out the autonomy conspiracy and the dangers that ensue therefrom which imperil Islamic principles, values, heritage, culture and civilization,

Considering that the Liberation of Al-Quds and its restoration to Arab sovereignty, as well as the liberation of the holy places from Zionist occupation, are a pre-requisite to the Jihad that all Islamic States must wage, each according to its means, . . .

1. Reaffirms that the problem of the Middle East and the Palestine Cause cannot be solved unless the following principles and conditions are implemented concurrently, without any exception and also reaffirms its commitment to these principles and conditions,
   (a) The cause of Palestine is the core of the Middle East problem and the crux of the Arab-Israeli struggle;
   (b) The Palestine Cause and the Middle East problem form an indivisible whole when dealing with the problem, or seeking a solution thereto hence any solution may not be a partial solution, concern some parties to the exclusion of others; or relate to some of the causes and not to others; nor can any partial peace be attained, for peace should be comprehensive and include all parties to the dispute, and should moreover, eliminate all the causes that led to it, in addition to being a just one;
   (c) A just peace in the region can only be achieved on the basis of total and unconditional withdrawal by Israel from all the occupied Palestinian and Arab territories, and on the recovery by the Palestinian people of their inalienable national rights including:
   —their right to their homeland, Palestine;
   —their right to return to their homeland and recover their

property in accordance with the UN General Assembly Resolutions;

—their right to self-determination without any foreign interference;

—their right to freely exercise sovereignty over their land and natural resources;

—their right to establish their national independent State in Palestine under the leadership of the Palestinian Liberation Organization.

(d) that Al-Quds is an integral part of the occupied Palestinian territory, and Israel must unconditionally and totally withdraw from it, and it should be restored to Arab sovereignty;

(e) that the P.L.O. is the sole legitimate representative of the Palestinian people and it, above is fully entitled to represent that people and to participate independently and on an equal footing in all Conferences, activities and international fora connected with the Palestinian cause and the Arab-Israeli conflict, with a view to achieving the inalienable national rights of the Palestinian people. No solution can be comprehensive, just and acceptable unless the P.L.O. participates in its formulation and accepts it as an independent party and on an equal footing and parity with the rest of the parties concerned. No other party is entitled to claim the right to represent or negotiate on the question of Palestine, its people, its territory and its rights, otherwise it shall be considered null and void and by no means legally binding.

(f) That Security Council Resolution 242 (1967) is not in keeping with the Palestinian and Arab rights and does not constitute a sound basis for the solution of the Middle East problem and the Palestine Question.

(g) That no Arab party concerned should unilaterally seek a solution to the Palestine Question or to the Arab-Zionist conflict, that resistance to the Camp David Accords, should be pursued, their consequences, effects or any initiative emanating therefrom voided, moveover, material and moral assistance should be extended to the Arab Palestinian People in the occupied Palestinian territories, and their resistance against the autonomy conspiracy reinforced.

2. Reaffirms that any solution that is not founded on all those principles and conditions can never lead to a just peace but, on the contrary, can only exacerbate tensions in the region and pave the way for the policies applied by the parties to the Camp David Accords to liquidate the question of Palestine and help Israel achieve its objec-

tives and expansionist, colonialist and racist policies. It would, more-over, encourage bilateral and partial solutions while disregarding the essence of the problem;

3. Reaffirms the right of the Arab States and the Palestine Liberation Organization to struggle militarily, politically and, by any other means, to liberate their occupied territories, secure the inalienable national rights of the Palestinian people and foil by all means possible any solution or settlement which is detrimental to such territories and rights; . . .

5. Reaffirms its full and effective support to the Palestinian people in their legitimate struggle under the leadership of the Palestine Liberation Organization, their legitimate and sole representative inside and outside the occupied homeland, with a view to liberating it, restoring their inalienable national rights in Palestine. All Member States shall commit themselves to safeguarding Palestinian unity, the independent character of Palestine Liberation Organization and non-interference in the internal affairs of Palestinian action.

6. Affirms
   (a) The commitment of Islamic States to liberate Al-Quds to become the capital of the independent Palestinian State, and to reject any situation which might infringe on the Arab right to full sovereignty over Al-Quds.
   (b) The commitment of all Islamic States to use all their means to foil the Israeli decision to annex Al-Quds and make it the capital of the Israeli entity, and decides to apply a political and economic boycott against those States which recognize this Israeli decision or participate in its implementation or establish their Embassies in Al-Quds Al Sharif;

7. Calls upon all countries throughout the world to abide by the United Nations resolutions by refraining from dealing with the Israeli occupation authorities and from any kind of relations that could be construed by Israel as a de facto recognition of its declaration that Al Quds has been the eternal and unified capital of the Israeli entity. It particularly calls upon all countries to refrain from:
   A. Signing any agreements in Al Quds;
   B. Making official visits to Al Quds;
   C. Conducting official talks in Al Quds;
   D. Presenting the Credentials of Heads of Diplomatic missions in Al Quds;

8. Calls upon member states to psychologically mobilize their people for Jihad to liberate Al Quds, through their official, non-official and otherwise mass media;

9. Emphasizes that any infringement on the resolutions of the Islamic

Conference Organisation on the Middle East problem and the cause of Palestine and Al Quds will weaken the struggle waged to liberate Al Quds and the occupied Palestinian and Arab territories and secure the inalienable national rights of the Palestinian people, undermine the struggle of the Organization against colonialism, foreign occupation, racism and Zionism and will be a reneging by Member States on their determination to put an end to Israeli occupation of the Palestinian and Arab territories and assist the Palestinian people to achieve their inalienable national rights;

10. Reaffirms its rejection and condemnation of the Camp David Accords signed on 17.9.1978, and the Israeli-Egyptian Treaty signed on 26.3.1979, and all the consequences and efforts ensuing therefrom and asks that they be resisted by all means and methods;

11. Strongly condemns any partial or separate solution and any agreement detrimental to the rights of the Arab nation and, the Palestinian people that would violate the principles and resolutions of the Islamic Conference Organization and the UNO, or that could impede the liberation of Al-Quds and the occupied Palestinian and Arab territories or prevent the Palestinian people, from securing and fully exercising their inalienable national rights;

12. Condemns the collusion between the Egyptian Regime, Israel and the United States in all fields and deems it a direct aggression against the right of the Palestinian people, their homeland and future, and a serious threat to the security and stability of Arab and Islamic States, and decides to support the suspension of its membership to the Non-aligned Movement;

13. Strongly condemns the Egyptian government for proceeding to normalize relations with the Zionist entity and considers it a denial of the principles of Jihad and a danger to Islamic principles, ideals, heritage, culture and civilization; and decides to suspend Egypt's membership in the Non-Aligned Movement. . . .

18. Calls upon all the States and Peoples of the world to refrain from extending military, manpower, material or moral support to Israel likely to encourage it in perpetuating its occupation of Al Quds and the Palestinian and Arab territories, and declares that such a continued support to Israel will compel Islamic States to take appropriate stands against them;

19. Deplores the attitude of these states that provide assistance and arms to Israel and considers that the real purpose of flooding Israel with this great quantity of weapons of war and destruction, is to establish it as a colonialist and racist base in the third world, in general, and in Africa and Asia, in particular. . . .

21. Invites member states which had recognized Israel to withdraw such

recognition and sever all kind of diplomatic, consular, economic, cultural, sports and touristic relations, as well as all forms of communication with Israel at all levels, official or otherwise, and requests the member states that have not yet severed such relations to do so;

22. Calls upon member states to take all measures within the United Nations, to:

   A. Request the U.N. General Assembly to refuse the credentials of the Israeli delegation to the UN General Assembly, as it represents an authority which aggressed against international legitimacy, and which made Al Quds its capital, and request the General Secretariat to take all necessary measures in this respect;

   B. Request the member states of the United Nations and its specialized institutions to assume their responsibility and face up to the continued rejection by Israel of United Nations resolutions, by applying appropriate penalties against Israel, in implementation of the provisions of Chapter VII of the UN Charter, and request the General Secretariat to take the necessary measures in this regard; . . .

24. Decides to have recourse to all Islamic states economic, potential and natural resources in a studied and planned manner with a view to:

   A. Weakening Israeli economy;

   B. Stopping the political, economic and financial assistance received by Israel;

   C. Bringing about political stands by countries in favour of the Palestine Question with a view to enabling the Palestine people recover their national inalienable rights;

   D. Endeavouring to turn national stands at the international level into friendly ones, and antagonistic or inimical stands into neutral or friendly ones;

25. Calls upon the Member States of the European Economic Community to fulfil their undertakings to the effect that their bilateral and multilateral agreements with Israel shall not be applied in the Palestinian and Arab occupied territories and endeavour to secure such a stand from other states that have similar agreements with Israel;

26. Invites states to pay up the capital of Al Quds Fund, and its Waqf in order to enhance the struggle and resistance of the Palestinian people;

27. Calls upon member states not to tolerate legislations enacted by the United States of America and other countries with a view to countering the Arab boycott, and to secure a strict implementation of the

boycott against Israel; stress its legitimacy and urge other states to adopt similar regulations.

Resolution No.5/3-P(IS)
Declaration of Holy Jihad

The Third Islamic Summit Conference, meeting at Mecca Al-Mukarrama and Taif from 19–22 Rabi-al-Awal 1401 H, corresponding to 25–28 January, 1981, . . .

Taking these facts into consideration, the Kings, Emirs and Presidents of Islamic States, meeting at this Conference and in this holy land, studied this situation and concluded that it could no longer be tolerated that the forthcoming stage should be devoted to effective action to vindicate right and deter wrong-doing; and have unanimously,

Decided:

To declare holy Jihad, as the duty of every Muslim, man or woman, ordained by the Shariah and glorious traditions of Islam;

To call upon all Muslims, living inside or outside Islamic countries, to discharge this duty by contributing each according to his capacity in the cause of Allah Almighty, Islamic brotherhood, and righteousness;

To specify that Islamic states, in declaring Holy Jihad to save Al-Quds al-Sharif, in support of the Palestinian people, and to secure withdrawal from the occupied Arab territories, wish to explain to the world that Holy Jihad is an Islamic concept which may not be misinterpreted or misconstrued, and that the practical measures to put it into effect would be in accordance with that concept and by incessant consultations among Islamic states.

Appendix 5:
Hamburg Symposium, 1983

Workshop 1*
Prospects for Cultural Exchange

The workshop discussed a large number of proposals and also the means of putting some of them into effect. It was recognized that many exchanges, both personal and institutional, already take place and that nothing should be done to hinder or complicate the successful working of these. Exchange and co-operation in many fields were discussed: exchange agreements between universities, exchanges between students and teachers and others, in the field of creative arts, of audio-visual materials, co-operation in translation, in transmitting Arabic publications to Europe, exhibitions and publication. Instead of making an ambitious list of numerous proposals the following concrete recommendations were made:

1. A general cultural agreement should be concluded between the Arab League and the European Community within the framework of which more specialized agreements could operate. Such an agreement should delineate the areas within which cultural co-operation and exchange could take place.
2. A small joint permanent committee within the Euro-Arab Dialogue should be set up to monitor the working of the agreement, to examine and accept proposals for future projects and to ensure their execution. . . .

Suggested projects

1. The publication twice yearly of a Euro-Arab journal devoted to specific topics with Arab and European contributors.
2. To invite Arab professional Unions and their members to conclude

*Euro-Arab Dialogue. The relations between the two cultures. Acts of the Hamburg symposium. April 11th to 15th 1983. English version edited by Derek Hopwood. (London: Croom Helm, 1983), 305–16. Extracts.

agreements with their European couterparts to further cultural co-operation and exchange. . . . Such agreements should also include the encouragement of periodical meetings between European and Arab Unions of Radio and Television and between Associations of Film Producers and Actors to promote joint productions.

3. The convening of small, specialized or professional seminars on selected themes. Among topics already suggested are the religious dialogue, Arab historiography, book publishing and librarianship, investigation of the contents of text books at all levels in the history of the two regions. The holding of a larger symposium every three years, to discuss inter alia the progress of the Euro-Arab Dialogue and of cultural co-operation.

4. The urgent publication of the catalogue of cultural and scientific institutions which has already been started under the auspices of the Dialogue.

Workshop 2

Social and Cultural Migration

3. The workshop noted the declaration on the "Principle governing the living and working conditions of migrant workers in the two regions" adopted in the fourth session of the Dialogue General Commission (Damascus, December, 1978).

It was felt that the declaration, though incomplete in some respects, is a landmarks in the path of Euro-Arab cooperation in the sphere of migration.

In this document it has been stated that "a migrant worker and the members of his family shall, in the country where they legally reside and work, enjoy equality of treatment as to living and working conditions, wages and economic rights, rights of association and the exercise of the basic public freedoms".

A declaration of principles, however, remains only a declaration, unless it is backed up by policies and programmes aimed at ensuring that the principles contained therein are implemented. It was felt that not enough was done to implement the tenets of the 'declaration' since its adoption. The present state of migrant workers is a testimony to this fact.

4. The workshop convened for about double the time planned in the official programme. . . .

Specifically, it is recommended that a permanent institution should be created to ensure that research and exchange of information is undertaken on a continuous basis to improve knowledge of the various aspects of migration between European and Arab countries and to formulate policies and programmes for the administration of migration with the purpose of ensuring the highest level of welfare for the migrants themselves and maximum benefit for both countries of origin and employment with a spirit of genuine cooperation among the countries involved in the Dialogue.

5. It is recommended that the social integration of migrant workers and their families in the host countries be facilitated by:

   a) giving equal rights in access to the housing market, the labour market and the educational system and to vocational and professional training,

   b) making the general public more aware of the cultural background of migrants, e.g. by promoting cultural activities of the immigrant communities,

   c) supplying adequate information on the culture of the migrant communities in the school curricula,

   d) creating special schooling and training facilities for those who have functional relationships with the immigrants (e.g. civil servants, medical staff, members of the police force, teachers, social workers, etc.),

   e) giving migrants access to the mass media in order to assure that migrants be in a position to receive regular information in their own language about their own culture as well as about the conditions of life in the host country,

   f) broadening cooperation between immigrant groups and the national population and taking measures to increase the participation of immigrant groups in trade union activities and explore their participation in political life.

6. It is recommended that the Arab countries of origin strengthen their cultural support to Arab migrants in Europe.

On the other hand, it is clear that more effective policies and programmes for the smooth reintegration of returning migrants are needed in the fields of job creation, housing, education of children, and social reintegration in Arab countries.

It is realized that rather severe constraints restrict the capabilities of Arab countries of emigration in this respect. It is hoped then that this situation would give rise to specific forms of cooperation between European and Arab countries, e.g. in the form of training of returning migrants in skills needed in their countries of origin.

Workshop 3

Co-operation in the Field of Language Teaching for Arabic and European Languages

Introduction

The participation of the workshop responsible for the elaboration of a programme on co-operation in the field of language teaching met several times. They were fully aware of the importance attached to the conception of this programme, as it constitutes a principle basis of the Euro-Arab Dialogue and is simultaneously an important instrument for the facilitation of its enforcement. They examined the recommendation elaborated at the symposium held in Venice from 28–30.3.77, and the work papers and documents submitted by the organizers and participants at the present symposium. Due to the results of the discussion and the cordial dialogue which took place at these sessions, the workshop presents the following recommendations:

The diffusion of the Arabic language and culture in the countries of the European community

1. A co-ordination of efforts which should be undertaken by the Arab countries in order to diffuse the Arabic language and culture in Europe as well as the establishment of an agreed form of co-operation among the Arab institutions employed in this domain.
2. In the European capitals the establishment of communal Euro-Arab cultural centres engaged in the diffusion of the Arabic language and culture.
3. A necessity to embark on a scientific study of the tradition of Arabic influences on European languages in order to illuminate the problems posed in translation and define the means necessary for attaining the desired efficiency, in order to contribute to the diffusion of Arabic culture in Europe.
4. Co-ordination and financial support of the research being carried out in Europe and Arab countries which concerns the diffusion of Arabic language and culture.

The teaching of the Arabic language

1. The necessity of taking into account the present reality of the Arab-Muslim civilization when teaching the Arabic language.
2. The necessity of promoting co-operation between European and

Arab experts in order to present students and the cultivated European public an objective picture of Islamic civilization and of contemporary Arab problems which might encourage them to orient themselves towards Arabic studies.

3.   The encouragement of European teaching institutions preoccupied with teaching the Arabic language and the study of Arab-Islamic culture and its diffusion, both at university and non-university level. Aiming at surmounting the obstacles which hinder the teaching of the Arabic language in public education.

4.   The necessity of extending and spreading teaching at different levels of both official and private education within the European Community, ranging from pre-school to secondary school, as well as at business level.

5.   Promoting the teaching of the Arabic language to children of migrants in the European Community thus responding to their legitimate aspiration of learning their national language.

6.   The necessity of establishing a centre for the distribution of periodicals, books and Arabic didactic texts in order to enable European readers to keep themselves informed on everything published in the Arab world. The European Community should agree on the choice of location in Europe and the ALECSO should be the responsible institution on the Arab side. . . .

The formation of experts

1.   The necessity of supplying a sufficient number of teachers from Arab countries specialized in teaching the Arabic language to Europeans and putting them at the disposal of institutions and universities on request.

2.   A necessity of co-operation between Arab and European universities with a view to training Europeans to teach the Arabic language, giving them the opportunity of studying at Arab universities and institutions specialized in the Arabic language as well as arranging educational programmes for them.

3.   The necessity of different kinds of exchanges among teachers, experts and researchers, especially in the organization of yearly seminars with a view to exchanging experience in the various spheres mentioned in these recommendations.

4.   The encouragement of both Arab and European scientific institutions to offer scholarships to European students who specialize in the Arabic language and culture, thus enabling them to study at Arab Universities and institutes.

The teaching of European languages in the Arab world

1. The teaching of European languages should be considered as being complementary to the teaching of the Arabic language, in as much as it represents an opening to Western civilization and a contribution to the reciprocal knowledge of both communities which might result in successful co-operation and cultural rapprochement.

Working party on co-operation in language teaching proposed five year working programme

Year One

1. Investigation of the situation and the needs of the Arabic language and culture in Europe and the European languages in the Arab Community. This investigation will be pursued by both sides, and serve as a basis for an approach for assistance to be made to the Arab League and to the European Community. . . .
    d) Plans for the teaching of Arabic to children of Arab communities in Europe. . . .
4. Co-ordination of the efforts of the Arab communities in the promotion of Arabic language and culture in Europe.
5. Immediate implementation should be given to the plans considered and approved by the sub-committee.

Years Two and Three

1. Meeting of the sub-committee to evaluate the results of work done in the previous stages.
2. Publication of the studies and the dictionaries prepared.
3. The establishment of joint Euro-Arab Cultural Centres in European Capitals to promote Arabic language and culture; the establishment of a programme of exchange visits at the levels of teachers, researchers and students.

Years Four and Five

3. Continuation of the implementation of the Five-Year Plan with regard to the formation and training of teachers on both sides, and responding to the needs of the teaching of the Arabic language and culture in Europe, and that of the European languages and culture in the Arab World.

Appendix 6
Council of Europe Parliamentary Assembly, 1991

Parliamentary Assembly of the Council of Europe

Forty-third Ordinary Session

Recommendation 1162 (1991)*

On the contribution of the Islamic civilisation to European culture

1. The Council of Europe has the statutory mission to safeguard and realise the spiritual and moral values which are the common heritage of its member states. Article 9 of the European Convention on Human Rights enshrines the right to freedom of thought, conscience and religion.

2. Multicultural Europe is based on humanist and religious traditions, which are the source of its dedication to freedom and human rights, as recalled by the Assembly in Resolution 885 (1987) on the Jewish contribution to European culture.

3. In a similar spirit, the Committee on Culture and Education held a colloquy in Paris in May 1991 on the contribution of the Islamic civilisation to European culture. The colloquy was organised in collaboration with the Western Institute for Islamic Culture (Madrid) and in association with Unesco.

4. The colloquy showed that, in addition to Christianity and Judaism, Islam in its different forms has over the centuries had an influence on European civilisation and everyday life, and not only in countries with a Muslim population such as Turkey. The new Europe as well is becoming increasingly subject to influences from Islam, not only through the regions of predominantly Islamic culture such as Albania

---

*Assembly debate on 19 September 1991 (11th Sitting) (see Doc. 6497, report of the Committee on Culture and Education, Rapporteur : Mr Lluis Maria de Puig). Text adopted by the Assembly on 19 September 1991 (11th Sitting).

302

or some southern republics of the USSR, but also by immigration from the wider Islamic world.

5. It must indeed be recognised that the Islamic world also embraces countries from Asia and Africa as well as the Middle East and the Maghreb.

6. Islam has, however, suffered and is still suffering from misrepresentation, for example through hostile or oriental stereotypes, and there is very little awareness in Europe either of the importance of Islam's past contribution or of Islam's potentially positive role in European society today. Historical errors, educational eclecticism and the over-simplified approach of the media are responsible for this situation.

7. The main consequence of such misrepresentation, to which many contemporary Muslims have contributed through their own lack of critical intellectual examination or intolerance, is that Islam is too often perceived in Europe as incompatible with the principles which are at the basis of modern European society (which is essentially secular and democratic) and of European ethics (human rights and freedom of expression).

8. While this incompatibility certainly does exist, as between Islamic fundamentalism and the cultural and ethical principles which the Council of Europe upholds, for example in regard to the treatment of women and respect for freedom of expression, it is not representative of Islam as a whole. It must be recognised that intolerance and distrust unfortunately exist on both sides. Islamic and non-Islamic.

9. The Assembly is aware of this situation, of the need for a better knowledge of the past so as better to understand the present and prepare the future, and of the valuable contribution that Islamic values can make to the quality of life through a renewed European approach on an overall basis to the cultural, economic, scientific and social fields.

10. Greater attention moreover should be given to co-operation with the Islamic world. The Council of Europe has already done a considerable amount of work on intercultural understanding and this [should] be further developed with specific reference to Islamic culture. Further co-operation should be sought with non-governmental institutions and organisations in this field, such as the Western Institute for Islamic Culture in Madrid, the Paris Institute for the Arab World and others.

11. The Assembly therefore recommends that the Committee of Ministers find room for consideration of the Islamic world in the intergovernmental programme of activities of the Council of Europe and in its recommendations to the governments of member states. The following measures are proposed :

In the field of education

i.   A balanced and objective account of the history of Islam should be included in education curricula and textbooks along the lines of the international research project : "Islam in textbooks".

ii.   There should be wider provision for the teaching of Arabic as a modern language in European schools.

iii.   Scientific research on Islamic matters should be encouraged, inter alia, by increasing the number of Arabic and Islamic professorial posts in universities. Islam should also be included in mainstream studies, for example Islamic history should be taught in history departments, Islamic philosophy in philosophy departments and Islamic law in law departments, and should not be relegated, as is often the case, to oriental language departments.

iv.   Similarly, in theology courses, a comparative approach should be encouraged, including Islamic, Christian and Jewish studies.

v.   An integrated teaching approach should be adopted to specific areas such as the Mediterranean basin, including studies on religion, philosophy, literature and history.

vi.   Student and teacher exchanges should be set up and developed within a framework of university co-operation between Europe and the Islamic world, along the lines of Recommendation 1032 (1986) on the creation of a Euro-Arab University. This could be called the "Averroës programme" in comparison with the existing "Erasmus" and "Demosthenes" programmes.

In the field of the media

vii.   The production, co-production and broadcasting of radio and television programmes on Islamic culture are to be encouraged.

In the field of culture

viii.   Places of cultural and intellectual expression are needed for immigrants from the Islamic world. The development of their own culture, however, should not entail their isolation from the society and culture of the host country.

ix.   Cultural itineraries of the Islamic world inside or outside Europe and cultural exchanges, exhibitions, conferences and publications in the fields of art, music and history should be encouraged. Museums have an important role to play in this respect.

x. Selected Islamic works, classic and modern, should be translated and published in a manner more conductive to greater understanding in Western society.

Administrative questions and everyday life

xi. Governments should encourage dialogue between Islamic communities and the competent authorities to provide for the religious requirements of their faith (such as holy days, prayer rules, dress and food), while respecting the customs of the host country, in addition to the usual provisions for the association and representation of immigrant and indigenous Islamic communities.

xii. The twinning of towns between Europe and the Islamic world, especially those which are geographically closer to Europe, should be encouraged.

In the field of multilateral co-operation

xiii. A real effort is necessary to provide a basis for a continuing dialogue between Europe and the Islamic world with a view to the reinforcement and development of all democratic and pluralistic tendencies. Particular attention can be given to direct co-operation with specific parts of this world, for example with the Arab countries around the Mediterranean (as a contribution to the possible development of a conference on security and co-operation in the Mediterranean) or with immigrant communities within Europe.

xiv. A positive dynamic should be given to this dialogue by tackling in future seminars key issues such as Islamic fundamentalism, the democratisation of the Islamic world, the compatibility of different forms of Islam with modern European society and, in general, the new problems posed by religions in contemporary society, whether the secular societies of the West or the traditional societies of the Third World. The problems posed by Islam should be examined in the same perspective as those posed by Christianity, by Judaism and by other religions in the world. Such studies will more surely help forward the historical process of the democratisation of traditional societies thanks to a broadening of the cultural horizons on which they are based.

12. The Assembly also asks the Committee of Ministers to invite inter-
    ested countries of the Islamic world to make similar initiatives on a
    reciprocal basis and, wherever appropriate, to accede to Council of
    Europe conventions and open partial agreements, with a view to
    harmonising legislation and developing intercultural under-
    standing.

Appendix 7:
Vatican Commission, 2003

Commission for Religious Relations with the Jews

Fourth European Day of Jewish Culture[1]

Reflections by Cardinal Walter Kasper[2]

Anti-semitism: A wound to be healed

Together with the faith of the Fathers and of the Torah, the Temple of Jerusalem—at least until Titus destroyed it in the year 70—was the heart of Judaism, with the exception of certain groups such as the Essenes and the Samaritans. The Temple was also one of the places for meeting and prayer of the first disciples of the Risen One, who were regarded by the authorities at times with suspicion, but with esteem by the people, with whom they shared their faith in the God of Abraham, Isaac and Jacob, of Sarah and Rebecca, of Rachel and Leah. They were all aware that they belonged to the one people of God with whom the Most High had made a Covenant with his promise to the Fathers which, after the Red Sea crossing, was sealed on Sinai and open to the promise and hope of universal renewal and redemption, in accordance with the messianic announcement of the prophets.

The Pharisee Gamaliel had wisely advised the Sanhedrin not to attempt to use force to quell a new spiritual movement which in Simon Peter and James had two charismatic leaders, and that may have interpreted correctly the Jewish tradition and the hope of Israel. Another Pharisee, a disciple of Gamaliel, young Saul of Tarsus, at first violently persecuted the followers of Jesus, but after an exceptional experience of conversion, held fast to the Gospel and became Paul, the Apostle to the Gentiles, who travelled around the Mediterranean and the empire until his martyrdom in Rome.

---

[1] *L'Osservatore Romano* English Weekly Edition, n. 40, October 1, 2003, 6. http://www.vati can.va/roman_curia/pontifical_councils/chrstuni/relati ons-jews-docs/rc_pc_chrstuni_doc _20030908_kasper-antisemitismo_en.html.

[2] Cardinal Walter Kasper, *President of the Pontifical Council for Promoting Christian Unity and of the Commission for Religious Relations with the Jews.*

Upon Israel, the one people of God, the Apostle grafted the wild olive of the Gentiles, and the Church of Christ slowly acquired a concrete form "upon the foundation of the apostles and prophets" (Eph 2: 20), in the two branches of *Ecclesia ex circumcisione* and *Ecclesia ex gentibus,* as admirably shown in the Paleo-Christian mosaic in the Church of Santa Sabina on the Aventine.

The corpus of the Sacred Scriptures—the Jewish ones of the *TaNaKH* (*Torah, Nevi'im and the Ketuvim*), which in the Christian canon came to be known as the Old Testament, as well as those of the New Testament— agrees in witnessing that God did not abandon his Covenant with the Hebrew (or "Judaic") people of the 12 tribes of Israel. Of course, what can appear to be a dangerous, exclusivist particularism is balanced, in the Scriptures themselves, by a twofold messianic universalism, both *ad intra,* in the tension between the Jewish Diaspora and the Jews of the Land of Israel (*Erez Israel*), and *ad extra,* in the tension between the Jewish people (*'am Israel*) and all the peoples called to enter into the same communion of peace and redemption of the first-born people of the Covenant.

Consequently, as a "messianic people," the Church does not replace Israel, but is grafted onto it, according to the Pauline doctrine, through adherence to Jesus Christ, the Saviour of the world, who died and rose; and this link forms a spiritual bond that is radical, unique and insuppressible for Christians. Although the contrasting concept—of an Israel *once (olim)* pre-chosen but later rejected by God for ever and now replaced by the Church—may have had widespread dissemination for almost 20 centuries, it does not in reality represent a truth of the faith, as can be seen both in the ancient *Creeds* of the early Church and in the teaching of the most important Councils, especially of the Second Vatican Council (*Lumen Gentium,* n. 16; *Dei Verbum,* nn. 14–16; *Nostra Aetate,* n. 4). Moreover, neither Hagar nor Ishmael were ever rejected by God, who made them "a great nation" (Gn 21: 18); and Jacob, the astute "usurper," received Esau's embrace in the end. The most recent document published by the Pontifical Biblical Commission on *The Jewish People and Their Sacred Scriptures in the Christian Bible* (2001), after recognizing the "surprising strength of the spiritual bonds that united the Church of Christ to the Jewish people" (n. 85), concludes by noting that "in the past, the break between the Jewish people and the Church of Christ Jesus might at times have seemed complete in certain periods and in certain places. In the light of the Scriptures, this should never have happened, because a complete break between the Church and the Synagogue is in contradiction to Sacred Scripture" (*ibid.*).

Thus, in the contemporary context, which cannot ignore the appalling slaughter of the *Shoah* in the 20th century, Cardinal Joseph Ratzinger, introducing this document, asks the question: "Did not the presentation of the Jews and of the Jewish people, in the New Testament itself, contribute to creating a hostility to this people which the ideology of those who wanted to suppress it has encouraged?" The document honestly admits that many passages in the New Testament that are critical of the Jews "served as a pretext for anti-Jewish sentiment and, effectively, have been used for this purpose" (n. 87). A few years earlier, Pope John Paul II himself had said that "in the Christian world—I do not say on the part of the Church as such—erroneous and unjust interpretations of the New Testament regarding the Jewish people and their alleged culpability have circulated for too long, engendering feelings of hostility towards this people" (*Address to Participants in a Symposium on "The Roots of Anti-Judaism in the Christian Milieu"*, n. 1, 31 October 1997; *ORE*, 5 November 1997, p. 1). So it was that "sentiments of anti-Judaism in some Christian quarters, and the gap which existed between the Church and the Jewish people, led to a generalized discrimination" towards the Jews over the centuries, in particular in Christian Europe (Holy See Commission for Religious Relations with the Jews, *We Remember: A Reflection on the Shoah*, 16 March 1998; *ORE*, 18 March 1998, n. III, p. 6).

During the 19th century, in a changed historical context that was bent on toppling the old regime that united Church and State, "there began to spread in varying degrees throughout most of Europe an anti-Judaism that was essentially more sociological and political than religious" (*ibid.*). This development of anti-Jewish feeling, with the addition of confused theories on evolution and the superiority of the "Aryan race," resulted in what was then called "anti-Semitism" characterized by explosions of violence, *pogroms* and the publications of anti-Jewish libel, such as the *Protocols of the Wise Men of Zion (Protocolli dei Savi Anziani di Sion)*. It was in this mindset, permeated by contempt and hatred for the Jews who were accused of dreadful crimes such as ritual homicide, that the unspeakable tragedy of the *Shoah* matured, the horrible plan of extermination programmed by the Nazi Government that struck down the European Jewish communities during the Second World War. The ideological premises of the *Shoah*, already widely divulged before the war in such works as *Mein Kampf* and *Der Mythus des zwanzigste Jahrhunderts* (the latter was put on the *Index*), did not encounter sufficient opposition, neither at the cultural level nor in the juridical context, nor among the Christian communities, even if reactions were registered, such as those of G. Semeria, G. Bonomelli or of the young A. Bea. Unfortunately, however, between the end of the 19th century and the first decades of the 20th, even very authoritative Catholic journals published articles in an anti-Semitic vein, and "more generally fanned anti-Jewish prejudices; they stemmed from the Medieval 'teaching of contempt,' that was a source of stereotypes and popular hatred" (J. Willebrands), so that it can be said, in this regard, that such an attitude offered a favourable context for the spread of modern anti-Semitism. It should also be noted that as the responsibility for these roots of hatred, in various ways and with rare exceptions, can be ascribed to both Western and Eastern Christendom, a combined ecumenical reaction is called for today.

The Vatican document *We Remember* (n. II) also declares: "The fact that the *Shoah* took place in Europe, that is, in countries of long-standing Christian civilization, raises the question of the relation between the Nazi persecution and the attitudes down the centuries of Christians towards the Jews" (*We Remember: A Reflection on the Shoah*, n. II). Although there were, before and during the *Shoah*, episodes of condemnation and reactions to anti-Semitism, both at a personal level with acts of heroism to the point of martyrdom, such as in the case of the Provost of Berlin, Bernhard Lichtenberg, and at the institutional level, with the condemnation of anti-Semitism (for example, on the part of the Holy Office in 1928 and on the part of Pope Pius XI in 1938), on the whole, "the spiritual resistance and concrete action of other Christians was not that which might have been expected from Christ's followers" (*ibid.*, n. IV). In this case too, indeed especially with regard to anti-Semitism and to the *Shoah*, we can justifiably speak of the need to embark on acts of repentance *(teshuvà)*, which ends in exemplary and concrete acts in which, "as members of the Church, we are linked to the sins as well as the merits of all her children" (*ibid.*, n. V). Certainly one of these acts was the one the Pope solemnly made on 12 March 2000 in St Peter's Basilica, and which he sealed on 26 March in Jerusalem at the Western or Wailing Wall of the Temple. We are all, therefore, called to share in our inner attitudes, prayers and actions in this same journey of conversion and reconciliation, because it is a question of the need to live *in capite et in membris*, not limited merely to a few authoritative, meaningful gestures or even high level documents.

This first fundamental engagement, of a spiritual and moral kind, concerns all of us as Christians, hence, we can say it has a marked ecumenical dimension. A second consequence, also of a theological kind, is the one that springs from the deep, radical and particular connection that unites the Church and the Jewish people "first-born of the Covenant" (Universal Prayer of Good Friday).

On the one hand, this bond impels us to respect and love the Jewish people, and on the other, it enables us to perceive in anti-Semitism a further dimension, in comparison with the general one of racism or religious discrimination, which anti-Semitism has in common with other forms of ethnic, cultural or religious hatred, as described in the document *The Church and Racism, Towards a More Fraternal Society* (Pontifical Commission *Iustitia et Pax*, 3 November 1988, I, n. 15; *ORE*, 13 February 1989, p. 7). It is not only a question of the cultural, social, political or ideological, and in a more general way "secular," dimensions of anti-Semitism which must also be a cause of concern to us, but of a specific aspect of it that was firmly condemned in 1928 by the Apostolic See when it defined anti-Semitism as "odium adversus populum olim a Deo electum" (*AAS* XX/1928, pp. 103–104). Today, 75 years later, the only modification we feel duty bound to make is the elimination of the word "olim" ("once"): this is no small thing, because in recognizing the perennial timeliness of the Covenant between God and his people, Israel, we in turn will be able to rediscover, with our Jewish brethren, the irrevocable universality of the vocation to serve humanity in peace and in justice, until the definitive coming of his kingdom. This is what the Pontiff also recommends to us in his Post-Synodal Apostolic Exhortation *Ecclesia in Europa* of last 28 June, recalling the "relationship which binds the Church to the Jewish people and of Israel's unique role in salvation history" (n. 56). Pope John Paul II continues, observing that "there is need for acknowledgment of the common roots linking Christianity and the Jewish people, who are called by God to a covenant which remains irrevocable (cf. Rom 11: 29) and has attained definitive fullness in Christ. Consequently, it is necessary to encourage dialogue with Judaism, knowing that it is fundamentally important for the self-knowledge of Christians and for the transcending of divisions between the Churches" (*ibid.*). Dialogue and collaboration between Christians and Jews "also implies that 'acknowledgment be given to any part which the children of the Church have had in the growth and spread of anti-Semitism in history; forgiveness must be sought for this from God, and every effort must be made to favour encounters of reconciliation and of friendship with the sons of Israel'" (*ibid.*). In this spirit of rediscovered brotherhood a new springtime for the Church and for the world can bloom once more, with the heart turned from Rome to Jerusalem and to the land of the Fathers, so that there too a just and lasting peace may quickly germinate for all and mature like a banner flying in the midst of the peoples.

Appendix 8:
Putrajaya Islamic Summit, 2003

Speech by Malaysian Prime Minister Datuk Seri Dr Mahathir Mohamad at the opening of the 10th Session of the Islamic Summit Conference on Oct 16, 2003*

ALHAMDULILLAH, All Praise be to Allah, by whose Grace and Blessings we, the leaders of the Organisation of the Islamic Conference (OIC) countries are gathered here today to confer and hopefully to plot a course for the future of Islam and the Muslim ummah worldwide.

On behalf of the Government and the people of many races and religions of Malaysia, may I extend a warm welcome to all and everyone to this 10th Session of the Islamic Summit Conference in Putrajaya, Malaysia's administrative capital.

It is indeed a great honour for Malaysia to host this Session and to assume the chairmanship of the OIC [Organization of the Islamic Conference]. I thank the members for their confidence in Malaysia's chairmanship.

May I also take this opportunity to pay a special tribute to the State of Qatar, in particular His Highness Shaikh Hamad Bin Khalifa Al-Thani, the Emir of the State of Qatar, for his outstanding stewardship of our organisation over the past three years.

As host, Malaysia is gratified at the high level of participation from member countries. This clearly demonstrates our continued and abiding faith in, and commitment to our organisation and our collective wish and determination to strengthen our role for the dignity and benefit of the ummah.

I would also like to welcome the leaders and representatives of the many countries who wish to become observers at this meeting because of their substantial Muslim population. Whether they are Muslims or not, their presence at this meeting will help towards greater understanding of Islam and the Muslims, thus helping to disprove the perception of Islam as a religion of backwardness and terror.

---

*The Star Online, News OIC 2003.

The whole world is looking at us. Certainly 1.3 billion Muslims, one-sixth of the world's population are placing their hopes in us, in this meeting, even though they may be cynical about our will and capacity to even decide to restore the honour of Islam and the Muslims, much less to free their brothers and sisters from the oppression and humiliation from which they suffer today.

I will not enumerate the instances of our humiliation and oppression, nor will I once again condemn our detractors and oppressors. It would be an exercise in futility because they are not going to change their attitudes just because we condemn them. If we are to recover our dignity and that of Islam, our religion, it is we who must decide, it is we who must act.

To begin with, the governments of all the Muslim countries can close ranks and have a common stand if not on all issues, at least on some major ones, such as on Palestine. We are all Muslims. We are all oppressed. We are all being humiliated. But we who have been raised by Allah above our fellow Muslims to rule our countries have never really tried to act in concert in order to exhibit at our level the brotherhood and unity that Islam enjoins upon us.

But not only are our governments divided, the Muslim ummah is also divided, and divided again and again. Over the last 1,400 years the interpreters of Islam, the learned ones, the ulamas have interpreted and reinterpreted the single Islamic religion brought by Prophet Muhammad S.A.W, so differently that now we have a thousand religions which are often so much at odds with one another that we often fight and kill each other.

From being a single ummah we have allowed ourselves to be divided into numerous sects, mazhabs and tarikats, each more concerned with claiming to be the true Islam than our oneness as the Islamic ummah. We fail to notice that our detractors and enemies do not care whether we are true Muslims or not. To them we are all Muslims, followers of a religion and a Prophet whom they declare promotes terrorism, and we are all their sworn enemies. They will attack and kill us, invade our lands, bring down our governments whether we are Sunnis or Syiahs, Alawait or Druze or whatever. And we aid and abet them by attacking and weakening each other, and sometimes by doing their bidding, acting as their proxies to attack fellow Muslims. We try to bring down our governments through violence, succeeding to weaken and impoverish our countries.

We ignore entirely and we continue to ignore the Islamic injunction to unite and to be brothers to each other, we the governments of the Islamic countries and the ummah.

But this is not all that we ignore about the teachings of Islam. We are enjoined to Read, Iqraq, i.e. to acquire knowledge. The early Muslims took this to mean translating and studying the works of the Greeks and other scholars before Islam. And these Muslim scholars added to the body of knowledge through their own studies.

The early Muslims produced great mathematicians and scientists, scholars, physicians and astronomers etc. and they excelled in all the fields of knowledge of their times, besides studying and practising their own religion of Islam. As a result the Muslims were able to develop and extract wealth from their lands and through their world trade, able to strengthen their defences, protect their people and give them the Islamic way of life, Addin, as prescribed by Islam. At the time the Europeans of the Middle Ages were still superstitious and backward, the enlightened Muslims had already built a great Muslim civilisation, respected and powerful, more than able to compete with the rest of the world and able to protect the ummah from foreign aggression. The Europeans had to kneel at the feet of Muslim scholars in order to access their own scholastic heritage.

The Muslims were lead by great leaders like Abdul Rahman III, Al-Mansur, Salah El Din Al Ayubi and others who took to the battlefields at the head of their forces to protect Muslim land and the ummah.

But halfway through the building of the great Islamic civilisation came new interpreters of Islam who taught that acquisition of knowledge by Muslims meant only the study of Islamic theology. The study of science, medicine etc. was discouraged.

Intellectually the Muslims began to regress. With intellectual regression the great Muslim civilisation began to falter and wither. But for the emergence of the Ottoman warriors, Muslim civilisation would have disappeared with the fall of Granada in 1492.

The early successes of the Ottomans were not accompanied by an intellectual renaissance. Instead they became more and more preoccupied with minor issues such as whether tight trousers and peak caps were Islamic, whether printing machines should be allowed or electricity used to light mosques. The Industrial Revolution was totally missed by the Muslims. And the regression continued until the British and French instigated rebellion against Turkish rule [that] brought about the downfall of the Ottomans, the last Muslim world power and replaced it with European colonies and not independent states as promised. It was only after World War II that these colonies became independent.

Apart from the new nation-states we also accepted the western democratic system. This also divided us because of the political parties and groups that we form, some of which claim Islam for themselves, reject the Islam of other parties and refuse to accept the results of the practice of democracy if they fail to gain power for themselves. They resort to violence, thus destabilising and weakening Muslim countries.

With all these developments over the centuries the ummah and the Muslim civilisation became so weak that at one time there was not a single Muslim country which was not colonised or hegemonised by the Europeans. But regaining independence did not help to strengthen the Muslims. Their states were weak and badly administered, constantly in a state of turmoil. The Europeans could do what they liked with Muslim territories. It is not surprising that they should excise Muslim land to create the state of Israel to solve their Jewish problem. Divided, the Muslims could do nothing effective to stop the Balfour and Zionist transgression.

Some would have us believe that, despite all these, our life is better than that of our detractors. Some believe that poverty is Islamic, sufferings and being oppressed are Islamic. This world is not for us. Ours are the joys of heaven in the afterlife. All that we have to do is to perform certain rituals, wear certain garments and put up a certain appearance. Our weakness, our backwardness and our inability to help our brothers and sisters who are being oppressed are part of the Will of Allah, the sufferings that we must endure before enjoying heaven in the hereafter. We must accept this fate that befalls us. We need not do anything. We can do nothing against the Will of Allah.

But is it true that it is the Will of Allah and that we can and should do nothing? Allah has said in Surah Ar-Ra'd verse 11 that He will not change the fate of a community until the community has tried to change its fate itself.

The early Muslims were as oppressed as we are presently. But after their sincere and determined efforts to help themselves in accordance with the teachings of Islam, Allah had helped them to defeat their enemies and to create a great and powerful Muslim civilisation. But what effort have we made especially with the resources that He has endowed us with.

We are now 1.3 billion strong. We have the biggest oil reserve in the world. We have great wealth. We are not as ignorant as the Jahilliah who embraced Islam. We are familiar with the workings of the world's economy and finances. We control 50 out of the 180 countries in the world. Our votes can make or break international organisations. Yet we seem more helpless than the small number of Jahilliah converts who accepted the Prophet as their leader. Why? Is it because of Allah's will or is it because we have interpreted our religion wrongly, or failed to abide by the correct teachings of our religion, or done the wrong things?

We are enjoined by our religion to prepare for the defence of the ummah. Unfortunately we stress not defence but the weapons of the time of the Prophet. Those weapons and horses cannot help to defend us any more. We need guns and rockets, bombs and warplanes, tanks and warships for our defence. But because we discouraged the learning of science and mathematics etc as giving no merit for the akhirat, today we have no capacity to produce our own weapons for our defence. We have to buy our weapons from our detractors and enemies. This is what comes from the superficial interpretation of the Quran, stressing not the substance of the Prophet's sunnah and the Quran's injunctions but rather the form, the manner and the means used in the 1st Century of the Hijrah. And it is the same with the other teachings of Islam. We are more concerned with the forms rather than the substance of the words of Allah and adhering only to the literal interpretation of the traditions of the Prophet.

We may want to recreate the first century of the Hijrah, the way of life in those times, in order to practise what we think to be the true Islamic way of life. But we will not be allowed to do so. Our detractors and enemies will take advantage of the resulting backwardness and weakness in order to dominate us. Islam is not just for the 7th Century A.D. Islam is for all times. And times have changed. Whether we like it or not we have to change, not by changing our religion but by applying its teachings in the context of a world that is radically different from that of the first century of the Hijrah. Islam is not wrong but the interpretations by our scholars, who are not prophets even though they may be very learned, can be wrong. We have a need to go back to the fundamental teachings of Islam to find out whether we are indeed believing in and practising the Islam that the Prophet preached. It cannot be that we are all practising the correct and true Islam when our beliefs are so different from one another.

Today we, the whole Muslim ummah are treated with contempt and dishonour. Our religion is denigrated. Our holy places desecrated. Our countries are occupied. Our people starved and killed.

None of our countries are truly independent. We are under pressure to conform to our oppressors' wishes about how we should behave, how we should govern our lands, how we should think even.

Today if they want to raid our country, kill our people, destroy our villages and towns, there is nothing substantial that we can do. Is it Islam which has caused all these? Or is it that we have failed to do our duty according to our religion?

Our only reaction is to become more and more angry. Angry people cannot think properly. And so we find some of our people reacting irrationally. They launch their own attacks, killing just about anybody including fellow Muslims to vent their anger and frustration. Their governments can do nothing to stop them. The enemy retaliates and puts more pressure on the governments. And the governments have no choice but to give in, to accept the directions of the enemy, literally to give up their independence of action.

With this their people and the ummah become angrier and turn against their own governments. Every attempt at a peaceful solution is sabotaged by more indiscriminate attacks calculated to anger the enemy and prevent any peaceful settlement. But the attacks solve nothing. The Muslims simply get more oppressed.

There is a feeling of hopelessness among the Muslim countries and their people. They feel that they can do nothing right. They believe that things can only get worse. The Muslims will forever be oppressed and dominated by the Europeans and the Jews. They will forever be poor, backward and weak. Some believe, as I have said, this is the Will of Allah, that the proper state of the Muslims is to be poor and oppressed in this world.

But is it true that we should do and can do nothing for ourselves? Is it true that 1.3 billion people can exert no power to save themselves from the humiliation and oppression inflicted upon them by a much smaller enemy? Can they only lash back blindly in anger? Is there no other way than to ask our young people to blow themselves up and kill people and invite the massacre of more of our own people?

It cannot be that there is no other way. 1.3 billion Muslims cannot be defeated by a few million Jews. There must be a way. And we can only find a way if we stop to think, to assess our weaknesses and our strength, to plan, to strategise and then to counter-attack. As Muslims we must seek guidance from the Al-Quran and the Sunnah of the Prophet. Surely the 23 years' struggle of the Prophet can provide us with some guidance as to what we can and should do.

We know he and his early followers were oppressed by the Qhuraish. Did he launch retaliatory strikes? No. He was prepared to make strategic retreats. He sent his early followers to a Christian country and he himself later migrated to Madinah. There he gathered followers, built up his defence capability and ensured the security of his people. At Hudaibiyah he was prepared to accept an unfair treaty, against the wishes of his companions and followers. During the peace that followed he consolidated his strength and eventually he was able to enter Mecca and claim it for Islam. Even then he did not seek revenge. And the peoples of Mecca accepted Islam and many became his most powerful supporters, defending the Muslims against all their enemies.

That briefly is the story of the struggle of the Prophet. We talk so much about following the sunnah of the Prophet. We quote the instances and the traditions profusely. But we actually ignore all of them.

If we use the faculty to think that Allah has given us then we should know that we are acting irrationally. We fight without any objective, without any goal other than to hurt the enemy because they hurt us. Naively we expect them to surrender. We sacrifice lives unnecessarily, achieving nothing other than to attract more massive retaliation and humiliation.

It is surely time that we pause to think. But will this be wasting time? For well over half a century we have fought over Palestine. What have we achieved? Nothing. We are worse off than before. If we had paused to think then we could have devised a plan, a strategy that can win us final victory.

Pausing and thinking calmly is not a waste of time. We have a need to make a strategic retreat and to calmly assess our situation.

We are actually very strong. 1.3 billion people cannot be simply wiped out. The Europeans killed six million Jews out of 12 million. But today the Jews rule this world by proxy. They get others to fight and die for them.

We may not be able to do that. We may not be able to unite all the 1.3 billion Muslims. We may not be able to get all the Muslim Governments to act in concert. But even if we can get a third of the ummah and a third of the Muslim states to act together, we can already do something. Remember that the Prophet did not have many followers when he went to Madinah. But he united the Ansars and the Muhajirins and eventually he became strong enough to defend Islam.

Apart from the partial unity that we need, we must take stock of our assets. I have already mentioned our numbers and our oil wealth. In today's world we wield a lot of political, economic and financial clout, enough to make up for our weakness in military terms.

We also know that not all non-Muslims are against us. Some are well disposed towards us. Some even see our enemies as their enemies. Even among the Jews there are many who do not approve of what the Israelis are doing.

We must not antagonise everyone. We must win their hearts and minds. We must win them to our side not by begging for help from them but by the honourable way that we struggle to help ourselves. We must not strengthen the enemy by pushing everyone into their camps through irresponsible and unIslamic acts. Remember Salah El Din and the way he fought against the so-called Crusaders, King Richard of England in particular. Remember the considerateness of the Prophet to the enemies of Islam. We must do the same. It is winning the struggle that is important, not angry retaliation, not revenge.

We must build up our strength in every field, not just in armed might. Our countries must be stable and well administered, must be economically and financially strong, industrially competent and technologically advanced. This will take time, but it can be done and it will be time well spent. We are enjoined by our religion to be patient. Innallahamaasabirin. Obviously there is virtue in being patient.

But the defence of the ummah, the counter-attack, need not start only after we have put our houses in order. Even today we have sufficient assets to deploy against our detractors. It remains for us to identify them and to work out how to make use of them to stop the carnage caused by the enemy. This is entirely possible if we stop to think, to plan, to strategise and to take the first few critical steps. Even these few steps can yield positive results.

We know that the Jahilliah Arabs were given to feuding, to killing each other simply because they were from different tribes. The Prophet preached the brotherhood of Islam to them and they were able to overcome their hatred for each other, become united and helped towards the establishment of the great Muslim civilisation. Can we say that what the Jahilliah (the ignorant) could do we, the modern Muslims cannot do? If not all at least some of us can do. If not the renaissance of our great civilisation, at least ensuring the security of the ummah.

To do the things that are suggested will not even require all of us to give up our differences with each other. We need only to call a truce so we can act together in tackling only certain problems of common interests, the Palestine problem for example.

In any struggle, in any war, nothing is more important than concerted and coordinated action. A degree of discipline is all that is needed. The Prophet lost in Jabal Uhud because his forces broke rank. We know that, yet we are unwilling to discipline ourselves and to give up our irregular and uncoordinated actions. We need to be brave but not foolhardy. We need to think not just of our reward in the afterlife but also of the worldly results of our mission.

The Quran tells us that when the enemy sues for peace we must react positively. True the treaty offered is not favourable to us. But we can negotiate. The Prophet did, at Hudaibiyah. And in the end he triumphed.

I am aware that all these ideas will not be popular. Those who are angry would want to reject it out of hand. They would even want to silence anyone who makes or supports this line of action. They would want to send more young men and women to make the supreme sacrifice. But where will all these lead to? Certainly not victory. Over the past 50 years of fighting in Palestine we have not achieved any result. We have in fact worsened our situation.

The enemy will probably welcome these proposals and we will conclude that the promoters are working for the enemy. But think. We are up against a people who think. They survived 2000 years of pogroms not by hitting back, but by thinking. They invented and successfully promoted Socialism, Communism, human rights and democracy so that persecuting them would appear to be wrong, so they may enjoy equal rights with others. With these they have now gained control of the most powerful countries and they, this tiny community, have become a world power. We cannot fight them through brawn alone. We must use our brains also.

Of late because of their power and their apparent success they have become arrogant. And arrogant people, like angry people will make mistakes, will forget to think.

They are already beginning to make mistakes. And they will make more mistakes. There may be windows of opportunity for us now and in the future. We must seize these opportunities.

But to do so we must get our acts right. Rhetoric is good. It helps us to expose the wrongs perpetrated against us, perhaps win us some sympathy and support. It may strengthen our spirit, our will and resolve, to face the enemy.

We can and we should pray to Allah S.W.T. for in the end it is He who will determine whether we succeed or fail. We need His blessings and His help in our endeavours.

But it is how we act and what we do which will determine whether He would help us and give us victory or not. He has already said so in the Quran. Again Surah Ar-Ra'd verse 11.

As I said at the beginning, the whole world is looking at us, the whole Muslim ummah is placing their hopes in this conference of the leaders of Islamic nations. They expect us not just to vent our frustrations and anger, through words and gestures, not just to pray for Allah's blessings. They expect us to do something, to act. We cannot say we cannot do anything, we the leaders of the Muslim nations. We cannot say we cannot unite even when faced with the destruction of our religion and the ummah.

We know we can. There are many things that we can do. There are many resources that we have at our disposal. What is needed is merely the will to do it, As Muslims, we must be grateful for the guidance of our religion, we must do what needs to be done, willingly and with determination. Allah has not raised us, the leaders, above the others so we may enjoy power for ourselves only. The power we wield is for our people, for the ummah, for Islam. We must have the will to make use of this power judiciously, prudently, concertedly. Insyaallah we will triumph in the end.

I pray to Allah that this 10th Conference of the OIC in Putrajaya, Malaysia, will give a new and positive direction to us, will be blessed with success by Him, Almighty Allah, Arahman, Arahirn.

Appendix 9:
High-Level Advisory Group Report, 2003

**Report by the High-Level Advisory Group established at the
initiative of the President of the European Commission***

Dialogue Between Peoples and Cultures in the Euro-Mediterranean Area

Extract pp. 34–36:

Make the Foundation the guardian of the dialogue**

The Foundation must be able to perform three essential functions without restriction. Firstly, it should be the guardian of the values and guiding principles of the dialogue, which will together form its **operating "software."** . . . Secondly, its **specification** must ensure that it can promote, launch and coordinate all the actions and initiatives that correspond to these principles and also assess the extent to which any ongoing initiative is compatible with these principles. If the Foundation is to fulfil its evaluation role fully and effectively it must waste no time in developing the appropriate methods and criteria and acquiring the necessary resources to apply them. . . .

This Foundation will not be a funding organisation, but will manage activities and networks of participants from civil society, either directly or via national networks that it will coordinate. It will provide the intellectual support, by organising cultural meetings and events and by bringing together existing skills and expertise. It will produce an inventory of needs and evaluate results, identifying and grouping together the resources available in civil society, collecting and disseminating information and promoting virtual communications. It will make recommendations to governments on supporting particular projects that it has analysed and considers to be relevant. . . .

The first condition is independence, the guarantee of its credibility and legitimacy.

---

*Version DEF, Brussels, October 2003.
**Underlined and bold as in the text

Apart from the formal independence from governments, international institutions and economic powers which is required and must be carved in stone, i.e. guaranteed by an appropriate international legal instrument, the Foundation must enjoy both financial and administrative independence and intellectual independence.

Financial and administrative independence means that the supervising authorities must not be able to interfere in the choice the Foundation makes about how it spends the money it is given and who its partners are to be. It will have to submit its accounts and produce results, in so far as these are quantifiable, but must never have decisions on the allocation of its budget imposed upon it. The same should apply to the national networks it coordinates.

Intellectual independence is also crucial. Political opportunism and sectoral interests must not be allowed to deflect the Foundation from its mission. It must have complete freedom of thought and freedom to propose and discuss, to choose its methodology, field of activity and intellectual partners, otherwise it will not be listened to or heeded or even taken seriously.

The second condition is that it be endowed with <u>sufficient financial and administrative resources</u> to covers its requirements. Clearly, the Foundation must have considerable resources, commensurate with the challenges it faces. Its activities are going to be expensive. It will need skilled staff who can act as catalysts for the activities carried out by the network and can call on a top-level academic committee that can give it irrefutable intellectual legitimacy in its relations with its partners. It will need competent administrators and experts on international, cultural and religious questions. It will also need an operating budget that is commensurate with its remit. Organising meetings, permeating the social fabric of 27 countries, running networks, archives and virtual libraries, maintaining permanent contacts with universities, research centres, NGOs and local associations, supervising, planning and monitoring, day after day, the progress being made in learning about the dialogue among young people, teacher training, changes in the media, school-twinning arrangements, all of this is costly in time, manpower and money. The disappointment that would be felt if it were to fail for lack of resources would be all the greater because of the high expectations being cherished.

This is why the Foundation must in time, be allowed to call on private sponsorship. We see this as a way to enabling it to obtain means commensurate with the ambitions role it should be assigned. It must, therefore, be allowed to draw on a substantial level of private funding, although it will be for the Euro-Ministerial Conference to decide the exact proportions. The diversity of its sources of funding will be both a guarantee of autonomy and an indication of the extent to which the Foundation has embedded itself. It is after all the calibre, originality and effectiveness of its initiatives that will determine whether it succeeds in winning support from private backers.

The third and final condition is visibility. The Foundation must be identifiable with a <u>place that is clearly visible and understandable</u>, wherever it may be.

Notes

Preface

1. Bat Ye'or, *The Dhimmi: Jews and Christians under Islam,* translated from the French by David Maisel, Paul Fenton and David Littman. With a preface by Jacques Ellul. Revised and enlarged English edition (Rutherford, NJ: Fairleigh Dickinson University Press, 1985).

2. Bat Ye'or, "Le dialogue Euro-Arabe et la naissance d'Eurabia," *Observatoire du monde juif* 4/5 (December 2002), English translation, "The Euro-Arab Dialogue and the Birth of Eurabia," http://www.dhimmitude.org/d_today_dhimmitude_issues.php; see also by the author, "Eurabia and Euro-Arab Antisemitism," FrontPageMagazine.com, April 5, 2004; "Eurabia, the Road to Munich," National Revue on Line, October 9, 2002; "European Fears of the Gathering Jihad," FrontPageMagazine.com, February 21, 2003; "Beyond Munich—The Spirit of Eurabia," FrontPageMagazine.com, July 2, 2004; Niall Ferguson, "EURABIA?" *New York Times Magazine,* April 4, 2004.

3. Pierre-André Taguieff, *La nouvelle judéophobie* (Paris: Mille et une Nuits, 2002); English translation by Patrick Cammiller, *Rising from the Muck: The New Antisemitism in Europe* (Chicago: Ivan R. Dee, 2004); Alexandre Del Valle, "Stratégies islamistes et nouvelle judéophobie en Europe," *Observatoire du monde juif* 4/5 (December 2002): 17–22; Per Ahlmark, "Europe errs in choice of foes," *The Australian,* Sidney, June 12, 2004. Jean-Claude Milner, *Les Penchants Criminels de l'Euopre démocratique,* Paris, Editions Verdier, 2004; Manfred Gerstenfeld, *Europe's Crumbling Myths. The Post-Holocaust Origins of Today's Anti-Semitism,* Jerusalem, Jerusalem Center for Public Affairs, 2003; Robert S. Wistrich, ed., *Antisemitism International,* Jerusalem, 2003.

4. Alexandre Del Valle, *Le Totalitarisme islamiste à l'assaut des démocraties,* with a preface by Rachid Kaci (Paris: Editions des Syrtes, 2002). See also Jeanne-Hélène Kaltenbach and Michèle Tribalat, *La République et l'Islam. Entre crainte et aveuglement* (Paris: Gallimard, 2002; Shmuel Trigano, *La démission de la République. Juifs et Musulmans en France,* (Paris: Presses Universitaires de France, 2003); Oriana Fallaci, *The Rage and the Pride* (New York: Rizzoli, 2002); Fallaci, *La Forza della Ragione* (Milan: Rizzoli, 2004).

5. See Gilbert Sewall, "Islam and the Textbooks," http://www.historytextbooks.org/islamreport.pdf., The American Textbook Council, 2003, 35 pp.; www.Campus-Watch.org.; Daniel Pipes, "Jihad and the Professors," *Commentary,* November 2002; and for all Pipes's writings on this subject, http://www.danielpipes.org/art/cat/47. Martin Kramer, *Ivory Towers on Sand: The Failure of Middle Eastern Studies in America* (Washington, DC: The Washington Institute for Near East Policy, 2001).

Chapter 1. Eurabia Revealed

1. Fallaci, *La Forza della Ragione,* 147.

2. Literally, "malicious joy."

3. See Arab press extracts reproduced by the Anti-Defamation League (New York), September 21, 2001.

4. Report on the situation of human rights in Iraq for the year 1994 by UN Special Rapporteur in Iraq, Max van der Stoel, E/CN. 4/ 1995/ 56, § 34. See Bat Ye'or, *Islam and Dhimmitude: Where Civilizations Collide* (Madison, NJ: Fairleigh Dickinson University Press), 2002, 234

for the decree dated June 4, 1994, ordering various mutilations as penalties. The article of Craig S. Smith, "Maimed Bodies, Tortured Minds," mentions this tragedy for the first time in a newspaper, *IHT*, April 25, 2003.

5. For the mild reactions to anti-Jewish aggressions from the French authorities, see Marc Knobel, "Les agressions anti-juives," *Observatoire du monde juif* 1 (November 2001), 17–21. For the rejoicing of Muslim children in French schools after the 9/11 attacks, see Emmanuel Brenner, "La tentation d'une libération de la parole antisémite," *Observatoire du monde juif* 4/5, (December 2002) 23–29.

6. *Jerusalem Post*, December 2, 2003.

7. Bat Ye'or, "L'antisionisme euro-arabe," in Collectif d'auteurs, *[nouveaux] visages de l'antisémitisme, haine—passion ou haine historique?* (Paris: NM7 éditions, 2001); "Euro-Arab Anti-Zionism" in Robert Spencer (Ed.), *The Myth of Islamic Tolerance: How Islamic Law Treats Non-Muslims*, Amherst, NY, 2005, Part 4, chapter 11.

8. John Vinocur, "Chirac arrives at a crossroads. President has to decide whether to try to limit U.S. power," *IHT*, April 23, 2003.

9. On this campaign see *ADL*, New York, *September 11 and Arab Media: The anti-Jewish and anti-American Blame Game*, November 2001, web site: www.adl.org; see also *MEMRI*, no. 274, September 21, 2001.

10. Arte, April 13 (8:45 pm), 2004. "Le 11 Septembre n'a pas eu lieu . . . ; Le grand complot; Tous manipulés."

11. See Marc Knobel, "Les sites internet musulmans francophones," *Observatoire du monde juif* 4/5 (December 2002), 2–6; and in the same issue, Michèle Tribalat, "islamiya.net, Quibla.com et Stcom.net. L'obsession anti-israélienne sur le net islamique," 7–16; Thomas Fuller, "Anti-Semitism infuses French debate on scarves," *IHT*, February 11, 2004.

12. See chapter 11.

13. Elaine Sciolino, "Led by Muslims, Paris peace rally again turns anti-Israeli," *IHT*, March 31, 2003; same journalist, "The new anti-Semitism/Jews feel unsafe again. On French streets, Mideast fallout," *IHT*, December 4, 2003; for the stabbing of Rabbi Gabriel Farhi in his synagogue in Paris on January 4, 2003, see France 2: http://www.france2.fr/semistatic/61-NIL-NIL-186685.html.

14. For the increased Judeophobia in France, see Alexandre Del Valle, "Stratégies islamistes et nouvelle judéophobie en Europe"; Pierre-André Taguieff, *La nouvelle judéophobie* (Paris: Fayard coll. Mille et Une Nuits, 2002); Robert Spencer, *Onward Muslim Soldiers: How Jihad Still Threatens America and the West*, (Washington DC: Regnery 2003), 73–74. Melanie Phillips, "The new anti-Semitism," *The Spectator*, March 22, 2003; Shmuel Trigano, *La démission de la République, Juifs et Musulmans en France* (Paris: Presses Universitaires de France, 2003).

15. *IHT*, November 7, 2003.

16. *IHT*, April 14, 2004. "Insurgents seize 4 Italians and a Frenchman," (AFP, AP).

17. Oriana Fallaci, *Oriana Fallaci intervista Oriana Fallaci*, Milan: *Corriere della Sera*, 2004, 102–3.

Chapter 2. Historical Background

1. Ibn Warraq, *Why I Am Not a Muslim* (Amherst, NY: Prometheus Books, 1995); Ibn Warrak, ed., *The Origins of the Koran* (Amherst, NY: Prometheus Books, 1999), *The Quest for the Historical Muhammad* (Amherst, NY: Prometheus Books, 2000), *What the Koran Really Says* (Amherst, NY: Prometheus Books, 2002), and *Leaving Islam: Apostates Speak Out* (Amherst, NY: Prometheus Books, 2003).

2. *MEMRI*, "Jihad against the U.S.: Al-Azhar conflicting Fatwas," *MEMRI* Special Dispatch No. 480, March 16, 2003, www.memri.org.

3. Spencer, *Onward Muslim Soldiers*, 31.

4. Ibid., 28–50.

5. Patrick Sookhdeo, *Understanding Islamic Terrorism: The Islamic Doctrine of War*, with a foreword by General Sir Hugh Beach, (Pewsey, Wilts/UK: Isaac Publishing, 2004), 158.

6. Samuel P. Huntington, *The Clash of Civilizations and the Remaking of World Order* (New York: Simon & Schuster, 1996).

7. Ismail Raji al-Faruqi, *Islam and Other Faiths* ed. Ataullah Siddiqui (Herndon, VA: The Islamic Foundation, The International Institute of Islamic Thought, 1998), 100. In the foreword to this collection of Faruqi's articles, his former student John Esposito referred to him as "a Muslim trailblazer of the twentieth century," vii.

8. Jihad warfare has been carefully documented for the conquest of Anatolia by Speros Vryonis Jr., in *The Decline of Medieval Hellenism in Asia Minor and the Process of Islamization from the Eleventh through the Fifteenth Century*, (1971; repr, Berkeley and Los Angeles: University of California Press, 1986). The process of conquest and Islamization of the Balkans, which proceeded well into the seventeenth century, was well described by Christian and Muslim sources and is better known than the Arab conquest of the Mediterranean Southern shore. For some sources, see Bat Ye'or, *The Decline of Eastern Christianity: From Jihad to Dhimmitude. Seventh-Twentieth Century*, with a foreword by Jacques Ellul. Translated from the French by Miriam Kochan and David Littman (Madison, NJ: Fairleigh Dickinson University Press, 1996).

9. In Spain, as well as in Byzantium and the Balkans, tributary Christian kingdoms had to provide military contingents.

10. Charles-Emmanuel Dufourcq, "A Propos de l'Espagne catalane et le Maghreb aux XIII^c et XIV^c siècles," *Revue d'Histoire et de Civilisation du Maghreb* 2 (1962): 44–45. See also by Dufourcq, "Berbérie et Ibérie médiévales: un problème de rupture," *Revue Historique* 92 (1968): 319–20. For the adaptation of *jihad* to modern times and the conditions for treaties and their abrogation, see Sookhdeo, *Understanding Islamic Terrorism*, 78–89.

11. Majid Khadduri, *The Islamic Law of Nations (Shaybani's Siyar)*, Baltimore: John Hopkins University Press, 1965. For primary source documents from Muslim and non-Muslim sources describing the initial five centuries of Arab Muslim *jihad* conquests and Islamization of the Near East, see Bat Ye'or, *Decline* 271–93; For primary source documents from exclusively Muslim sources regarding the *jihad* conquests and Islamization of the Indian subcontinent, see H. M. Elliott and John Dowson, *The History of India As Told By Its Own Historians—The Muhammadan Period,* 8 vols. (London, 1867–77). Detailed modern analyses of the *jihad* conquests and Islamization of North Africa and the Iberian peninsula, specifically, are provided by Evariste Levi-Provençal, in *Histoire de L'Espagne Musulmane*, vol.1; for Anatolia and the Balkans, see Joseph Laurent, *Byzance et Les Turcs Seldjoucides Dans L'Asie Occidentale Jusqu'en 1081* (Nancy: Berger-Levrault, 1913 [1919]); Apostolos E. Vacalopoulos, *The Origins of the Greek Nation—The Byzantine Period, 1204–1461* (New Brunswick, NJ: Rutgers University Press, 1970); Vacalopoulos, *The Greek Nation, 1453–1669* (New Brunswick, NJ: Rutgers University Press, 1976); and Speros Vryonis, Jr., *Decline of Medieval Hellenism.* A concise narrative summary of the initial century of Arab Muslim conquests is provided by Demetrios J. Constantelos in "The Moslem Conquest of the Near East as Revealed in the Greek Sources of the Seventh and Eight Centuries," *Byzantion* 42 (1972); 325–57; while Moshe Gil's comprehensive analysis, *A History of Palestine, 634–1099*, includes an extensive elucidation of the first 465 years of *jihad* campaigns in historical Palestine. Finally, K. S. Lal provides a modern review of a millennium of *jihad* and Islamization on the Indian subcontinent in *The Legacy of Muslim Rule in India* (New Delhi: Aditya Prakashan, 1992) and *Theory and Practice of Muslim State in India* (New Delhi: Aditya Prakashan, 1999).

12. Since the slavery system, mainly of Christians, was one of the pillars of the Muslim empires, information on this subject is found in several source books and modern studies. Vryonis examines this aspect extensively in his book *Decline of Medieval Hellenism*; see also Vryonis, "Seljuk Gulams and Ottoman Devshirmes" in *DER ISLAM* ed. C. H. Becker and Berthold Spuler (Berlin: Walter de Gruyter, 1965), 224–52; see also Maria-Mathilda Alexandrescu-Dersca, "Le Rôle des Esclaves en Roumanie Turque au XVe siècle," *Byzantinische Forschungen* 2 (1987): 15–28. David Ayalon, *The Mamluk Military Society. Collected Studies.* London: Variorum Reprints, 1977. For the eunuch institution extensively practiced in Islamic lands, see Jan Hogendorn, "The Hideous Trade: Economic Aspects of the 'Manufacture' and Sale of Eunuchs," *Paideuma* 45 (1999) 137–60. Muslims generally do not acknowledge their own history of war and conquests, but in an article of January 14, 2004, Sallah 'Issa, an Egyptian editor of the independent weekly *Nahdat Misr* alluded to Muslim invasions in the Middle Ages of "parts

of Asia, Africa, and Europe," see *MEMRI* Special Dispatch—Egypt/Reform Project, No. 703, April 29, 2004.

13. Bassam Tibi, "War and Peace," in *Islamic Political Ethics: Civil Society, Pluralism, and Conflict*, ed. Sohail H. Hashmi, with a foreword by Jack Miles (Princeton, NJ: Princeton University Press, 2002), 178.

14. This collaboration has been examined, mainly with the Turks, by Vryonis in *Decline of Medieval Hellenism*, as well as in Greek, Serbian, and Bulgarian studies. For Spain, see Dufourcq, *La Vie Quotidienne dans l'Europe Médiévale sous Domination Arabe* (Paris: Hachette, 1978). and "Le Christianisme dans les pays de l'Occident musulman 'des alentours de l'an mil jusqu' aux temps almohades," in *Etudes de Civilisation Médiévale (IX–XII siècles). Mélanges offerts a Edmond-René Labande.* (Poitiers: CESCM, 1974), 241–45.

15. This process is well documented by Vryonis in *Decline of Medieval Hellenism* and by Armenian chroniclers in the seventh to the tenth centuries. For documents on Mesopotamia and the Mediterranean islands, Sicily, south of Italy, see Bat Ye'or, *Decline.*

16. Many authors have denounced the entrenchment in Europe of Islamic terrorist cells. In his book, *Le Totalitarisme Islamique*, Alexandre Del Valle has minutely detailed the Islamist network spread all over Europe. See also Desmond Butler, "Europe-wide Network Enlists Fighters for Iraq," *New York Times*, December 6, 2003; Robert Wistrich, "Hate Britain," *JC*, May 16, 2003.

17. Abbasali Amid Zanjani, *Minority Rights According to the Laws of the Tribute Agreement: A Survey of Some Purports of the International Rights from the Viewpoint of the Islamic Jurisprudence.* (Teheran International Publishing Co., 1997).

18. Ibid., 254.

19. Ibid., 258.

20. Ibid., 262.

21. Ibid., 295.

22. Case No. Xmas/M/42.

23. *Al-Muhajiroun, The Voice, The Eyes and The Ears of the Muslims*, London, press release dated December 21, 1999, www.almuhajiroun.com.

24. The tensions within the Islamic societies confronted with modernization and Westernization were abundantly reported in the nineteenth century's European diplomatic correspondence and by contemporary analysts, see Abdolonyme Ubicini, *Lettres sur la Turquie, ou Tableau Statistique, religieux, politique, administratif, militaire, commercial, etc. de l'Empire ottoman depuis le Khatti-Cherif de Gulkhané (1839). Accompagné de Pièces Justificatives*, revised 2nd ed. vol. 1, *Les Ottomans*; vol. 2, *Les Raias. (Grecs, Arméniens-Catholiques, Israélites, Latins)* (Paris: Librairie Militaire de J. Dumaine (Anselim), 1853/1854); Edouard Engelhardt, *La Turquie et le Tanzimat ou Histoire des Réformes dans l'Empire Ottoman depuis 1826 jusqu'à nos jours*, (Paris: Librairie Cotillon & Librairie Conseil d'Etat, vol. 1, 1882; vol. 2, 1884); Bat Ye'or *Islam and Dhimmitude*, 223.

25. *MEMRI*, Special Report—no. 10, September 26, 2002; see also Spencer, *Onward Muslim Soldiers, How Jihad Still Threatens America and the West*, Washington, D.C.: Regnery, 2003; "Europe: Jihad in the Making?", chap. 2; Sookhdeo, *Understanding Islamic Terrorism*, 172–87.

26. Al-Faruqi, *Islam and other Faiths*, 100.

27. Ayatullah Morteza Mutahhari, "The Quiddity of Jihad," http://www.aalulbayt.org/ html/eng/books/jihad/3.htm, from *Jihad The Holy War of Islam and its Legitimacy in the Quran*, trans. Mohammad Salman Twhidi, 1985. For classic and modern legal Muslim texts on *jihad*, see Andrew Bostom, *The Legacy of Jihad. Islamic Holy War and the Fate of Non-Muslims*, (New York: Prometheus Books, 2005).

Chapter 3. Knitting the Threads Together

1. Michael Curtis, *Verdict on Vichy. Power and Prejudice in the Vichy France Regime*, Arcade Publishing, New York, 2002, 293.

2. Henry Laurent, "Le Mufti et la France de la IVᵉ République," *Revue d'Etudes Palestiniennes* 81 (Autumn 2001), 70–87.

3. Ibid., 70.

4. Ibid; Lukacs Hirszowicz, *The Third Reich and the Arab East* (London: Routledge & Kegan Paul; Toronto: University of Toronto Press, 1966); Zvi Elpeleg, *The Grand Mufti Haj Amin al-Hussaini, Founder of the Palestinian National Movement*, London: Frank Cass, 1993; Martin Gilbert, *Second World War* (London: Weidenfeld & Nicolson, 1989), 265. The French Vichy regime sent arms and helped the pro-Nazi Arab uprising in Iraq; see Curtis, *Verdict on Vichy: Power and Prejudice in the Vichy France Regime* (New York: Arcade, 2002), 262.

5. Pierre Lyautey, "Le nouveau rôle de la France en Orient," *Comptes rendus des Séances de l'Académie des Sciences d'Outre-Mer*, May 4, 1962, 176, in Jacques Frémeaux, *Le monde arabe et la sécurité de la France depuis 1958* (Paris, Presses Universitaires de France, 1995), 46.

6. Ibid.

7. Elie Kedourie, "Going Third World à la Française," *Middle East Quarterly*, Summer 2004, vol. 11:3, 65–68.

8. Raymond Aron, *De Gaulle, Israël et les Juifs* (Paris: Plon, 1968), 96–98; after the war, except in some cases, most of the ministers, civil servants, politicians, and intellectuals of the Vichy regime pursued their careers, see Curtis, *Verdict on Vichy*.

9. August 25, 1957. For a more detailed list of Nazis, with their function during the war, and their Arabic names and activities in Egypt and Syria, see Institute of Jewish Affairs, *Pattern of Prejudice*, London, May–June 1967; Michel Tatu in *Le Monde*, June 9, 1967; M. S. Arnoni, *Le Nationalisme Arabe et les Nazis*, Tel-Aviv, August 1970; Yahudiya Masriya, *Les Juifs en Egypte* (Geneva: Editions de l'Avenir, 1971), 66–69.

10. For the links between the Palestinians and the European Nazi and fascist groups see Alain Geismar, *L'engrenage terroriste* (Paris: Fayard, 1981); and especially Claire Sterling, *The Terror Network* (New York: Holt, Rinehart & Winston and Reader's Digest Press, 1981).

11. James Parkes, *Antisemitism* (London: Vallentine-Mitchell, 1963), 109–18; see also Robert Wistrich, *Hitler's Apocalypse: Jews and the Nazi Legacy* (London: Weidenfeld & Nicolson, 1985). Pierre-André Taguieff has extensively researched on the Arab-Nazi-Fascist links in *Rising from the Muck: The New Anti-Semitism in Europe*, and in *Les Protocoles des Sages de Sion*, 2 vols. (Paris: Berg International, 1992). See also Alexandre Del Valle, *Le Totalitarisme Islamiste*, 91–98.

12. Aron, *De Gaulle*, 121.

13. Frémeaux, *Le monde arabe*, 53.

14. January 25–26, 1969. See *Second International Conference, Cairo 1969*, UN Library, Geneva.

15. Ibid.

16. In *Bulletin d'informations*. Délégation Permanente de la Ligue des Etats Arabes. Geneva. May 1, 1970, no. 7, 7.

17. Ibid., 6.

18. "Le directeur de 'Témoignage Chrétien' dénonce la propagande sioniste," *Informations Arabes*, no. 15, Geneva, November 30, 1970, 6.

19. Saleh A. Al-Mani, *The Euro-Arab Dialogue: A Study in Associative Diplomacy*, ed. Salah Al-Shaikhly (London: Frances Pinter, 1983), 48. See also Jacques Bourrinet, ed., *Le Dialogue Euro-Arabe* (Paris: Economica, 1979).

20. *Bulletin d'Informations*, no. 22, Centre d'Information Arabe, July 1971, Geneva. For French and European neo-Nazis activities from the 1950s, see Christian Delacampagne "L'Antisémitisme en France (1945–1993)," in *Histoire de l'Antisémitisme 1945–1993*, under the direction of Léon Poliakov (Paris: Seuil, 1994).

21. *Energy and Europe: EEC Energy Policy and Economy in the Context of the World Energy Crisis*, written by Mary Mauksch et al., European News Agency, Brussels, vol. 1, Feb.1975, 73; and vol. 2; see also *Studies* and part 1, *Report by the Commission on the behaviour of the oil companies in the Community during the period from October 1973 to March 1974*, Commission of the European Communities, 1976 (series 26).

22. *Documents d'Actualité Internationale* (henceforth *DAI*), Direction de la Documentation française, Ministère des Affaires Etrangères, no. 1, 1974, 2–3.

23. This hegemonic and imperialist policy was mainly voiced by the Ba'ath party and the Syrian Social Nationalist Party, two movements strongly influenced by Nazism and popular among some Eastern Christians, including their clerics.

24. Antoine Morison, *Relation Historique d'un voyage nouvellement fait au Mont Sinaï, et à Jerusalem. On trouvera dans cette relation un détail de ce que l'auteur a vu de plus remarquable en Egypte,*

en Arabie, . . . sur les côtes de Syrie et en Phoenicie . . . et le gouvernement politique de l'Empire ottoman, etc. (Paris: Antoine Dezallier, 1705), 245, 292–96.

25. "Conférence des Chefs d'Etat Arabes (Alger, 26–29 novembre 1973) Déclaration de politique Générale (Alger, 28 novembre 1973)" in *DAI*, no. 7, 1974, 122–26.

26. Yehoshafat Harkabi, *Palestinians and Israel* (Jerusalem: Keter, 1974), 281.

Chapter 4. Emergence of the Euro-Arab Bloc

1. See Al-Mani, *Euro-Arab Dialogue,* 70–73, 111; Bourrinet, *Le Dialogue Euro-Arabe,* 4. Analyzing the formula of the EAD, John Waterbury writes, "The eventual bargaining took place in the form of a trade-off: the Arab political demands against European economic objectives," in "Les implications politiques et diplomatiques du dialogue international," in Bourrinet, 25; Françoise de la Serre, "Conflit du Proche-Orient et Dialogue Euro-Arabe: La Position de l'Europe des Neuf," in Bourrinet, 79–94.

2. Al-Mani, *Euro-Arab Dialogue,* 48.

3. *Report on Islamic Summit 1974: Pakistan. Lahore, 22–24 February 1974,* (Karachi), 222–23.

4. April 2, 1974.

5. September 16, 1974.

6. See www.Medea, European Institute for Research on Mediterranean and Euro-Arab Cooperation.

7. *Report on Islamic Summit 1974,* 228.

8. As this issue of *DAI* has disappeared from the collection of the Library at the United Nations in Geneva, references are from Bourrinet, *Le Dialogue Euro-Arabe,* 331–35: *DAI,* 1977, no. 16–17, 315–19.

9. Al-Mani, *Euro-Arab Dialogue,* 70–73.

10. Bat Ye'or, *Islam and Dhimmitude,* 253.

11. Al-Mani, *Euro-Arab Dialogue,* 73.

12. Ibid., 70–71.

Chapter 5. A New Political and Cultural Entity

1. Comité Européen de Coordination des Associations d'Amitié avec le Monde arabe, Paris, Lucien Bitterlin (publication director), 16 Rue Augereau, 75007 Paris. The current monthly (2004), *France-Pays Arabes,* retains the subtitle *Eurabia.* See p. 273.

2. Georges Vaucher, *Trois Mythes de l'Ancien Testament dont il faut atténuer le caractère raciste pour que la paix vienne en Terre Sainte* (Geneva: *Eurabia,* 1978). The Franco-Arab Solidarity Association (ASFA) was a Gaullist group, presided by Louis Terrenoire, former information minister. Vaucher was the representative in Switzerland of *Eurabia* and of the *Groupe d'étude sur le Moyen-Orient,* both at the same Geneva address, opposite the Arab League office.

3. In 2004: around six hundred members in eighteen national Parliaments of countries members of the Council of Europe as well as in the European Parliament. www.medea.be/index.html?page=0&lang=en&idx=0&doc=1020.

4. *Eurabia,* 2 July 1975. The article emphasized that this issue had been studied by a large number of experts from the Association de Solidarité Franco-Arabe (Association for Franco-Arab Solidarity) and from the general assembly of the Parliamentary Association for Euro-Arab Cooperation in Strasbourg.

5. *Eurabia,* 1975, no. 2, 1. At its 18th General Conference from October 17 to November 23, 1974, UNESCO refused to include Israel in any world region, thereby excluding it from all UNESCO activities and funds. This was an exceptional measure that simply eradicated the spiritual existence of Israel from the nations of the world. This resolution was backed by the communist and Arab bloc. An important number of eminent scholars, intellectuals, writers, and artists protested. See *Le Monde,* December 1–2, 1974; Eric Werner, *L'Imposture. En Marge*

de la 18e Conference Generale de l'UNESCO, (Geneva: Centre d'Information et de Documentation sur le Moyen-Orient, 1975).

6. *Eurabia* (1975), no. 2, 12–16.

7. Bourrinet, *Le Dialogue Euro-Arabe*, 296–301.

8. The Joint Memorandum is reproduced in ibid., 296–306.

Chapter 6. The Spiral

1. The main bodies of the EC then comprised:

1. A Commission, the executive body, whose work was to define, initiate, and implement policies.

2. The Council of Ministers constituted by the ministers of the national governments. At the 1974 Paris summit, France's President Giscard d'Estaing and West Germany's Chancellor Schmidt were instrumental in establishing the European Council, a body constituted by the heads of government that directs policy development from the highest political level. The European Council coordinates EU policy in several domains and particularly on economic, foreign, and security matters.

3. The European Parliament, with legislative, budgetary, and supervisory functions, and, from 1979, elected by direct popular vote.

4. A Court of Justice.

2. Al-Mani, *Euro-Arab Dialogue*, 71.

3. Edmond Völker, ed., *Euro-Arab Cooperation*, Europa Instituut, University of Amsterdam, Amsterdam (Leyden: A.W. Sijthoff, 1976), 179.

4. Ibid., 176–77.

5. Ibid., 215.

6. John Laffin, *The PLO Connections* (London: Corgi, 1982); Christopher Dobson, *Black September: Its Short, Violent History* (London: Robert Hale, 1974 & 1975).

7. Al Mani, *Euro-Arab Dialogue*, 60–61.

8. Ibid., 61.

9. Ibid.

10. Ibid., 135.

11. See chapter 8.

12. *Report on Islamic Summit, 1974,* al-Tohami's discourse, 195–219; extracts 198–202, 204, 215, 217.

Chapter 7. Political Alignment of the European Community

1. *DAI*, no. 35, September 2, 1977, Council of Europe (London, June 29–30, 1977), 137. Declaration of the Nine on The Middle East (London, June 29, 1977) (Source: Ministère des Affaires étrangères, Paris) Official Texts, 666–67 (French).

2. *DAI*, 1977, no. 16, 315–19.

3. Brussels Declaration, November 1973. See chapter 3.

4. *Official Records of the General Assembly. Thirty-second Session. Plenary Meetings*, vol. 1, Sept.20–Oct. 13, 1977, United Nations, New York, 1978.

5. See Articles 8 and 9 of the Communiqué.

6. In article 6 of the declaration published at the end of its fourth session.

7. Fez Islamic Conference, 1980, article 12; Al-Mani, *Euro-Arab Dialogue*, 113.

8. *Europe Arab World: From Clashing on Petroleum to Cooperating for a New Economic Order* (Forli, Italy: Pio Manzù International Centre, December 1979) 77–79.

9. Ibid., 125–27.

10. *Groupe d'études sur le Moyen Orient*, 80 (Geneva, December 1979).

11. See www. Medea.be./European Institute for Research on Mediterranean and Euro-Arab Cooperation/information files/Venice Declaration and Euro-Arab Dialogue.

12. Article 6.
13. Article 7.
14. Article 8.
15. Article 9.
16. Kenneth Cragg, *The Arab Christian: A History in the Middle East,* 275.
17. Bat Ye'or, *Decline,* 219–17. See also Ellul foreword, 20.
18. Foremost among them: James Parkes, Jacques Ellul, Paul Giniewski, Pierre-André Tagu-ieff, Robert Wistrich, William Nicholls, Rabbi Marvin Hier, Rabbi Abraham Cooper, and Shi-mon Samuels of the Simon Wiesenthal Center, and David G. Littman at the UNCHR in Geneva since 1986.
19. Robert S. Wistrich, *Hitler's Apocalypse,* 247. For a condensed analysis of French anti-Zionist policy and its pro-Arab and pro-Palestinian influence in the EEC, see "France, French Interests and Policies," in *Political Encyclopedia of the Middle East,* ed. Avraham Sela, 259–62. (Jerusalem, 1999)
20. *L'Événement du Jeudi,* September 13–19, 1990. Jean-Pierre Chevènement, France's min-ister of defense and president of the organization "France-Iraq," resigned his post before the Gulf War began in January 1991, rather than associate with a government that participated in the coalition against Iraq. In an open letter, Odai al-Tayi, ex-counselor to the Iraqi ambassa-dor in Paris, urged France to renew with its traditional anti-American, pro-Arab policy; see *Le Figaro,* May 31, 1993.
21. *L'Evénement du Jeudi,* "France-Irak, L'argent de la Corruption," September 13–19, 1990, Paris. For Berque's appraisal of terrorism against Israel, see Bat Ye'or, *Islam and Dhimmi-tude,* 215; Elie Kedourie, "Going Third World," *MEQ,* Summer 2004, 65–68.
22. See chapter 11.
23. *Euro-Arab Dialogue. The relations between the two cultures. Acts of the Hamburg symposium, April 11th to 15th 1983.* English version ed. Derek Hopwood (London: Croom Helm, 1983), 9.
24. Walid Phares, *Lebanese Christian Nationalism: The Rise and Fall of an Ethnic Resistance* (Boulder, CO: Lynne Riener, 1995), 219. For the Syrianization of Lebanon, see also Habib C. Malik, *Between Damascus and Jerusalem: Lebanon and Middle East Peace* (Washington DC: The Washington Institute for Near East Policy, 1997).
25. Sherwin B. Pomerantz, in *Jerusalem Post* (Comment and Opinion), December 1, 2003; see also "Britain Orders End to Import of Products from Israeli Illegal Settlements," London, July 6, 2002, http://www.islamOnline.net/English/News/2002-07/06 article57.shtml; and Yahia Abu Zakaria, "Swedish Public Figures Urge Israeli Boycott," Stockholm, January 18, 2003, www.islamOnline.net; Julie Stahl, "EU labeling of Israeli Products Described as Anti-Semitic Boycott," CNSNews.com Jerusalem Bureaux Chief, August 6, 2004.

Chapter 8. The Cultural Alignment

1. It is difficult to quantify illegal and legal Muslim mass immigration in Europe since this subject was labeled "xenophobic" and "racist." To this must be added an important Euro-pean movement of conversion to Islam. Alexandre Del Valle provides some figures for West-ern European countries in his detailed book, *Le Totalitarisme islamiste.* According to Huntington, "By the mid-1990s, approximately 4 million Muslims lived in France and up to 13 million in Western Europe overall." Samuel P. Huntington, *The Clash of Civilizations and the Remaking of World Order* (New York: Free Press, 1996), 200. This low figure can safely be dou-bled today for both France and Europe.
2. Hopwood, *Euro-Arab Dialogue: The Relations;* see the recommendations of the Venice Seminar, 317–23.
3. Ibid. At the opening session in the University's great audience hall in Cà Dolphin, sev-eral personalities gave welcome speeches—including Ambassador Cesare Regard, the Italian representative to the European Group of coordination for the Euro-Arab Dialogue. The names of the participants are listed.
4. Hopwood, *Euro-Arab Dialogue: The Relations,* 320–21.
5. Most of the authors published in Bourrinet discussed the functionality of the Dialogue.

6. The choice of the word "dialogue" to define this all-encompassing political and economic network between states is attributed to French Minister of Foreign Affairs Michel Jobert in 1973; see de la Serre, in Bourrinet, *Le Dialogue Euro-Arabe,* 82.

7. Del Valle, *Le Totalitarisme Islamiste,* 410–29.

8. This trend is studied in Bat Ye'or, *Islam and Dhimmitude,* 209–13.

9. Al-Mani, *The Euro-Arab Dialogue,* 69.

10. Hopwood, *Euro-Arab Dialogue: The Relations,* 305–07.

11. Article 3.

12. Ibid., 308–11.

Chapter 9. Foreign Policy

1. Mary Mauksch, *Energy and Europe,* 1:75.

2. Ibid., 1:77.

3. Ibid., 2:3–4.

4. Ibid., 2:4–5.

5. Neil Nugent, *The Government and Politics of the European Union* (New York: Palgrave Macmillan, 2003), 47.

6. Ibid., 67.

7. www.medea.be/site.html.

8. This is established by MEDEA's information files.

9. http://europa.eu.int/comm/external_relations/euromed/bd.htm.

10. Bat Ye'or, *Islam and Dhimmitude,* 198.

11. For a short overview of the situation of the Copts see Nabil A. Malek, "The Copts: From an Ethnic Majority to a Religious Minority," in *Acts of the Fifth International Congress of Coptic Studies,* ed. David W. Johnson Washington August 12–15, 1992, vol. 2, Papers from the Sections, part 2, The International Association for Coptic Studies (Rome: C.I.M., 1993), 299–311. See also Bat Ye'or, *Islam and Dhimmitude,* chap. 8.

12. Spencer, *Onward Muslim Soldiers*; see particularly chapter 2.

13. Israeli, *Islamikaze: Manifestation of Islamic Martyrology* (London: Cass, 2003), 75. It is a fact that Islamists justify their terrorist war against infidels by Qur'anic injunctions and by *shari'a* laws. On this, see also Anne-Marie Delcambre, *L'Islam des Interdits,* (Paris: Desclée de Brouwer, 2003).

14. Israeli, *Islamikaze,* 88.

15. Sookhdeo, *Understanding Islamic Terrorism,* 219–33, see also appendix 4, " 'Bin Laden' audiotape," and appendix 6 "The Zarqawi Document"; Daniel Pipes, "Muslims Love Bin Ladden," *New York Post,* October 22, 2002.

16. For the politization of NGOs and their influence in international bodies, see Gerald M. Steinberg, "NGOs Make War on Israel," *MEQ* (Summer 2004), 13–25.

Chapter 10. An Anti-Zionist, Antisemitic Policy

1. See chapter 6.

2. Edmond Völker, *Euro-Arab Cooperation,* 178.

3. Ibid., 179.

4. See chapter 7.

5. *Report on Islamic Summit, Lahore,* 198.

6. Ibid., 199–200.

7. Al-Mani, *Euro-Arab Dialogue,* 134.

8. Venice Declaration, 1980.

9. The population comprised Arabs, Turcomans, and nineteenth-century Muslim settlers from Circassia, Algeria, Egypt, Syria, and Turkey. Christian refugees fleeing the massacres in Cilicia, Iraq and Syria after WWI also settled there. The territory covered 78 percent of the

League of Nations' designated area of Palestine, and was made off-limits to Jews by Great Britain, the mandatory power.

10. This was their position from 1973 on. See chapter 3 and the EAD Venice Seminar, appendix 1.

11. *IHT*, April 28, 2004; see also Herb Keinon, "Europe pressing U.S. on Israeli settlements;" of JPonline edition, August 4, 2004.

12. *IHT*, April 27, 2004.

13. *Telegraph*, May 2, 2004.

14. "Ex-U.S. envoys protest Mideast Policy" (*AFP, Reuters*) *IHT*, May 5, 2004.

15. *PAEAC meets British Presidency of the EU, 29/4/1998*, Documents, PAEAC, MEDEA, European Institute for Research on Mediterranean and Euro-Arab Cooperation. http://www.medea.be/index.html.

16. See chapter 9.

17. *Euro-Arab Parliamentary Dialogue, Damascus, 1998. Euro-Arab Dialogue, PAEAC, MEDEA*.

18.The section of this Conference's Communiqué on "Cultural cooperation and mutual respect for cultural values" will be examined in chapter 11.

19. Dore Gold, *Hatred's Kingdom: How Saudi Arabia Supports the New Global Terrorism* (Washington, DC: Regnery, 2003), 190–91; for the incitement to Jihad and the call to destroy America, *see MEMRI*, Special Report, Saudi Arabia/Jihad and Terrorism Studies Project, no. 29, June 24, 2004.

20. Syrian FM talks to Euro-Arab parliamentary meeting on Middle East developments, *Syria-Regional, Politics, 7/13/1998*. www.arabicnews.com/ansub/Daily/Day/980713/1998071308.html.

21. Ibid.

22. Speech by Mr. Henning Gjellerod, MP, Co-Chairman of the PAEAC, at PAEAC, MEDEA site.

23. October 27–28, 1998.

24. http://www.medea.be/index.html?page = &lang = &doc = 1023; see also the PAEAC files on MEDEA.

25. Melissa Radler, "View from the Left," *International Jerusalem Post*, December 26, 2003.

26. Thomas Fuller, "European poll calls Israel a big threat to world peace," *IHT*, October 31, 2003.

27. *Yediot Aharonot*, Jerusalem, November 2, 2003.

28. Margaret Brearley, "Bi-focal Vision: Israel and the Intifada in the British Press," *Antisemitism International, 2003. An Annual Research Journal of the Vidal Sassoon International Center for the Study of Antisemitism*, Hebrew University, Jerusalem, December 2003, 47; see also Julie Burchill, "Beyond the Facts: Good, Bad and Ugly," where the author denounces the anti-Semitism of the newspapers, *Guardian*, November 29, 2003.

29. *Financial Times*, July 7, 2003.

30. Speech by The Rt. Hon. Christopher Patten. SPEECH/01/49, European Parliament—Joint debate—Brussels, January 31, 2001, http://europa.eu.int/comm/external_relations/news/patten/speech_01_49.htm. See Steinberg, "NGOs Make War on Israel."

31. See chapter 9.

32. Robert S. Wistrich, "Editor's Diary" in *Antisemitism International, 2003*, 7.

33. "Threat on head scarves anger French Muslims," *IHT*, (*AP*) December 13–14, 2003. See also the most detailed factual record of the situation in France, under the direction of Emmanuel Brenner, *Les territoires perdus de la République. Antisémitisme, racisme et sexisme en milieu scolaire*, (Paris: Fayard, Mille et une Nuits, 2002; 2nd edition, 2004); and Emmanuel Brenner, *"France, prends garde de perdre ton âme . . ." Fractures sociales et antisémitisme dans la République*, (Paris: Fayard, Mille et une Nuits, 2004); Nidra Poller, "Betrayed by Europe: An Expatriate's Lament," *Commentary* (New York) 117, no. 3 (March 2004): 21–29.

34. Bertrand Benoit in Berlin, *Financial Times*, http://news.ft.com/world/; November 22, 2003.

35. Marc Perelman, Forward staff, "E.U. Accused of Burying Report on Antisemitism Pointing to Muslim Role. Politics Trumped Truth, Scholar Charges," *Forward* (New York), November 28, 2003. http://www.forward.com/images/forward.mini.hed.gif and http://www.forward.com/images/rule.gif

36. Ibid.

37. Barry Kosmin and Paul Iganski, "Israel in the British Press. Crossing the Line from Criticism to Bigotry," *IHT*, September 8, 2003; for the following discussion see *IHT*, September 16, 2003.

38. *Observatoire du monde juif* no. 8/9 (November 2003); Sara Leibovich-Dar, "Brain damage," *Haaretz Magazine*, November 21, 2003, 8–11.

39. Paul Marshall, "Bethlehem and Beyond," *NRO*, December 24, 2003.

Chapter 11. The New Euro-Arab Culture

1. *MEDEA's information files. Euro-Arab University.*

2. See chapter 8, note 8.

3. www.medea.be/index.html?page = &lang = &doc = 1144.

4. *MEDEA's information files*, Euro-Mediterranean Forum, Final Declaration (1st meeting, Brussels, October 1998).

5. Its 22nd session convened in the Belgian Senate and Chamber of Representatives.

6. www.medea.be/index.html?page = &lang = &doc = 1144.

7. Ibid.

8. *MEMRI*, "Saudi Opposition Sheikhs on America, Bin Laden, and Jihad," *MEMRI* Special Dispatch No. 400, July 18, 2002, www.memri.org.; and *MEMRI*, Special Report No. 10, "Friday Sermons in Saudi Mosques: Review and Analysis," www.memri.org, September 26, 2002. For a survey of recent *jihad*, see Spencer, *Onward Muslim Soldiers*, chap. 1; for an analysis in depth of the religious motivations of the modern jihadists, see Sookhdeo, *Understanding Islamic Terrorism.*

9. Warraq, *Leaving Islam.*

10. *MEDEA's information files. Pressure on Israel (by the Western World).*

11. Fraser Nelson, "The Poisonous Return of Anti-Semitism," TheScotsman.com, June 23, 2003; Melanie Phillips, "London: A Leftist Axis of Anti Semitism," *Hadassah*, September 4, 2003; Spencer, *Onward Muslim Soldiers*, 73–74.

12. Israeli scientific and technological performance arouses jealousy. This boycott is intended to impose a regression upon Israel.

13. Patrick Healy, *Boston Globe*, A1, February 20, 2003.

14. Diana Jean Schemo, in *IHT*, "The Scientists," July 2, 2003, 5.

15. The South is generally a euphemism for the Arab-Muslim countries.

16. http://194.235.129.80/euromesco/publi_artigo.asp?cod_artigo = 86822., Paper 20, February 2003, *Eastern Enlargement and the Euro-Mediterranean Partnership: A Win-Win Game?* Arab-Muslim countries are only referred to as Southern Mediterranean countries or by the "Euro Mediterranean Partnership." The word "Arab" is usually avoided.

17. www.ifri.org/front?id = ifri/publications/publications_en_ligne_1044623469287/publi_P_publi_eco_ce_oct___1045670053108.

18. John Vinocur, "A European Doomsday Scenario. French Research Group Paints a Gloomy Economic picture," *IHT*, May 14, 2003.

19. Anthony Browne, "Britain on the Brink," *The Times* (London), January 28, 2003.

20. For modern *jihad*, see Yossef Bodansky, *Bin Laden: The Man Who Declared War on America* (New York: Random House, 1999); Spencer, *Onward Muslim Soldiers;* Del Valle, *Le Totalitarisme Islamique.*

21. Bernard Bridel, "Pour Jacques Delors, l'islam fait aussi partie des valeurs européennes," *Le Temps* (Geneva), October 11, 2003, from an interview of Delors in *La Repubblica.*

Chapter 12. Arab and Muslim Unaccountability

1. Charles Bloch, *Le IIIe Reich et le monde*, Notre Siècle, series editor J.-B. Duroselle (Paris: Imprimerie Nationale, 1986), 432.

2. Alain Boyer. *L'Islam en France*, (Paris: Presses Universitaires de France, 1998), 44.

3. Bat Ye'or, *Islam and Dhimmitude*, 131–39; Jonathan Frankel, *The Damascus Affair: "Ritual Murder," Politics and the Jews in 1840* (Cambridge: Cambridge University Press, 1997).

4. Pierre-André Taguieff, *Prêcheurs de haine. Traversée de la Judéophobie planétaire* (Paris: Editions Fayard/Mille et une nuits, 2004).

5. Boyer, *L' Islam en France*, 16. See Nicolas Beau, *Paris, Capitale Arabe* (Paris: Seuil, 1995), for an extensive description of the Franco-Arab connections among businessmen, neo-Nazis, politicians, journalists, and intellectuals.

6. See chapter 2, on resolution 15.

7. Chapter 3.

8. Douglas Davis, "Documents show British official in Jerusalem urged understanding of Munich massacre," Jpostcom, January 1, 2003.

9. Yehoshafat Harkabi, *Palestinians and Israel* (Jerusalem: Keter Publishing House, 1974), 282. On Palestinian terrorism see, Jillian Becker, *The Rise and Fall of the Palestine Liberation Organization* (London: Weidenfeld and Nicolson, 1984); Benjamin Netanyahu, ed., *Terrorism: How the West Can Win*, (London: Weidenfeld and Nicolson, 1986); Wistrich, *Hitler's Apocalypse*.

10. Henry Delfiner, "The Socialist International and the Rise of Yasir Arafat," *Midstream* (Nov.–Dec. 2002); see also Wistrich, *Hitler's Apocalypse*.

11. Jacques Frémeaux. *Le Monde Arabe et la Sécurité de la France depuis 1958*, Politique d'Aujourd'hui (Paris Presses Universitaires de France, 1995).

12. Ibid., 86.

13. Martin Kramer, *Ivory Towers on Sand: The Failure of Middle Eastern Studies in America* (Washington, DC: Washington Institute for Near East Policy, 2001); Abdel Latif Tibawi, *Second Critique of English Speaking Orientalists and Their Approach to Islam and the Arabs* (London: Islamic Cultural Center, 1979).

14. John Laffin, *The PLO Connection: How Has the Wealthiest, Most Bloodthirsty Terrorist Organisation in the World Become Accepted—Even Respectable?* (London: Gorgi Book, 1982).

15. Frémeaux, *Le Monde Arabe*, 293.

16. www.telegraph.co.uk/news/main.jhtml?xml = /news/2003/10/15/wbish15.xml.

17. Mouna Naïm, in *Le Monde*, April 4, 1996.

18. *Le Temps*, Geneva, July 11, 2003.

19. Laffin, *PLO Connection*, 60.

20. Sciolino, "Led by Muslims," *IHT*, March 31, 2003, 3.

21. *IHT*, March 13, 2003.

22. "2nd Issue of "Voice of Jihad Al-Qa'ida Online Magazine," *MEMRI Special Dispatch*, Jihad and Terrorism Studies, No. 60131, October 31, 2003.

23. Ibid.

24. Elaine Sciolino, "Mideast comes next. France and U.K. agree," *IHT*, April 10, 2003.

25. Elaine Sciolino, "Led by Muslims," *IHT*, March 31, 2003.

26. John Vinocur, "France: Veto is debated," *IHT*, March 6, 2003.

27. Von Matthias Küntzel, "Islamic Terrorism and Anti-Semitism: The Mission against Modernity," Presentation at the University of Yale conference on "Genocide and Terrorism— Probing the Mind of the Perpetrator," April 11, 2003.

28. *IHT*, August 4, 2003.

29. *IHT*, June 27, 2003.

30. *Star Online*, OIC, 2003.

31. In France, a French Muslim of Moroccan or Algerian origin can repudiate his wife (or wives) under Algerian or Moroccan law; Catherine Simon, "Les Répudiées de la République," *Le Monde*, June 11, 2004.

Chapter 13. The Andalusian Utopia

1. Bat Ye'or, *Decline*, 169–70; see her lecture, "Myths and Politics: The Tolerant Pluralistic Islamic Society: Origin of a Myth," sponsored by the Lord Byron Foundation for Balkan Studies, The International Strategic Studies Association, Symposium on the Balkan war: Yugosla-

via: Past and Present, in Chicago, August 31, 1995, on www.dhimmitude.org/archive/LectureE1.html.

2. See chapter 14.

3. Charles-Emmanuel Dufourcq, *La Vie Quotidienne;* this book examines the Arab conquest and colonization of Andalusia—see chapter 1, "Les Jours de Razzia et d'Invasion." For the centuries of *jihad* in Andalusia, see Paul Fregosi, *Jihad in the West: Muslim Conquests from the Seventh to the Twenty-first Century* (New York: Prometheus Books, 1998).

4. Evariste Lévy-Provençal, *Histoire de l'Espagne Musulmane* (Paris: Maisonneuve, 1950), 1:150.

5. Dufourcq, *La Vie Quotidienne,* 42; see also, by the same author, "Le christianisme," 237–46; and for a later period, Dufourcq, "Les Mozarabes du XIIè siècle et le prétendu 'Evêque' de Lisbonne," in *Revue d'Histoire et de Civilisation du Maghreb,* vol. 5 (Algiers: Faculté des Lettres d'Alger, 1968), 125–30.

6. Dufourcq, *La Vie Quotidienne,* chapter 2. Land expropriation and the confiscation of *dhimmi* property by Arab colonists are mentioned in numerous chronicles from the eighth century onward in the Eastern part of their empire. It led to the abandonment of their lands by the native *dhimmi* peasantry in a similar way as that described by Dufourcq in Andalusia; see Bat Ye'or, *Decline,* 100–136, 305–30.

7. Lévy-Provençal, *Histoire,* 1:157–91.

8. Evariste Lévy-Provençal, *Séville musulmane au début du XIIè siècle. Le traité sur la vie urbaine et les corps de métiers d'Ibn Abdun,* translated from Arabic with notes, Islam d'hier et d'aujourd'-hui (Paris: 1947; repr., Maisonneuve, 1948), 2:108–28.

9. Roger Arnaldez, "La Guerre Sainte selon Ibn Hazm de Cordou," in *Etudes d'Orientalisme dédiées à la mémoire de Lévi-Provençal,* 2 vols. (Paris: Maisonneuve et Larose, 1962), 2:457.

10. *Muhammad Messenger of Allah. Ash-Shifa of Qadi 'Iyad,* trans. Aisha Addarrahman Bewley, (Granada: Medinah Press, 1999), 371–47. See Samuel Shahid, "Rights of non-Muslims in an Islamic State," in Robert Spencer, ed., *The Myth of Islamic Tolerance. How Islamic Law Treats Non-Muslims,* Part 2, ch. 1.

11. Dufourcq, *La Vie Quotidienne,* 9–10.

12. Del Valle, *Le Totalitarisme,* 328.

13. http://www.united-church.ca/., see "That we may know each other."

14. Al-Azhar, The Fourth Conference, C.—On Civilization and Society: (2) and (3), 927.

15. Many of these writings sought to compensate for the declarations of the Second Vatican Council of the Catholic Church (1962–65), as well as the "Orientations" of the French episcopate (1973) and of the Vatican (1975), on the theological, spiritual, and cultural relationship between Judaism and Christianity.

16. *Assembly debate* on September 19, 1991 (11th Sitting) (see Doc. 6497, report of the Committee on Culture and Education, Rapporteur: Mr de Puig). *Text adopted by the Assembly* on September 19, 1991 (11th Sitting).

17. 885 (1987).

18. Resolution 1162.

19. 1032 (1986).

20. Council of Europe, Parliamentary Assembly, *The Contribution of the Islamic Civilisation to European Culture,* Strasbourg, 1992, Doc. 6497.

21. Ibid., 15.

22. Ibid., 170–71.

23. Ibid., 50–51.

24. James Robson, trans., *Mishkat Al-Masabih* (Lahore: Sh. Muhammad Ashraf, 1975), 1:636.

25. Ibid., 52–54.

26. www.telegraph.co.uk/news/main.jhtml?xml = /news/2003/07/08/wmosq08.xml.

27. Mark McCallum, "Muslim Call to Thwart Capitalism," Story from BBC News, July 12, 2003. For the origin and policy of the *al-Murabitun* and their links with the Islamists see Del Valle, *Le Totalitarisme Islamiste,* 327–30.

28. "A New Dialogue with Islam," *Q-News, The Muslim Magazine,* 297 (October 1998).

29. Bat Ye'or, *Decline,* chap. 9, "Characters of Dhimmitude," and by the same author, *Islam and Dhimmitude,* 103–8. For a refutation of the negationist Muslim view on history, see Robert

Spencer "The Myth of Islamic Tolerance," in Spencer, ed. *Myth of Islamic Tolerance*, Part 1, ch. 1.

30. Bruno Etienne, *La France et l'islam*, (Paris, 1989), 180, without specifying place or date.

31. Qur'an 3:60; see Heribert Busse, *Islam, Judaism, and Christianity: Theological and Historical Affiliations*, translated from the German by Alison Brown (Princeton: Markus Wiener Publishers, 1998. See also Ismail Raji al-Faruqi, *Islam and Other Faiths*, chaps. 3 and 5; Mark Durie,"Isa, the Muslim Jesus," answering-islam.org/Intro/islamic_jesus.html.

32. See chapter 13.

Chapter 14. Palestinianism

1. This trend has been examined in Bat Ye'or, *Islam and Dhimmitude*, chapter 9 and pp. 386–96. See also Bat Ye'or, "Juifs et Chretiens sous l'Islam: Dhimmitude et Marcionisme" *Commentaire* (Paris) 25, no. 97 (Spring 2002), 105–16; for the English translation of this article, www.dhimmitude.org/d_today_christian_antizionism.php.

2. Kenneth Cragg, *The Arab Christian*.

3. See the perspicacious review of Cragg's *The Arab Christian* by Habib Malik, in *The Beirut Review* 3 (Spring 1992), 109–22.

4. For a discussion of this subject, Bat Ye'or, *Islam and Dhimmitude*, 272–78 and by the same author, "Juifs et Chrétiens," 105–16; see Hayek, *Le Christ et l'Islam* (Paris: Seuil, 1959).

5. Bat Ye'or, *Islam and Dhimmitude*, 359.

6. Naim Stifan Ateek, *Justice and only Justice: A Palestinian Theology of Liberation* (Maryknoll, NY: Orbis Books, 1989); Cragg, *Arab Christian;* see in *Observatoire du monde juif* 6/7 (June 2003), "Les chrétiens et le conflit proche oriental. Le dialogue judéo-chrétien à l'épreuve"; Bat Ye'or in the same issue, "La 'compassion' assassine," 14–18; and "Les déchirures des Chrétiens d'Orient," 24–26; English translation in www.dhimmitude.org.

7. Commission Biblique Pontificale, *Le Peuple Juif et ses Saintes Ecritures dans la Bible Chrétienne*, with a preface by Cardinal Joseph Ratzinger (Paris: Le Cerf, 2001).

8. St. Augustine, fourth century. See William Nicholls, *Christian Antisemitism: A History of Hate* (Northvale, NJ: Jason Aronson, 1993). On the policy of the popes in early Christianity, Nicholls writes: "They fully believed the Christian myth of the Christ-killing Jews, and the theology of supersession, based on it. The Jewish law had been abolished and replaced by the new, spiritual law of the Church, which they administered. In particular the popes inherited the theology of Augustine, according to which the Jews where destined to survive until the second coming of Christ as a witness to their crimes. They were to be *preserved, but in misery"* (221; italics in the text). For St. Augustine's declarations on the Jews, see Jules Isaac, *Genèse de l'antisémitisme* (Paris: Calman-Lévy, 1956), 166–72; Jean Juster, *Les Juifs dans l'Empire Romain. Leur Condition Juridique, Economique et Sociale* (Paris: Paul Geuthner, 1914), 45–119 and 227–232; Marcel Simon, *Verus Israel, Etudes sur les Relations entre Juifs et Chrétiens dans l'Empire Romain (135–425)* (Paris: de Boccard, 1964), 118–20; English translation *Verus Israel: A Study of the Relations between Christians and Jews in the Roman Empire (AD 135–425)*, trans. H. McKeating Littman Library of Jewish Civilization (New York: Oxford University Press, 1986), 91–95; see also James Parkes, *The Conflict of the Church and the Synagogue: A Study in the Origin of Antisemitism* (New York: Atheneum, 1969); and recently David I. Kertzer, *Unholy War: The Vatican's Role in the Rise of Modern Anti-Semitism* (London: Macmillan, 2002).

9. See Bat Ye'or, *Islam and Dhimmitude*, chapter 9.

10. Mark Durie, "Yes Amrozi, we do remember Khaibar," *Quadrant*, November 2003; David G. Littman, FrontPageMagazine.com, "Islamists' Perpetual Jihad," August 15, 2003, www .frontpagemag.com/articles/Printable.asp?ID = 9393., being an oral statement delivered to the UN Sub-Commission on Human Rights (Geneva) for the World Union for Progressive Judaism on August 12, 2003.

11. www.ikv.nl/ikv/docs/english/sharing-stories.html. Jan Jaap van Oosterzee, "Sharing Stories. *Evaluation of the Euro-Arab education exchange between schools in Palestine and the Netherlands.* 2000–2001"; on this subject see also Bat Ye'or, *Islam and Dhimmitude*, 389–92. The mimicry of Jewish history under Nazi occupation in Holland is particularly evident in the *Olive*

Branch from Jerusalem Newsletter from the Holy Land, initiated by Father Raed Awad Abusahlia, chancellor of the Jerusalem Latin patriarchate, in October 2000 at the start of Palestinian attacks.

12. Agence de presse internationale catholique (Apic), November 15, 2002. See also "Mgr. Sabbah: l'occupation est la source de tous les maux." http://www.upjf.org/documents/ showthreod.phh?threadid = 2789.

13. *BFS Overseas,* "News from the Holy Land, Muslim Convert Butchered," July 29, 2003. According to *shari'a* (Islamic law), any Muslim male who apostatizes faces the death penalty. Barnabas Fund is campaigning for a change in Islamic teaching on apostasy. A petition has been launched, copies of which can be obtained from the address below, or downloaded from www.barnabasfund.org/Apostasy/petition.htm. In Britain's House of Commons, ninety-two MPs put their name to an Early Day Motion calling for an end to the punishment of apostates. www.barnabasfund.org/News/Archive/United%20Kingdom/UK-20030702.htm. and www .barnabasfund.org/Apostasy.htm. It was finally signed by 88,890 persons in 32 countries.

14. *Le Temps,* Geneva, April 28, 2003. Sergio Minerbi writes that during the desecration of the Church of the Nativity in Bethlehem by two hundred armed Palestinians "The huge catholic machinery was spreading strong anti-Israel propaganda in various degrees." in "The Vatican and the Standoff at the Church of the Nativity," http://www.jcpa.org, March 15, 2004, no. 515.

15. Shmuel Trigano, *La démission de la République,* 45–53; *Observatoire,* December 2002; *Antisemitism International, 2003,* "Antisemitism and Prejudice in the Media," 66–69.

16. Pierre-André Taguieff has extensively researched and written on racism and antisemitism.

17. Alexandre Del Valle, "L'Islamisation de l'Intifada ou le fondement religieux du conflit israélo-palestinien," *Le Lien,* no. 181, Supplément, I–VIII, Paris, March 15, 2002. Alexandre Del Valle, a researcher and prolific Catholic writer, has been harassed for his forceful denunciation of Islamism and Judeophobia.

18. Oriana Fallaci wrote a passionate condemnation of antisemitism and a defense of Europe in *The Rage and the Pride*; see also her latest courageous study, *La Forza della Ragione.* For a Muslim woman's progressive view, see Irshad Manji, *The Trouble with Islam* (Toronto: Random House, 2003).

19. *MEMRI,* no. 93, May 1, 2002.

20. *MEMRI,* no. 400, July 18, 2002.

21. Official statement of July 4, 2002, see *MEMRI,* Special Dispatch—Reform in the Arab and Muslim World/Jihad and Terrorism, No. 405, July 30, 2002.

22. Malka Hillel Shulewitz, ed., *The Forgotten Millions: The Modern Jewish Exodus from Arab Lands* (New York: Continuum, 1999); Shmuel Trigano, ed., *L'exclusion des Juifs des pays arabes. Aux sources du conflit israélo-arabe,* (Paris: Pardes, 2003); Moïse Rahmani, *L'exode oublié. Juifs des pays arabes,* with a preface by Alexandre Del Valle (Paris: Raphaël, 2003); also David G. Littman, "The Forgotten Refugees: An Exchange of Populations," December 3, 2002, www .nationalreview.com/comment/comment-littman/20302.asp; in UN document, E/CN.4/ Sub.2/2003/NGO/35 (July 17, 2003) for Sub-Commission on Human Rights (2003), www .unhcr./ch/Huridocda/Huriodoca.nsf/(Symbol)/E.CN.4.Sub.2.2003.NGO.35.En? Open document—and reproduced in a forthcoming volume, Robert Spencer, ed., *The Myth of Islamic Tolerance. How Islamic Law Treats non-Muslims* (New York: Prometheus Books, 2005), Part 5.

23. Mordechai Nisan, *The Conscience of Lebanon: A Political Biography of Etienne Sakr (Abu-Arz)* (London: Cass, 2003), chap. 3; Nisan, *Minorities in the Middle East. A History of Struggle and Self-Expression* (Jefferson, N.C.: 1991; repr., McFarland, 2002); Walid Phares, *Lebanese Christian Nationalism*; Frederick P. Isaac, *Indigenous Peoples under the Rule of Islam,* (USA: Xlibris Corporation, 2002).

24. Nisan, *Conscience,* 25.

25. Jillian Becker, *Rise and Fall,* 124.

26. For the terrible tragedy of the Indonesian Christians, see Bat Ye'or, *Islam and Dhimmitude,* 414–17.

27. "What is happening in Indonesia," www.anglicanmedia.com.au/old/2002/401.htm.

28. It has also obfuscated the genocide and atrocities perpetrated against Kurds in Iraq and the nearly 150,000 dead in the civil war in Algeria since 1992, as well as the continuous Christian exodus from Arabized countries. For persecutions of Christians in Iraq, death threats,

stolen goods, ransoming abducted children, see Katherine Zoepf, "Christians flee Iraq as attacks on them rise," *IHT*, August 5, 2004.

29. Reuters, "Solana: Mideast Peace Vital for Arab Reforms," March 3, 2004; see also Neil MacFarquhar, "Arab States Start Plan of Their Own Mideast," *IHT*, March 4, 2004.

30. Yahya Abu Zakaria, "Swedish Foreign Ministers Boycott Israeli Products," Stockholm April 20, 2003, *IslamOnline.net*.

31. John Vinocur, "In U.S., Schröder offers support of Bush's Mideast plan," *IHT*, February 27, 2004.

32. Ibid.

33. Busse, *Islam, Judaism, and Christianity*.

34. Norman Daniel, *Islam and the West* (Edinburgh: Edinburgh University Press, 1960).

35. Permanent Delegation of the Arab League, *Information Bulletin*, no. 7, Geneva, May 1, 1970.

36. United Nations, press release, GA/PAL/44, August 29, 1984.

37. Moshe Gil, *A History of Palestine 634–1099* (Cambridge: Cambridge University Press, 1992).

38. See Bostom, *The Legacy of Jihad*, for a selection of scholarly assessments on this subject.

Chapter 15. Conditioning Minds

1. Arthur Stanley Tritton, *The Caliphs and Their Non-Muslims Subjects: A Critical Study of the Covenant of Umar* (1930; repr., London: Frank Cass, 1970).

2. Antoine Fattal, *Le Statut Légal des Non-Musulmans en Pays d'Islam* (Beirut: Imprimerie Catholique, 1958).

3. *MEMRI, Special Report*, no. 10, September 26, 2002.

4. Patrick Sookhdeo, *A People Betrayed: The Impact of Islamization on the Christian Community in Pakistan* (Pewsey, Scotland: Christian Focus Publications and Isaac Publishing, 2002).

5. Charles Churchill, *The Druzes and the Maronites under Turkish Rule from 1840 to 1860*, with an introduction by Robin Bidwell (1993) (Reading, England, Garnett Publishing, 1994; original ed. London: Bernard Quaritch, London, 1862), 20–30.

6. Edouard Engelhardt, *La Turquie et le Tanzimat ou Histoire des Réformes dans l'Empire Ottoman depuis 1826 jusqu'à nos jours* (Paris: Librairie Cotillon & Librairie Conseil d'Etat, vol. 1, 1882, vol. 2, 1884).

7. Bat Ye'or, *Islam and Dhimmitude*, 79, 128–30.

8. Ibid, *Islam and Dhimmitude*, 221, 281–84, 287–88, 398–99. See also Sandro Magister, "The Church and Islam: 'La Civiltà Cattolica' Breaks the Ceasefire," http://213.92.16.98/ESW_stampa_articolo/1,2400,41931,00.html, and the web sites of Rev. Stephen Sizer, http://www.sizers.org/, and Steve Motyer.

9. Al-Faruqi, *Islam and Other Faiths*, 149.

10. Kramer, *Ivory Towers*; Frederick P. Isaac, *Indigenous Peoples*.

11. Al-Faruqi, *Islam and other Faiths*, 149; see also Khaled Abou el Fadl, "The Rules of Killing at War: An Inquiry into Classical Sources," *Muslim World* 89, no. 2 (April 1999), 144–57. For a thorough critic of el-Fadl's contradictions see Andrew Bostom, "Khaled Abou El Fadl: Reformer or Revisionist?" El Fadl: http://www.secularislam.org/articles/bostom.htm.

12. Fregosi, *Jihad in the West*.

13. The aggressiveness of the *jihad* is played down by Fernand Braudel in his book on the Mediterranean. The incrimination of the Church and the European kingdoms constitutes a major historical and political trend today, expressed by Cragg, in *The Arab Christian*, among many others. For a sharp critique of Cragg see Habib C. Malik, *The Beirut Review* 3 (Spring 1992): 109–22, published by the "Lebanese Center for Policy Studies." ed. Paul Salem, Beirut.

14. Daniel Pipes, "Harvard Loves Jihad," *New York Post*, June 11, 2002, see also http://www.danielpipes.org/pf.php?id = 419; same author, *Militant Islam reaches America*, (New York: W. W. Norton & Co., 2002). Pamela Ferdinand, "Harvard Student Gives Speech Citing 'Jihad,'" *Washington Post*, June 7, 2002, A03; Ibn Warraq, "The Genesis of a Myth," in Spencer, *The Myth*, Foreword.

15. This view appears in John Esposito, *Islam: The Straight Path* (Oxford: Oxford University Press, 1994), ix, 32; Esposito, *The Islamic Threat: Myth or Reality?* (Oxford: Oxford University Press, 1992). For a discussion of this position, see Bat Ye'or, *Islam and Dhimmitude*, 312–16, and Pipes, www.Campus-Watch.org.; Pipes, "Jihad and the Professors," *Commentary*, November 2002; Andrew G. Bostom "Endowing Denial," http://frontpagemag.com/Articles/ReadArticle.asp?ID = 7802., FrontPageMagazine.com, May 13, 2003.

16. Excerpts from the May 2, 2003, Friday Sermon delivered by the Sheikh Jamal Shakir Al-Nazzal at the Great Mosque in Falouja, Iraq. *MEMRI Special Dispatch Series*, No. 500, May 6, 2003.

17. Mawardi, *al-Ahkam as-Sultaniyyah. The Laws of Islamic Governance*, trans. Asadullah Yate (London: Ta-Ha Publishers, 1996), 210–11. These views are taught by Muslim jurists, sunni and shi'i.

18. Zanjani, *Minority Rights*, 326–29 and passim. For a modern appraisal of the rights of non-Muslim in contemporary Iran, see Reza Afshari, *Human Rights in Iran. The Abuse of Cultural Relativism* (Philadelphia: University of Pennsylvania Press, 2001).

19. Louis Massignon, Fernand Braudel, Jacques Berque, Georges Corm, Edward Said, Norman Daniel, Rashid al-Khalidi represented the think tanks of this majority—and nearly unanimous—trend.

20. 'Iyad Ibn Musa al-Yahsubi, *Muhammad Messenger of Allah. Ash Shifa of Qadi 'Iyad*, trans. Aisha Abdarrahman Bewley (Madinah Press, 1991), 373. A whole section is devoted to "The judgements concerning those who think the Prophet imperfect or curse him," 371–447. For recent examples of an accusation of blasphemy and defamation of Islam at the U.N. Commission on Human Rights, see René Wadlow and David Littman "Dangerous Censorship of a UN Special Rapporteur" in *Justice* 14 (September 1997): 10–17; and David Littman "Universal Human Rights and 'Human Rights in Islam'" *Midstream* (Feb.–March 1999): 2–7; Littman, "Islamism Grows Stronger at the U.N.," *Middle East Quarterly* (September 1999): 61–63. These three articles will appear in the forthcoming book, edited by Robert Spencer, *The Myth of Islamic Tolerance*.

21. Al-Yahsubi, *Muhammad*, 386.

22. Ibid., 409.

23. For the modern anti-Western views, see Spencer, *Onward Muslim Soldiers*; Sookhdeo, *Understanding Islamic Terrorism;* Daniel Pipes, "Europe's Threat to the West," *New York Sun*, May 18, 2004.

24. Symposium: *The Muslim Persecution of Christians*, Jamie Glazov with Bat Ye'or, Paul Marshall, Habib Malik, Walid Phares, October 10, 2003; see also *Christians in Egypt: The Humiliation Continues*, http://www.laciviltacattolica.it.

25. *IHT*, April 11, 2003.

26. *The History of al-Tabari (Ta'rikh al rusul wa'l-muluk)*, ed. Ehsan Yar-Shater, vol. 12, trans. and ann. Yohanan Friedman (Albany: State University of New York Press, 1992), 167.

27. Bat Ye'or, *Decline*, 121–24.

28. See chapter 9.

29. Euromed Synopsis, No. 248, November 13, 2003.

30. "Spain pays to head off Moroccan migration," *IHT*, December 10, 2003.

31. Dufourcq, *La Vie Quotidienne*, 20, and chap.1, "Les Jours de Razzia et d'Invasion"; see also Habib C. Malik, "Political Islam and the Roots of Violence," in *The Influence of Faith: Religious Groups and U.S. Foreign Policy*, ed. Elliott Abrams (Washington, DC: Ethics and Public Policy Center, 2001).

32. Vryonis, *Decline of Medieval Hellenism*; Peter Balakian, *The Burning Tigris. The Armenian Genocide and America's Response*, New York: Harper Collins, 2003.

33. Jovan Cvijic, *La Péninsule Balkanique. Géographie Humaine.* (Paris: Armand Colin, 1918).

34. *L'Evénement du Jeudi*, Paris, September 13–19, 1990.

35. Brian Knowlton, "U.S. officials softens criticism of Syria," *NYT* and *IHT*, April 16, 2003, p. 3.

36. Barry James "France steps up efforts to smooth things over," *IHT*, April 17, 2003; and see *IHT*, October 30, 2003.

37. *Wall Street Journal*, September 9, 2003.

38. Israeli, *Islamikaze*.

39. Quoted in ibid, 194, cited by *Al-Hayat al-Jadida* (Palestinian Authority) October 10, 2001.

40. Quoted by L. P. Harvey, *Islamic Spain* (Chicago: University of Chicago Press, 1990), 57.

41. Dore Gold, *Hatred's Kingdom,* 111. Such declarations by modern Islamic scholars and clerics abound, see Sookhdeo, Israeli, Gold, and Spencer.

42. Gold, *Hatred's Kingdom,* 221.

43. Per Ahlmark, "Combatting Anti-Semitism Now and Then," in *Justice* 34 (Winter 2002).

44. *New York Observer,* May 10, 2004, 4; this article appears as an afterword, written for an anthology, ed. Ron Rosenbaum, *Those Who Forget the Past: The Question of Anti-Semitism* (New York: Random House, 2004). The expression "The Modern *Hep! Hep! Hep!*"—used by George Eliot in her 1878 essay—comes from the abbreviation of the Latin, *Hierosolyma est perdita* (Jerusalem is destroyed). Cynthia Ozick writes: "*Hep!* was the cry of the Crusaders as they swept through Europe annihilating one Jewish community after another" [the first Crusade of 1096].

45. Spencer, *Onward Muslim Soldiers,* 28–50.

46. David G. Littman, "Islam Grows Stronger at the UN," *MEQ,* Sept. 1999, vol. 6, no. 3, 59–64. Many of his articles and UN statements have been published in Robert Spencer, ed., *The Myth of Islamic Tolerance,* mainly in Part 5; "Human Rights and Human Wrongs at the United Nations."

47. Sandro Magister, "Bush and God: A Puzzle for the Church in Europe," www.chiesa., March 31, 2003; and Ernesto Galli della Loggia "The Non-Existent Crusade," editorial, *Corriere della Sierra,* April 6, 2003.

48. 2003 WorldNetDaily.com.

49. Tom Leonard, Media Editor, "Christians 'Are Easiest Target for TV Satire'" *Daily Telegraph,* filed December 29, 2003, at www.telegraph.co.uk/; and *Apic,* January 5, 2004.

50. *NYT* and *IHT,* February 23, 2003.

51. Coalition for the Defense of Human Rights, see Dhimmi.com.

Chapter 16. The Islamization of Christianity

1. Michel Hayek, *Le Christ de l'Islam.*

2. Busse, *Islam, Judaism, and Christianity.*

3. Qur'an 2:100; 16:103.

4. The oneness of the Revelation is mentioned several times in the Qur'an.

5. Al-Faruqi, *Islam and Other Faiths,* pp. 152–53.

6. Ibid, p. 219.

7. Rossi de Gasperis: "La Shoah spirituale attuata dagli arabocristiani," at www.chiesa, http://213.92.16.98/ESW_articolo/0,2393,32295,00.html; see also Sandro Magister, *Is Europe a Province of Islam? The Danger Is Called Dhimmitude,* at www.chiesa, http://213.92.16.98/ESW_articolo/0,2393, 41028,00.html.

8. James Parkes, *Conflict;* Nicholls, *Christian Antisemitism.*

9. Steve Motyer, in *Evangelical Alliance: Day Consultation on the Holy Land,* London, June 26, 2003. See also Rev. Stephen Sizer, www.sizers.org.

10. Alain Besançon, *Le Malheur du siècle. Sur le communisme, le nazisme et l'unicité de la Shoah* (Paris: Fayard, 1998), p. 108 and 68.

11. Habib Malik, "Christians in the Land Called Holy," *First Thing* 89 (January 1999).

12. Michel Hayek, *Le Christ de l'Islam,* 15. Tarif Khalidi, ed. and trans., *The Muslim Jesus: Sayings and Stories in Islamic Literature,* in the series Convergences: Inventories of the Present, ed. Edward W. Said (Cambridge, MA: Harvard University Press, 2001).

13. Youakim Moubarac, *L'Islam et le Dialogue Islamo-Chrétien, Pentalogie Islamo-Chrétienne* (Beirut: Edition du Cénacle Libanais, 1972–73) 3:156.

14. Moubarac, *Pentalogie,* 5:63, 213–14. See the Declaration of the "Islamic-Christian Conference," March 2–6, 1969, Cartigny, Switzerland, under the auspices of the World Council of Churches, in Moubarac, *Pentalogie,* 3:305–6.

15. Zanjani, *Minority Rights According to the Law of the Tribute Agreement,* 251–53.

16. *La Civiltà Cattolica* 3680 (October 18, 2003).

17. From the Greek name *Philistia* for the land of the Philistines, a people of Aegean origin that occupied Gaza and its neighborhood from the twelfth century B.C.E. at the same period as the Israelites. The Latinized name *Palaestina* was given to Judea by the Emperor Hadrian in 135 when he crushed the Jewish resistance to Roman rule. After a general massacre, he also ordered as a punishment that no Jews could live in Jerusalem, which he called *Aelia Capitolina* and consecrated to the cult of Jupiter. Under Byzantium's rule, the Church restored with the greatest severity this lapsed prohibition, and transmitted it to the new Arab rulers in the seventh century, who tolerated only a very restricted Jewish presence in Jerusalem. While Hadrian's prohibition was linked to a circumstantial political war, the Church, on the other hand, made it the essential component of its anti-Jewish teaching and replacement theology. This trend has fed the entire anti-Zionist Church war until today, and the modern Western refusal to acknowledge Jerusalem as the capital of Israel.

18. Al-Faruqi, *Islam and Other Faiths*, 188.

19. Ibid., 190.

20. Ibid., xviii.

21. Ibid., 93.

22. Ibid., 75.

23. See quote from Father Abusahlia, chancellor of the Latin patriarchate in Jerusalem, Bat Ye'or, *Islam and Dhimmitude*, 387.

24. Al-Faruqi, *Islam and Other Faiths*, 211–40, from an article published in *Seminar of the Islamic-Christian Dialogue*, Popular Office of Foreign Relations, Socialist Peoples Libyan Arab Jamahiriya, Tripoli, 1981, 229–64.

25. Al-Faruqi, *Islam and Other Faiths*, 216–17.

26. Jacques Ellul, *Islam et judéo-christianisme*, with a preface by Alain Besançon (Paris: Presses Universitaires de France, 2004). Besançon, a Catholic, and Ellul, a Protestant, discuss this subject from a Christian viewpoint.

27. http://www.cccu.org/docLib/20030402_Malikaddress.pdf.

28. Wolfram Reiss, Rostock University, "La représentation du Christianisme dans les manuels scolaires en Egypte. Résultats d'une enquête et propositions pour des améliorations," November 2002. www.religioscope.com/dossiers/manuels/2002_01_reiss_a.htm and www.religioscope.com/pdf/manuels/Reiss.pdf. Arnon Groiss, compiled, trans. and ed., Report: *Jews, Christians, War and Peace in Egyptian School Textbooks* (New York/Jerusalem: Center for Monitoring the Impact of Peace (CMIP), March 2004); see also by the same editor, *The West, Christians and Jews in Saudi Arabian Schoolbooks* (New York/Jerusalem, CMIP, January 2003), and Arnon Groiss ed., *La democratie en danger, l'enseignement scolaire saoudien*, preface by Antoine Sfeir, Center for Monitoring the Impact of Peace (CMIP) (Paris: Berg International, 2004).

Chapter 17. Eurabia Against America

1. See chapter 2.

2. Ahmed Youssef, *L'Orient de Jacques Chirac. La politique Arabe de la France*, with a preface by Jean Lacouture (Monaco: Editions du Rocher, 2003); the whole speech is reproduced on 189–202.

3. John F. Burns, "Palestinian ends case with message," *IHT*, September 30, 2003.

4. *IHT*, April 26–27, 2003.

5. Brian Knowlton, "Saying U.S. approach to Syria isn't working, EU seeks cooperation," *IHT*, October 10, 2003. This method has been tested since 2000. The EU has been funding Palestinian jihadists, calling them not terrorists but victims of American and Israeli policies.

6. *IHT*, December 5, 2003.

7. Rachel Ehrenfeld, "EuroCash. What Does the Palestinian Authority Do with European Money?" National Review Online, December 10, 2003; see also by the same author, *Funding Evil: How Terrorism Is Financed and How to Stop It*. FrontPageMagazine.com, January 15, 2004. The author is director of the New York-based American Center for Democracy.

8. Euromed Report, 66 EN, Romano Prodi, president of the European Commission, "Sharing Stability and Prosperity," speech delivered at the Tempus Meda Regional Conference, Bibliotheca Alexandrina, Alexandria, October 13, 2003.

9. Commission of the European Communities. Communication from the Commission to the Council and the European Parliament, to prepare the VI Meeting of Euro-Mediterranean Ministers of Foreign Affairs, Naples, December 2–3, 2003 (Barcelona VI), Brussels, October 15, 2003. COM (2003) 610 final.

10. Report by the High-Level Advisory Group established at the initiative of the president of the European Commission, *Dialogue Between Peoples and Cultures in the Euro-Mediterranean Area*, version DEF, Brussels, October 2003.

11. Ibid., 9.

12. Ibid., 10.

13. Ibid., 11.

14. Ibid., Executive Summary, 2.

15. Ibid., 29.

16. Ibid., 13.

17. Ibid., 30.

18. Ibid., 17.

19. Ibid., 22. These essential principles of the dialogue needed to be broken down into five other principles of action for the success of the partnership: 1) equity; 2) co-ownership and shared responsibility; 3) transversality, meaning the idea that any question and initiative "in a given context/axis (North, South, North-South/South-North) has repercussions in the others"; 4) cross-fertilization; and 5) cooperation.

20. Ibid., 23.

21. Ibid., 10.

22. Ibid., 36.

23. Ibid., 35–36.

24. European Cultural Foundation, *Beyond Enlargement: Opening Eastwards, Closing Southwards?* Toledo, November 13–16, 2003. beyond_enlargement.pdf.

25. Said's name, incidentally, means southern Egypt, more precisely Nubia.

26. *IHT*, May 5, 2004. "Aznar admits one failing in fight against terrorism," (*Reuters, AP*)

27. Patrick E. Tyler and Don Van Natta Jr., "Call to Jihad rising on Europe's streets. Hundreds of angry Muslims are answering," *NYT* and *IHT*, April 27, 2004.

28. See also Euromed Report, no. 71 + , December 12, 2003.

29. Thomas Fuller, "Spending up in Europe budget plan," *IHT*, February 11, 2004.

30. *Arab Human Development Report 2002. Creating Opportunities for Future Generations* (United Nations Development Programme, New York): see also the 2003 Report.

31. Elisabeth Bumiller, "Bush Faces a Hostile Reception in Ireland," *IHT*, June 26, 2004.

32. François Heisbourg, "L'Europe sous la menace d'un terrorisme de destruction massive," *Le Temps*, June 21, 2004.

33. "Bush calls on Muslim nations to reform," from news reports, *NYT* and *IHT*, June 30, 2004.

34. Alain Hertoghe, *La Guerre à Outrance. Comment la presse nous a désinformés sur l'Irak* (The War without Mercy. How the press disinformed us on Iraq) (Paris: Calmann-Lévy, 2003). See also John Vinocur, "Author Sees Anti-U.S. Reporting: Journalist Fired for Book Critical of French Newspapers," *IHT*, December 29, 2003. Vinocur mentions the anti-American bias in England, France, and Germany. For an in-depth analysis of Euro-American relationship, see Niall Ferguson, "The End of Power," *Wall Street Journal Europe*, June 21, 2004, and his latest book, *Colossus: The Price of America's Empire* (London: Penguin, 2004).

Chapter 18. The Backlash of the Parnership

1. Martin Holland, *The European Union and the Third World* (New York: Palgrave, 2002).

2. Council of the European Union, "Strengthening the European Partnership with the Arab World," 6. http://www.ueitalia2003.it/NR/rdonlyres/72193E5B-19DB-455E-8F66-915B561E6563/0/1212DocSolanaMondoArabo_en.pdf.

3. Presidency Conclusions, Brussels European Council, December 12, 2003, http://ue.eu.int/pressData/en/ec78364.pdf.

4. Paragraph 55.

5. Commission of the European Communities, Communication from the Commission to the Council and the European Parliament: "Reinvigorating EU actions on Human Rights and democratisation with Mediterranean partners, Strategic guidelines" COM (2003) 294 final, Brussels, May 21, 2003. http://europa.eu.int/comm/external_relations/human_rights/doc/com03_294.pdf.

6. Pew Research Center for the People and the Press, "A Year after Iraq War," March 16, 2003, http://people-press.org/reports/display.php3?ReportID=206. See also ISIC Briefing 18, "Calls for Jihad Widespread in Islamic World," April 11, 2003.

7. Menahem Milson, "Reform vs. Islamism in the Arab World Today," *MEMRI*, Special Report—No. 34, Sept. 15, 2004.

8. *Boston Globe*, March 20, 2004. For Saddam's support of terror, see Deroy Murdock, "Saddam Hussein's Philanthropy of Terror," *American Outlook*, (Fall 2003).

9. John Vinocur, "Criticism of U.S. Obscures Growing Disunity on Continent," *IHT*, January 20, 2004.

10. Louis René Beres and Michael L. Messing, "What happens to the 'Merely Wounded.' The radiology of suicide bombing terrorism," Isralert@aol.com source http://www.freeman.org.

11. http:/www.copticpope.org/downloads/audio/qi6032004.zip ; *La Revue Copte* 1, no. 3 (March 2004), 7–8. See U.S. Copts Association. www.copts.net/index.asp.

12. Radio Vatican, November 6, 2003, see also www.upjf.org, November 23, 2003.

13. Pauline Jelinek, "US, Spanish Officials Spar on Iraq, Terrorism," *Boston Globe*, March 18, 2004.

14. "Terror Group Warns Spain on U.S. Support," Associated Press, April 5, 2004.

15. "Prodi would end Italy's role in Iraq" (AP, Reuters) *IHT*, March 29, 2004.

16. Andrew Hussey, "Profile Tariq Ramadan," *New Statesman*, June 21, 2004, 32.

17. "Anglicans' ex-leader angers Britain's Muslims with criticism of Islam" (AFP, AP), *IHT*, March 27–28, 2004.

18. Thierry Meyer, "Les musulmans britanniques appelés par leurs pairs à combatre le terrorisme," *Le Temps*, Geneva, April 1, 2004.

19. Amber Haque, ed., *Muslims and Islamization in North America: Problems & Prospects* (Maryland: Amada Publications and A.S. Noordeen, 1999). "Islamization of Knowledge in North America," 13–66. See also Daniel Pipes, "Think like a Muslim," *New York Post*, February 11, 2002.

20. Amber Haque, 61.

21. Ibid., 66.

22. Isma'il Raji al-Faruqi, *Al Tawhid: Its Implications for Thought and Life*. Islamization of Knowledge Series no. 4 (1982; repr. Herndon, VA: International Islamic Publishing House and Institute of Islamic Thought, 1995), 105–111.

23. For the situation in French schools, see Emmanuel Brenner, *Les territoires perdus*. Marie Brenner, "Daughters of France, Daughters of Allah," *Vanity Fair*, April 2004, 190–209. For antisemitism in Belgium see Adi Schwartz, "Between Lesser and Greater Evils," *Haaretz Magazine*, Nov. 21, 2003, 12–15.

24. Susan L. Douglass, *Strategies and Structures for Presenting World History with Islam and Muslim History as a Case Study*, The Council on Islamic Education (Beltsville, Md.: Amana Publications, 1994).

25. Ibid., 45.

26. Edward W. Said, *Orientalism* (London: Routledge & Kegan Paul, 1978), 204. This quotation is taken from the excellent critique of E. Said by Ibn Warraq, "Debunking Edward Said: Edward Said and the Saidists: or Third World Intellectual Terrorism," http://www.secularislam.org/articles/debunking.htm. Reprinted in Spencer, *The Myth*. Part 6.

27. Caroline Cox and John Marks, *The "West," Islam and Islamism: Is Ideological Islam Compatible with Liberal democracy?* (London: Civitas, 2003). For the cultural war see Keith Windschuttle,

"The cultural war on Western civilization," (The survival of culture: V), *New Criterion*, January 1, 2002.

28. For details, see Glenn R. Simpson "A Small Virginia Town Takes Center Stage In U.S. Financing Probe," *Wall Street Journal Europe*, June 21, 2004.

29. See Shammai Fishman, "Ideological Islam in the United States: 'Ijtihad' in the Thought of Dr. Taha Jabir al Alwani," translated from Hebrew by Dr. Tzemah Yoreh, first published in Hebrew in *Jamaa* 11 (2003), Ben Gurion University, Beer Sheva, www.e-prism.org.

30. Hayek, *Le Christ de l'Islam*, 264.

31. Simon Sebag Montefiore "A Dangerous Time to Be a Jew." *New Statesman*, June 28, 2004. www.newstatesman.com/site.php3?newTemplate = NSArticle_World&newDisplayURN = 200406280017.

32. Brenner, *Les territoires perdus*, and *"France, prends garde de perdre ton âme . . .".*

33. Presidency Conclusions, Euro-Mediterranean Conference of Ministers of Foreign Affairs, Naples, December 2–3, 2003. http://www.ueitalia2003.it/NR/rdonlyres/D33FB0C7-4B19–4F4D-B9FB-1003734AC339/0/1202ConclusionsEuromed_EN_.pdf.

34. *Jerusalem Post*, January 15, 2004.

35. House of Commons International Development Committee, *Development Assistance and the Occupied Palestinian Territories*, Second Report of Session 2003–04, Volume 1, HC 230–I [incorporating HC 1107–i to–iv, Session 2002–03], 74. http://www.parliament.the-stationery-office.co.uk/pa/cm200304/cmselect/cmintdev/230/230.pdf.

36. *Le Temps*, Geneva, February 4, 2004.

37. Stockholm International Forum 2004, January 17–February 7. For antisemitism in Sweden and its denial, see Ilya Meyer, "Whither the White Buses?" *The International Jerusalem Post*, July 2, 2004.

38. www.politicalcartoon.co.uk/html/exhibition/html.

39. Ilka Schröder, "Europe's Crocodile Tears," *Jerusalem Post*, February 19, 2004.

40. Extract from Euromed synopsis 270 http://europa.eu.int/comm/external_relations/euromed/synopsis/synopsis270_fr.pdf.

41. High-Level Advisory Group, *Dialogue Between Peoples and Cultures*, 3.

42. Ibid.

43. Israeli, *Islamikaze*, 350, see the chapter "The Western War against Islamikaze" and its subsection "The Rising Danger of Domestic Islam in the West."

44. High-Level Advisory Group, *Dialogue Between Peoples and Cultures*, 18.

45. Ibid., 19

46. Ibid., 24.

47. Ibid., 26

48. Ibid., 29.

49. Ibid., 29.

50. Ibid., 32.

51. Alan Cowell, "Britain to Tighten Immigration Rules for Eastern Laborers," *IHT*, February 24, 2004. Britain was among the last countries of the EU to adopt this measure. However, European politicians continuously evoke the need for immigration.

52. Yehia Abu Zakaria, "Who killed Anna Lindh?," Stockholm, September 14, 2003, IslamOnline.net.

53. Wolfram Reiss, "La Représentation du Christianisme dans les Manuels Scolaires Egyptiens."

54. Center for Monitoring the Impact of Peace. Report: *Jews, Christians, War and Peace in Egyptian School Textbooks*, compiled, translated and edited by Dr. Arnon Groiss, 2004, www .edume.org; see also "Antisémitisme et négationisme dans le monde arabo-musulman: la dérive," Centre de Documentation Juive Contemporaine, Paris, 2004; Association for World Education, "Jihad & Martyrdom as taught in Egyptian primary/preparatory/secondary school text books," written statement submitted by the Association of World Education to the UN Sub-Committee on Human Rights, 56th session (July 23–August 13), E/CN.4/Sub.2/2004/NGO/27, and oral statement on August 10, 2004. It was published on Frontpage Magazine, October 1, 2004, www.fronpagemag.com/Articles/Printable.asp?ID = 15302.

Conclusion

1. *BBC NEWS* Europe, "Spain proposes cultural alliance," September 23, 2004.

2. Tariq Ramadan, "Critique des (nouveaux) intellectuels communautaires," Oumma .com, October 3, 2003. On Ramadan, see Del Valle, *Le Totalitarisme,* 160–69; 258–59; Spencer, *Onward Muslim Soldiers,* 63–69.

3. Associated Press, January 9, 2004.

4. *Le Figaro,* November 7, 2003.

5. Melanie Phillips, "The Moral Bankruptcy of the Church of England," June 30, 2004, www.melaniephillips.com/diary. See Will Cummins's article in the *Telegraph* on July 7, 2004. Cummins mentions the joint letter of the Archbishop of Canterbury, Dr. Rowan Williams, with the Archbishop of York, Dr. David Hope, to Prime Minister Tony Blair criticizing his policy on Iraq and the "Holy Land." On this last point, he criticized the Christian Zionists for their "interpretations of the Scriptures from outside the mainstream of the tradition," who "were fostering an uncritical and one-sided approach to the future of the Holy Land." He writes that many clergymen "have been working with Islamic leaders" and that "double standards" weaken Western governments. Maybe for the archbishop the mainstream interpretation means that the West should work with Islamic leaders to destroy Israel, a policy now openly advocated.

Bibliography

Abrams, Elliott, ed. *The Influence of Faith: Religious Groups and U.S. Foreign Policy.* Washington DC: Ethics and Public Policy Center and Rowman & Littlefield, 2001.

Abu Zakariya, Yehia. "Who killed Anna Lindh?" Stockholm, Sept. 14, 2003, Islam online.net.

Afshari, Reza. *Human Rights in Iran. The Abuse of Cultural Relativism,* Philadelphia: University of Pennsylvania Press, 2001.

Alexandrescu-Dersca, Maria-Mathilda. "Le Rôle des Esclaves en Roumanie Turque au XVe siècle." *Byzantinische Forschungen* 2 (1987): 15–28.

Arnaldez, Roger. "La Guerre Sainte selon Ibn Hazm de Cordou." In *Etudes d'Orientalisme dédiées à la mémoire de Lévi-Provençal,* 2 vols., 2:445–59. Paris: Maisonneuve & Larose, 1962.

Arnoni, M. S. *Le Nationalisme Arabe et les Nazis.* Tel-Aviv: August 1970.

Aron, Raymond. *De Gaulle, Israël et les Juifs.* Paris: Plon, 1968.

Arte. "Le 11 Septembre n'a pas eu lieu . . . ; Le grand complot; Tous manipulés." April 13 (8:45pm), 2004.

Ateek, Naim Stifan. *Justice and Only Justice: A Palestinian Theology of Liberation.* Maryknoll, N.Y.: Orbis Books, 1989.

Ahlmark, Per. "Combatting Anti-Semitism Now and in the Past." *Justice* 34 (Winter 2002): 6–8.

Ayalon, David. *The Mamluke Military Society.* London: Variorum Reprints, 1979.

al-Azhar (Academy of Islamic Research). *The Fourth Conference of the Academy of Islamic Research.* English ed. Cairo: General Organization for Government Printing, 1970.

al-Baghawi, *Mishkat Al-Massabih,* see Robson.

Balakian, Peter. *The Burning Tigris. The Armenian Genocide and America's Response.* New York: HarperCollins, 2003.

Barnabas Fund. "News from the Holy Land, Muslim Convert Butchered." www .barnabasfund.org/Apostasy.htm.

Bat Ye'or. "L'antisionisme euro-arabe." In Collectif d'auteurs, *[nouveaux] visages de l'antisémitisme, haine – passion ou haine historique?,* 23-70. Paris: NM7 éditions, 2001.

———. "Euro-Arab Anti-Zionism" [French, 2001, above]. Translated by Nidra Poller. In Spencer, Robert, ed. *The Myth of Islamic Tolerance.* Part 4, ch. 4.

———. "La 'compassion' assassine." *Observatoire du monde juif* 6/7 (June 2003): 14–18. English translation at www.dhimmitude.org.

———. "Les déchirures des Chrétiens d'Orient." *Observatoire du monde juif* 6/7 (June 2003): 24–26.

———. *The Decline of Eastern Christianity under Islam. From Jihad to Dhimmitude.*

Seventh-Twentieth Century. [French, 1991] Translated by Miriam Kochan and David Littman with a foreword by Jacques Ellul. Madison, NJ: Fairleigh Dickinson University Press, 1996.

―――. *The Dhimmi: Jews and Christians under Islam.* [French 1980] Translated by David Maisel, Paul Fenton, and David Littman. With a preface by Jacques Ellul. Revised and enlarged English edition. Rutheford, NJ: Fairleigh Dickinson University Press, 1985.

―――. "Le dialogue Euro-Arabe et la naissance d'Eurabia." *Observatoire du monde juif* 4/5 (December 2002): 44–55. English translation: "The Euro-Arab Dialogue and the Birth of Eurabia" at http://www.dhimmitude.org/d_today_dhim mitude_issues.php.

―――. "Eurabia and Euro-Arab Antisemitism." FrontPageMagazine.com, April 5, 2004.

―――. "Eurabia, the Road to Munich." National Revue on Line, October 9, 2002.

―――. "European Fears of the Gathering Jihad." FrontPageMagazine.com, February 21, 2003.

―――. *Islam and Dhimmitude: Where Civilizations Collide.* Madison, NJ: Fairleigh Dickinson University Press, 2002.

―――. "Juifs et Chrétiens sous l'islam. Dhimmitude et Marcionisme." *Commentaire* (Paris), 25, no. 97. (Spring 2002): 105–16. English translation at http://www. dhimmitude.org/archive/by_dhimmitude_ marcionism_en.pdf

―――. "Myths and Politics: the tolerant pluralistic Islamic society: origin of a myth." Lecture at Lord Byron Foundation for Balkan Studies, The International Strategic Studies Association, Symposium on the Balkan war: Yugoslavia: Past and Present, August 31, 1995. www.dhimmitude.org/archive/LectureE1.html.

―――. With Paul Marshall, Habib Malik and Walid Phares. Moderator: James Glazov. Symposium: *The Muslim Persecution of Christians,* October 10, 2003, FrontPage Magazine.com.

Beau, Nicolas. *Paris, Capitale Arabe.* Paris: Seuil, 1995.

Becker, Jillian. *The PLO: The Rise and Fall of the Palestine Liberation Organization.* London: Weidenfeld & Nicolson, 1984.

Benoit, Bertrand. "Bertrand Benoit in Berlin." *Financial Times,* November 22, 2003.

Beres, Louis René and Michael L. Messing, "What happens to the 'merely Wounded'. The radiology of suicide bombing terrorism," January 27, 2004. israpundit.com/archives/004492.html.

Besançon, Alain. *Le Malheur du siècle. Sur le communisme, le nazisme et l'unicité de la Shoah.* Paris: Fayard, 1998.

Bewley, Aisha Addarrahman. Trans. *Muhammad Messenger of Allah. Ash-Shifa of Qadi 'Iyad.* Granada: Medinah Press, 1999.

Bloch, Charles. *Le IIIe Reich et le monde.* Notre Siècle, edited by J.-B. Durselle. Paris: Imprimerie Nationale, 1986.

Bodansky, Yossef. *Bin Laden: The Man Who Declared War on America.* New York: Random House, 1999.

Bostom, Andrew G. "Endowing Denial." FrontPageMagazine.com, May 13, 2003.

―――. "Khaled Abou El Fadl: Reformer or Revisionist?" http://www.secularislam .org/articles/bostom.htm.

————. *The Legacy of Jihad. Islamic Holy War and the fate of non-Muslims.* Amherst, NY: Prometheus Books, 2005.

Bourrinet, Jacques, ed. *Le Dialogue Euro-Arabe.* Paris: Economica, 1979.

Boyer, Alain. *L'Islam en France.* Paris: Presses Universitaires de France, 1998.

Brearley, Margaret. "Bi-focal Vision: Israel and the Intifada in the British Press." In *Antisemitism International, 2003,* 47–53. Vidal Sassoon International Center for the Study of Antisemitism, Jerusalem: Hebrew University, December 2003.

Brenner, Emmanuel. "La tentation d'une libération de la parole antisémite." *Observatoire du monde juif* 4/5 (December 2002), 23–30.

————. (Under the direction of) *Les territoires perdus de la République. Antisémitisme, racisme et sexisme en milieu scolaire.* 2002. Reprint, Paris: Mille et une Nuits, 2004.

————. *"France, prends garde de perdre ton âme . . ." Fracture sociale et antisémitisme dans la République.* Paris: Mille et une Nuits, 2004.

Brenner, Marie, "Daughters of France, Daughters of Allah," *Vanity Fair,* April 2004, 109–209.

Bridel, Bernard. "Pour Jacques Delors, l'islam fait aussi partie des valeurs européennes." *Le Temps,* Oct. 11, 2003.

Browne, Anthony. "Britain on the Brink." *London Times,* January 28, 2003.

Bumiller, Elisabeth. "Bush Faces a Hostile Reception in Ireland." *IHT,* June 26, 2004.

Burchill, Julie. "Beyond the Facts. Good, Bad and Ugly." *Guardian,* November 29, 2003.

Burns, John F. "Palestinian ends case with message." *IHT,* Sept. 30, 2003.

Busse, Heribert. *Islam, Judaism, and Christianity: Theological and Historical Affiliations.* Translated from the German by Alison Brown. Princeton Series on the Middle East. Princeton: Markus Wiener Publishers, 1998.

Butler, Desmond. "Europe-wide Network Enlists Fighters for Iraq." *New York Times,* December 6, 2003.

Centre de Documentation Juive Contemporaine. *Antisémitisme et négationisme dans le monde arabo-musulman: la dérive.* Paris, 2004.

Center for Monitoring the Impact of Peace (CMIP), see Groiss.

Churchill, Charles. *The Druzes and the Maronites under Turkish Rule from 1840 to 1860.* With an Introduction by Robin Bidwell (1993). Reading England: Garnett Publishing, 1994. (Original ed. London: Bernard Quaritch, 1862).

Commission Biblique Pontificale. *Le Peuple Juif et ses Saintes Ecritures dans la Bible Chrétienne.* Preface by Cardinal Joseph Ratzinger. Paris: Le Cerf, 2001.

Commission for Religous Relations with the Jews. See Kasper, Cardinal Walter.

Commission of the European Communities. Communication from the Commission to the Council and the European Parliament: "Reinvigorating EU actions on Human Rights and democratisation with Mediterranean partners, Strategic guidelines." COM (2003) 294 final, Brussels, May 21, 2003. http://europa.eu.int/comm/external_relations/human_rights/doc/com03_294.pdf.

————. Communication from the Commission to the Council and the European Parliament, to prepare the VI Meeting of Euro-Mediterranean Ministers of Foreign Affairs, Naples, 2–3 December 2003 (Barcelona VI). Brussels, October 15, 2003. COM (2003) 610 final.

————. Report by the Commission on the behaviour of the oil companies in the

Community during the period from October 1973 to March 1974. 1976 (series 26).

———. Report by the High-Level Advisory Group established at the initiative of the President of the European Commission, *Dialogue Between Peoples and Cultures in the Euro-Mediterranean Area*. Version DEF, Brussels, October 2003.

Constantelos, Demetrios J. "The Moslem Conquest of the Near East as Revealed in the Greek Sources of the Seventh and Eight Centuries." *Byzantion* 42 (1972): 325–57.

Council of Europe, Parliamentary Assembly. *The Contribution of the Islamic Civilisation to European Culture*. Strasbourg, 1992. Doc. 6497.

Council of the European Union. "Strengthening the European Partnership with the Arab World." http://www.ueitalia2003.it/NR/rdonlyres/72193E5B-19DB-455E-8F66-915B561E6563/0/1212 DocSolanaMondoArabo_en.pdf.

Cowell, Alan. "Britain to Tighten Immigration Rules for Eastern Laborers." *IHT*, February 24, 2004.

Cox, Caroline, and John Marks. *The "West," Islam and Islamism: Is Ideological Islam Compatible with Liberal democracy?* London: Civitas, 2003.

Cragg, Kenneth. *The Arab Christian: A History of the Middle East*. London: Mowbray, 1992.

Cummins, Will. *Telegraph*, July 7, 2004.

Curtis, Michael. *Verdict on Vichy: Power and Prejudice in the Vichy France Regime*. New York: Arcade Publishing, 2002.

Cvijic, Jovan. *La Péninsule Balkanique: Géographie Humaine*. Paris: Armand Colin, 1918.

Davis, Douglas. "Documents Show British Official in Jerusalem Urged Understanding of Munich Massacre." Jpost.com, January 1, 2003.

Delacampagne, Christian. "L'Antisémitisme en France (1945–1993)." In *Histoire de l'Antisémitisme 1945–1993*, dir. Léon Poliakov, 121–64. Paris: Seuil, 1994.

Delcambre, Anne-Marie. *L'Islam des Interdits*. Paris: Desclée de Brouwer, 2003.

Delfiner, Henry. "The Socialist International and the Rise of Yasir Arafat." *Midstream* (Nov.–Dec. 2002): 4–8.

Del Valle, Alexandre. "L'Islamisation de l'Intifada ou le fondement religieux du conflit israélo-palestinien." *Le Lien*, no. 181, Supplément, I–VIII, March 15, 2002.

———. "Stratégies islamistes et nouvelle judéophobie en Europe." *Observatoire du monde juif* 4/5 (December 2002): 17–30.

———. *Le Totalitarisme islamiste à l'assaut des démocraties*. With a preface by Rachid Kaci. Paris: Editions des Syrtes, 2002.

Dobson, Christopher. *Black September. Its Short: Violent History*. London: Robert Hale, 1974 & 1975.

Documents d'Actualité Internationale. Direction de la Documentation française, Ministère des Affaires Etrangères.

———. "Conférence des Chefs d'Etat Arabes (Alger, 26–29 novembre 1973) Déclaration de politique Générale (Alger, 28 novembre 1973)." No. 7, 1974.

———. "Conseil Européen (London, 29–30 June 1977)." 137. Déclaration des Neuf sur le Moyen-Orient (June 29, 1977) N° 35, September 2, 1977.

Douglass, Susan L. *Strategies and Structures for Presenting World History with Islam and*

Muslim History as a Case Study. The Council on Islamic Education. Beltsville, Md.: Amana Publications, 1994.

Dufourcq, Charles-Emmanuel. "Berbérie et Ibérie médiévales: un problème de rupture." *Revue Historique* 92 (Paris, 1968): 293–324.

———. "Le christianisme dans les pays de l'Occident musulman des alentours de l'an mil jusqu'aux temps almohades." In *Etudes de Civilisation Médiévale (IX–XII siècles). Mélanges offerts à Edmond-René Labande,* 237–46. Poitiers: CESCM, 1974.

———. "Les Mozarabes du XIIè siècle et le prétendu 'Evêque' de Lisbonne." In *Revue d'Histoire et de Civilisation du Maghreb,* 5 (1968), 125–30. Algiers: Faculté des Lettres d'Alger.

———. "A Propos de l'Espagne catalane et le Maghreb aux XIIIe et XIVe sièles." In *RHCM,* 2 (1967), 32–53.

———. *La Vie Quotidienne dans l'Europe Médiévale sous Domination Arabe.* Paris: Hachette, 1978.

Durie, Mark. "Yes Amrozi, we do remember Khaibar." *Quadrant,* November 2003.

———. "Isa, the Muslim Jesus." See answering-islam.org/Intro/islamic_jesus.html.

———. "What is happening in Indonesia." See www.anglicanmedia.com.au/old/2002/401.html.

Ehrenfeld, Rachel. "EuroCash. What does the Palestinian Authority do with European money?" *NRO,* December 10, 2003.

———. "Funding Evil: How Terrorism is Financed and How to Stop It." FrontPage-Magazine.com, January 15, 2004.

Elliott, H. M., and John Dowson. *History of India As Told By Its Own Historians—The Muhammadan Period.* 8 vols. London, 1867–77.

Ellul, Jacques. *Islam et judéo-christianisme.* Preface by Alain Besançon. Paris: Presses Universitaires de France, 2004.

Elpeleg, Zvi. *The Grand Mufti Haj Amin al-Hussaini, Founder of the Palestinian National Movement.* London: Frank Cass, 1993.

Engelhardt, Edouard. *La Turquie et le Tanzimat ou Histoire des Réformes dans l'Empire Ottoman depuis 1826 jusqu'à nos jours.* Paris: Librairie Cotillon & Librairie Conseil d'Etat, vol. 1, 1882, vol. 2, 1884.

Esposito, John L. *Islam: The Straight Path.* Oxford: Oxford University Press, 1994.

———. *The Islamic Threat. Myth or Reality?* Oxford: Oxford University Press, 1992.

Etienne, Bruno. *La France et l'islam.* Paris: Hachette, 1989.

Euromed Report. No. 71 +, December 12, 2003.

Euromed Synopsis. No. 248, November 13, 2003. http://europa.eu.int/comm/external_relations/euromed/bd.htm.> [check Euromed Synopsis, N° 270, <http://europa.eu.int/comm/external_relations/euromed/synopsis/synopsis 270 _fr.pdf [chap. 18].

Euro-Mediterranean Conference of Ministers of Foreign Affairs, Naples, December 2–3, 2003. Presidency Conclusions. http://www.ueitalia2003.it/NR/rdonlyres/D33FB0C7-4B19-4F4D-B9FB-1003734AC33 9/0/1202ConclusionsEuromed_EN_.pdf.

Euro-Mediterranean Parliamentary Forum (Brussels). Final Declaration. October 27–28, 1998.

Euro-Mediterranean Study Commission (EuroMeSCo). *Eastern Enlargement and the Euro-Mediterranean Partnership: A Win-Win Game?* Paper 20, February 2003.

European Council. Presidency Conclusions. (Brussels, 12 December 2003). http:// ue.eu.int/pressData/ en/ec/78364.pdf.

European Cultural Foundation. *Beyond Enlargement: Opening Eastwards, Closing Southwards?* Toledo, November 13–16, 2003. beyond_enlargement.pdf.

European Institute for Research on Mediterranean and Euro-Arab Cooperation (MEDEA). MEDEA's information files. "Euro-Arab University." www.Medea.be.

———. MEDEA's information files. "Euro-Mediterranean Forum, Final Declaration (1st meeting, Brussels, October 1998)." www.Medea.be.

———. MEDEA's information files. "Pressure on Israel (by the Western World)." www.Medea.be.

———. "Syrian FM Talks to Euro-Arab Parliamentary Meeting on Middle East Developments." Syria-Regional, Politics, 7/13/1998. www.arabicnews.com/ansub/ Daily/Day/980713/1998071308.html.

———. "Venice Declaration and Euro-Arab Dialogue." www.Medea.be.

el Fadl, Khaled Abou. "The Rules of Killing at War: an Inquiry into Classical Sources." *Muslim World* 89, no. 2 (April 1999): 144–57.

Fallacci, Oriana. *The Rage and the Pride.* New York: Rizzoli, 2002.

———. *La Forza della Ragione.* New York: Rizzoli, 2004.

———. *Oriana Fallaci intervista Oriana Fallaci.* Milan: Corriere della Sera, 2004.

al-Faruqi, Isma'il Raji. *Al Tawhid: Its Implications for Thought and Life.* Islamization of Knowledge Series no. 4. 1982. Reprint, Herndon, VA: International Islamic Publishing House and Institute of Islamic Thought, 1995.

———. *Islam and Other Faiths.* Edited by Ataullah Siddiqui. With a foreword by John Esposito. Herndon, VA: The Islamic Foundation, The International Institute of Islamic Thought, 1998.

———. "Islam and Other Faiths." In *Seminar of the Islamic-Christian Dialogue.* Tripoli: Popular Office of Foreign Relations, Socialist Peoples Libyan Arab Jamahiriya, 1981.

Fattal, Antoine. *Le Statut Légal des Non-Musulmans en Pays d'Islam.* Beirut: Imprimerie Catholique, 1958.

Ferdinand, Pamela. "Harvard Student Gives Speech Citing 'Jihad.'" *Washington Post,* p. A03, June 7, 2002. *New York Times Magazine,* April 4, April 2004.

Ferguson, Niall. *Colossus: The Price of America's Empire.* London: Penguin, 2004.

———. "The End of Power." *Wall Street Journal Europe,* June 21, 2004.

———. "EURABIA?" *New York Times Magazine,* April 4, 2004.

Fishman, Shammai. "Ideological Islam in the United States: 'Ijtihad' in the Thought of Dr. Taha Jabin al-Alwani" trans. from Hebrew by Tsemah Yoreh (*Jamaa* 11 (2003), Ben Gurion University) Beer Sheva www.e-prism.org.

Frankel, Jonathan. *The Damascus Affair: "Ritual Murder," Politics and the Jews in 1840.* Cambridge: Cambridge University Press, 1997.

Fregosi, Paul. *Jihad in the West. Muslim Conquests From the Seventh to the Twenthy-first Centuries.* New York: Prometheus Books, 1998.

Frémeaux, Jacques. *Le Monde Arabe et la Sécurité de la France depuis 1958.* Politique d'Aujourd'hui. Paris: Presses Universitaires de France, 1995.

Fuller, Thomas. "Anti-Semitism infuses French debate on scarves." *IHT,* Feb. 11, 2004.

———. "European poll calls Israel a big threat to world peace." *IHT*, October 31, 2003.

de Gasperis, Rossi. "La Shoah spirituale attuata dagli arabocristiani" www.chiesa; http://213.92.16.98/ESW_articolo/0,2393,32295,00.html.

Geismar, Alain. *L'engrenage terroriste.* Paris: Fayard, 1981.

Gerstenfeld, Manfred. *Europe's Crumbling Myths. The Post-Holocaust, Origins of Today's Anti-Semitism.* Foreward by Emile L. Fackenheim. Jerusalem: Jerusalem Center for Public Affairs, 2003.

Gil, Moshe. *A History of Palestine, 634–1099.* Translated from Hebrew by Ethel Broido. Revised ed. Cambridge: Cambridge University Press, 1992.

Gilbert, Martin. *Second World War.* London: Weidenfeld & Nicolson, 1989.

Gjellerod, Henning. Speech. At PAEAC, MEDEA site.

Gold, Dore. *Hatred's Kingdom. How Saudi Arabia Supports the New Global Terrorism.* Washington DC: Regnery, 2003.

Groiss, Arnon, compiler, trans., and ed. *Report: Jews, Christians, War and Peace in Egyptian School Textbooks.* New York/Jerusalem: Center for Monitoring the Impact of Peace (CMIP) 2004. www.edume.org.

———. *The West, Christians and Jews in Saudi Arabian Schoolbooks.* New York/Jerusalem: CMIP, January 2003. www.edume.org

Haque, Amber, ed. *Muslims and Islamization in North America: Problems & Prospects.* Maryland: Amada Publications and A.S. Noordeen, 1999.

Harkabi, Yehoshafat. *Palestinians and Israel.* Jerusalem: Keter Publishing House, 1974.

Harvey, Leonard Patrick. *Islamic Spain, 1250 to 1500.* Chicago: University of Chicago Press, 1990 [paperback, 1992].

Hayek, Michel. *Le Christ de l'Islam.* Texts presented, translated and with notes by Michel Hayek. Paris: Seuil, 1959.

Healy, Patrick. *Boston Globe,* A1, February 20, 2003.

Heisbourg, François. "L'Europe sous la menace d'un terrorisme de destruction massive." *Le Temps,* Geneva, June 21, 2004.

Hertoghe, Alain. *La Guerre à Outrance. Comment la presse nous a désinformés sur l'Irak.* Paris: Calmann-Lévy, 2003.

Hirszowicz, Lukacs. *The Third Reich and the Arab East.* London: Routledge & Kegan Paul; Toronto: University of Toronto Press, 1966.

Hogendorn, Jan. "The Hideous Trade: Economic Aspects of the 'Manufacture' and Sale of Eunuchs." *Paideuma* 45 (1999), 137–160 (Goethe University, Frankfurt).

Holland, Martin. *The European Union and the Third World.* New York: Palgrave, 2002.

Hopwood, Derek, ed. English version. *Euro-Arab Dialogue. The relations between the two cultures. Acts of the Hamburg symposium, April 11th to 15th 1983.* London: Croom Helm, 1983.

House of Commons International Development Committee, *Development Assistance and the Occupied Palestinian Territories,* Second Report of Session 2003–04, Volume 1, HC 230–I [incorporating HC 1107–i to–iv, Session 2002–03]. http://www.parliament.the-stationery-office.co.uk/pa/cm200304/cmselect/ cmintdev/230/230.pdf.

Huntington, Samuel P. *The Clash of Civilizations and the Remaking of World Order.* New York: Simon & Schuster, 1996; London: Free Press, Simon & Schuster, 2002.

Hussey, Andrew. "Profile Tariq Ramadan." *New Statesman,* June 21, 2004.

Institute of Jewish Affairs, *Pattern of Prejudice.* London, May–June 1967.

Institute for the Study of Islam and Christianity (ISIC). *Calls for Jihad Widespread in Islamic World,* London: ISIC Briefing. No. 18, April 18, 2003.

Isaac, Frederick P. *Indigenous Peoples under the Rule of Islam.* USA: Xlibris Corporation, 2002.

Isaac, Jules. *Genèse de l'antisémitisme.* Paris: Calmann-Lévy, 1956.

Israeli, Raphael. *Islamikaze: Manifestation of Islamic Martyrology.* London: Cass, 2003.

James, Barry. "France steps up efforts to smooth things over." *IHT,* April 17, 2003.

Jelinek, Pauline. "US, Spanish Officials Spar on Iraq, Terrorism." *Boston Globe,* March 18, 2004.

Johnson, David W., ed. *Acts of the Fifth International Congress of Coptic Studies, Washington, 12–15 August 1992.* Vol. 2, Papers from the Sections, part 2. Rome: International Association for Coptic Studies, C.I.M., 1993.

Juster, Jean. *Les Juifs dans l'Empire Romain. Leur Condition Juridique, Economique et Sociale.* Paris: 2 vols. Paul Geuthner, 1914.

Kaltenbach, Jeanne-Hélène, and Michèle Tribalat. *La République et l'Islam. Entre crainte et aveuglement.* Paris: Gallimard, 2002.

Kasper, Walter. Cardinal. "Anti-semitism: A wound to be healed." In *Osservatore Romano* English Weekly Edition (Vatican City), no. 40, October 1, 2003, 6. See Commission for Religious Relations with the Jews.

Kedourie, Elie. "Going Third World à la Française." *MEQ* (Summer 2004) 65–68.

Keinon, Herb. "Europe pressing U.S. on Israeli settlements." JPonline edition, Aug. 4, 2004.

Kertzer, David I. *Unholy War: The Vatican's Role in the Rise of Modern Anti-Semitism.* London: Macmillan, 2002.

Khadduri, Majid. *The Islamic Law of Nations (Shaybani's Siyar),* Baltimore: Johns Hopkins University Press, 1965.

Khalidi, Tarif. ed. and trans., *The Muslim Jesus: Sayings and Stories in Islamic Literature.* Convergences: Inventories of the Present, ed. Edward W. Said. Cambridge, MA: Harvard University Press, 2001.

Knobel, Marc. "Les agressions anti-juives." *Observatoire du monde juif* 1 (November 2001), 17–21.

———. "Les sites internet musulmans francophones." *Observatoire du monde juif* 4/5 (December 2002): 2–6.

Knowlton, Brian. "Saying U.S. approach to Syria isn't working EU seeks cooperation." *IHT,* Oct. 10, 2003.

———. "U.S. officials soften criticism of Syria." *IHT,* April 16, 2003.

Kosmin, Barry, and Paul Iganski. "Israel in the British Press: Crossing the Line from Criticism to Bigotry." *IHT,* September 8, 2003.

Kramer, Martin. *Ivory Towers on Sand: The Failure of Middle Eastern Studies in America.* Washington, DC: Washington Institute for Near East Policy, 2001.

von Küntzel, Matthias. "Islamic Terrorism and Anti-Semitism: The Mission against Modernity." Presentation at the University of Yale conference on "Genocide and Terrorism—Probing the Mind of the Perpetrator," April 11, 2003.

Laffin, John. *The PLO Connection: How Has the Wealthiest, Most Bloodthirsty Terrorist*

Organisation in the World Become Accepted—even Respectable? London: Gorgi Book, 1982.

Lal, K. S. *The Legacy of Muslim Rule in India.* New Delhi: Aditya Prakashan, 1992.

———. *Theory and Practice of Muslim State in India.* New Delhi: Aditya Prakashan, 1999.

Laurent, Henry. "Le Mufti et la France de la IVe République." *Revue d'Etudes Palestiniennes* 81 (Autumn 2001): 70–85.

Laurent, Joseph. *Byzance et les Turcs Seldjoucides dans l'Asie Occidentale jusqu'en 1081.* Nancy: Berger-Levrault, 1913 [1919].

Leibovich-Dar, Sara. "Brain damage." *Haaretz Magazine.* Nov. 21, 2003.

Leonard, Tom. "Christians 'Are Easiest Target for TV Satire.'" *Telegraph.* Filed December 29, 2003.

Lévy-Provençal, Evariste. *Histoire de l'Espagne Musulmane.* Vol. 1. Paris: Maisonneuve, 1950.

———. *Séville musulmane au début du XIIè siècle. Le traité sur la vie urbaine et les corps de métiers d'Ibn Abdun.* Translated from Arabic with notes. Vol. 2. Islam d'hier et d'aujourdshui. 1947. Paris: Maisonneuve 1948.

Ligue des Etats Arabes (Délégation Permanente), *Bulletin d'information* 7 (Geneva, May 1, 1970), article 3: 6–7: "Pour la Vérité et la Justice. La Conférence des Chrétiens pour la Palestine."

———. "Le directeur de 'Témoignage Chrétien' dénonce la propagande sioniste." 15 (November 30, 1970).

Littman, David G. "The Forgotten Refugees. An Exchange of Populations." December 3, 2002, www.nationalreview.com/comment/comment-littman/20302.asp; in UN document, E/CN.4/Sub.2/2003/NGO/35 (July 17, 2003) for Sub-Commission on Human Rights (2003), www.unhcr./ch/Huridocda/Huriodoca.nsf/ (Symbol)/E.CN.4.Sub.2.2003.NGO.35.En? Open document.

———. "Islamism Grows Stronger at the U.N." *Middle East Quarterly* (September 1999) 59–64. See also in Spencer, *The Myth of Islamic Tolerance,* Part 5, "Human Rights and Human Wrongs at the United Nations," chapter 1.

———. "Islamists' Perpetual Jihad." Oral statement delivered to the UN Sub-Commission on Human Rights (Geneva) for the World Union for Progressive Judaism on August 12, 2003. FrontPageMagazine.com. August 15, 2003. www .frontpagemag.com/articles/Printable.asp?ID=9393.

———. "Universal Human Rights and 'Human Rights in Islam'" *Midstream* (Feb.–March 1999) 2–7. See also in Spencer, *The Myth of Islamic Tolerance.* Part 5, ch. 2.

———. See Wadlow

della Loggia, Ernesto Galli. "The non-Existent Crusade." Editorial, *Corriere della Sera,* Milan, April 6, 2003.

Lyautey, Pierre. "Le nouveau rôle de la France en Orient." Comptes rendus des Séances de l'Académie des Sciences d'Outre-Mer, Paris, May 4, 1962.

MacFarquhar, Neil. "Arab States Start Plan of Their Own Mideast." *IHT,* March 4, 2004.

Magister, Sandro. "Bush and God: A Puzzle for the Church in Europe." www .chiesa. March 31, 2003.

———. "Is Europe a Province of Islam? The Danger is Called Dhimmitude." www .chiesa; http://213.92.16.98/ESW_articolo/0,2393, 41028,00.html.

———. "The Church and Islam. "La Civiltà Cattolica" Breaks the Ceasefire." http://213.92.16.98/ESW_stampa_articolo/1,2400,41931,00.html.

Malek, Nabil A. "The Copts: From an Ethnic Majority to a Religious Minority." In *Acts of the Fifth International Congress of Coptic Studies*, ed. David W. Johnson, vol. 2, Papers from the Sections, part 2, 299–311. Washington, August 12–15, 1992. Rome: International Association for Coptic Studies, C.I.M., 1993.

Malik, Habib C. "The Arab Christian: A History in the Middle East." (Book Reviews). *The Beirut Review* 3 (Spring 1992): 109–22.

———. *Between Damascus and Jerusalem: Lebanon and Middle East Peace*. Washington DC: Washington Institute for Near East Policy, 1997.

———. "Christians in the Land Called Holy." *First Thing* 89 (January 1999).

———. "Political Islam and the Roots of Violence." In Abrams, *Influence of Faith*, 113–48.

al-Mani, Saleh A. *The Euro-Arab Dialogue. A Study in Associative Diplomacy*. Edited by Salah Al-Shaikhly. London: Frances Pinter, 1983.

Maoz, Moshe, ed. *Studies on Palestine During the Ottoman Period*. Jerusalem. Magnes Press, 1975.

Marshall, Paul. "Bethlehem and Beyond." *NRO,* December 24, 2003.

———. "World Silence over Slain Muslims." *Boston Globe,* October 13, 2003.

———. See Bat Ye'or. Symposium.

Masriya, Yahudiya [Bat Ye'or]. *Les Juifs en Egypte*. Geneva: Editions de l'Avenir, 1971.

Mauksch, Mary, et al. *Energy and Europe: EEC Energy Policy and Economy in the Context of the World Energy Crisis*. Brussels: European News Agency, vol.1, Feb. 1975; vol. 2 in collaboration with Pol Carrewyn and Christopher Redman, 1975.

Mawardi, Abu'l Hasan. *Al-Ahkam as-Sultaniyyah. The Laws of Islamic Governance*. Translated by Asadullah Yate. London: Ta-Ha Publishers, 1996.

McCallum, Mark. "Muslim Call to Thwart Capitalism." Story from BBC News, July 12, 2003.

Messing, Michael L. See Beres.

Meyer, Ilya. "Whither the White Buses?" *International Jerusalem Post,* July 2, 2004.

Meyer, Thierry. "Les musulmans britanniques appelés par leurs pairs à combattre le terrorisme." *Le Temps,* Geneva, April 1, 2004.

Middle East Media Research Institute (MEMRI). "Egypt/Reform Project." *MEMRI,* SDS, 703, April 29, 2004.

———. "Excerpts from the 2 May 2003 Friday Sermon delivered by Sheikh Jamal Shakir Al-Nazzal." *MEMRI, SDS,* 500, May 6, 2003.

———. "Friday Sermons in Saudi Mosques: Review and Analysis." *MEMRI, Special Report,* 10, September 26, 2002.

———. "Jihad against the U.S.: Al-Azhar Conflicting Fatwas." *MEMRI, SDS,* 480, March 16, 2003.

———. "Reform in the Arab and Muslim World/Jihad and Terrorism. Official statement of July 4, 2002." *MEMRI, SDS,* 405, July 30, 2002.

———. "Saudi Opposition Sheikhs on America, Bin Laden, and Jihad," *MEMRI, SDS,* 400, July 18, 2002.

———. 2nd Issue of "Voice of Jihad Al-Qa'ida Online Magazine." *MEMRI, Special Dispatch—Jihad and Terrorism Studies,* October 31, 2003.

Milner, Jean-Claude. *Les Penchants Criminels de l'Europe démocratique.* Paris: Editions Verdier, 2004.

Milson, Menahem. "Reform vs. Islamism in the Arab World Today," *MEMRI,* Special Report No. 34 September 15, 2004.

Ministère des Affaires étrangères, Paris. Declaration of the Nine on The Middle East (London, June 29, 1977). Official Texts. See *Documents d'Actualité.*

Montefiore, Simon Sebag. "A Dangerous Time to Be a Jew." *New Statesman,* June 28, 2004. www.newstatesman.com/site.php3?newTemplate = NSArticle_World& newDisplay URN = 200406280017.

Morison, Antoine. *Relation Historique d'un voyage nouvellement fait au Mont Sinaï, et à Jerusalem. On trouvera dans cette relation un détail de ce que l'auteur a vu de plus remarquable en Egypte, en Arabie, . . . sur les côtes de Syrie et en Phoenicie . . . et le gouvernement politique de l'Empire ottoman, etc.* Paris: Antoine Dezallier, 1705.

Motyer, Steve. "Israel in God's Plan." In *Evangelical Alliance. Day Consultation on the Holy Land.* London, June 26, 2003.

Moubarac, Youakim. *L'Islam et le Dialogue Islamo-Chrétien, Pentalogie Islamo-Chrétienne.* Vol. 3. Beirut: Edition du Cénacle Libanais, 1972–73.

al-Muhajiroun. The Voice, The Eyes and The Ears of the Muslims. London. www.almu hajiroun.com.

Murdock, Deroy. "Saddam Hussein's Philanthropy of Terror." *American Outlook,* Fall 2003.

Mutahhari, Ayatullah Morteza. "The Quiddity of Jihad." In *Jihad The Holy War of Islam and its Legitimacy in the Quran.* Translated by Mohammad Salman Twhidi. 1985. http://www.aalulbayt.org/html/eng/books/jihad/3.htm.

van Natta Jnr., Don. See Tyler Patrick.

Nelson, Fraser. "The Poisonous Return of Anti-Semitism." TheScotsman.com., June 23, 2003.

Netanyahu, Benjamin, ed. *Terrorism: How the West Can Win.* London: Weidenfeld and Nicolson, 1986.

Nicholls, William. *Christian Antisemitism: A History of Hate.* Northvale, NJ: Jason Aronson Inc., 1995.

Nisan, Mordechai. *The Conscience of Lebanon. A Political Biography of Etienne Sakr (Abu-Arz).* London: Cass, 2003.

———. *Minorities in the Middle East: A History of Struggle and Self-Expression.* 1991. Reprint, Jefferson, N.C. North Carolina: McFarland, 2002.

Nugent, Neil. *The Government and Politics of the European Union.* New York: Palgrave Macmillan, 2003.

van Oosterzee, Jan Jaap. "Sharing Stories: Evaluation of the Euro-Arab Education Exchange Between Schools in Palestine and the Netherlands. 2000–2001." www .ikv.nl/ikv/docs/english/sharing-stories.html.

Parfitt, Tudor. *The Jews in Palestine, 1800–1882.* Studies in History, 52. London: Royal Historical Society, Boydell Press, 1987.

Parkes, James. *Antisemitism.* London: Valentine Mitchell, 1963.

———. *The Conflict of the Church and the Synagogue: A Study in the Origin of Antisemitism.* 1934. Reprint, New York: Atheneum, 1969.

Parliamentary Assembly of the Council of Europe. Resolution 1162, 1991.

———. Resolution 885, 1987.

———. Assembly debate on September 19, 1991. Text adopted (11th sitting). Document 6497, report of the Committee on Culture and Education, Rapporteur: Mr. de Puig. Recommendation 1162 (1991) on the Contribution of the Islamic civilisation to European culture.

Parliamentary Association for Euro-Arab Cooperation (PAEAC/APCEA). "Euro-Arab Parliamentary Dialogue, Damascus, 1998. Euro-Arab Dialogue." Documents PAEAC / MEDEA at www.medea.be/index.html

———. "PAEAC meets British Presidency of the EU, 29/4/1998." Documents PAEAC / MEDEA.

Patten, Christopher. SPEECH/01/49, European Parliament—Joint debate—Brussels, January 31, 2001. http://europa.eu.int/comm/external_relations/news/patten/speech_01_49 .htm.

Perelman, Marc. "E.U. Accused of Burying Report on Antisemitism Pointing to Muslim Role. Politics Trumped Truth, Scholar Charges." *Forward*, New York, November 28, 2003. www.forward.com/images/forward.mini.hed.gif.

Pew Research Center for the People and the Press. "A Year after Iraq War," March 16, 2004. http://people-press.org/reports/display.php3?ReportID = 206.

Pfaff, William. *IHT*, April 26–27, 2003.

Phares, Walid. *Lebanese Christian Nationalism: The Rise and Fall of an Ethnic Resistance.* Boulder, CO: Lynne Riener Publishers, 1995.

Phillips, Melanie. "London: A Leftist Axis of Anti Semitism." *Hadassah*, September 4, 2003.

———. "The Moral Bankruptcy of the Church of England." June 30, 2004. www .melaniephillips.com/diary.

———. "The New Anti-Semitism." *The Spectator*, March 22, 2003.

Pipes, Daniel. "Europe's Threat to the West." *New York Sun,* May 18, 2004.

———. "Harvard Loves Jihad." *New York Post,* June 11, 2002.

———. "Jihad and the Professors." *Commentary,* November 2002.

———. *Militant Islam Reaches America.* New York: W.W. Norton & Co., 2002.

———. "Think like a Muslim." *New York Post,* February 11, 2002.

———. "Muslims Love Bin Ladden." *New York Post,* October 22, 2002.

———. www.Campus-Watch.org.

Poller, Nidra. "Betrayed by Europe: An Expatriate's Lament." *Commentary* 117, no. 3 (March 2004): 21–29.

Pomerantz, Sherwin B. "Comment and Opinion." *Jerusalem Post,* December 1, 2003.

Prodi, Romano. "Sharing Stability and Prosperity." Speech at the Tempus Meda Regional Conference, Bibliotheca Alexandrina, Alexandria, October 13, 2003. Euromed Report, 66 EN.

de Puig, Lluis Maria. "Explanatory Memorandum." In *The Contribution of the Islamic Civilisation to European culture,* 13–17. Council of Europe. Parliamentary Assembly, Strasbourg, 1992.

Radler, Melissa. "View from the Left." *IJP*, December 26, 2003.

Rahmani, Moïse. *L'exode oublié. Juifs des pays arabes.* With a preface by Alexandre Del Valle. Paris: Raphaël, 2003.

Ramadan, Tariq. "Critique des (nouveaux) intellectuels communautaires." Oumma.com, October 3, 2003.

———. "Version Homme". *AP,* January 9, 2004.

Reiss, Wolfram. "La représentation du Christianisme dans les manuels scolaires en Egypte. Résultats d'une enquête et propositions pour des ameliorations." Rostock University, 2002. www.religioscope.com/dossiers/manuels/2002_01_reiss_a.htm and http://www.religioscope.com/pdf/manuels/Reiss.pdf.

Report on Islamic Summit 1974: Pakistan. Lahore, 22–24 February 1974, Karachi. 1974.

La Revue Copte. Vol.1, no. 3 (March 2004). www.copticpope.org/downloads/audio/qi6032004.zip.

Robson, James. *Mishkat Al-Massabih* [al-Baghawi]. Translated with explanatory notes by James Robson, 2 vols. SH. Muhammad Ashraf, Lahore, 1975.

Rosenbaum, Ron, ed. *Those Who Forget the Past: The Question of Anti-Semitism.* New York: Random House, May 2004.

Said, Edward W. *Orientalism.* London: Routledge & Kegan Paul, 1978.

Sallah 'Issa. Special Dispatch, in *Nahdat Misr.* January 14, 2004. See *MEMRI,* English translation, "Egypt Reform Project," No. 703, April 29, 2004.

Schemo, Diana Jean. "The Scientists." *IHT,* 5, July 2, 2003.

Schröder, Ilka. "Europe's Crocodile Tears." *Jerusalem Post,* February 19, 2004.

Schwartz, Adi. "Between Lesser and Greater Evils." *Haaretz Magazine,* November 21, 2003, 12–15.

Sciolino, Elaine. "Led by Muslims, peace rally again turns anti-Israeli." *IHT,* March 31, 2003.

———. "Mideast comes next. France and U.K. agree." *IHT,* April 10, 2003.

———. "The new anti-Semitism/Jews feel unsafe again. On French streets, Mideast fallout." *IHT,* December 4, 2003.

de la Serre, Françoise. "Conflit du Proche-Orient et Dialogue Euro-Arabe: La Position de l'Europe des Neuf." In Bourrinet, *Le Dialogue Euro-Arabe,* 79–94.

Second International Conference [in Support of the Arab Peoples], *Cairo 1969.*

Sela, Avraham, ed. "France, French Interests and Policies." In *Political Encyclopedia of the Middle East.* Jerusalem, 1999, 257–62.

Seminar of the Islamic-Christian Dialogue. Tripoli: Popular Office of Foreign Relations, Socialist Peoples Libyan Arab Jamahiriya, 1981.

Sewall, Gilbert. "Islam and the Textbooks." The American Textbook Council, 2003. http://www.historytextbooks.org/islamreport.pdf.

Shahid, Samuel. "Rights of non-Muslims in an Islamic state." In Robert Spencer, ed. *The Myth of Islamic Tolerance,* Part II, ch. 1.

Shulewitz, Malka Hillel, ed. *The Forgotten Millions: The Modern Jewish Exodus from Arab Lands.* New York: Continuum, 1999.

Simon, Catherine. "Les Répudiées de la République." *Le Monde,* June 11, 2004.

Simon, Marcel. *Verus Israel, Etudes sur les Relations entre Juifs et Chrétiens dans l'Empire Romain (135–425).* Paris: de Boccard, 1964. English translation: *Verus Israel. A Study of the Relations Between Christians and Jews in the Roman Empire (AD 135–425).* Translated by H. McKeating. Littman Library of Jewish Civilization. Oxford: Oxford University Press, 1986.

Simonet, Henri. In *Official Records of the General Assembly. Thirty-second Session. Plenary Meetings.* Vol. 1, 20 Sept.–13 Oct. 1977, United Nations, New York, 1978.

Sizer, Stephen. *Evangelical Alliance Consultation on the Holy Land, 26th June 2003,* London, 1–14; and http://www.sizer.org.

Smith, Craig S. "Maimed Bodies, Tortured Minds." *IHT,* April 25, 2003.

Sookhdeo, Patrick. *A People Betrayed: The Impact of Islamization on the Christian Community in Pakistan*. Pewsey, Scotland: Christian Focus Publications and Isaac Publishing, 2002.

———. *Understanding Islamic Terrorism: The Islamic Doctrine of War*. With a foreword by General Sir Hugh Beach. Pewsey, Scotland: Isaac Publishing, 2004.

Spencer, Robert, ed. *The Myth of Islamic Tolerance. How Islamic Law Treats non-Muslims* Prometheus Books, 2005.

———. *Onward Muslim Soldiers: How Jihad Still Threatens America and the West*. Washington, D.C.: Regnery, 2003.

Steinberg, Gerald M. "NGOs Make War on Israel." *MEQ* (Summer 2004) vol. 11:3, 13–25.

Sterling, Claire. *The Terror Network*. New York: Holt, Rinehart & Winston and Reader's Digest Press, 1981.

van der Stoel, Max. Report on the situation of human rights in Iraq for the year 1994 by UN Special Rapporteur in Iraq. E/CN. 4/ 1995/ 56. Commission on human rights, Geneva.

al-Tabari. *The History of al-Tabari (Ta'rikh al rusul wa'l-muluk)*. Vol. 12, *The Battle of al-Q ādisiyyah and the Conquest of Syria and Palestine*. Translated and annotated by Yohanan Friedmann. Edited by Ehsan Yar-Shater. Albany: State University of New York Press, 1992.

Taguieff, Pierre-André. *La nouvelle judéophobie*. Paris: Mille et une Nuits, 2002; English translation, see below *Rising from the Muck*.

———. *Prêcheurs de haine. Traversée de la Judéophobie planétaire*. Paris: Editions Fayard / Mille et une nuits, 2004.

———. *Les Protocoles des Sages de Sion*. 2 vols. Paris: Berg International, 1992.

———. *Rising from the Muck: The New Anti-Semitism in Europe*. Translated by Patrick Camiller. Chicago: Ivan R. Dee, 2004.

Tibawi, Abdel Latif. *Second Critique of English Speaking Orientalists and their Approach to Islam and the Arabs*. London: Islamic Cultural Center, 1979.

Tibi, Bassam. "War and Peace." In *Islamic Political Ethics: Civil Society, Pluralism, and Conflict,* edited by Sohail H. Hashmi with a foreword by Jack Miles, 175–93. Princeton: Princeton University Press, 2002.

Tribalat, Michèle. "islamiya.net, Quibla.com et Stcom.net. L'obsession anti-israélienne sur le net islamique." *Observatoire du monde juif* 4/5 (December 2002): 7–16.

Trigano, Shmuel. *La démission de la République, Juifs et Musulmans en France*. Paris: Presses Universitaires de France, 2003.

———, ed. *L'exclusion des Juifs des pays arabes. Aux sources du conflit israélo-arabe*. Paris: Pardès, 2003.

Tritton, Arthur Stanley. *The Caliphs and their Non-Muslim Subjects. A Critical Study of the Covenant of Umar*. 1930. Reprint, London: Frank Cass, 1970.

Tyler, Patrick E. and Van Natta, Jr., Don. "Call to Jihad rising on Europe's streets. Hundreds of angry Muslims are answering." *New York Times/IHT*, April 27, 2004.

Ubicini, Abdolonyme. *Lettres sur la Turquie, ou Tableau Statistique, religieux, politique, administratif, militaire, commercial, etc. de l'Empire ottoman depuis le Khatti-Cherif de Gulkhané (1939). Accompagné de Pièces Justificatives*. Revised 2nd ed. Vol. 1, *Les Ottomans*; vol. 2, *Les Raias. (Grecs, Arméniens-Catholiques, Israélites, Latins)*. Paris: Librairie Militaire de J. Dumaine (Anselim), 1853/1854.

United Nations. *Arab Human Development Report 2002. Creating Opportunities for Future Generations.* New York: United Nations Development Programme. Sponsored by the Regional Bureau for Arab States, 2002.

———. *Arab Human Development Report 2003. Building a Knowledge Society.* New York: United Nations Development Programme. Sponsored by the Regional Bureau for Arab States, 2003.

Vacalopoulos, Apostolos E. *The Origins of the Greek Nation—The Byzantine Period, 1204–1461.* New Brunswick, NJ: Rutgers University Press, 1970.

Vaucher, Georges. *Trois Mythes de l'Ancien Testament dont il faut atténuer le caractère raciste pour que la paix vienne en Terre Sainte.* Geneva: *Eurabia,* Centre d'Information Arabe, 1978.

———. Groupe d'étude sur le Moyen-Orient, *Bulletin d'information* N° 74, October 1, 1977.

Vinocur, John. "Author Sees Anti-U.S. Reporting: Journalist Fired for Book Critical of French Newspapers." *IHT,* December 29, 2003.

———. "Chirac Arrives at a Crossroads. President Has to Decide Whether to Try to Limit U.S. Power." *IHT,* April 23, 2003.

———. "Criticism of U.S. Obscures Growing Disunity on Continent." *IHT,* January 20, 2004.

———. "A European Doomsday Scenario. French Research Group Paints a Gloomy Economic Picture." *IHT,* May 14, 2003.

———. "France: Veto is debated." *IHT,* March 6, 2003, 4–17.

———. "In U.S., Schröder Offers Support of Bush's Mideast Plan." *IHT,* February 27, 2004.

Völker, Edmond, ed. *Euro-Arab Cooperation.* Europa Instituut, University of Amsterdam. Leyden: A.W. Sijthoff, 1976.

Vryonis, Speros, Jr. *The Decline of Medieval Hellenism in Asia Minor and the Process of Islamization from the Eleventh through the Fifteenth Century.* 1971. Reprint, Berkeley and Los Angeles: University of California Press, 1996.

———. "Seljuk Gulams and Ottoman Devshirmes." In *DER ISLAM,* edited by C. H. Becker and Berthold Spuler, 224–52. Berlin: Walter de Gruyter, 1965.

Wadlow, René, and David Littman. "Dangerous Censorship of a U.N. Special Rapporteur." *Justice* 14 (September 1997), 10–17. *See also in* Spencer, *The Myth of Islamic Tolerance.* Part 5, chapter 3.

Warraq, Ibn. "Debunking Edward Said: Edward Said and the Saidists: or Third World Intellectual Terrorism." http://www.secularislam.org/articles/debunking .htm; and in Spencer, ed. *The Myth,* Part 6, ch. 1.

———, ed. *Leaving Islam: Apostates Speak Out.* New York: Prometheus Books, 2003.

———, ed. *The Origins of the Koran.* New York: Prometheus Books, 1999.

———, ed. *The Quest for the Historical Muhammad.* New York: Prometheus Books, 2000.

———, ed. *What the Koran Really Says.* New York: Prometheus Books, 2002.

———. *Why I Am Not a Muslim.* New York: Prometheus Books, 1995.

———. "The Genesis of a Myth." In Spencer, ed. *The Myth,* foreword.

Waterbury, John. "Les implications politiques et diplomatiques du dialogue international." In Bourrinet, *Le Dialogue Euro-Arabe,* 21–28.

Werner, Eric. *L'Imposture. En Marge de la 18ᵉ Conference Générale de l'UNESCO.* Geneva: Centre d'Information et de Documentation sur le Moyen-Orient, 1975.

Windschuttle, Keith. "The cultural war on Western civilization." The survival of culture: V. *The New Criterion,* New York, January 1, 2002.

Wistrich, Robert S. "Editor's Diary." In *Antisemitism International, 2003.* Vidal Sassoon International Center for the Study of Antisemitism. Jerusalem: Hebrew University, December 2003.

———. "Hate Britain." *JC,* May 16, 2003.

———. *Hitler's Apocalypse: Jews and the Nazi Legacy.* London: Weidenfeld & Nicholson, 1985.

Youssef, Ahmed. *L'Orient de Jacques Chirac. La politique Arabe de la France.* With a preface by Jean Lacouture. Monaco: Editions du Rocher, 2003.

Zanjani, Abbasali Amid. *Minority Rights According to the Laws of the Tribute Agreement. A Survey of Some Purports of the International Rights from the Viewpoint of the Islamic Jurisprudence.* Teheran International Publishing Co., 1997.

General Index

Abd-al-Rahman, Salim, 204
Abdul Rahman III, 314
Abdullah, 49
Abraham, 113, 173, 174, 212–13, 220,
  223, 307; Ibrahim Al Khalil, 71, 113,
  172, 213
Abrahamism, 173–74, 213
Abrams, Elliott, 340n. 31
Abu Abbas, 156
Abu Dhabi, 56
Abu Hajjer, 158–59
Abusahlia, Raed Awad, 222, 338n. 11,
  342n. 23
Achille Lauro, 156
Ackerman, Gary, 127
Adam, 174
Adinolfi, Gaetano, 171
Afghanistan, 27, 119, 160, 183, 193, 204
Afro-Arab cooperation, 152
Afshari, Reza, 340n. 18
Agha Shahi, 85, 276
Ahlmark, Per, 205, 324n. 3, 341n. 43
AIPU, 135
Akaba, Gulf, 43–44
Akin, James, 116
Al Quds Committee, 274, 277, 280;
  Fund, 280, 288, 294. *See also* Jerusalem
Albania, 200, 302
ALECSO. *See under* Arab League
Alexandrescu-Dersca, Maria-Mathilda,
  326n. 12
Algeria, 24, 40–41, 89, 91, 104, 107, 109,
  118, 142, 147–49, 160, 201, 203, 226,
  246, 274; civil war, 201
Ali Ben Khader. *See* Baumann, Walter
Altern, Erich (Ali Bella), 42
al Alwani, Taha Jabir, 345n. 29
America. *See* U.S.
American University of Paris, 160
Amman, 86, 114, 151–54, 266, 281
Amrozi, 178, 337n. 10

Anatolia, 35, 143, 173, 193
Andalusia, 147, 163–75, 191, 196–97,
  202, 236; Almoravids, 172; Amirate of
  Cordova, 166; and dhimmitude, 191;
  Cerdagne, 165; Ceuta, 197; Cordova,
  165, 166; dhimmitude in, 165–66;
  dogma of, 163; Eurabian model, 147;
  Granada, 131, 133, 172, 197, 314; history of, 165; immigration issue, 163,
  165; Islamic, 341; Merida, 165; Mozarabs, 165, 166, 172; Murabitun, 172;
  Muslim, 257; *muwalladun*, 166; political aspects of, 164, 191; Saragossa,
  165; Septimania, 165; Seville, 166,
  251; Toledo, 165–66, 238–39; Utopian model, 161, 163–75, 269. *See also*
  dhimmitude; Eurabia
Anna Lindh Foundation. *See under*
  Lindh
Annan, Kofi, 265
Ansars, 318
anti-Americanism, 10, 12, 24, 26–28, 41,
  69, 75, 88, 102, 108, 116, 125, 132,
  140, 151, 155, 161, 186, 203, 206–7,
  225–28, 230, 235, 239, 241–42, 244,
  247, 265–69; Arab, 71–77, 247; European, 12, 24, 26, 75, 126, 207, 225–42;
  French, 44, 125; international, 126; Islamic, 267
anti-Arab/Muslim, 25, 71, 186
anti-Israel, 25–26, 44–45, 58, 63, 68–69,
  71–74, 82, 86, 89, 102, 104, 109, 111,
  113, 125–26, 134, 150–151, 154, 156,
  188, 206, 218, 226, 230, 239, 260, 267;
  Catholic Pedagogical Centre (KPC),
  179; Churches, 177
anti-Judaism, 188, 214–16, 309; Christian, 214, 217, 220. *See also* antisemitism; Judeophobia
antisemitism, 10, 12, 15, 25–29, 46, 96,
  113, 123–24, 126–28, 161, 177, 186,

363